WITHDRAWN

GRAMLEY LIBRARY
Salem Academy and College
Winston-Salem, N. C. 27108

SOUTHERN LITERARY STUDIES

Louis D. Rubin, Jr., *Editor*

Selected Letters of John Crowe Ransom

PS
3535
.A635
Z48
1985

Selected Letters of

JOHN CROWE RANSOM

Edited, with an Introduction, by

THOMAS DANIEL YOUNG *and* GEORGE CORE

Louisiana State University Press

Baton Rouge and London

GRAMLEY LIBRARY
Salem Academy and College
Winston-Salem, N. C. 27108

Copyright © 1985 by Louisiana State University Press
All rights reserved
Manufactured in the United States of America

Designer: Barbara Werden
Typeface: Linotron Primer
Typesetter: G & S Typesetters, Inc.
Printer and Binder: Edwards Brothers, Inc.

Vanderbilt University and the Mellon committee of the College of Arts and Sciences, University of the South, furnished subventions toward defraying the production costs of this book.

"A Naturalist Looks at Sentiment" by George Core was first published (in slightly different form) in the *Virginia Quarterly Review*, LIII (Summer, 1977), 455–74. Six of John Crowe Ransom's letters to Allen Tate between the years 1923 and 1927 were first published under the title "Art as Adventure in Form" in the *Southern Review*, XII (Autumn, 1976), 776–97. John Crowe Ransom's poem "The Eye Can Tell" also first appeared in the *Southern Review*, XIX (Autumn, 1983), 836–37, printed by permission of Helen Ransom Forman.

Library of Congress Cataloging in Publication Data

Ransom, John Crowe, 1888–1974.
Selected letters of John Crowe Ransom.

(Southern literary studies)
Includes index.
1. Ransom, John Crowe, 1888–1974—Correspondence.
2. Poets, American—20th century—Correspondence.
3. Critics—United States—Correspondence. 4. Editors—United States—Correspondence. I. Young, Thomas Daniel, 1919– . II. Core, George. III. Title. IV. Series.
PS3535.A635Z48 1985 811′.52 [B] 84-10006
ISBN 0-8071-1168-6

To the memory of Allen Tate
and for Louis D. Rubin, Jr.

As he grew into an outsider without ceasing to be an insider, it was as if everything to which he was native took on a special quality, an exact identity, a microscopic reality, which, only for what it was, had a value because it was wholly free from his outsiderness. This is what happens to things we love. He picked it up and took it with him. He drew a picture of it, many pictures of it, in his books. The greater the value he set on it, the dearer it became, the most closely he sought out its precise line and look, the more it became a legend, the peculiar legend of things as they are when they are as we want them to be, without any of the pastiche of which the presence vulgarizes so many legends and possibly everything legendary in things, not as they are, but as we should like them to be.

WALLACE STEVENS
"John Crowe Ransom: Tennessean"
(1948)

CONTENTS

ACKNOWLEDGMENTS

We are grateful to the following libraries for allowing us to publish materials from their holdings: the Collection of American Literature from the Beinecke Rare Book and Manuscript Library at Yale University (letters to Cleanth Brooks, F. O. Matthiessen, and Robert Penn Warren); the Berg Collection of the New York Public Library (letter to Babette Deutsch); the Chalmers Library of Kenyon College (letters to William Empson, R. W. B. Lewis, Robert Lowell, and Denham Sutcliffe); the Columbia University Libraries (letters to Lionel Trilling); the duPont Library at the University of the South (letters to Alexander Guerry, W. S. Knickerbocker, and Monroe K. Spears); the Firestone Library at Princeton University (letters to R. P. Blackmur and Allen Tate); the Huntington Library (letters to Wallace Stevens); the Lily Library at Indiana University (letters to Josephine Piercy, Newton P. Stallknecht, and Louis Untermeyer); the Magill Library at Haverford College (letters to Christopher Morley); the Olin Library at Washington University (letters to Robert Duncan and Mona Van Duyn); the Tennessee State Library and Archives (letters to Annie Ransom, Ellene Ransom, and Mr. and Mrs. John James Ransom); the Jesse E. Wills Collection of Vanderbilt University Library (letters to Donald Davidson, James H. Kirkland, Caroline Gordon, Robert Graves, Edwin Mims, Andrew Lytle, Arthur Mizener, and Randall Stewart). We thank Robie Macauley, Valerie Eliot, and Richard Wilbur for letting us publish letters to them that remain in their hands.

We are indebted most to the late Robb Reavill Ransom, who allowed us to consult books and papers in her family's possession and who granted us permission to publish the entire correspondence. (This permission has been renewed by her daughter, Helen Ransom Forman.) Allen Tate assisted us greatly by identifying various matters alluded to in these letters and by making astute suggestions for establishing dates and the identities of many persons mentioned in them. Robert Penn Warren has also been most helpful.

Our special thanks go to Louise Durham for typing the many stages that this manuscript went through before reaching its final stage. We also wish to thank Mary Lucia Snyder Cornelius for proofreading and Audrey Johnston Reynolds for help in typing and photocopying. We are deeply appreciative to Trudie Calvert for her superb copyediting. The Research Council of Vanderbilt University generously provided grants for collecting Ransom letters from various depositories, for photocopying and transcribing the letters, and for typing the manuscript.

We profoundly appreciate the support and encouragement of our wives, Arlease Lewis Young and Susan Darnell Core.

Selected Letters of John Crowe Ransom

INTRODUCTION
A Naturalist Looks at Sentiment

HIS INTRODUCTORY ESSAY was undertaken in an effort to penetrate the masks of John Crowe Ransom. For years we had assumed that logic provided the driving force behind the man's cheerful public exterior and his far more complex private character. Allen Tate persuasively argued that logic was Ransom's ultimate standard of judgment, the value to which everything else in his nature—emotion, ambition, passion—was subordinated. Superficially Tate's argument appears to be unassailable, yet when one considers the most important decisions in Ransom's life (as they are revealed in the authorized biography, *Gentleman in a Dustcoat*), the issue becomes problematic. Most of his major decisions—such as entering matrimony and teaching English rather than philosophy or classics (or teaching any discipline rather than writing for a living)—were made in a spirit that was anything but coldly logical.

Our hunch was that the dualism that underlies John Ransom's poetry and criticism must also inform his life. Thus began our investigation of Ransom's complicated attitude toward sentiment—the theme of this correspondence that joins literary and domestic matters. The investigation led immediately and directly to examining his relations with various friends during the last sixty years of his life, especially the central relationship with Tate. Considering the connection between a major theoretical critic who almost incidentally or casually became a great minor poet and a poet whose practical criticism not only is superior to his own poetry but is superior to that of any southerner of his time illuminates the public and private selves of both principals. In each case one sees to what extent knowledge was carried to the heart.

The essay that follows is an account of the role sentiment played in the life of John Crowe Ransom, a history of the ways in which the curve of his behavior touched the shape of his thought as that behavior and thought are revealed in the letters printed in this volume. Our procedure is biographical, with critical excursions.

I

"Sentiment is not useful, nor moral, nor even disciplinary; it is simply aesthetic," Ransom observes in "Sentimental Exercise." Sentiment's homely but powerful surety will irrupt in everyday life at expected and unexpected turns all the same, and it will affect even the business world. Its near cousins—familiarity, nostalgia, respect, tenderness, affection for the object, love—are "all subjective or emotional terms." In its mysteriousness, irrationality, and perfect inutility, sentiment reminds us of poetry; and indeed Ransom believed that sentiment and poetry share the common ground of aesthetics. "Sentiment is aesthetic, aesthetic is sentiment," he writes.

"The true poetry," the author says elsewhere in *The World's Body*, "has no great interest in improving or idealizing the world. . . . It wants only to know the untechnical homely fulness of the world." The sentiments, "the flowers of civilization," constitute essential parts of that fullness.

Art affords the poet the opportunity to join sentiment and aesthetics, Ransom argues: the poet can use his sentiments, "when nourished by properties and privacies, and by rites and ceremonies," as one dimension of the experience in which his poetry must be rooted. He might, for instance, write a lyric about the ritual of the fox hunt or the ceremonies of death. On the other hand, like the businessman or the scientist, he might, willingly or not, let friendship's demands intrude upon his life and his art. Aristotle, Ransom reminds us, argues that friendship is "the occasion of a great extension of knowledge." "If the interest is not a cognitive one," he adds, "I believe the phenomenon of friendship is unaccountable."

What, we might ask, is the purpose of an essay devoted to sentiment that appears in the middle of a book devoted to literature and aesthetics? "The sentiments," Ransom answers, "furnish the race with a much larger volume of [aesthetic] experience than the arts do." Sentiment is not limited to artists, and it achieves perfection in human attitude and intention that is not found in the cold remove of form and in the rigorous concentration of knowledge. Ransom is quick to stress that the world's body exists outside art, which touches the lives of relatively few people. "It is the sentiments which attend us daily, and keep us constantly, or at least recurrently, up to the decent level of our historic humanity," he concludes.

Our next question is, What part did sentiment play in Ransom's life and in the making of his art? It is a critical commonplace that in his poetry he avoided sentimentality by the use of aesthetic distance—the observer in Ransom's lyrics is posted far from the action that he describes—and by the employment of subtle and sometimes devastating irony. The poet achieves this distance and control and balance in the writing of poetry that is often homely and mundane in subject. Ransom's criticism is only a little less mannered and ironic: even though the critic seems polite and desultory, the control is severe. In both the poetry and the criticism the tough reasonableness in argument is complemented and buttressed by perspicuous grace of expression. This is not to say that the personae are the same: quite the contrary. In "The Tense of Poetry" Ransom observes that "prose is the supremely single and exclusive experience, possible only by an abridgement of personality." The poet in contrast assumes a mask and a costume for the discharge of his office; he does not abridge his personality but assumes the character of others; in this guise he enters and explores the world of make-believe, which Ransom insists is dramatic, not real. So we should not expect the critic and the poet to be one and the same. What of the man himself?

John Ransom never entertained the notion that life imitates art, and he always stressed the relative importance of art to life. "Life must come first," Robert Penn Warren heard him say. He held fast to that principle throughout his long and full life. The citadel of Ransom's life was the family—first his father's, then his own (which he called acquired), then (by the same extension) those of his children and grandchildren. In that fastness he created a world of love, loyalty, discipline, and joy, one in which art had small place. Croquet and poker and the Cleveland Browns were as important in his household as poetry. "Anyone who ever entered his house would have known it to be the habitat of a deep joy in life—a place where work was play and play was work, because of an abounding energy and the intensity of the life-sense," Warren has written in his tribute (*Southern Review*, Spring, 1975).

If Ransom could dispassionately describe the marriage bond as a social propriety which safeguards the physical attachment of the sexes, he could also observe that "the parties have such an imperious animal use for each other that the romantic relation had better be encouraged." Ransom experienced sexual urgency and tenderness as well as the drive of the intellect and the reach of the imagination. No one who has read "Lost Lady," "The Equilibrists," and "Judith of Bethulia" can doubt as much.

The private life was always guarded, of course (and here we take the sanctity and richness of that world as a given). The circle of Ransom's immediate family stood inviolable amidst the making of poetry, the launching of critical campaigns, the creation of the *Fugitive* and the *Kenyon Review*, the rise of Agrarianism, the removal to Gambier, the founding of the Kenyon School of English, the death of colleagues—amidst the attendant blood, toil, sweat, and tears of a career that began in the backwater of a small southern university and reached its pinnacle in a considerably smaller and more obscure midwestern college.

Touches of the warm and full domestic life of the Ransom household appear regularly in Ransom's letters to Warren. About the time that he was writing "Sentimental Exercise" he invited the Warrens to his house in Nashville for Thanksgiving. "We'll bridge, eat, drink (if there's any liquor), ride, or sit upon the ground and tell sad stories of the deaths of kings" (November 6, 1934). In May, 1935, he reported on the last of his children: "Young Jack is a very lusty and eager youth, especially at 2 and 6 a.m., when he wants his bottle. A promising fellow but needs a great deal of discipline; quite unformed intellectually." In April, 1942, Ransom's interests turned momentarily toward canine parturition: "Dooley (I think you know this wretch) has tried a second time to raise a family, and a second time she had to have a Caesarian. She's doing pretty well though it's worse than the other time, and she has two spotted pups to show." One regularly finds mention of the doings of children and pets in Ransom's letters to Warren, the youngest of the Fugitives. The relation of the older man to the younger was avuncular (almost that of father to son) in their show of friendship and sentiment; on a professional basis it was entirely different: Ransom treated Warren as an equal. That respect is evident from his reaction to *John Brown: The Making of a Martyr* through his high praise of *Brother to Dragons* (which appeared in part in the *Kenyon Review*) to his more restrained praise of *You, Emperors*. (Ransom always thought more highly of Warren's poetry and criticism than of his fiction.)

Robert Penn Warren was one of the two friends with whom Ransom had a sustained relationship of many years' standing. The other friend was Allen Tate, and in this relationship one can see the essential nature of both men. Ransom's letters to Tate became at once almost exclusively professional, after he had accepted Tate as a colleague and no longer thought of him as a precocious but trying student. His letters to Tate deal chiefly with matters of poetic practice and critical theory and with the practical politics of the literary world: there is little that goes beneath the surface of his domestic life and a good deal less about Tate's. Ransom must have quickly sensed that Tate was uninterested in domestic matters, his own or those of anyone else. (Tate observed rightly in 1968 that Ransom's "life has been so perfectly private that it could bear any public scrutiny." The same could not have been said of Tate.)

Ransom and Tate were southern gentlemen of an older time, regardless of their relation to modernism and the modern world as men of letters. Ransom assumed a mask in public as an ambassador to the unseemly modern world as deliberately as he assumed his masks as poet and critic. Behind the smiling public face was a man who was profoundly skeptical and who was driven by ambition. (He spoke from experience in saying that "a human aspiration is probably the strangest and most characteristic of human behaviors.") His manners were as nearly perfect and as controlled as his meters. With Tate the matter was different and more complicated. Certainly the "severe and courteous formality" that Andrew Lytle witnessed at 27 Bank Street in New York City in 1926 was habitual; and just as certainly he was "the soonest friendly, / But then the soonest tired," as Mark Van Doren observed. Malcolm Cowley put the matter in still another way: "He had the best manners of any young man I had known, in America or in France. I thought he used politeness not only as a defense but sometimes as an aggressive weapon against strangers." For Tate manners were a sword; for Ransom they were a shield. Neither personal convention could have been perfected anywhere in this country but the South. The grave rites and ceremonies of John Crowe Ransom and Allen Tate were not restricted to their poetry and prose, needless to say.

The two men seldom resorted to formality with one another after 1924, and there is little or no ceremony in the correspondence written in the ensuing half-century. Ransom deliberately avoids certain subjects or alludes to them elliptically. He often mentions Tate's family as well as his own, but the enlivening domestic details that regularly appear in his letters to Warren seldom occur in those to Tate. The friendship was chiefly intellectual ("It astonishes me frequently to find how close is our agreement in many departments of thought; and so deep that it is probably permanent," he wrote Tate in September, 1933); but it had a sustained social intercourse to undergird the intense commitment to the community of letters that is the common basis of the relation.

Tate's commitment to his profession was greater than Ransom's, especially regarding the human dimension: he was far less interested in his family but much more concerned about his friends, virtually all of whom were writers. Caroline Gordon, a productive and committed author, had many of the same drives and instincts as her husband; their involvement in domestic life was clearly secondary to their involvement in art. (One thinks of their life together in relation to winters with Hart Crane, summers with Malcolm Cowley and, later, Ford Madox Ford and Robert Lowell; of fellowships and academic appointments, of publishing jobs and of books. It was a world with little room for children and pets, for bridge and golf and croquet, for gardening, carpentry, and cooking, for the Little League and the Cleveland Browns.) Ransom's center was invariably in his family, not in his intellectual pursuits, fierce and total as they were. He forged his identity as the most industrious and responsible child in a large close-knit family; Tate found his identity in rebelling against his family—first his father and mother, then his older brother Ben (his putative father). As the youngest child in a loose-knit family that traveled from place to place in the upper South, gradually dissipating its resources and its strength, Tate had to find his way outside the family circle. He created his identity in large measure in an alien spirit, responding perversely to his mother's fear that he would injure his mind and fall into "melancholia because of excessive application to books." Tate became a literary prodigal, prodigal in his commitment to letters and ideas. Ransom in contrast was exceptionally close to his father; Tate could not have been more distant from his father (who "always spoke to me impersonally as if he were surprised that I was there"). The relation recurred with Tate's own children. But he did not look for a father figure in Ransom, who could not have abided such a relationship.

If, then, Ransom and Tate had much in common as southern men of letters who were raised and educated in the piedmont South, there were also sharp differences in temperament and in extraliterary values which might have driven them asunder. Such a breach did occur on literary grounds in the Waste Lands controversy of 1927; but afterward, nothing similar occurred in the next half-century. In that crisis Tate won the battle and proved his mettle, and thereafter Ransom accepted him as an equal, not merely as a persistent balky former student. It was the crucial turning point in an association that endured for an astonishing length of time—a friendship that profoundly affected the mature lives of both men. The complexion of that friendship is as complicated as the intellection of its principals.

II

In "A Southern Mode of the Imagination" Allen Tate said that John Crowe Ransom taught Andrew Lytle, Cleanth Brooks, Warren, and himself "Kantian aesthetics and a philosophical dualism, tinged with Christian theology, but ultimately derived from the Nicomachian ethics." In the same year, 1959, Ransom wrote his essay for Tate, "In amicitia." In it he mentions his fondness for a "sort of pagan bible" entitled *The Nicomachean Ethics*. "In this treatise friendship is regarded as the sum and crown of the common single virtues. In its high form Aristotelian friendship requires both intellectual and moral maturity; its best exercise is when two well qualified friends talk long and fruitfully together with perfect understanding." Ransom continues: "To the best of my knowledge there has been an excellent understanding between us for more than thirty years; and I have felt as pleased and comfortable in his company as in any which I have been offered."

Ransom once indicted Aristotle for reducing myth to metaphysics, but Aristotle remained his favorite philosopher and his favorite example of the practical critic. Ransom wrote three full-length essays devoted to Aristotle, the last of which is "The Literary Criticism of Aristotle" (1948). His theoretical essays are in large part responses to Aristotle, Kant, and Hegel; the literary examples are drawn from Shakespeare more than from any other poet, Milton included. Ransom depreciated Shakespeare as a sonneteer, but he had great respect for Shakespeare's artistry as a dramatist and for the energy of his language: hence his first two essays on Aristotle, "Poetry: I. The Formal Analysis" and "Poetry: II. The Final Cause" (1947), depend heavily upon *Hamlet, Julius Caesar, A Midsummer Night's Dream, Antony and Cleopatra,* and other Shakespearean plays as underpinning; and indeed Ransom detached "The Iconography of the Master" from "The Final Cause" for *Beating the Bushes*, creating a separate essay on Shakespeare's imagery, diction, and teleology. (There he remarks in passing: "In naturalistic speculation, a man is nothing less than a biological and psychological organism. I cannot see why he should be more; provided of course the whole man can be figured organically, including the poet in the man.") This is to say that Ransom's best criticism often resulted from his renewed engagement with Aristotle and Shakespeare. That is the case with his essays from "On Shakespeare's Language" (1947) through "The Literary Criticism of Aristotle" (1948); it is true of his essays on the cathartic and mimetic principles which appear in *The World's Body*.

John Crowe Ransom was temperamentally and philosophically an Aristotelian in many respects (Aristotle "is a naturalist, and I guess I am," he wrote to Tate in April, 1948). "The Greek philosophers after all had not attained unto a religion," he wrote in *God without Thunder* (1930), explaining: "Aristotle had been a pure metaphysician, with no Gods and only Principles." His "natural religion" was much the same as the Greeks', and in 1959 he said: "I . . . confess that my regular piety is that of a pagan."

If Ransom was Aristotelian in his paganism and naturalism, in his emphasis on the importance of the world's body, and in his general approach to art, Tate in contrast was far more drawn to Coleridge than to Aristotle for his critical principles; and his great example as a classic poet was Dante, not Shakespeare. There is nothing so revealing in a personal sense about the differing tastes in criticism and poetry as the fact that Tate's criticism often concerns ideas (for example, his attacks upon humanism and positivism), whereas Ransom's is over and again devoted to sentiment. On the one hand, the stress is on values; on the other, on sensibility. The thought of the two men meets in the "general idea that poetry can be an undemonstrable form of knowledge" (as Tate has framed the equation) and in their common revulsion toward science and technology. Ideas for Tate often took on a religious cast; for Ransom the tonality was more rigorously philosophical; the meeting ground between the two was myth. Ransom also shunned the religious valuation as strenuously as Tate often sounded it. For all his fascination with miraculism Ransom was a naturalist; Tate was a supernaturalist. Ransom realized that fundamental difference as early as 1924 and wrote to Tate: "Do you not . . . stake everything on the chance of recovering some cosmological values out of the debris? . . . I simply renounce Cosmology and Magic. . . . It is quite a quaint idea that we are to find this world out there somewhere transcending sense. And there are no formulas. The formulas are the specific delusions." Ransom adverted to this general subject from time to time in the 1920s and 1930s, clinching his point in a letter written in mid-September, 1936: "You are looking, I believe, for something special in the aesthetic experience, whereas I can see only an ordinary scientific or animal core *plus* glittering contingency."

"We are of the literary estate," Ransom wrote of himself and Tate in 1959. The literary estate, needless to say, is not limited to the community of the Fugitives or the Agrarians at their closest, when the *Fugitive* and the Agrarian symposia were at high tide. It is a country of the mind, and the writer is often alone with the alone in that country. In such circumstances it is understandable that the writer would seek authority and solace outside himself and depend upon religion or philosophy. Allen Tate did that throughout his career, even if he did not join the Catholic church until he was well into middle age. It was he who argued the religious position in *I'll*

Take My Stand; he returned to that theme repeatedly over the years. In his preface to *Memoirs and Opinions* (1975) he asserts that a philosophy of literature is invalid "without religious authority to sustain it." What is of crucial importance is that Tate joined life and literature in the religious, or supernatural, dimension of man's experience, whereas Ransom insisted that the same intersection occurs in the world's body—the realm of mundane human intercourse and of nature itself. He can therefore conclude in "The Literary Criticism of Aristotle" that "the thing which will best certify our humanism" is "something as impractical as gentleness, or love, whose organ is sensibility." He decides that this love of nature, "if nature means 'everything in the world,'" is necessary for art.

After presenting his "crude sketch of a natural history of sentiment and sensibility" in the same essay, Ransom says that the arts exist for the "most perfect expression" of sentiment and sensibility, and he returns to the argument of "Sentimental Exercise." The equation is that the sentiments, "those irrational psychic formations," are "alternative forms of aesthetic knowledge." A sentiment therefore illustrates the world's body more fully than an idea, for any idea is ultimately reductive. In the "general psychic economy" the "sentimentalist employs his wits and transforms himself into a man of sensibility; and now he has infinite resources. Poetry lies before him, and the future of poetry is immense. Now the whole of nature . . . becomes the object of his affection." This natural history, one quickly perceives, applies to John Crowe Ransom himself.

In such passages one can also deduce considerable evidence for Ransom's natural religion as well as the grounds of his aesthetics. The cardinal aspect of his piety has already been stated: "Life must come first." Art must therefore imitate life, must draw its sustenance from life's precious objects: hence "human affections are vastly and inconspicuously diffused among the objects of poetry, as among those of common experience." Ransom accordingly could not ignore the affective element in literature: he wrestles with it over and again, especially in "Poetry: The Formal Analysis." There he demonstrates that "poetry is language in the pathetic mode," not in the logical mode; it is a "discourse in the 'pathetic mode' if we emphasize the feelings which attend it."

Ransom's explorations in aesthetics caused Donald Davidson grief, and he objected to their narrowness and formalism in a letter to Tate (January 2, 1943), saying that he held them to be "a misuse of his great gifts." This bent was to Davidson another instance of Ransom's perplexing nature and of his treason to the South. "He is a mystery," Davidson observed to Tate in 1938, "but a mystery so friendly & homely & cheerful that you are always forgetting his capacity for turning up with an entirely new perspective." In 1974 Tate wrote of Ransom that "the actions of this logical man were unpredictable." To a certain extent that statement is perfectly true, but the logic of Ransom's relations is in retrospect consistent to an astonishing degree. He would not have seen "Art and the Human Economy" (1945) as a move leading to the loss of the "friendship of his old friend Donald Davidson," as Tate put it in his memorial essay for Ransom; he would have considered that friendship terminated by his move from Vanderbilt to Kenyon and by his earlier loss of interest in the South as a subject for endeavor, particularly Agrarianism. In September, 1936, he had written to Tate: "What is true in part for you (though a part that is ominously increasing) is true nearly in full for me: *patriotism* has nearly eaten me up, and I've got to get out of it." In leaving Vanderbilt Ransom divested himself of Agrarianism and patriotism at once.

As one comes to perceive the subtlety and persistence of John Ransom's investigations of sentiment, he realizes that the critic stands less on the side of logic than on the side of sensibility. Ransom said to Warren that he viewed man as a kind of "oscillating mechanism," and such poems as "Painted Head" indicate that Ransom was remarkably balanced in his dualism; and that dualism was not confined to his poetry. The sympathetic imagination accommodates both sense and sensibility. It remains for us to see how Ransom's imagination operated when affection was directly involved.

III

In Book 8 of *The Nicomachean Ethics* Aristotle examines friendship. He finds that there are three ascending orders of friendship which are based respectively upon utility, pleasure, and a common pursuit of the good. Aristotle's anatomy is convincing, indeed inexorable, in its logic. Friendships based upon use and pleasure are "only incidental; for it is not as being the man he is that the loved person is loved, but as providing some good or pleasure. Such friendships, then, are easily dissolved, if the parties do not remain like themselves; for if the one party is no longer pleasant or useful the other ceases to love him." In contrast, the highest order of friendship lies between men who are "friends for their own sake, i.e. in virtue of their goodness. These, then, are friends without qualification." Such friendship is based not only upon love but upon a state of character. "In loving a friend," Aristotle believes, "men love what is good for themselves; for the good man in becoming a friend becomes a good to his friend."

Such was the friendship of Ransom and Tate once it had been forged and tempered. Initially it was based upon what Aristotle calls "inequality between the parties, e.g. that of father to son and in general of elder to younger." But once Ransom had accepted Tate as a colleague their association was thereafter founded on the bedrock of equality. In July, 1927, he wrote to Tate in the midst of the Waste Lands dispute: "Your duplicity is charming from an intellectual point of view, but there's also a sentimental one. It was a regular bolt from the blue." After the chill following this argument had abated, there were no equally strong incidents in the ensuing half-century. There were often occasions for misunderstanding and disagreement, to be sure. The friends might have exchanged sharp words over many matters—the converging goals of the *Kenyon Review* and the *Sewanee Review* (while Tate was editor of the latter), the failure of Tate to respond positively to many of Ransom's invitations to write for his quarterly, the composition of the faculty of the Kenyon School of English (and, later, of the Indiana School of Letters), the propriety of Tate's relations with his wives, and so forth. But nothing of the kind occurred. The relation might have actually been strengthened by the fact that the men seldom saw one another. ("Perhaps in more of those thirty years than not we met no oftener than two or three times the whole year long," Ransom remarked in 1959.) Aristotle observes that "distance does not break off the friendship absolutely, but only the activity of it." In close quarters under continuing circumstances Tate's wrathfulness and his compulsion for gossip and controversy would have inevitably clashed with Ransom's discretion, reticence, and reserve. "Readily enthusiastic, he could be as readily bored," Mark Van Doren said of Tate. "He would change in an instant from a child who remembered nothing to an old man who remembered everything, and suddenly, like the soul in Emily Dickinson's poem, would close the valves of his attention."

The friendship fortunately was never put to that test. It was to remain principally a literary relation based upon the life of the mind. "Ever after the Agrarian movement I believe that Tate and I conducted our lives in much the same fashion; in a free society we assumed the right to live simply and to keep company with friends of our own taste, and with increasingly unpopular books in the library. We lived in an old-fashioned minority pocket of the culture, so to speak," Ransom wrote in his essay for Tate.

Ransom's friends at Kenyon were primarily his managing editor at the review, Philip Blair Rice, and the chairman of the English department, Charles Coffin. He was also close to the college's president, Gordon Keith Chalmers. All these men suddenly died in 1956, but Ransom continued his work at the *Kenyon Review*, even though "the joy of the enterprise must by then have been gone," as George Lanning later observed. A less responsible man, a weaker man, might have been prompted to retire. Ransom continued as editor for another three years, until his successor (who otherwise would have been Rice) was found and appointed. It must have been a lonely time, but as ever he had his family.

In his earlier life John Ransom had a wide circle of acquaintances, but these connections were based in large part upon the fortuities of his location and of his commitment to particular interests shared by others. Ransom's regular correspondence with Christopher Morley and Robert Graves in the period immediately preceding the publication of *Poems about God* until the publication of *Grace after Meat*, 1917–1925, is illustrative of the occasional nature of his friendships. He had met Morley while they were both Rhodes scholars at Oxford. Morley then helped him place *Poems about God* with Holt, and at the same time Morley sent out individual titles for consideration by various magazines while Ransom was in France during the war. After the war Ransom thought that he would take an editorial or journalistic position in New York City, and he planned to stop by Philadelphia to see Morley. Instead he returned to teach at Vanderbilt in the fall of 1919, and the correspondence of the preceding two years lapsed. In one of his last letters he closed by saying: "I'm surely going East next year!" He did not, and the friendship came amicably to an end.

Ransom's relationship with Robert Graves was similar in many respects, but the men never met and knew each other only through correspondence. Graves was intensely interested in Ransom's poetry and placed *Grace after Meat* with the Hogarth Press. Graves also wrote the foreword and acted in an editorial capacity in seeing the collection through the press. He and Ransom also shared certain critical interests. But when *Grace after Meat* was in print and the *Fugitive* (which published Graves) had ceased publication, letters between the two men ceased.

These friendships were based on utility. "Those who love for the sake of utility love for the sake of what is good for themselves," Aristotle declares. "The useful is not permanent but is always changing. Thus when the motive of friendship is done away, the friendship is dissolved, inasmuch as it existed only for the ends in question." Ransom needed help, especially while he was in France during World War I and his mail was often held up and censored; and Morley, with his excellent sources in the publishing world, provided that help. The case with Graves was more complicated, but the upshot was the same. In both instances the associations ended cordially, and there was no ill feeling. The same was true of Ransom's friendship with Samuel Chew at the Hotchkiss School in 1913–1914, when both men were teaching there. He and Chew saw one another several times a day for six months or more, and they discussed literature and literary theory at length, obviously taking great pleasure in one another's company; but the bond was not strong enough to survive the test of separation and distance. This was another of Ransom's incidental friendships—warm and deep for the time being but not enduring. None of them was ever renewed.

There is no substantial reason to account, however briefly, for Ransom's many other friendships; but it is necessary to dwell momentarily on his associations with Davidson, Coffin, and Rice. (We neglect altogether the relations with such younger men as Randall Jarrell, Peter Taylor, and Robie Macauley, which in this connection are of considerably lesser significance.)

In March, 1938, Davidson wrote to Tate: "I am beginning to see myself as Ransom's Captain Carpenter. . . . Yet I tell myself that the long years of fellowship that have tied us all together have made the alliance something that cannot be casually broken. It is unthinkable that the communion

GRAMLEY LIBRARY
Salem Academy and College
Winston-Salem, N. C. 27108

should cease, and it won't." It did cease, nevertheless, between Ransom and Davidson after a relation that had persisted for a quarter-century; and it was restored only when Ransom returned to Vanderbilt to teach for a semester in 1961. Davidson was grieved by the rupture and said so to Tate in October, 1945: "John is and has been his own master; and furthermore there have been other occasions when he swung an axe wildly, not much regarding his friends." The friendship was nourished primarily, once again, on shared causes—especially the *Fugitive* and Agrarianism. Ransom lost interest in writing poetry and in pursuing southern campaigns. In his own defense he might have said wryly that no natural law forced him to fight permanently under the southern banner. Being a man with an absolute sense of his own identity, he could assume a new tack without a crippling loss of psychic energy. Davidson, on the other hand, required, almost desperately (as James H. Justus has pointed out), "the consolations of community, of a cohesive, philosophically consonant group of true believers."

Ransom regularly found Davidson's gloominess and indecisiveness troublesome (his words for Davidson's temperament included fretfulness and orneriness), and it is startling and instructive to read his comments on Davidson and Warren, cheek by jowl, in a letter dated October 25, 1932. The older man "is still one of the most intransigent spirits incarnated since Saul of Tarsus. . . . Our rebel doctrines are good for us all but Don, and very doubtful there, because they are flames to his tinder." Then a crisp compliment on the younger man: "Red is as good a head and heart as I've known and it's a pleasure to be with him."

Strong friendship did not exist between Ransom and Davidson as it did between Ransom and Warren and between Ransom and Tate, relations that battened over the years. Part of Tate's genius, despite his irascibility, lay in his happy talent for striking up and developing friendship; in this and other ways he was the linchpin of the Nashville group. Davidson did not possess the gift of sociability, and this fault made it difficult for him to develop and hold friendship. Friendship between virtuous men which is directed toward the good is infrequent, as Aristotle says. "Such friendship," he argues, "requires time and familiarity; as the proverb says, men cannot know each other till they have 'eaten salt together.'" Davidson's refusal to engage regularly in social life meant that his friendship would be partial at best, but his remarkable kinship with Tate endured despite the social deprivation. Despite his naturally remote and circumspect disposition Ransom was an extremely sociable man, an eminently clubable man with a remarkable common touch. It is impossible to imagine Davidson or Tate playing poker at the town dump with his neighbors, as Ransom did at Gambier. Davidson and he were of radically different temperaments—the one a fretful puritan, the other a cheerful naturalist.

John Ransom's relation to Philip Rice was, so far as one can infer, very similar to his relation to Warren: as colleagues they were equals; on a social basis the relation of the older man to the younger inclined toward the avuncular. In June, 1938, Ransom wrote to Tate: "Each time I have been with [Rice] I have liked him better." In the ensuing eighteen years the friendship deepened. The connection was not only professional but social, and Ransom felt as at ease with Rice at the dinner table and during the cocktail hour as in the office. Unfortunately, he did not go on record about his sentiments for Rice, and the same holds true for his still greater friendship with Charles Coffin. Of their deaths he said nothing to Tate in correspondence and little to Warren. "Within six months we have lost Rice, Chalmers, and Coffin; a very dreary record. I can't feel that the place is quite the same without them. And I guess of the three that I was closest to Charles," he wrote to Warren in late August, 1956.

It is an understatement worthy of Ransom the elegiac poet: the sentiment is so guarded from sentimentality that one is mystified and perturbed, but then he might remember the friar in "Necrological" who "sat upon a hill and bowed his head / As under a riddle, and in a deep surmise / So still that he likened himself unto those dead." (In 1974 Ransom would be buried beside Coffin and Rice.) Of Ransom's place in the Gambier community Ronald Berman has observed: "In the middle of all that sainted normalcy he was cold and in a useful way without illusions." At such points in John Crowe Ransom's life one is struck by the sense that the man's sensibility was too fine to have been violated by the contingencies of our mortality.

IV

"We, for our curse or our pride, have sentiments," Ransom remarks in "Forms and Citizens." "They are directed towards persons and things; and a sentiment is the totality of love and knowledge which we have of an object that is private and unique." It is the burden of being human—the agony and the glory. And Ransom was profoundly and unalterably committed to what he called the common actuals of life.

In "Art Worries the Naturalists" the critic argues that to understand the ontology of nature one must "deploy the numerous action we call religion; or the one we call art; or . . . the numerically still larger one which we might call sentimental attachment, this being for individual natural objects, or for persons and social objects, all of them apparently inviolable and respected in their own objective natures." (Without that respect the beholder would be a monstrous Platonist to Ransom.) He explains: "In these kinds of behavior the object appears to us as a dense area of contingency, that is, a concretion, a reality on which we cannot take our usual firm grip, and a foreign if not unfriendly being. Toward this object the human creature assumes suddenly a new humility; it figures in religion as a sense of awe, in art as a sense of beauty, and in sentimental life as an uncritical affection."

Uncritical affection—that is, one's usual attitude for his immediate family and closest friends—was for Ransom characteristic and natural. At the same time in such matters he was deeply private and reticent, and in his distaste for sentimentality he always protected his response to sentiment, which takes its most usual form in love, which Ransom called "the dense natural context of an imperious human action" or one's affection for "the familiar individual objects of nature." That umbrella will cover the artistic transaction (including the critical performance), and it will apply nearly as well to the human transaction—in this instance to the friendship between two poet-critics who were imperious in differing ways. Tate's arrogance and quick temper were matched by Ransom's remoteness and powerful ambition. And both men were strong-willed and both possessed remarkable senses of their own natures, their own capabilities.

In "Reflections on Gandhi" George Orwell writes that "the essence of being human is that one does not seek perfection, that one *is* sometimes willing to commit sins for the sake of loyalty, that one does not push asceticism to the point where it makes friendly intercourse impossible, and that one is prepared in the end to be defeated and broken up by life, which is the inevitable price of fastening one's love upon other human individuals." It is a statement that John Crowe Ransom would have assented to, and it acutely describes the man's behavior. Tate sought perfection through art and was seldom prepared for defeat in his dealings with humankind. Davidson practiced asceticism to the point that it cut him off from the possibilities of friendship at its most profound. Neither man truly lived a full and natural life, although one can greatly admire their separate virtues (including loyalty) as men of letters and sages—Tate the paradoxical combination of sensualist and religionist, Davidson the stern puritan. Ransom in contrast led an exemplary life, putting each thing in its own place, whether it was the drama of Shakespeare or the play of the Cleveland Browns. His was a life not merely literary.

Tate declared after Ransom's death that "logic was the mode of his thought and sensibility." One must modify that statement to "logic was the mode of his thought." In his hierarchy of values Ransom placed the sentiments, especially affection and love, at the top; religion and art fell further down the list. So too did logic. He was the man—and the poet and critic—who insisted on the primacy of life itself.

The common actuals of life, the known familiars, the precious objects made up the world's body for John Crowe Ransom just as they do for humanity at large, and he never tried to kick free of humanity into the rarefied atmosphere of art. Art, he insisted, must always reflect the world of everyday life. ("The work he did was implicitly a criticism of the good life as we commonly imagine it," Berman has pointed out.) Ransom stated his beliefs plainly and unmistakably to Tate in 1927: "The poet, again, will simply refer concept to image, with the intention and with the effect of showing how the concept, the poor thin thing, is drowned in the image, how the determinate is drowned in the contingent, and how, ultimately, this world can neither be understood nor possessed. In the poet's art we will have to see, if we are willing to look at all, the Objectivity of the World; this is a dreadful, an appalling, a religious, and a humble attitude to which we will come perforce after the conceited Subjectivism into which we have been persuaded by the practical and the scientific life alike. The issue will take place on its most emotional and poignant plane, of course, when the concepts referred back to reality are the dearest concepts."

That is the Man of Sensibility addressing the Man of Idea. Both are men of letters. The Man of Sensibility says that "the poet perpetuates in his poem an order of existence which in actual life is constantly crumbling beneath his touch." The Man of Idea retorts that "actuality and poetry are respectively and even reciprocally one." The Man of Sensibility replies, gently but firmly: "Life must come first."

BIBLIOGRAPHICAL NOTE

The essays by John Crowe Ransom to which we principally allude appear in *The World's Body* (1938), in *Beating the Bushes* (1972), and in the *Kenyon Review* (IX–X, 1947–1948). Ransom's "In amicitia" and the essays by Mark Van Doren, Andrew Lytle, and Malcolm Cowley are included in *Allen Tate and His Work*, edited by Radcliffe Squires (Minneapolis: University of Minnesota Press, 1972). The quotations from the Tate-Davidson letters appear in *The Literary Correspondence of Allen Tate and Donald Davidson*, edited by John Tyree Fain and Thomas Daniel Young (Athens: University of Georgia Press, 1974). Ransom's letters to Robert Penn Warren are located in the Beinecke Library of Yale University. Ransom's letters to Tate are in the Allen Tate collection at the Firestone Library of Princeton University. The passages from Tate's criticism appear in his *Essays of Four Decades* (Chicago: Swallow Press, 1968), in *Memoirs and Opinions* (Chicago: Swallow Press, 1975), and in "Gentleman in a Dustcoat" (*Sewanee Review*, LXXVI [Summer, 1968]). Ronald Berman's "Confederates in the Backfield: Mr. Ransom and the Cleveland Browns" was published in the *New Republic* (October 4, 1975), and Warren's tribute to Ransom appeared in the *Southern Review* (XI [Spring, 1975]). James H. Justus's "Two Men of Letters of the *Fugitive* World" was written for the *Southern Literary Journal* (VII [Spring, 1975]). We have used W. D. Ross's translation of Aristotle's *Nicomachean Ethics* (Oxford: Clarendon, 1925).

EDITORIAL NOTE

A Mask and an Unveiling

OHN CROWE RANSOM was an unpretentious man of tidy habits that sprang naturally from his disciplined and unassuming nature. Although he had an absolute sense of his own identity and of his ability as a poet, critic, editor, teacher, and ambassador of letters, he did not cherish the notion that his personal life and its trappings were important to the world at large. This sense led him all his mature life to view books, periodicals, and correspondence as the mere tools and appurtenances of his trade—items that could easily be dispensed with and just as easily replaced if necessary. Ransom's attitude toward a book, even a handsome new edition, was casual at best; *indifferent* is a better word to describe his feeling toward books: he willingly lent them or gave them away, he lost them, he abused them, whether they belonged to him or to a friend or a student. The impulse to collect and accumulate books or the other objects of teaching and scholarship he would have deemed, if asked, academic and antiquarian—for us quaint, materialistic, stuffy. The finished text, his own or that of another author, was all that mattered to him—not the stages of revision that marked each draft in manuscript and proof; and he wished to possess any text only in an intellectual sense.

Fortunately Ransom's powerful disinclination to save letters of any variety—incoming or outgoing—was not shared by many of his correspondents. Hence many of his letters to various members of his father's family; to friends and colleagues such as Cleanth Brooks, Donald Davidson, Allen Tate, and Robert Penn Warren; and to various acquaintances, especially contributors to the *Kenyon Review*, have survived.

Helen Ransom Forman, Ransom's daughter and an author in her own right, remembers a correspondence that her father carried on with T. S. Eliot over the course of some months. The subject: the nature of poetry. As each letter came in on Faber & Faber stationery Ransom would carefully consider it, gravely meditate for several days on what Eliot had said and on what he would say in response, and then write or type his reply without making a copy; afterward he would chuck Eliot's letter into a wastebasket and post his own, leaving no record of the transaction.

In conversation Donald Davidson described a scene that profoundly impressed him. As Ransom was preparing to leave Vanderbilt after twenty years to teach at Kenyon, he burned his accumulated papers in a trash barrel in his office. Davidson happened upon the conflagration and its maker as the flames devoured the letters and other documents that until then had eluded Ransom's fell hand.

Even at the *Kenyon Review* correspondence and manuscripts were treated casually, and many letters were not saved and filed. In his last years as editor Ransom had a secretary, but nobody could change his deeply ingrained habits; and at various times the files of the first series of the *Kenyon Review* were discarded in part.

In the fifty-odd years of his life as an American man of letters John Crowe Ransom must have misplaced, lost, thrown out, and destroyed at least a half million dollars' worth of correspondence. Toward the end of his life Allen Tate over and again complained petulantly that Ransom had not preserved Tate's letters to him, which doubtless were among Tate's best; but Ransom's behavior toward his friend in this regard was perfectly evenhanded and democratic: he treated T. S. Eliot, foundation heads, university presidents, department chairmen, insurance agents, and landladies in precisely the same fashion. Hence there can probably be no book involving Ransom such as *The Literary Correspondence of Donald Davidson and Allen Tate* (1974).

It is all too easy to keep looking for letters (as this manuscript goes to press we are still searching) and to postpone making a final selection of what is available. We are persuaded that we have seen the vast majority of Ransom's extant letters and that this selection constitutes a representative and significant cross-section of his correspondence and touches on every important aspect of his life and thought. Only one source of letters has been denied to us: Ransom's letters to Yvor Winters. These letters have little chance of rivaling his letters written during the same period to Tate and Warren.

II

The reader naturally wonders what principles the editors have followed in choosing the letters that are reproduced in this book. At the outset we decided to be as inclusive as possible in our choices, and we are grateful to the director and the publications committee of the Louisiana State University Press for their generosity in this connection. But in the last stage of the editing we dropped ninety-five letters. Nevertheless, a very substantial selection remains, a selection that in no way has been emasculated by the pruning necessitated by economic considerations.

The letters included here are principally directed to Ransom's father, mother, and sisters and to his friends of long standing, especially Tate and Warren. We have deliberately preserved sequences of letters written to the same correspondents over many years, but in no case does every extant letter to a given correspondent appear in our selection.

In several instances, chiefly those of Christopher Morley and Robert Graves, the reader will find sequences of letters written to friends and acquaintances associated only with certain phases in Ransom's life. We have also included letters to authors such as Babette Deutsch and Richard Wilbur who occasionally contributed to the *Kenyon Review*, in part to show Ransom's behavior as an editor.

In every instance the given letter has been chosen to show essential aspects of Ransom's personal or professional life, the development of his thought, the cast of his temperament. Most of the letters were chosen first and foremost for their literary value—the insight that they provide into literary history.

III

Even if it were possible to provide facsimile reproductions of letters in a published collection, or to present the letters precisely typeset in diplomatic transcription, no reader would want to thread through such a minefield. An edition in either form would be impossibly difficult to follow with interest and pleasure.

Within the limits of typographical practice and of editorial convention, Ransom's letters are presented here as he wrote them. The punctuation, capitalization, paragraphing, and spelling (including many British and other variant forms) are Ransom's with rare exceptions. These exceptions mostly involve obvious (infrequent) lapses that are chiefly typographical. Ransom was a careful writer under all circumstances. Because the errors are rare and almost invariably result from haste or oversight, there is seldom any point in reproducing them. Several lapses that are substantively significant (such as the misspelling of Allen Tate's given name in the first letter to him) have been retained.

After careful consideration we decided not to show whether a letter is written in longhand or typed; and since Ransom forgot to sign only two letters included here, we have seen this fact as a further reason not to use the notations *ALS* and *TLS*, *AL* and *TL*. Ransom wrote in a clear, flowing script that is almost never difficult to read easily, and his hunt-and-peck typing also rarely causes problems in legibility. There are no missing or blotted or torn pages. Whether the given letter is autograph or typed copy, its text is seldom difficult to establish. This information about a letter's provenance is therefore of little moment.

We have standardized headings and closings. We always show the full name of the person being addressed and the full date (to the extent that it can be determined). We show the place of the letter's origin only when that place changes; the overwhelming majority of these letters was written from Oxford and Hawarden, England, before World War I; from France (especially Saumur) during that war; and subsequently from Nashville, Tennessee, and Gambier, Ohio.

We have not standardized usage with the exception of a few typographical forms. For instance, the abbreviation of United States appears consistently as U.S., and the initials for persons' names are spaced as follows: A. T., J. C. R. If the abbreviations A.M. and P.M. are capitalized by Ransom, they are printed here in small capital letters; in the same way the abbreviations MS and MSS appear here in small caps if the author has capitalized those abbreviations. Words Ransom wrote in all capital letters are reproduced in capitals and small capitals.

Every letter is presented here in full (including all marginalia and postscripts). The ellipses are therefore Ransom's, but the number of points in these now follows standard usage. Marginalia have been silently inserted at appropriate places in Ransom's letters—without editorial notation.

Brackets enclose the material that has been provided by the editors. These insertions chiefly involve surnames when the reader might encounter difficulty in identifying a person from his or her Christian name or nickname. The index contains every name in full, including the nickname for each case in which one applies. The only other editorial interpolations within the text are the occasional silent expansion of obscure abbreviations (such as Ch. Ch. for Christ Church, Oxford).

The arch expression of the omniscient editor, [*sic*], has not been used. In this and other ways we have presented a text as free of editorial garnish as possible.

We have provided notes on the assumption that most readers will not read the correspondence from beginning to end and that all readers will read some letters independently and out of sequence. Hence the notes are occasionally repetitious. In each case they are given to make the letter as self-explanatory and independent as is reasonably practicable, and the same principle applies to editorial insertions.

Notes have been provided with the principal intention of characterizing the people, publications, and ideas that touched upon Ransom in an intellectual sense—the things that helped shape his mind. The letters here chiefly reveal the life of the mind that Ransom lived rather than his quotidian existence or social life. Therefore we have not identified many of the people whom he saw in passing while studying at Christ Church, Oxford, as a Rhodes scholar; nor have we given much information about the many officials representing universities and foundations with whom Ransom dealt over the last six decades of his life.

We have endeavored to make the notes as readable and as uncluttered as possible, still giving the essential information: hence, in general, we provide full bibliographical details only when articles and books have been written by Ransom and the inner circle of the Fugitives and Agrarians; the other titles, especially books, are usually cited only by date, omitting the place of publication and the publisher.

We urge the reader to repair to the chronology of Ransom's life and to the index as often as seems necessary and useful.

The proof has been checked not only against the final typescript provided to the publisher but against the original letters whenever a question has arisen. The reader should assume that the text of each letter is printed correctly, within the limits here described. The text faithfully represents the letters as they were first written by Ransom and read by his correspondents.

IV

John Crowe Ransom does not stand among the great letter-writers that this country has produced over the past one hundred years or more—Henry James, Henry Adams, Mark Twain, Edmund Wilson, E. B. White, and Nunnally Johnson. But there is no need to apologize for Ransom in this connection: he holds his own among most of his contemporaries. Of the major southern writers who have published since 1925 probably only Allen Tate is stronger as a letter-writer. We believe Ransom the equal of Caroline Gordon and Flannery O'Connor, who were both superb in this department, and superior to Conrad Aiken, John Peale Bishop, Donald Davidson, and William Faulkner.

To observe at this date that Ransom is a master of prose style seems sententious and supererogatory. It is germane to note that he forged that style early: he wrote good letters even as a young man. Although he often let his intellect play freely as he wrote a letter, covering every shade of thought clearly and succinctly and forcefully in letter after letter, he seldom gave full rein to his literary impulses (in terms of narrative and description and scene). Ransom's wit and irony also seldom achieve full expression in his letters. For him, as we have already implied, the letter was chiefly an instrument—not an end in itself.

Ransom was a guarded man who did not reveal his intimate life to anyone; nor did he intrude into others' personal lives or engage in controversy, public or private. His letters, good as they are, would be better had he not been so guarded in his relations; but to expect him to let down his guard is to ask for another person of wholly different temperament and character.

"All writing is both a mask and an unveiling," E. B. White remarked to his biographer in February, 1964. John Crowe Ransom, as we have shown, was far more interested in assuming a mask than in unveiling himself. He would have agreed fully with another remark in White's letters: "A man who publishes his letters becomes a nudist—nothing shields him from the world's gaze except his bare skin. A writer, writing away, can always fix things up to make himself more presentable, but a man who has written a letter is stuck with it for all time—unless he is dishonest." The man who wrote the letters in this book knew all that before White wrote it in June, 1975, and did his best to prevent our presenting him to the world in his bare skin, exposed to the world's cold eye and caught in his own nakedness and modesty. But there is nothing here for Ransom to be ashamed about, and we are unreconstructed and unregenerate when it comes to presenting these letters. We hope their readers will share our delight in them, for the letters are not merely literary documents for the scholars of the present and the future to study devotedly. They embody the record of the life of a man of letters whose zest for mundane life and whose talent for high art are endlessly fascinating.

A CHRONOLOGY

John Crowe Ransom, 1888–1974

1888	John Crowe Ransom was born April 30, in Pulaski, Tennessee, the third of the four children of John James Ransom (1853–1934) and Sara Ella Crowe Ransom (1859–1947); his siblings were Annie Phillips, Richard B. (Dick), and Ella Irene (Ellene).
1891–1899	Ransom lived in four Middle Tennessee communities served by his father, a Methodist minister: Spring Hill, Franklin, Springfield, and Nashville. Educated at home until he was ten, Ransom entered public school in October, 1898.
1899	In September entered the Bowen School in Nashville; Angus Gordon Bowen, the headmaster, Ransom wrote many years later, "did more for my . . . education than any other man."
1903	In June he was graduated at the head of his class from Bowen, and in September he entered Vanderbilt University.
1905–1906	Taught sixth and seventh grades at Taylorsville (Mississippi) High School.
1906–1907	Taught Latin and Greek at the Haynes-McLean School in Lewisburg, Tennessee.
1907–1909	Reentered Vanderbilt; selected for Phi Beta Kappa at the end of his junior year; elected editor of the *Observer*, the undergraduate literary magazine, in the spring of 1908; on June 16, 1909, was graduated from Vanderbilt at the head of his class.
1909–1910	Senior master and co-principal of Haynes-McLean, he taught Latin and Greek to the sixth form and was chief academic officer of the school.
1910–1913	At Christ Church College, Oxford, as Rhodes scholar; read "The Greats" (the School of *Literae Humaniores*) and in summers traveled extensively in the British Isles and on the Continent; his degree from Oxford was deemed the "best of the Seconds."
1913–1914	Taught Latin at the Hotchkiss School in Lakeville, Connecticut, where he met and shared literary ideas with Samuel

Claggert Chew, a member of the English department; read English literature seriously for the first time and began to formulate his ideas on the nature and function of poetry in conversations with Chew and in letters to his father.

1914–1917 In September, 1914, joined the faculty of Vanderbilt University as instructor of English; published his first essay, "The Question of Justice," in the *Yale Review* (July, 1915); in fall of 1914 began a series of informal discussions of philosophy and literature with a group of students and friends, later known as the Fugitives: Donald Davidson, Alec B. Stevenson, William Yandell Elliott, Stanley Johnson, and Sidney Mttron Hirsch; summer of 1915 read his first poem, "Sunset," to Davidson; on May 12, 1917, reported with Davidson to Officers' Training Camp at Fort Oglethorpe, Georgia; during summer read to Davidson some of the poems later to appear in *Poems about God.*

1917–1919 Was commissioned in August, 1917, and assigned to Field Artillery Training Base in Saumur, France; sent to the front as a member of the Fifth Field Artillery in January, 1918; in April, 1918, reassigned to Saumur as instructor; Alec Stevenson and William Frierson, later members of the Fugitive group, attended the artillery school while Ransom was an instructor; on May 13, 1918, sent complete draft of *Poems about God* to Christopher Morley, who had been at Oxford with Ransom and who helped him find a publisher, Henry Holt and Company; upon recommendation of Robert Frost the book was published in spring 1919; enrolled at the universities of Grenoble and Nancy in spring and summer of 1919 while awaiting orders to return to United States for discharge; first poems appeared in print: "One Who Rejected Christ," *Independent* (July 27, 1918); "Roses," *Contemporary Verse* (December, 1918); "Darkness" and "Under the Locusts," *Independent* (June 28, 1919); at Nancy first saw copies of *Poems about God.*

1919–1925 Arrived in New York in mid-August, uncertain of future plans; explored possibility of career in publishing in New York or in teaching in an eastern university; arrived in Nashville in late August and decided to return to Vanderbilt to be near aging parents; in the fall of 1919 Fugitive group met at home of Sidney Hirsch's brother-in-law, James M. Frank, at 3802 Whitland Avenue; in January, 1920, met Robb Reavill, of Denver, Colorado, to whom he was married on December 22, 1920; in November, 1921, Allen Tate began attending Fugitive meetings and discussions of the group, which soon were almost exclusively concerned with poems written by its members; daughter Helen born January 17, 1922; in April, 1922, the first of nineteen issues of the *Fugitive* appeared (most of Ransom's best poetry was published in this little periodical); in 1922 began correspondence with Robert Graves; review of *The Waste Land*, to which Tate responded, appeared in *Literary Review* (July 14, 1923); in spring of 1923 Tate brought Robert Penn Warren to Fugitive meeting; during 1923 published twenty-one poems, all but three in the *Fugitive*; a son, Reavill, was born September 14, 1923; *Chills and Fever* was accepted by Alfred Knopf in May, 1924, and a few weeks later, with assistance from T. S. Eliot, Graves convinced Hogarth to bring out *Grace after Meat* in England; received serious consideration for Pulitzer prize in poetry, which went to Edwin Arlington Robinson, in 1924; Ransom's first serious critical essays appeared in the *Fugitive*: "Mixed Modes" (March, 1925); "Thoughts on the Poetic Discontent" (June, 1925); "A Doctrine of Relativity" (September, 1925); the last issue of *Fugitive* appeared in December, 1925.

1926–1930 Spent leave from Vanderbilt during fall of 1925 composing a book-length manuscript on the nature and function of poetry, entitled "The Third Moment," and later destroyed because it was "hopelessly abstract"; a detailed summary of the ideas he hoped to include in this manuscript is included in letter to Tate (September 5, 1926); in January, 1927, *Two Gentlemen in Bonds* appeared and was hailed by reviewers as a major achievement by one of the most important poets of the era; promoted to professor of English at Vanderbilt in June, 1927; in 1926 his correspondence with Tate turned from discussion of literary theory toward the concepts of society and culture presented in *I'll Take My Stand* (1930), to which Ransom contributed the introduction and an essay; at work, beginning in 1928, on *God without Thunder* (1930); published "Classical and Romantic," on September 14, 1929, an essay in which he outlined the basic thesis of *The World's Body* (1938); 1927–1930: the discussions resulting in *I'll Take My Stand* occurred; in 1930–1931 Ransom engaged in a series of public debates with Stringfellow Barr, William S. Knickerbocker, and William D. Anderson on principles of Agrarianism.

1931–1940 The Ransoms spent the academic year 1931–1932 in England on Guggenheim fellowship; Ransom published "The State and the Land" (*New Republic*, February, 1932) and "Land! An Answer to the Unemployment Problem" (*Harper's*, July, 1932); began work on essays to appear in *The World's Body* and published first two: "A Poem Nearly Anonymous" and "A Poem Nearly Anonymous: A Poet and His Formal Tradition" in May and September, 1933; published "Modern with the Southern Accent" (April, 1935) and "What Does the South Want?" (April, 1936) in the *Virginia Quarterly Review*; the latter is Ransom's contribution to the second Agrarian symposium, *Who Owns America?* (1936); his son John James (called Jack) born April 12, 1935; left Vanderbilt to become professor of poetry at Kenyon College in Gambier, Ohio, in September, 1937; published "Shakespeare at Sonnets" in *Southern Review* (Winter, 1938); *The World's Body* appeared from Scribners in late winter 1938; during winter of 1937–1938 began discussions with Gordon Chalmers, president of Kenyon, about publication of a review; first issue of *Kenyon Review* appeared in January, 1939; began work on *The New Criticism* in summer of 1938 and published first essay to appear in the book in *Southern Review* in winter 1939; became Carnegie professor of poetry at Kenyon in spring 1939 and declined offer to become chairman of the English department of the Woman's College of North Carolina at Greensboro.

1941–1950 *The New Criticism* appeared, from New Directions, in spring of 1941; in spring of 1942 *Southern Review* (old series) was discontinued, and the *Kenyon Review* took over "all unexpired subscriptions"; during 1944 and 1945, with the assistance of Doubleday, Doran and Company, the *Kenyon Review* offered a first prize of $500 and a second prize of $250 for the best short stories "submitted by a writer who has not published a book of stories"; *Selected Poems* appeared from Knopf in spring of 1945 and reviews indicate Ransom's reputation as a poet was already firmly established; from 1945 to 1947 the Rockefeller Foundation supported a series of *Kenyon Review* fellows; from 1948 through 1950 this foundation supported the Kenyon School of English, which had on its faculty the most celebrated writers and critics of the time and attracted to Gambier many returning veterans and other students seriously interested in the study of literature; on December 30, 1947,

Ransom became a member of the National Institute of Arts and Letters; the summer 1948 issue of the *Sewanee Review* was devoted to "a tribute to Ransom on his sixtieth birthday"; Ransom spent the academic year 1949–1950 as visiting professor at Indiana University.

1951–1959 In the summer of 1951 the Kenyon School of English moved to Indiana University and became the School of Letters; on January 22, 1951, he received the Bollingen prize in poetry for 1950 and a few weeks later the Russell Loines Award in Literature from the National Institute of Arts and Letters; in 1951 Ransom edited, with introduction, *The Kenyon Critics*; from 1953 to 1955 *Kenyon Review* offered a fellowship each year to a poet, a writer of fiction, and a critic; among those receiving these awards were Irving Howe, Flannery O'Connor, W. S. Merwin, R. W. B. Lewis, Howard Nemerov, and Richard Ellmann; the fellowships were renewed for 1956–1958 and attracted, among others, Delmore Schwartz, James Wright, Andrew Lytle, J. F. Powers, Elizabeth Spencer, Leslie Fiedler, and Francis Fergusson; Ransom taught at School of Letters three summers: 1952, 1954, and 1958; published two of his most important critical essays in the mid-1950s, both in the *Kenyon Review*: "The Concrete Universal: Observations on the Understanding of Poetry, I" (Autumn, 1954) and "The Concrete Universal: Observations on the Understanding of Poetry, II" (Summer, 1955); on January 13, 1956, he presented "New Poets and Old Muses," as one of the Gertrude Clarke Whittal poetry lectures at the Library of Congress; returned to Vanderbilt for the Fugitives' reunion May 3–5, 1956; became honorary consultant in American literature for the Library of Congress; received the Creative Arts Committee Award in Poetry from Brandeis University on January 28, 1958; retired from teaching in the spring of 1958 and from the editorship of the *Kenyon Review* in the spring of 1959.

1960–1974 Visiting professor at Northwestern University for the winter term, 1960; participant in Vanderbilt Literary Symposium on April 20–21; returned to Vanderbilt as visiting professor, fall 1960; on December 4, 1962, received $5,000 award from the Academy of American Poets for distinguished poetic achievement; in April, 1963, a new edition of *Selected Poems* appeared; *John Crowe Ransom: A Tribute from the Community of Letters* appeared; and the spring issue of *Shenandoah* was a "Tribute to John Crowe Ransom on His Seventy-Fifth Birthday"; the *Kenyon Review* sponsored a symposium on the subject: "Quo Vadimus? Or the Books Still Unwritten," with Allen Tate, Robert Penn Warren, Robert Lowell, Robie Macauley, and Stephen Spender as participants; published essay on Wallace Stevens in *Kenyon Review* (Winter, 1964); in winter of 1964 made extended lecture trip to California; on March 10, 1964, received National Book Award for *Selected Poems* (1963); wrote essay on "Gerontion" for *Sewanee Review* (Spring, 1966); on December 16, 1966, elected to membership in the American Academy of Arts and Letters; in July, 1966, received $10,000 from the National Endowment for the Arts, an award made to a small number of "distinguished senior American writers"; on April 28, 1967, Martin College in Pulaski, Tennessee, gave a dinner honoring Ransom on his eightieth birthday; with other Agrarians participated, in mid-April, 1968, in Southern Literary Festival at the University of Dallas; a dinner was held in his honor at Kenyon on April 30, 1968, at which Allen Tate was the principal speaker; a third edition of *Selected Poems* appeared in April, 1968, and *The World's Body*, with a lengthy postscript, was reissued by the Louisiana State University Press at the same time; on May 9, 1968, received Emerson-Thoreau Medal and an award of $1,000 from the American Academy of Arts and Sciences; made last public appearance at Kenyon College on February 27, 1973, in presenting Robert Penn Warren, who was in Gambier to read his poetry; his poem "Four Threesomes or Three Foursomes" appeared in *Sewanee Review* for summer 1973; died in his sleep in Gambier, Ohio, on July 3, 1974; was cremated, and his ashes were buried behind the Chalmers Library on the Kenyon College campus.

1911–1920

HE EARLIEST known letters from John Crowe Ransom are two he wrote to his sister Annie during the spring of his freshman year at Vanderbilt. There are no letters from his other student years at Vanderbilt or from his earliest teaching (one year at Taylorsville [Mississippi] High School and two years at the Haynes-McLean School in Lewisburg, Tennessee). In the fall of 1910, however, he went to the University of Oxford as a Rhodes scholar and enrolled in Christ Church College. Apparently his family saved all of the letters he wrote from there.

Ransom's American friends at Oxford were very surprised that he chose "to read 'The Greats' because this School of pure learning was the most prestigious" of all the programs offered in the university. To enter it one must be able to read with ease, speed, and accuracy both Latin and Greek. But Ransom, unlike those friends, had studied both languages for eight years and had taught them for two before entering Oxford, so he was prepared to meet the academic challenges of the university's most demanding program.

Soon after Ransom enrolled in Oxford, he began a routine which he continued as long as he was there. Once each week, and often more frequently, he wrote a letter home. Although these letters were obviously intended for the entire family, he wrote alternately to his father (John James Ransom), his mother (Ella Crowe Ransom), and his two sisters, Annie and Ellene. These letters are filled with the details of his life at Oxford and his travels during his frequent vacations in Great Britain and on the Continent, but Ransom obviously attempted to stress the activities that he thought would be most interesting to the person to whom the letter was addressed. Those to his mother often included an explanation of his domestic arrangements—where he was living, the kind and quality of food available, his daily schedules of sleep, work, exercise, and entertainment, his travels, and other activities. Those to his father discuss in detail his reading and writing, precisely how he was attempting to satisfy the demands of his tutors, and how well he thought he was succeeding. The letters to his sisters are filled with accounts of his social life: the clubs he joined and why, the young ladies he met, the dramatic and musical entertainments he enjoyed.

These letters to his family are an amazingly complete record of an important period in Ransom's life. The rigorous academic discipline to which he willingly subjected himself gave him a thorough knowledge of the classical cultures, which was essential to many of his future literary endeavors; his experiences with a foreign way of life helped him to form convictions that he would retain throughout his life: that ritual and ceremony, form and pageantry are necessary ingredients of a formal culture. This prolonged introduction to British culture exaggerated a natural tendency toward a formality of manner that puzzled and often irritated even his best friends.

After he was graduated from Oxford, with a degree which his tutor assured him was "almost a First, at least the best of the Seconds," Ransom accepted a position at the Hotchkiss School in Lakeville, Connecticut. His letters to his family during that period follow much the same pattern he had established at Oxford. The most important of these, perhaps, are those he wrote to his father, detailing and complementing some of the discussion he was having with Samuel Claggert Chew, a member of the English department at Hotchkiss and later a well-known scholar of English literature. Ransom was reading English literature seriously for the first time and was establishing some critical positions he would maintain for the remainder of his life (see, for example, the theory of poetry outlined in the letter to his father on February 4, 1914). But readers of Ransom's later Agrarian essays may be surprised to find him in one letter arguing the advantages of city life over country life.

In the fall of 1914 he joined the English department of Vanderbilt University, where he remained until he reported for officers' training at Fort Oglethorpe, Georgia, on May 12, 1917. From there, and later from his stations in France, he wrote his family, as specifically as the censors would permit, the details of his activities as an officer in the field artillery. He was also writing to Christopher Morley, who had secured a publisher for Ransom's first book of poems, *Poems about God* (1919), sending revisions, publications, instructions, and new poems. In 1919 Ransom wrote Morley several letters in an attempt to find a position in New York because he was not certain he wanted to return to Vanderbilt. He wanted a place in an eastern college or university or, better still, a position in publishing or literary journalism in or near New York, the literary center of the country.

To John James Ransom

July 16, [1911]

Dear Father:

I am sending you my *opus magnum*, which I would like to have you hand on to Dr. Alexander.[1] It is somewhat belated, though not so much as you had thought; I did not get my official commission from headquarters until late in Term, and then Dr. Alexander told me to "take my time."

I send it to you with the hope that you will look it over with an eye to corrections where you think they are necessary. Perhaps the *Review* won't care for my English typist's English spelling.

As to remuneration, if that is to be a feature of the matter, please ask Dr. Alexander to turn that over to you at my request. I should like for Dick to have it; I wish I had some money to send him from here, but it may be that some other journalistic ventures of mine this summer will come to something.

Please ask Dr. Alexander to send copies of the number in which my article is to appear to the following: two to me; one to Dr. Richard W. Jones, Tufts College, Mass.; one to Mrs. A. M. Crane, 42nd St., Riverview, Norfolk, Va.; and one to Paul W. Terry, 978 Fourth Ave., Louisville, Ky. I suppose Bishop Denny, Mr. Ferguson and the Vanderbilt people will see the *Review* anyhow.

If Dr. Alexander would consider favourably an article on Ibsen, I should like very much to know about it. I have been reviewing my Ibsen this summer and am starting a new article. I had to tear up my first article when I had studied the subject better.

After this extent of "shop talk," I had better be saying that I hope that all are well, including Lucile and Ella Crowe,[2] and that you are not troubled with hot weather. London has been very unpleasant for nearly a week, with the thermometer approaching 90° as an upper and 75° (at midnight) as a lower limit. That is very disagreeable weather for England, where the humidity is so great. I shall be here through this week, at shifts between Ibsen and the dentist, who have much in common. I had allowed my teeth to go untended (except for the tooth-brush) for two years, and I find there are several alterations to be made.

Sunday afternoon I visited Hyde Park to see how the right of free speech worked. The strikers (of London dock-workers), and the suffragettes were holding demonstrations, and had a hundred thousand hearers; and there were various lesser lights, including Joachim Kaspary, who presented the "Propaganda of Humanitarian Deism, for the Conversion of Jews, Christians, Mohammedans, Atheists and other Misbelievers and Sinners."[3] The suffragettes had some able speakers, including two M.P.'s and Miss Sylvia Pankhurst, who spoke at Nashville last winter, whose mother is here in prison, and whose sister, Miss Christabel, has been at large for several months hiding from the police.[4] The strikers were considerably roused by some "fighting" speeches, and their part of the programme ended with a riot in which eleven men were sent to the hospital.

I had a fine letter from Ellene a few days ago; and this morning one from Omar Reynolds, an old pupil of mine in Taylorsville, who is now at Millsaps.[5]

With love to all.

Aff'ly, your son,
John C. Ransom

---

1. The Reverend Dr. Grosse Alexander (1852–1915) was editor of the *Methodist Quarterly Review.*

2. The wife and daughter of his brother Dick.

3. Joachim Kaspary was apparently a maverick socialist agitator; he was not associated with any organized socialist movement during this period.

4. Sylvia Pankhurst (1882–1960), the daughter of British suffragette leader Emmeline Pankhurst and a writer and representative for the movement.

5. Ransom taught in Taylorsville (Mississippi) High School during the 1905–1906 academic year.

To Sara Ella Crowe Ransom

Munich, October 1, 1911

Dear Mother:

Annie's letter came last Wednesday and was much enjoyed. Later a postal from her and one from Harlin saying that Dick and his bride had passed through. Harlin said she was certainly good-looking, which was no more than I expected. I hope Dick does well in Florida.

This is the last home letter I shall write from Munich for some time. I am planning to clear out for London next Sunday, and will write you from there, unless I change my plans. I hope to finish my summer's work, though not to my satisfaction, next Saturday, and then have a few days to spend in London before school opens Oct. 13, a week from next Friday. I have not done justice to many of the sights of London; during my last stay there I was too busy seeing Coronation to attend to museums, picture-galleries, etc. I hope to make several trips to the Museum next week; it is very interesting to anyone studying Greek history.

I have enjoyed my stay here fairly well, though just now I am rather tired of work and ready for a change. The bad weather has set in here in earnest, and the city is not so attractive under these conditions.

Last night I attended a performance of Wagner's *Tannhäuser* at the Royal Bavarian Opera House, standing-place, one mark (a quarter). I was much surprised and pleased to see how well it was given. I had thought the Dresden Opera, from its reputation, was far ahead of this, but it is not the case; they are two of a kind. I heard *Tannhäuser* in Dresden. I think it is the most popular of Wagner's operas, perhaps. To-night Caruso sings here in Verdi's *Aida*. But *Stehplatz*[1] is five M[arks] each and all were sold two weeks ago to a crowd that stood in line more than twenty hours. Several other good operas are to be given this week, and Schumann-Heink, the soprano, sings in one of them.[2]

I have been much interested lately in the newspapers, especially the accounts of the Canadian elections, which disappointed me very much, the war between Italy and Turkey, and the Johnson-Wells prize-fight in London.[3] The Methodists in London started the movement against the fight between the negro and the white man and used the big Johnson-Jeffries fight in America as an illustration.[4] The Methodists in England certainly seem to take their religion more seriously than most of the English, especially the Established Church.

I am much interested, of course, in Conference. I have not learned yet just when nor where it opens, but I imagine, not till the last of October. I suppose it will be well in November before I learn the results. Am sorry I can't help with the packing; I believe book-packing used to be my specialty.

A year ago to-day I sailed from Philadelphia. I imagine I have changed somewhat in that time, but mainly for the better, I hope.

Love to all,

Affectionately, your son,
John C. Ransom

(Most of the Rhodes Scholars call me Crowe, and I came near signing my name to this letter in English style, J. Crowe Ransom.)

---

1. Standing room.

2. Ernestine Schumann-Heink (1861–1936), Austro-American singer.

3. The fight between Jack Johnson and Bombardier Wells aroused much criticism in London because a black man (Johnson) was matched against a white man (Wells).

4. Jack Johnson successfully defended his title against James Jeffries on July 4, 1910. Many, particularly sports writers, were looking for the white fighter who could defeat Johnson; thus the expression the *Great White Hope* was applied to Jeffries.

To John James Ransom

Oxford, October 29, 1911

Dear Father:

I did not write last Sunday, because I did not feel very much like anything that strenuous. I had a three days' siege of the "flu," abbreviation for influenza, or what we call the "grippe." However, I am very much myself again now, after staying close in my room for several days. This is the first instance of any trouble with my health since I came over; besides that I have not had even a single cold of any consequence. My normal weight seems somewhat above what it was at home and my general health apparently all I could ask.

I have never been able to learn just when Conference met, so that I don't know whether your appointment was made last Monday, or is to be made tomorrow. The latter, I should think. If you or Mother have not already done so, please write me the results as soon as you get this. At any rate, I suppose Murfreesboro will no longer be our home address, and you will leave Ellene to represent us there. I believe she was away at school in Fayetteville for a while, so that she probably won't get very homesick. I hope she will not work too hard, and am glad to hear that she is going to play basket-ball.

I have enjoyed my two weeks in Oxford (except when I had to stay in) very much after a sixteen weeks' vacation. I have been very busy with my duties as Treasurer of the American Club, with entertaining the American "Freshers," and with my regular work for my tutors. The American Club is not doing so well as I should like; the men of my year are disposed to make too much of a joke out of the programs, and are rather boisterous in Parliamentary procedure, setting, as I think, a bad example for the Freshers. This is after the fashion of the English clubs, but I think the American Club ought to be somewhat more serious and dignified.

I have a new Philosophy tutor this term, or rather, I have gone back to the one I had the first term, Mr. Blunt. He is a very fine scholar and a severe critic. I am to do Logic and Metaphysics with him this term—a hard subject.

All the "Greats" tutors of this college (there are four) have been down, one or more at a time, with the influenza this term. In fact, it has been a sort of epidemic here the last ten days, and is always the stock malady of Oxford.

Next Tuesday I go to a Hallowe'en party, four to ten-thirty, at Sir James Murray's home. Hallowe'en is strictly a Scotch institution and not observed in England except by the Scotch families. I am invited to spend Christmas week with them; this is a rare chance to see an English Christmas first-hand, and ought to be a very pleasant affair for me. I appreciate the invitation very much. The Rhodes Scholar from New Hampshire, [Joe] Worthen, a very fine fellow, was given the same invitation, but he had already committed himself to a vacation in France. As for myself, I had about decided to go to Hawarden again; it is a place where I can get fine company, good accommodations, and all the books I can read. I had thought of studying in the fine Shakespeare library there. If I stay in England, as I am planning, I can come back to Oxford and the Murrays' for the week without great expense.

Since I began this letter I have gotten your letter with the news of Conference. I did not think Conference had met so early.

I hope Arlington will prove a pleasant place to live in.[1] I imagine your duties will not be so arduous as they would be on a District.[2] However, I am sorry the salary is not greater. I hope you have no pressing obligation to meet just now. I would like to be of some help, but am having all I can manage to meet the debts that I had to make in order to come over here. I shall do my best, but doubt whether I can do more than pay off my necessary debts and avoid any new ones during my Scholarship.

Is Arlington on the railroad, and what sized town is it? I can't locate it at all in my memory. I am sorry that Annie won't be able to carry out her plans.[3] It seems that I am the fortunate member of the family now, but I hope this will not always be true.

When I first came over, I planned a visit home this Christmas vacation. But the financial situation has caused me to change my mind. Quite a number of the Rhodes Scholars of my year are going home for Christmas, however.

I am about to take up a new sport here, though I have not settled whether it will be hockey or Lacrosse. I suppose the reason for my influenza was that I was doing nothing in the way of out-door sports. The rowing club is monopolized by the Freshers, who are learning how, and there would be little rowing for me this term. Besides, I am doubtful whether I care to go through another training season, as I would have to do if I rowed next term. I think the training is rather severe on the stomach, if nothing else, and it ruins the term for working purposes. To-morrow I think I shall go out for Lacrosse.

I was invited to join the Chess Club of the University, and a member of the team invited me to his rooms for a game, to see whether I was good varsity material. But the influenza came on in the meantime, and I had to call it off.

For some reason the books which I used in Germany have not come yet, though I shipped them from Munich over three weeks ago. I am writing to the German shipping company whose receipt I have for the box.

My collection of books has grown to such an extent that I shall have to have another small book-case when I get my box in. My books include the Encyclopedia, which is very useful in every subject which I have to work up; a complete Grate's Greece, 12 vols., a bargain from a London book-shop; a good number of text and reference books for use in Greek history; philosophical books; a small German library (mostly philosophy); and some books of general literature, such as Shakespeare, 6 vols. of Carlyle, a complete Emerson, the poets, and miscellaneous books, including a number of the Everyman Library (which cost 1 shilling each here, and 35¢, I believe, in America). I shall not make any further additions to my library, at least of any consequence except as I need books in my course. I do considerable reading on Sundays, and some in the vacations. But most of my time here is taken up with preparing two essays weekly. I am applying myself somewhat better than last year and gradually increasing my "pace." I admire the Oxford training very much, but just now am rather disgusted with the pedantic style in which the "Greats" people talk and write. They compose very quickly and smoothly, but have too great a fondness for big words.

I shall address this letter to Murfreesboro, being uncertain as to your present P.O. address.

Love to Mama, Annie and Ellene.

Aff'ly, your son,
John C. Ransom

---

1. A community then immediately outside Nashville, now a part of the city.

2. John James Ransom had just finished a term as the presiding elder (district superintendent) of the Murfreesboro district of the Methodist church.

3. Annie, Ransom's older sister, had planned to study music, perhaps in New York, under a professional teacher. She had been taught by her mother since early childhood, and the family considered her a gifted musician.

To Sara Ella Crowe Ransom

November 14, [1911]

Dear Mother:

Your letter arrived day-before-yesterday, Saturday, and Annie's a few minutes ago. Her letter made the best record of any that have passed between the two places, so far as I know; its time was only eight days.

I am much interested in the news from Arlington. Am glad to hear that you are so pleasantly situated, though it is a pity the salary is no greater.[1] I should think living there ought to be very nice. I would like very much to pay you a visit, but that will have to be post-poned somewhat. I have been away from Tennessee now for more than a year, and am more convinced than ever that it is the best place I have seen. Oxford is a delightful experience, but I should think that no American could ever be content in England. The differences are really more than surface-deep. On the whole, I am inclined to believe that people over here don't regard life in so healthy a way as Americans do—certainly they don't seem to enjoy it so much. There is much said to the effect that Americans are distinguished as *practical* people; but I would say, on the contrary, that they are the only nation of idealists that I know anything about. The politics of Europe is specially enlightening; the nations, like most of the individuals I have met, are basely utilitarian and the United States seems the only country whose foreign policy is fair and just; and the people and publications here can't believe that that is the case, but are always making out a case for America's (as they call us) secret motives.

I did not mean to get off such a tirade. But Annie's letter told about so many nice people and nice things that it started me thinking along that line. I am glad to know that the bother of moving is over and you can settle down quietly again. What do the people think of Papa's sermons? That reminds me, the sermons we hear in Oxford (that is, in the Anglican churches) are rather tame affairs; the Europeans for the most part seem to take their religion rather mildly.

I am to go presently (at 10 P.M.) to see Mr. Bell, a young "don," or professor, of this college whom I was with in Hawarden. We played chess together there a good deal, and I believe that is what he has asked me in for, to-night. I have finally gotten in upon one of the few gravel tennis courts in Oxford and am enjoying some fine games. My playing has much improved.

I have just learned that one of the new Americans in this college, Osborne, of Indiana, is down with inflammatory rheumatism and has been taken to the hospital.[2] That is hard luck for a man just starting out.

Yesterday I had a letter from an old Kappa Sigma friend, Willard Steele, of Cumberland and Vanderbilt. He and Mrs. Steele, who was recently Miss

Kate Hinds, of Lebanon, another good friend of mine, are in London for the winter. I hope to see them there sometime.

The Americans are making busy preparations just now for Thanksgiving. Dr. Dixon, from Moody's church in Chicago, now in Spurgeon's Tabernacle, London, will preach in the morning, and we are to have a big dinner that evening.

Love to all,

Aff'ly, your son,
John C. Ransom

1. The salary at the Arlington Methodist Church in 1910 was $1,000. J. J. Ransom may have earned a little more because he had recently completed a term as presiding elder.

2. James I. Osborne, a Rhodes scholar at Christ Church from 1911 to 1914.

To John James Ransom

November 20, [1911]

Dear Father:

Have spent a pleasant week since I wrote last, but nothing of great importance has happened. Think I have had no letter from home since Annie's of last Monday.

How do you like the new home and church? I would like to know something about the parsonage, garden, neighbourhood, and other features. I suppose that having only one church to attend to will be something of a rest to you. Are you doing any special reading or study of any kind?

I have not accomplished much work somehow this term, so far as quantity goes, but think my work has much improved in quality. My tutor, Mr. Blunt, has taken sick and I have been assigned for my Philosophy work to Mr. Steward, a very old man and lecturer on Plato. I took him a paper to-day on Aristotle's theory of Justice, and he complimented it very highly. I am perhaps giving a disproportionate amount of study to Aristotle's Ethics; but it is so far ahead of most works on the subject, which are usually one-sided.

In talking over my History "collection" (college examinations) with Mr. Dundas, I seemed to surprise him very much by telling him that there had been a great deal of open cheating in the examination. That is really a very ordinary thing here, I believe. He invited me to take tea with him this afternoon to discuss the morals of Oxford; but he failed to come in until rather late and asked me to come to-morrow instead.

The Americans are making great preparations for the Thanksgiving celebration which has become an annual thing here. The morning service will not be held in Christ Church Cathedral, as usual, because the preacher is a non-Conformist and the cathedral pulpit can only be occupied by a Conformist. The preacher is Rev. Dixon, now pastor at the Spurgeon Tabernacle in London, and just come from the Moody Tabernacle in Chicago. He was here being entertained the other day; I found that he was from North Carolina, an old friend of Sam Jones, and acquainted with Nashville.

The dinner will be as near a duplicate of Thanksgiving dinners at home as can be gotten in England. The dinner committee has been occupied several weeks with tasting samples of mince pies and training the cook. The speakers will be Englishmen of prominence here and members of the Club.

In three weeks the term will be over and I shall go to Hawarden, where I spent my second vacation, for the six weeks. It is a splendid place for reading, working and playing chess. I intend to take up golf there for recreation, as that is about the only sport the place affords besides walking and biking. I have declined the Murrays' invitation to spend Christmas week with them; am sorry to say that it is rather dangerous to accept entertainment in an English home where there are marriageable daughters.

The new Freshmen from America seem to be a rather fine lot of fellows. They still advertise themselves by their American ways and clothes, but I think they will prove a very popular lot.

Wednesday I shall take a day off to catch up with my correspondence; this includes a letter to Ellene, who probably gets a little homesick sometimes.

Love to Mother, Annie and Ellene.

Affectionately, your son,
John C. Ransom

To Sara Ella Crowe Ransom

January 8, 1912

Dear Mother:

We are having a considerable snow-storm for this part of the world. The snow has now gotten two or three inches deep and to-night is still coming down. Last night we had a good deal of ice and the snow had a dry surface to fall upon. It is a rather pleasant sight; but it interfered with our golf this afternoon, although a few days ago we did play clear through a sleet-storm. If the snow is light, golfers use a red ball and play right on; but two inches of snow is enough to hide the ball entirely.

Saturday it was raining so hard that instead of having our usual golf game we took the train to Liverpool for the afternoon. We visited the art gallery there and had a very pleasant holiday. Saturday is always a "slack" day here.

Stuart and I have become considerably interested in a prospective trip to Norway and Sweden next summer. Jim Crowe[1] is coming over to spend a month with me, and Stuart (Va.) and Bland (O.),[2] who are at Hawarden with me, will complete our party. We expect to take some walking excursions in Germany or some boat trips through the northern seas. Stuart has some lady friends in Norway, whom he met in Germany last year; and the World's Olympic Games at Stockholm furnish another attraction.

I am enjoying Oxford terms and the many vacations in various places, but I will be perfectly ready to come home when my time is up: I shall begin about a year from now upon my search for a good position in some college as near Nashville as possible. I should like best to teach philosophy, but am not averse to Greek. I am thinking of teaching at least three or four years, that is, until I make some financial headway, for the family's sake and my own. The probability is that I shall teach for some years longer and perhaps indefinitely, because I am planning to embark upon some publishing ventures and teaching is most closely connected with that sort of enterprise. I shall be very glad when I am through with these preliminaries and down at work in a settled position.

I hope you enjoyed the Christmas holidays; am sure you were glad to have Ellene at home.

Love to all.

Aff'ly, your son,
John C. Ransom

---

1. James Crowe, Ransom's cousin, called Pat by the family, was graduated from Vanderbilt in 1914. After a brief career as a journalist in New York, he joined the Army Air Corps and was killed when his plane crashed while he was on duty on the Western front in 1918.

2. Ransom's references here characterize his mention of other Rhodes scholars. William Alexander Stuart (1889–1976), a graduate of the University of Virginia, who was at Balliol College, became a distinguished attorney. William John Bland (1887–1918), a graduate of Kenyon College, who was at Lincoln College, was commissioned a major after a brief career as an attorney and was killed in action in France, as were others of Ransom's fellow Rhodes scholars.

To John James Ransom

January 29, 1912

Dear Father:

Your letter received last week, and one from Mother to-day. I am very glad to hear that her hand is not in any serious trouble.

You wrote about the note which required my signature for Mr. Morgan, but did not enclose it as you said. I thought of enclosing a statement authorizing the holder of the note to consider me as joint security, but I have not particulars as to date and think it would be worthless, legally, to do so. But I will gladly sign it if you will send it. As I have said, I am very sorry not to be able to give you any assistance now. I hope this state of things will not continue more than three or four years longer; and think that a safe estimate provided I can have reasonable luck in getting me a position.

I have just come from a meeting of the Twenty Club. I am Secretary for this term and consequently am now attired in evening raiment. The Club is a very important body, at least in its own estimation, and requires of its officers a great amount of dignity and scrupulousness.

I have taken up a new sort of work for this term or perhaps longer. That is Psychological Laboratory, under Mr. Wm. Macdougall. The Laboratory is quite a good one, although not nearly so elaborate as the Harvard one and several others. Mr. Macdougall is an extremely able man; he is the author of "Social Psychology," and "Mind and Matter" and I think is bound to make a considerable name for himself with these books and others that he will write. He is quite a young man yet. The class in the Laboratory is very small, and consists mainly in Americans; but his lecture courses are very popular. I am very doubtful as to the value of experimental psychology; all that it has done so far has been to "elaborate the obvious." But since I intend to teach philosophy, if I can find the patience, and in any case wish to inform myself to some extent on all the branches of philosophy, I concluded that a term, at least, in this study would be worth while. Of course this is quite separate from my regular work with my tutors. That goes on regardless. At present I am making a study of the Judgement, and its history in Logic.

Ormond, the Rhodes Scholar from New Jersey, spent Saturday with me.[1] We were engaged in writing a book. That is, a good lady here with nothing better to do is planning a book on Oxford and asked us to give her some of the details of Oxford life, of which she has no first-hand knowledge.

We have had several days of fine, clear, cold weather. To-day there has been good skating. The Christ Church Meadows, and all other low places along the river, have been flooded several weeks from the back-waters of the Thames, and there is no lack of skating rinks. But it does not seem cold; and people go hatless and overcoat-less all over the town. My bed-room and sitting-room windows are down as far as they will go now, as always. All this is possible by reason of the magical cold tub with which the day always starts at Oxford.

Mother's letter has set me to thinking much about coming home this summer; but I can't decide one way or the other yet.

I hope all are well and not minding the weather.

Love to all.

Aff'ly, your son,
John C. Ransom

---

1. A. H. Ormond, a graduate of Princeton, was in Oriel College from 1910 to 1913 and subsequently practiced law in New Jersey until 1967.

To Sara Ella Crowe Ransom

February 4, 1912

Dear Mother:

I enjoyed your last letter very much, receiving it five or six days ago. I am glad to hear that your hand is getting better. I hope that both you and Papa are taking advantage of the quiet surroundings of the new home and enjoying a good rest from the hard labours of the Murfreesboro work.

This morning I had a good, long letter from Ellene. She seemed to be enjoying herself, but I think perhaps she is working too hard. She ought to take numerous evenings "off" and visit Suzanna, Cousin Bessie and the other kinfolks. But she seems to think that the ladies at Soulé would object. I hope you will write her and them and impress it upon them that she is to get away from her responsibilities occasionally.

We have had some very surprising weather here for the past week. There have been exactly seven days of skating and the ice is now thicker and the weather colder than ever. If I had known that the cold snap would be so prolonged, I would have gotten some skates at the first and perhaps would now be an accomplished performer on the ice. But as it is, I have not been out for skating at all, taking my "exer" in other forms. I am joining a tennis club, which plays on a private gravel court, for the rest of term. This sounds like a strange form of sport for this sort of weather, and so it would be; but the probability is that it will soon be warm again, and it is safe to count on a good number of suitable tennis-days in the remaining six weeks of term.

I enjoy the cold weather very much in certain ways. It is disagreeable to have to get out of bed in the morning with the temperature of the bed-room at 25° F, take a cold "tub," dress and rush off to a chilly chapel service at 8 o'clock, before breakfast. But my rooms are all the more comfortable by the contrast. My rooms, as I am sure I have told you, are in the "garret" of Peckwater, somewhat cramped compared with the rooms on lower floors, but extremely warm and pleasant in cold weather. I am breakfasting with McLean this term; we alternate between his rooms, which are next door, and mine. After we finish reading the newspaper, I spend the morning at work; I have given up lectures for the time being. Luncheon at 1 is a light affair. I have my exercise and bath in the next three hours and come in to tea. I do some further work before Hall (or dinner in Hall) at 7:30; and after Hall I am free to read, write, visit, entertain, attend a club-meeting or go to the picture show. Four meals a day are not quite enough for Oxford men and after Hall they meet in some one's rooms for "coffee"; which consists in a coffee-and-hot-milk compound ("harf and harf") and cake and fruit.

After doing a pretty good week's work I have enjoyed to-day more than most Sundays. My amusements consisted, first, in reading one of Shakespeare's plays for the first time—Cymbeline, which I liked fairly well; and next, in attending a tea followed by a private violin recital, given by the Rhodes Scholar from New Hampshire, Worthen, of New College. He played Humoresque, also Raff's Cavatina and Massenet's Meditation, from the opera Thais. He is a very good performer, although he does not have time to keep up his practice. He is the President of the American Club now, and has announced his engagement (during the Christmas holidays) to a Wellesley girl, a member of the Wellesley quartet, a violinist and a pianist (all in one). I have never seen a man so pleased with the world as he is at present.

After Hall to-night (which is exceptionally good on Sundays), I had an Englishman in to coffee. We read together some of Browning's poems, including Saul, Fra Lippo Lippi and Andrea del Sarto. After this letter and one or two others I shall arrange my blankets in sufficient numbers and turn in.

I am having a nice time of it in the Psychological Lab. The class is so small and its members so irregular that sometimes only one or two attend. Mr. McDougall is a very fine man, and extremely affable. I also attend an informal Lecture of his on the Psychology of Ethics, which meets shortly after the Laboratory class once a week. Last Thursday he invited me to share his tea with him between times; which he made on an alcohol lamp in the Laboratory and improved with condensed milk.

I have been thinking a good deal about your suggestion as to coming home for the summer. It had not occurred to me, because I thought I had better see as much as possible while over here and summer of course is the time for sight-seeing. But the idea of going home appeals to my inclinations and, I am inclined to think, would be no less profitable than the other. Perhaps I had better not express myself too definitely, because various things might intervene, but I think I am safe in saying that I shall come if nothing prevents. But I had rather not advertise my plans so that I can take people by surprise. In the meantime I shall try to get ahead with my work so as to have as much time as possible free in the summer. Is there room enough to have Jim Crowe with me a week or two? He was coming over here, but may not do so if I write him.

Love to all.

Aff'ly, your son,
John C. Ransom

To Annie Ransom

February 19, 1912

Dear Annie:

Before dinner-time I have about an hour and a half in which to attend to some of my arrears in correspondence. I am writing in the college J.C.R. (Junior Common Room). This is an undergraduate club which provides luncheon, tea, newspapers, comfortable chairs and stationery. The J.C.R. also supplies "hotters" and cake for teas in the undergraduates' rooms. All their china and plate is marked with these initials, which happen to correspond with my own. Consequently I can pretend to be serving teas in style, with my own initials on everything, when I have people from other colleges who do not know about our institutions.

I have had a very fine experience this afternoon. I played in my first game of hockey. The Christ Church first hockey team is not very successful and one or two enterprising men decided to get up a second team. We played a team of graduates, some of whom are said to have played on the varsity. They were much surprised when we beat them, 6 to 4. Hockey is a splendid, rough game and I don't know when I have enjoyed an athletic occasion so much before. I did rather well for my first appearance. My regular game here is tennis, but the weather has not been at all propitious up to date.

I am beginning to look around for "digs" (diggings, if you prefer) for next year. I managed to get permission, against the letter of the rules, to go into unlicensed "digs." They are not under regulations as to hours, absences, etc., and are considered safer places for undergraduates. The unlicensed "digs" are less expensive, but still no one complains that they are too cheap. Either sort of lodgings is much less expensive than living in college, but at the same time less pleasant.

Saturday I attended the ceremony of conferring degrees. A friend of mine, Nicholson, who roomed next to me last year, took his B.A., for which he had been qualified since last summer's examinations. During the summer he took part in a bicycle accident, coming out with his leg broken in two or three places. He has just "come up" for the rest of the year to study Theology. He is handicapped with a considerable limp. His record in Schools (the Final Examinations) was unusually fine; he was one of the few "Firsts," which is the highest distinction to be won here outside of the prizes and scholarships in special subjects.

Mr. and Mrs. Wylie had me to dinner with them last Thursday night. As you know, he is the Home Secretary of the Rhodes Trust and the man who oversees us and presents the cheques. He and Mrs. Wylie are very nice to the Rhodes Scholars and entertain almost continually. Thursday night they had some young ladies and several other Rhodes Scholars out.

Mr. Wylie, as I may have mentioned before, has had a bad accident himself, very much like that in Nicholson's case. While out riding last term, he was thrown from his horse and his leg badly broken. He has just recently gotten up from bed and will never be able to walk without limping.

I have a pretty big week's work ahead of me. Besides my two regular essays, in History and Philosophy, I have undertaken to write another to be read in the informal class which Mr. McDougall, the University Psychologist, is holding. It is to be based on a book by Ribot, not yet translated from the French.[1] Another man was to have gotten up the paper, as I did not know any French, but he was hit by a hockey ball and the Doctor advised him not to read. He has agreed to get people to translate the book (which has 186 pages) for me on condition that I write the essay.

"Toggers," or "Torpids," the winter boat races, begin on next Thursday and continue till the next Wednesday. I took part in "Toggers" last year, but this year I did not go in for rowing on account of my recollection of the training season. Training is not compatible with work, and, besides that, I am doubtful as to whether it is of very great benefit to be stuffed twice a day for four weeks. The table is the most strenuous feature of English rowing.

I have not heard much of interest musically this term. There seems to be a scarcity of great performers here this winter. But the Balliol Sunday night concerts are always good, with sometimes an exceptionally fine singer or violinist. What pieces are you playing most now? I am very fond now of Mendelssohn's Jägerlied; think it is my favourite piano piece. Humoresque is my choice for the violin, and probably Liszt's Hungarian Rhapsodie No. 2 for an orchestra. But I am not certain on any of these.

Sunday I received a batch of Lewisburg *Gazettes* for January and February. They are building the railroad at last, it seems, and the town is evidently enjoying something of a "boom."

Hope all are well. Love to Father, Mother and Ellene.

Aff'ly, your brother,
John C. Ransom

1. Théodule Armand Ribot (1839–1916) was a pioneer in experimental psychology.

To John James Ransom

March 26, [1912]

Dear Father:

Your letter received to-day. I am very glad to hear of the steps you have taken in the matter of my getting some journalistic work for this summer. I am writing to Mrs. Cole thanking her for her interest. I do not know her address, and so am enclosing the letter in this. I will be still further obliged if you will address and post it. I hope that you and she together can get some sort of position for me.

I am still undecided as to my profession. But, other things being equal (which means finances in my case), I think a few years of journalism would be better for me than the same time spent teaching. Journalism calls for more enterprise than teaching. I could without much effort devote myself to scholarship, especially Philosophy, in which I feel that I might win some recognition. But at present I am rather averse to philosophizing because it makes life so anaemic for the man who gives himself up to it. And I do not think it is especially useful to the other people.

I am also obliged for your suggestion to Dr. Alexander about my writing him an article. I shall be very glad to do this. But I suppose this has no financial interest, has it? Shall I wait for him to write, or does he understand that I have undertaken the article?

I am glad to hear that you are all well. I have had a very pleasant week since I wrote. I am staying at Foxcombe Hill, Berkshire, with three other Americans, McLean, of Texas, Bland, of Ohio, and Worthen, of New Hampshire. Bland and Worthen have "Schools," or Final exams, next Term, and are making severe preparations. They are taking the B.C.L. (Bachelor of Civil Law) Schools, which are much the hardest of the Law Schools. McLean takes his B.Sc. in Pathology in June, and goes into Oxford (four miles) daily to the Laboratory to carry on his experiments. He is discovering some law about the composition of the blood, something I am not qualified to understand. He worked a year at Johns Hopkins before coming over.

Our land-lady supplies us with a liberal table and our lodging arrangements are entirely comfortable. Our place is called Hill View, and commands a fine sweep of country towards Abingdon. We coast on our bikes almost to Oxford and our air here is so much better that it seems to be of a different country.

Our amusements consist in golf, tennis, riding and walking. There are some fine old villages within five or six miles, enough of them, I should think, to occupy us during our whole stay here. Yesterday we biked four miles to the Frilford Golf course and spent the entire afternoon playing eighteen holes. This course is the best in this part of England, better than the three which are nearer Oxford. But my playing was very bad; I seem to be following out the usual rule of getting steadily worse. To-day we went in to Oxford for a game of tennis. McLean couldn't leave the Lab., and Barbour, of Mich., who is staying near here, made the fourth man.[1] He is working for a B.Litt. in Law; his subject is one that no one has ever worked up, The History of Consideration in Contract, and his thesis is based on a study of thousands of French cases in the eleventh and twelfth centuries, which no other [person] alive has read. He is a great friend of Anderson, Principal of the Murfreesboro School, and a very nice man.

To-day I had a letter from Mr. John Murray, my tutor, insisting on my joining his party in Brittany. I had expected to stay on here the whole vac., but now I suppose I shall spend the latter half with him on the Continent. He has selected a place near St. Malo, where he says there are good tennis courts.

I am making a study of Ibsen this vac., preliminary to writing a general review of his work for our new literary club.[2] I had already read two or three of his plays, and I am very much interested in the study.

Last Sunday Worthen and I went over to Garsington, five miles the other side of Oxford, to spend the day with Miss Crocker. She is an American lady who has taken it upon herself to entertain the Rhodes Scholars and other Americans in Oxford. She has twenty or thirty to tea every Sunday of Term, and she performs a great service as an advisor on English etiquette. She is at Garsington for a few weeks. She has an interesting relic of the Wesley family which I am to take to you when I leave.

The coal-strike continues, as you have seen. Coal is higher than it has ever been since the close of the Franco-German War. It now sells at 46/ per ton; or over $11.00. A million strikers and about twelve hundred thousand workmen other than coal-miners are out of work. The train service is much disorganized. Many poor people are starving. There is no prospect of an early settlement and matters are likely to get much worse. Fortunately for the housekeepers, the spring has become very mild and the warm weather season is almost here. But the manufacturers all over the country are gradually closing down and there is sure to be much distress. It seems that in many directions hard times are ahead for England.

With love to all.

Aff'ly, your son,
John C. Ransom

1. Willard T. Barbour, a graduate of the University of Michigan, earned a B.Litt. in jurisprudence at Oriel College in 1912. He became an attorney and businessman in Nashville.

2. Ransom and some of his friends, including William Alexander Stuart and Christopher Morley, had founded the Hermit Crabs, a literary club. The organization of this group generally resembled that of the Fugitives.

To Sara Ella Crowe Ransom

April 4, 1912

Dear Mother:

I have been pretty well supplied with home mail the past week. Annie's letter came a few days ago, one from Ellene just afterwards, and yours and Father's to-day.

I went in to Oxford this afternoon to see if I could find Annie's picture, "Sir Galahad," there; but I had forgotten that on Thursdays the shops close at 1 p.m. in order to give the employees a half-holiday. To-morrow I shall try again.

My interest in journalism has considerably revived since Papa's and Mrs. Cole's efforts in my behalf. I have about given up my intentions of going home for the summer, although I had never fully decided to do that. I shall like it very much if I can get some news-correspondence work to do during the summer. I would be willing to take six or eight weeks of the summer from work (i.e., my studies) for that purpose. If I can get a decent salary to start with, I think I shall go into journalistic work as soon as I am out of Oxford; otherwise I shall have to take up teaching, at least temporarily.

I have not heard from Mrs. Cole at all, but suppose you addressed my letter to her which I enclosed about two weeks ago.

The past week has been a very pleasant one, though uneventful. Sunday I went in to tea at Sir James Murray's. I talked with him more fully than I had ever done, there being other young men to entertain the ladies in the room. He has a wonderful stock of information; I have never seen him at a loss for the fact he wants.

Joe Worthen, one of our four here, has been taking some pictures of our golf-games and of some English country scenes about here. In my next letter I shall send some of them. One of them ought to give a pretty good view of an English thatch-roof cottage; they are very plentiful here.

Besides my work in Greek History, I have managed to do some reading in Ibsen, which I have found extremely interesting. I have read about half of his works, and expect to read them all during the vacation in preparation for an essay which I am to read early in term before our new club. I also spend at least an hour a day reading the English newspapers. I read the *Telegraph* completely through, which is quite an achievement.

We have had some perfect weather for several days, after getting a bad start at the beginning of the vacation. The countryside is brightening up visibly every day, and will keep on doing so for about six weeks; then England will be the prettiest country to be found.

I leave for Brittany early next week, to join my tutor's party. He and I probably go together from Oxford.

I hope you are having a pleasant Easter.

Love to all.

Aff'ly, your son,
John C. Ransom

To Sara Ella Crowe Ransom

A TRIP TO BRITTANY AND OTHER THINGS

May 8, 1912

Dear Mother:

As I said on the post-card, I have been very negligent as to writing of late. Sunday is my usual day for writing, but my last few Sundays have been pretty well taken up with other things. I shall try not to miss my regular weekly letter after this. I think this must be my first offence.

Perhaps I had better write of my trip to Brittany. I wrote a letter just as I was leaving there, but it did not suit me on re-reading it, and I tore it up without finding time just then to write another.

We were in Dinan just two weeks. Our party consisted of my young Philosophy tutor, John Murray, and six undergraduates—all "loyal Britishers" except myself. We had some lively international arguments, but of course I was considerably outnumbered. However, I enjoyed this amusement very much. It was the first time I had been entirely away from Americans, I think, for anything like so long a time.

Dinan is a very picturesque town, of about 12,000 population. I think I never saw in a small place such a variety of scenes. The town is built up from the Rance valley and is very precipitous in places. The mediaeval buildings are abundant and some of the streets are so steep and narrow as to suggest anything rather than modern comfort. *La belle Rance* is a lovely stream and as a great concession to the tourists, is provided with luxurious boats—of which we made some use.

Market day (Thursday) is the finest sight that Dinan affords to my way of thinking. The country people bring in their produce and fill the streets all day. They wear the old-fashioned Breton peasant costume, which means, for the women, black dresses and tiny white bonnets with long, stiffly-ironed strings hanging down behind. The peasants in this section are rather fine-looking specimens physically. The women seem to do more than their share of the farm work; they drive in their pigs and calves, done up in a sort of harness (i.e. the pigs and calves), and seem to do most of the buying and selling. The pigs are all white, and evidently household pets. I have seen the women, when their pigs refused to go, stop and scratch their backs a few minutes, after which the pigs would become perfectly obedient. The calves are much more troublesome and there seems to be no recognized method of dealing with the refractory ones except simply to wear them out with sheer patience.

The valley of the Rance claims a good deal of space in Baedeker and perhaps I ought to refer to it. We went both up and down the river with fine results. Among other excursions we went to tea with an American gentleman who had just bought a very fine chateau above the river about six miles below Dinan. He was a Col. Jones, of Washington, and had a very pretty niece, Miss Emerson. He seemed to be a man of some wealth and influence, and said he had been an intimate friend of Senator Cormack's. My English friends, and, for that matter, the English colony at Dinan in general, of which I shall have more to say, were not favourably impressed with Col. Jones; partly because of the matter of accent, which was American, partly because he was the wealthiest man in the neighbourhood (this applies only to the feelings of the English colony), and partly because he always told his guests how much everything of his had cost, a habit which is not American, I trust. But for all that he had a lovely place on the cliffs, and he was a very strong character, in spite of his weaknesses. I was very much struck with the fact that my English friends did not see this. It seems that the English attach so much importance to what is "good form," meaning English form, that they fail to estimate fairly people and institutions to which their standards will not apply.

I was much surprised that Col. Jones could not detect the American in my accent; but on the other hand, it never escapes an Englishman with whom I talk for any considerable time. I think it best, when in Rome, to adopt the Roman accent; but I imagine I shall have a good deal to unlearn some months hence.

Our party was supposed to be a reading-party, and certainly bore that appearance with a tutor at its head. Of course you know that reading is Oxford parlance for working at texts. But we became involved in the social activities of the English colony at Dinan to such an extent that we did not get very far with our programme. There are more than a hundred English residents in Dinan, largely for reasons of climate, most of them extremely nice. We met them in very rapid succession from our first Sunday at the Dinan English Church onwards. Then we had entertainments in our honour, ranging from ordinary tea-parties to all day picnics on the river. Our tutor is rather shy and timid with the ladies, and he was quite unequal to exercising any discrimination with the invitations, with the results that we had a very delightful season socially in Dinan, but not a very profitable reading party. But I think no one regrets that, because, after all, we could not have done much in the time, and it is a great deal to have had such a pleasant fortnight. We all hope to repeat the experience next spring. The only fatality was in the case of a young Welshman, who has Schools, or final examinations, this June; he fell violently in love with a pretty girl and has not been able to attend to his work properly in consequence.

Crossing the channel was rather an experience on both occasions. We had a small boat (comparatively) and a rough sea, going; the combination proved my undoing, though I was not by any means alone. It was my first serious experience of sea-sickness, and I was agreeably surprised that it was not worse. For our return journey, which was not so rough, we made preparations by taking some patent medicine guaranteed to prevent seasickness. It did; but it also left me stupid and "groggy" for several days.

Summer term at Oxford is a wonderful institution and I am prepared for the most pleasant eight weeks I have yet had here. My experience is that Oxford improves upon acquaintance, and you know that my first impressions were very pleasant ones. The days are becoming long and warm, and they seem to be best fitted for reading in easy chairs, punting lazily on the Cher, and taking tea in pretty gardens. At least, that is my present feeling in the matter, but it may be because I have just come from an hour with a tutor, for which I have been making severe preparations for several days. For I have a really great teacher in philosophy this term—Mr. Blunt—and I want to get a good deal out of him while I can. I am also beginning on my Roman history this term, so that I don't seriously intend to "slack" to any great extent. Besides the interest of my work, I have other incentives in the pleasant vacation I have just had and the prospects ahead for the summer. A letter received yesterday from James Crowe says he is certainly coming to see me, and we are planning to tour Norway and Sweden.

I am playing tennis for my "exer" this term, varied by occasional games of golf. The Christ Church tennis and cricket fields are very fine to look at. But they have been needing rain badly, up till two nights ago. In spite of the traditional showers, April of this year broke all records for dryness, having less rainfall than any month in the history of the weather bureau, that is, for a hundred years. Consequently the spring is rather well advanced and Oxford is almost in her full glory. The architecture of Oxford was evidently meant for rain and fog such as it gets in the autumn and winter terms. Peckwater Quadrangle, where I live, looks as if dropping to pieces with age, and is most impressive in the cold rains. It will look strange next week when every window is filled with flower-boxes of blazing geraniums and all sorts of red, yellow and purple things. The fine thing about Oxford in summer term is the natural beauties of the trees, the gardens and the playing-fields, but the venerable look of the architecture presents a great contrast.

The prettiest walk in Oxford, I think, is around the "House" (which means Christ Church) meadows. The meadows are just back of one part of the college, which Ruskin built, and are in the form of a circle, enclosed by the famous "Long" and "Broad" walks, the Isis (which is the classical Oxford rendering of the Thames) and the Cherwell (pronounced Ch*ar*). It is a twenty-minutes walk, and much frequented by the American tourists who are beginning to arrive.

My presidential term at the American Club has been inaugurated very successfully and I am expecting to have a very good term. The Club at present is in most flourishing condition.

The independence of the American Colonies has been recognized for the first time in the history of Oxford this term in having a university lecture course on an American history subject; the lecture is on the American Civil War, and given by an American, Dr. James Ford Rhodes.[1] I heard the first instalment Saturday, but was considerably disappointed. He is considered here the greatest of American historians, but I thought him rather ordinary; and besides, he seemed to me unjust to the Southern side.

The Americans are to meet Dr. Rhodes at tea this afternoon, and I must hurry to complete this letter and start out for that function.

I have had two letters from Father in the past week or ten days and shall answer Sunday. Please tell him that I shall send him my Ibsen paper in about ten days, I hope. I read it in a rather unfinished state to the Club[2] the other night, and after touching it up pretty freely will forward it for Dr. Alexander, if he has use for it. I shall also start upon the article on *Oxford* at once and hope to send that this month. It is hard to find extra time at Oxford; consequently I won't make any definite promises.

Yesterday I received Ellene's Apple-Blossom programme. I should like to have heard her perform. I shall write to her to-night if I can. I am considerably behind with my correspondence. I was much pleased a few days ago to have a good letter from Dick.

I hope you are all well and enjoying the spring-time. Did Annie receive her picture?

With love to all.

Aff'ly, your son,
John C. Ransom

1. James Ford Rhodes (1848–1927), an American historian, author of *History of the Civil War, 1861–1865; History of the United States from the Compromise of 1850*; and other works.

2. The Hermit Crabs.

To Ellene Ransom

June 10, 1912

Dear Ellene:

I have been living so strenuously this term that I have been neglectful of my duties of correspondence. I have had my usual work to do, and in addition to that my duties as president of the American Club, which took a good deal of time; some literary undertakings; and above all, a lot of social affairs which take time and trouble, without seeming to accomplish anything. Altogether this has been the busiest term I have had, and I do not think I shall let another one become so busy.

I had a letter from Annie a few days ago, in which she says she hasn't ever received the picture of "Sir Galahad" which I sent her. I hope it has now turned up. I sent it before I went to Brittany, about April 1, I should think. I imagine the customs officers have held it up, as they are a very uncertain quantity. Both her name and my name were on the package. I am sorry it should be lost, as it was a very nice copy of the picture, though small, and cost ten "bob."

I received your recital invitation and also heard good reports from various places as to how it came off. I suppose you are at home resting for the summer by this time. Don't be too ambitious and work hard at home; I imagine you have done a good year's work already at Soulé.

About ten days ago I had a letter from Father, written and posted last Dec. 14. It had travelled to England, Italy and various other European countries, and it is something of a wonder that I ever received it [at] all after so long a time. It seems that the college servants here mis-sent it, when it arrived in the vacation, to the address of another Rhodes Scholar travelling in Italy; consequently I missed my Christmas letter.

The American Club has had a very good term. We have taken up the practice of holding joint debates with college societies. Saturday night we entertained the Arnold Society of Balliol College with a joint debate in our Hall on the motion—"That this House welcomes the prospect of the return of T. Roosevelt to the Presidency." They selected the affirmative and beat our speakers by a substantial majority. T. R. is not very popular with the Rhodes Scholars. A good majority of them are Democrats and nearly all the Democrats are for Woodrow Wilson.

The Literary Club which I had the honour of starting about the end of last term has had a very flourishing infancy. We have studied four literary men, Ibsen, Wilde, Stevenson and Synge, the Irish play-wright; and above all, there has been a good number of "contributions" or original articles in the nature of stories, essays and poems. I embarked upon a poetic enterprise, at one time, but became discouraged and substituted a less ambitious venture. I also wrote at great length upon the "Ethics of Ibsen," early in the term, and since then have occupied my spare time with re-reading Ibsen and un-writing my treatise. At present the latter work is about completed and I am now preparing to re-write. I am certain we have the finest literary club in Oxford; by that I mean the most inspiring and useful, if not composed of the ablest men; though, personally, I am very well satisfied with ourselves on the latter point.[1] One of the members is Stuart, of Virginia, who used to edit the U. of Virginia Magazine.

Since returning to Mr. Blunt for my "tutorials" in Philosophy my interest in that subject has revived very greatly and I think I can say I have had a good term in that department. I won't go into the nature of my work here, because I imagine that you haven't done a great deal in philosophy; at least I hope so. Mr. Blunt has complimented me rather highly (for him) and I think perhaps I have gotten hold of some original points.

Outside of these humble achievements I am not at all satisfied with my summer term. I have done little enough with my Roman history. In fact, I did my Greek history (which I concluded last term) in a somewhat perfunctory way, and I liked my tutor in that department much better than my tutor in Roman history. I am much interested in the personalities and the political developments of history and I enjoy the texts from a literary standpoint; but I have no enthusiasm for the intricate details, such as the organization of an army and the problems of dates, which take up such a large part of the attention given to the histories.

I have had a good deal of "society" this term. Of course everything social comes to a head in Eights Week, and I had to take part in a great many more tea-parties and river picnics than I liked.[2] But the undergraduates, when they have accepted North Oxford hospitality, are duty bound to return the favour when special college occasions take place. Next year I think I shall lead a retired life, as I am afraid that social tea-parties are not worth while.

About a week ago we had a very pleasant occasion, when the Congress of Americanists visited Oxford. The Americanists held their 18th Annual meeting in London during the week before. They are archaeologists who are studying Red Indians, cave-dwellers, and other things American; they themselves are not necessarily American, but include French, German, Italian and Spanish people, and the Americans among them are very largely South Americans. The Oxford archaeologists entertained a hundred of them. As President of the American Club I provided ten American undergraduates to help with the entertainment, at their request. We had a busy day. The American Club made some useful friends both among the Americanists and among the Oxford faculty.

Recently some of us have heard from Mr. Griffiths, American Consul-General in London, who has visited us several times, to the effect that his niece is going to visit him, and that she and his wife wish to come to Oxford the week after Term, which begins June 23, and would like to see some of Oxford life under the guidance of some of the American Rhodes Scholars. He describes his niece (who is from Indiana) as "eighteen, very pretty and fond of dancing." We are trying to arrange to entertain them with some river-parties, college breakfasts, etc., and so I shall probably "stay up" a little later than Term, which expires Saturday, June 22.

I have not yet heard finally from Jim Crowe as to our plans for the summer, nor heard at all from the Hearst newspapers to whom I announced my readiness to do some writing on the scenes of our prospective travels. In case neither of them comes to satisfactory terms with me, I am thinking somewhat about coming home. I think it would do me a great deal of good to see the folks, and to revive my impressions of America in order to test my comparative views of Europe and America. Perhaps the main reason I have in mind, however, is simply the pleasure it would give me to stay a little time at home. Still, it is an expensive trip, and that is an objection very much to the point with a Rhodes Scholar. When I first mentioned it in my letters, I was on the point of trying to arrange by correspondence some profitable work at home; but Father and Mother rather discouraged the idea of my coming and I did nothing about it. On the whole, it is more probable that I shan't come home this summer, but still it is possible that I may.

This reminds me that the Rhodes Trust has just ordered Mr. Wylie, the Secretary here, to take a vacation at their expense, and to spend it in America. So he and Mrs. Wylie have just sailed for an extensive American trip. They are very fine people, and wonderfully hospitable to the Rhodes Scholars. He was formerly a "Greats" Don at Brasenose College and she is a graduate of one of the affiliated woman's colleges. They have four pretty little children; and I think their plan for the summer is to stay about six weeks in New England, where Mrs. Wylie was born, after which she will return to them; and then for him to go west by the northern route and return by the southern.

Father said in his letter of Dec. 14 that he would like to see some specimen essays of mine. I shall copy one or two of my essays on Plato and send them along with the articles I am preparing for the Methodist Review. Dr. Alexander wrote me to send him the article on Oxford, and I shall send along my article on Ibsen, hoping that he will appreciate its merits and accept it.

Tell Mother that I shall see if I can't write more regularly than I have done the past two months. I hope you are all well.

Love to all.

Aff'ly, your brother,
John C. Ransom

1. The Hermit Crabs.

2. Eights Week is the social and athletic event of the Oxford calendar. Each May the "bump races" are held. Each crew attempts to bump the boat in front of it until the winner holds pride of place at the head of the river.

To John James Ransom

June 19, [1912]

Dear Father:

I have not heard from home for the last few days, and so have heard nothing definite about my uncle's condition. However, I hope he has grown stronger.

I am sending some old essays which I have copied in very small script in order to enclose. This is in answer to your letter of Dec. 4, which I only received a few weeks ago. I have a large collection of essays, historical and philosophical, and did not know which to send; these two I have written this term. Perhaps they show as well as any what I am thinking about, though the essay on Plato is short and inadequate. The other is a logic paper and encountered considerable opposition from my tutor; but I am building up my Theory of Knowledge along the lines indicated.[1]

I have had a rather severe term and feel somewhat bagged out. Two essays a week, club duties of several descriptions; and social functions in excess have kept me going pretty strenuously for this debilitating climate. I have not had time and energy left from all this round to write the articles for Dr. Alexander, though I have done some work in preparation. Term is over on Saturday the 22nd and I plan to amuse myself with reading and sightseeing for about a month before working on my books, doing nothing more severe than writing the articles for Dr. Alexander, which is a kind of work that I enjoy.

That is my plan if I do not decide to come home, which appears quite possible. I have not heard lately from Jim Crowe and so am led to believe that he is not coming as he gave me to understand. In that case I am not free to come home. I have not heard from Mr. Graves about some correspondence-work that I offered to do, so that here is another uncertainty. In any case, it may be my business as a Rhodes Scholar to stay and employ my time to advantage in travelling; I have not fully argued that question out yet.

I have just had a card from Joe Ransom, who is in London, starting on his European tour.[2] I shall see him Saturday. Late advices from Lewisburg predict that Mr. and Mrs. Summar are to make a European tour this summer, so that I expect to find them here at any time.[3] It will be a great pleasure to see old friends here.

Yesterday I had a "collection," or college examination, on the Roman history I have done this term. I think I did very well. But of course collections do not count on university standing, they only give the tutor signs of a man's progress or his special needs.

I have made arrangements to go out into "digs" or lodgings next year. McLean, Davis of Ind. (now Pres. of the Amer. Club) and Lange of Ok. (varsity runner and lacrosse player) are to occupy a place with me. Our landlady's husband is a fish and poultry dealer, and we expect good fare.

I hope all are well. I shall write at greater length after Term.

Love to all.

Aff'ly, your son,

---

1. Ransom apparently had begun to consider his theories of cognition, which he developed in the 1920s and which appear in *God without Thunder* (1930), *The World's Body* (1938), and elsewhere.

2. Joe Ransom, a cousin, with whom Ransom served briefly in the army in 1918.

3. M. M. Summar, headmaster of the Haynes-McLean School, where Ransom taught in 1906–1907 and in 1909–10.

To Sara Ella Crowe Ransom

Freiburg, Germany, July 24, 1912

Dear Mother:

I have done a bit of travelling since I wrote last. I have added Brussels, Heidelberg and Freiburg to my list of achievements. But my acquaintance with Brussels is not worth boasting about, being limited to what I could learn of the place in a two hours' stop for breakfast.

We left London at last on Saturday night, crossed without mishap by the 3-hour Dover-Ostende route, and reached Brussels at the break of a very dingy dawn. Travelling third class, we had to make frequent changes, because the through-trains are usually limited to first and second. We had tea at Cologne, then proceeded up the Rhine, which was very fine in the moonlight. At 12.30 we had to stop at Mannheim for ten hours' sleep, after which we easily managed the small remaining distance to Heidelberg.

Quite a colony of Rhodes Scholars are at Heidelberg, and it is certainly a reasonable act to choose that place for the summer vacation. I have never seen finer hills, nor prettier streets, nor a more impressive old castle. The most aristocratic of the German universities is located there, and gives the town an air of wealth and culture. I spent twenty-four pleasant hours there, and enjoyed, as much as anything else, seeing the Oxford men again after a month away from Oxford.

Yesterday afternoon I came on alone to Freiburg, where I am now located for four or six weeks of work. The University of Freiburg is Prof. Severy's[1] old Alma Mater, and is especially distinguished for its Medical Department. McLean, of Vanderbilt, Southwestern, Johns Hopkins and Oxford, is just completing a 6-week's semester in the Department of Pathology. I am staying here at the same place with him at present, but will be alone after another week, when he goes on to Munich.

I was agreeably surprised, after my pleasant impressions of Heidelberg, to find Freiburg such a lovely place, but it is quite equal to Heidelberg or any other city. It is in the Black Forest and surrounded by the most splendid wooded mountains. We took an excursion tramp several miles out this afternoon, and, with that as a specimen of what the country affords, I shall not be in the city very many afternoons. I shall take several all day tramps as well.

The city impresses as being extremely flourishing and up-to-date. There are no manufacturers here, happily for its good looks; but there is no end of handsome streets and public buildings and of pretty homes. After the dirt of English cities it seems very clean and new. Then there is plenty of shade, so that some of the streets are as fine as Main Street, Murfreesboro, or as Peachtree Street, Atlanta. By the way, the front yards of American cities will always make them more attractive to me than European cities, with their walled and hedged gardens.

Germany is very agreeable after spending nearly a year, except for two weeks at Easter, in England. I am not sure that I have done the Germans justice although it probably hasn't hurt them seriously—in my admiration for the English. One or two things that strike me especially just now are the German genius for citizenship, which gives them the finest municipal and state advantages that a government has ever secured to its members, as I should imagine; and their superior manners.[2] I don't mean formalities—which may be a part of the same thing, but which at any rate makes them kind, courteous and mutually agreeable. The Germans sometimes appear awkward, but they nearly always try to be pleasant and polite.

During my prolonged stay in London I had the pleasure of meeting some very fine American girls, all from Evanston, Ill., the seat of Northwestern (Methodist) University. One of them I particularly admired, a society girl of Chicago, of which Evanston is a suburb. Unfortunately she is older than I.

I have a good lot of work to do this summer, principally in Roman History.

But I am also much interested in some literary ventures. Just now I am trying to finish an article on Ibsen which may never appear in print but which I am going to send to the *Atlantic Monthly*. Then there are some descriptive sketches and short stories in my head. The principal difficulty is that I work rather slowly on things of this sort, but perhaps it comes more quickly with practice.

I suppose you are at home again by this time. I had a letter from Annie since I wrote last. I hope Ella C. thrives these hot days.[3]

Bob Blake will be married before this letter arrives. I met his wife almost as soon as he met her, in Oxford, and she is a fine girl, but I am not certain whether as fine as Bob's first girl.

Love to Father, Annie, Ellene, Dick, Lucile and Ella Crowe.

Aff'ly, your son,
John C. Ransom

---

1. Professor at the Vanderbilt Medical School.

2. Ransom's first publication, outside of church and school magazines, was "The Question of Justice," *Yale Review*, IV (July, 1915), 684–98. In this essay he emphatically expresses his admiration of the German character.

3. Ella Crowe Ransom, his brother Dick's daughter, was named for her grandmother.

To John James Ransom

August 5, 1912

Dear Father:

I enjoyed your letter of about five days ago very much. I haven't got it here to refer to just now, as it is in another coat that McLean is bringing from Badenweiler to-night, where I left him playing in the tennis tournament.

Speaking of books, the Home University Series is published in England too, and has the advantage of selling for a shilling per volume. I have bought a number of them, and have several with me now, including Prof. McDougall's book, Smith's *English Language*, and Lord Hugh Cecil's *Conservatism*. I studied for a term in the Experimental Laboratory under Prof. McDougall. I am somewhat disappointed in *Conservatism*, because I expected it to be a philosophical treatment of the conservative attitude of mind, while in fact it is only a political party hand-book. These three books are in the latest series of ten, and a prize is given over here for the best essay on any one of the ten. I bought them and brought them with that in mind. The essays must be in by Sept. 1, so that is another literary labour before me.

My other literary enterprises have not made much progress for a week, owing to my walking excursion with McLean through the Black Forest. My article on Ibsen seems never to get done, because I always find faults with it when I reread it. It is a difficult subject. But I shall let it go to-morrow or next day, regardless and if it is not accepted, I can do it over then. I am sending it first to the *Atlantic Monthly*. I hope to get one of my descriptive sketches and a short story done this week. I got "impressions" enough to write a long article on my last week's trip.

I think I wrote you a card from Hintergarten last Wednesday. That is a station well up in the mountains, where we left the train and struck out on foot. A little further on we had a fine view of Titisee, a lake of over a mile long, the most-visited scene of any of the country places in the Schwartzwald. It took us two hours and a half, a half hour under the conventional time, to reach the Feldberg, the highest point attained in the whole Forest, being about 1500 meters *über das Meer*. There we lunched liberally and looked about us. Another two hours and a half brought us to a little teahouse at Notschrei, where we had another rest; and a final stage of three hours to Belchen, almost as high as Feldberg, where we spent the night.

The walking that day was all very fine and the weather conditions ideal. We made about 43 kilometers, about 27 miles, through the woods and up and down the hills. McLean was pretty well fagged out at Belchen, but I think I was never in such good walking form.

But the next morning we had to finish our trip in a steady rain. We had intended to go to Badenweiler by way of Blauen, which commands a fine view of the Rhine. But owing to the clouds, which prevented us from seeing very far, we gave that up and took the shortest route, about 24 kilometers, which we accomplished by one-thirty. I did not mind the rain in the least. The pine forests were very fragrant, and the paths were firm under foot. We had on some stout walking suits, which would not be damaged by getting wet, and when once we got to Badenweiler, we had clean and dry things awaiting us.

At Badenweiler I stayed till Saturday night and took train back to Freiberg. I left McLean still playing in the tournament. I met all the players, ladies and gentlemen, and thought them a fine set of people. The Germans have none of the stiffness of the English. Tennis is coming on at a great rate with the Germans. In fact, the younger generation seems to be largely giving up its beer and sausages for sports and for a more wholesome diet. I am bound to say that the Germans strike me as a very strong and sound people.

One very good lady player was Miss Pendleton, an American from Washington, whose father was once Minister to Sweden. She has been studying French and German, and if her French is as good as her German, she is certainly a young lady of talents. She is very good-looking as well.

McLean returns tonight or tomorrow, but stops only a few hours to get his things, and then goes on to Munich. Then I shall be alone for perhaps the rest of the summer.

I hope you don't find it so very hot now. Love to Mama, Annie and Ellene and, when you write, to Dick, Lucile and the baby. I wrote him a short time ago.

Aff'ly, your son,
John C. Ransom

To John James Ransom

September 2, 1912

Dear Father:

I received your letter about the middle of the last week. I had postponed my usual Sunday letter in order to enclose some essays which I had not yet finished. I finally did finish them, after a fifteen-hours' session on Friday, and immediately sent them on by *Eilpost* to the English publishers of the Home University Library, whose announcement of their prize competition I enclose. Then yesterday I sat down to "copy the copy" for sending home. I send the essay on Conservatism, but regret to announce that the maid has made away with my manuscript and notes on Psychology. This gives me a better opinion of her philosophical attainments, but certainly depreciates her value as a serving-maid.

I am sorry that I did not write the essay on Conservatism sooner, in order to let it settle down for a final revision. On re-reading it I see plentiful evidences of haste and undigested ideas, though the thought in the main seems to me correct. I had written an essay on the book some weeks ago, but Friday morning I consigned it to oblivion and began on an entirely new line, with the result you see.

I have done a good deal of writing this summer, and it has helped greatly to clear up my ideas on whatever subjects I was considering. But I am never satisfied that I have reached the bottom of a subject. I usually write an article and let it stand for a time; then when I go back to it, find an entirely new line of thought opening up; and rewrite the whole thing, and repeat the process indefinitely. I find that I never know exactly my own thoughts till I write them down; and then I see their errors.

Yesterday I read Maine's *Ancient Law*, which I suppose is the last of the great books on the origin of the State. It is strictly an inference from historical facts, and on that ground severely criticizes the Social Contract theorizings of Hobbes, Locke, Rousseau and the political philosophers generally. My copy of the book cost a shilling and is a volume of *The New Universal Library*, published by Routledge and Sons; I see it is also published in America by E. P. Dutton & Co., New York.

I was somewhat surprised to learn that Dr. Ivy found one of my private letters available for publication. I shall write him a letter, perhaps a little longer and more carefully worked out, within two or three weeks. Shall send it to you, and you can judge whether he would want it.

I shall be here only a week longer, then back to England, most probably to my old stand at Hawarden. I have gotten rather tired of leading the metaphysical existence that I do here where I can get no regular out-door physical exercise, and it is with golf on my mind that I turn to England. I have had some splendid tramps into the Black Forest, but the last two or three weeks there has scarcely been a day that it has not been raining or threatening rain in the afternoon when I wanted to go out. My mind was made up a few days ago by an unfortunate experience. I was tramping comfortably through the low forest, and finally came out in the open of the Günthersthal. There I found a considerable storm threatening, which I had not seen from the woods. Before I could get to a house, I was rained upon, hailed at, blown about, and finally deprived of the services of an excellent umbrella for which I had paid 9 M. 50 pfg. the day previous.

I shall go to Basle, the "Golden Gate of Switzerland," with some Oxford friends now in Heidelberg; and after staying about there a day or two, make my way by easy stages back to Oxford and Hawarden. I am very fond of the latter place, and perhaps that will be my subject for Dr. Ivy.

Am beginning to-day on Aristotle's Ethics, which I shall run through rapidly in the hopes of completing it before my Heidelberg friends come for me. I suppose it is the most important single book required for my course. I am very fond of it, and have read it several times, but it is very loosely put together, and requires much study.

I am in fine health, and spirits, though beginning to feel a bit cramped from staying indoors and confining my sporting instincts to Swedish calisthenics. I am getting more and more anxious to get home, as the time passes. I have become very intensely American within the last few months, I hardly know from what reasons. My plans for occupying myself at home are very indefinite; but it seems necessary for me to teach at least two years as the only certain means of making above my living expenses and meeting old obligations. I am anxious, too, to find leisure to write some *Studies in Democratic Theory*—assuming that I shall have already made such studies. I think the principles of democracy are often obscured even by leaders in democratic government, and it is time for a general discussion.

I hope you are all well and enjoying your fried chickens. It seems a pity that the girls don't read more literature. With love to Mama, Annie, Ellene, Dick and family.

Your aff'te son,
John C. Ransom

To Annie Ransom

Hawarden, September 11, [1912]

Dear Annie:

I have made another shift of base since I wrote home last. This is familiar ground again, as I have been here more time than anywhere else in the vacations, except possibly in London.

I had Papa's letter about Wednesday or Thursday of last week. I was much alarmed to hear that some of my letters had "gotten into print" again, for fear that this will expose me to my other correspondents. When I write a number of letters at one time, they usually turn out to be much alike. But it may be that my standing with what few correspondents I have is too secure to be affected, even when they find out how professional my style of correspondence is. I hope so.

I had a fairly interesting, but very tiresome, journey of over two days from Freiburg to Hawarden. I left Freiburg very dramatically on Sunday afternoon, getting up from the dinner table to make some hurried farewells and take my leave of Pension Kircher. I only got as far as Mannheim, four hours away, on that day. My friend Davis, of Indiana and Queen's, more recently of Vienna, the Balkan States and Constantinople, was to meet me there with tickets for a performance of Carmen that night. That sounds like bad business for Sunday nights, but it is quite customary in Germany. However, I was restrained against my will from breaking the Sabbath, because he had been too late to get tickets: *alles ausverkauft* [all sold out]. I went with him back to Heidelberg, where he is staying, a few miles off the main line from Mannheim, and spent the evening with him and other Americans, exchanging accounts of our travels. The crowd which had gone East had had some fine experiences. They also brought back some beautiful silks and laces and beads and other fine Eastern stuffs which they had haggled out of Turkish bazar-keepers.

It is thirteen hours from Mannheim to Ostende, even with only one change at Cologne. The schedule reads 7.42 to 7.42, but I found that I had to go over the hour of 3.15 to 4.15 twice, because at the German-Belgian frontier-station, Herbesthal, the time-belt changes. This way of doing will be disagreeable next summer, when I am crossing the Atlantic; 24 hours a day then will be long enough when I am started in that direction.

The rain for which I was leaving Freiburg pursued me clear to the edge of the continent. It rained so much, I could hardly see the fine scenery from Mainz to Cologne, as you go down the Rhine. Another difficulty was that my compartment in the train was crowded, as generally happens when a III *Klasse Wagen* is appended to a *schnellzug* with good connections, and I was not quite enterprising enough to get the place by the window. So I had to read an *Ainslee's* which the Heidelberg Americans had discarded, and watch the people in my compartment, for most of my amusement. It is a very hard matter to lay down any general propositions about the Germans, or any other people, because you find so many exceptions if you keep an open eye. I watched the Germans as closely as I could on this journey, as it might prove to be my last chance of first-hand observation. Then when I landed in England, I watched English faces all day, to compare them while my memory was fresh. Being as fair as I can, I incline much to the English side of the comparison. While there are many fine faces in Germany, and much character in them, and while many courtesies and pleasantries come up when one has a tiresome journey to make with them, still I have not seen in either English or American faces, though possibly in French, anything like the great proportion of coarse and brutal expressions that strike one very forcibly when travelling in Germany.

The crossing was very rough, in consequence of much wind, and I wasn't altogether successful in dealing with it. I am not such a good sailor as my ocean voyage led me to believe. Crossing the Channel in a small ship is a better test than Atlantic experiences under the usual conditions. But I never *suffer* from sea-sickness, as do most people who are afflicted with it; it is an unpleasant episode of only a few minutes with me, after which I turn over and go to sleep.

In London, where I arrived at a very dreary day-break, I spent two hours, making a purchase or two; and at Oxford three or four, changing books and clothes and attending to business. My belongings had not been transferred from The House (which is Oxford for Christ Church) to the house, which four of us have engaged as our head-quarters for next year. I found the latter in a state of great confusion, due to the recent arrival of twins in the family. I hope that they will prove to be law-abiding British twins, but I am fearful of next year, as twins can be very noisy if they will.

Last night at ten I reached Hawarden, just in time for Compline. The house is full of guests, mostly Conformist parsons, and I got the last room. Some of the guests I remember quite well as having been here with me before, and the general average of them is very pleasant and sociable.

Unfortunately the train officials failed to put my luggage off here, and I am not yet settled down to business. The matron found me a suit of pyjamas which some unknown guest had left here in the past. He was evidently a man of great stature.

It has not rained since I reached England, but it threatens to snow, and the fires are going this morning. But the golf course is still in use and at golf one forgets about the weather.

I hope you have had a pleasant summer. Conference time is approaching, of course. I wish I could get the Sunday Tennessean-American for three months. If you will subscribe for me, I shall send you a dollar bill which is in my trunk at Oxford. I want to keep up with the political and the football news; but I haven't time to read a paper from home daily, besides reading the English papers.

I hear that you and Ellene are doing a good deal of society, and that Mama provides so much fried chicken that you are all tired of it.

I was very sorry to hear about Papa's accident, and his scar. A scar is a great asset for a German face, and the students cultivate them painfully; but I suppose it provokes more curiosity than admiration at first sight in America.

Thank Mama for the pictures of Ella Crowe. She will no doubt uphold the family traditions.

Love to all, aff'ly, your brother,
John C. Ransom

To Sara Ella Crowe Ransom

September 22, 1912

Dear Mother:

I have had letters from you and Father since I wrote last. I was glad to hear that my Oxford article had found its way (under Father's direction) into the October *Review*.[1] The fact is, when I wrote it, I had no idea of the dates of publication, or I would have hurried it on sooner, which I should have done anyway.

The weather has undergone a great improvement since I entered England, though I do not claim all the credit. The summer, on the whole, has been notorious all over Europe for its rain and chill; and England, as usual, gets the worst of it. But the two weeks I have spent in Hawarden have about saved the reputation of the whole season; almost as fine as early October in Tennessee, except that the scenery is not quite so spacious and the atmosphere not quite so bracy. This, for instance, has been a remarkable Sunday; just twelve hours [of] solid sunshine, as good as America could do on this particular day, and a real achievement for English sky.

The best way to use a day like this, I imagine, is to put on old things and tramp through the fields and the woods; provided it doesn't conflict too seriously with a regular working program, or with Sunday observances. But I didn't even go the Sabbath Day's journey, being too much interested in a volume of George Meredith's, *Beauchamp's Career*, which I started after working-hours yesterday. Not many pleasures are superior to that of discovering a new author; and as one gets on in experiences it becomes rarer and harder to discover them equal to Meredith. I shall have to add him to my library as rapidly as I can.

After *Beauchamp's Career* I browsed through the Library an hour or two, mostly in the Modern Philosophy section, but winding up with some scattering operations in Bryce's *American Commonwealth*, and a glance at Walt Whitman. That is a favorite Sunday-afternoon occupation at St. Deniol's. There are fifty thousand books on its shelves, enough for everybody in the house to finger.

I have revived my golfing-interests completely, and find the game as exciting as ever. The St. Deniol's program is something as follows: Breakfast at 8.30, work till luncheon at 1.15, golf and bath till 4.30, work till dinner at 8.00, and then amusement for the evening. Seven hours a day of Tacitus is all I care to do, but a round of golf in the middle makes that amount able to be managed very comfortably.

A fine lot of men have been staying here, and more in numbers than I had seen before. The twentieth and last room is occupied. Most of the guests are Church of England parsons, and most of the others are Church of England laymen, though the rules of the foundation extend the privileges of the Library to all students alike. The Conformist preachers are very sociable people, and usually well supplied with good stories, so that I am often reminded of assemblies of Methodist preachers at home; but there are at least two differences. The Conformists keep the Common Room pretty well filled with the smoke from their pipes and the chatter from their card tables; though many do not join in either. And secondly, in spite of the fine principles and charming manners which they usually display, I think one is obliged to see sometimes that they are lacking somewhat in the best Christian charity, for their attitude towards non-Conformist bodies is rather snobbish than charitable, or even fair.

I would like very much to get hold of some foot-ball news. And Conference news, when the time comes for that.

I hope all are well and prosperous. Annie and Ellene haven't written in some time. I suppose Father is very busy winding up his year.

Love to all.

Aff'ly, your son,
John C. Ransom

1. Ransom is apparently referring to "Oxford," which appeared in the *Methodist Quarterly Review* for October, 1912.

To John James Ransom

November 21, [1912]

Dear Father:

I believe I have not had a letter from home in ten days or so. But on the other hand it has been eight days since I wrote last.

I was very glad in a way that we were to be at Arlington another year, since it seems to be such a pleasant location; but I sincerely hope the trustees will see that they should raise your salary.

All the Americans here, with very few exceptions (perhaps one out of ten), were much gratified over Wilson's election. I should certainly have cast my vote that way, though I don't think the country would have fared badly under either of the other candidates. It seems to have been a remarkably fine crop of candidates. But Teddy wasn't quite "safe," I should think, though I have no doubts of his honesty; and Taft was too "safe."

Philosophy *versus* Science continues to occupy a large part of our attention in this house, 167 Walton Street. Davis (Ind.) and I represent Philosophy, and McLean stands for Science, his case being conducted by Lange (Jurisprudence and Oklahoma).[1] We have acquired a good deal of notoriety in this way, and I am sorry to say our place is headquarters for a large number of other undergraduates, "digging" in this neighbourhood who are gradually developing a taste for abstruse discussions. I never imagined that scientific, legal, engineering and generally practical men, from such states as Arizona and Kansas, could ever become interested in the abstractions of philosophy, but the enticements of that study do seem to have gotten hold of them. People hereabouts have become afraid to express any positive opinions nowadays, due to the standing menace of philosophical criticism.

In a more official capacity, I am working today on an Essay for my philosophy tutor, John Murray, which is to try to reconcile Determinism with Free Will. It is a very difficult paper, but I have almost constructed my outline, and if the result seems worthy, I shall send it to you. I have had a very good term so far as Philosophy goes, though I haven't done my duty by the Roman History.

Last week I had the double pleasure of taking a handsome Tennessee girl to hear a renowned pianist. These were, respectively, Miss Hefley, of whom I have spoken as the Memphis P[residing]. E[lder].'s daughter, and Paderewski. I am not able to find my programme for Annie, but I remember very distinctly some of my favourites which he played, including Chopin Op. 37; Chopin's Opus including the Funeral March (I can't recall the number);[2] Liszt's Campanella; Beethoven's Op. 109; and, for an encore, Mendelssohn's Jägerlied, which I first learned from Annie. I am not qualified as a musical critic, but I can say definitely that Paderewski gave me more pleasure than any pianist I have ever heard at a single concert, and that he almost disturbed my conviction that I preferred violin to piano music.

Thanksgiving plans are much under discussion now. The preacher is to be Dr. Len K. Broughton, formerly of Atlanta, now of London. Among the dinner speakers is Price Collier, author of books on England, Germany, and other subjects, a much-travelled American. I am down for that purpose, too, though I was warned that I was a very late choice of the Committee, the others whom they approached not being able for various reasons to make the speech. They have not given me my subject yet.

A Mississippi Rhodes Scholar, Rogers, of Southwestern Pres. University at Clarkesville, is joining in with me to entertain two ladies from Tennessee at the dinner.[3] One is Miss Hefley, and the other a Miss Palmer, from Nashville, now studying in London. I wrote and invited her under the impression that she was Miss Ophelia Palmer of Murfreesboro, but she informs me that she is Miss Evy Lee Palmer, of Nashville. It seemed to Rogers and me that that was near enough to justify an invitation, and so we repeated it and were successful.

If you should hear of any positions as teacher going begging at a salary of $1800 or $2000 per year, I would like to hear of them. My preference of subjects would be Philosophy, and I shall not contract for any other sort of position until I have thoroughly tried the philosophical market.

I hope you have a pleasant Thanksgiving. I should like to help deal with Mother's turkey, to hear your sermon, and to accompany Annie and Ellene to the Vanderbilt football game.

Love to all,

Aff'ly, your son,
John C. Ransom

1. Elmer Holmes Davis (1890–1958), a graduate of Franklin College, would become a reporter for the New York *Times*, a free-lance writer (novelist and essayist), and finally a news analyst for CBS and ABC. During World War II he directed the Office of War Information. Dougald Kenneth McLean (1886–1922) and Ransom shared a more common background than Ransom shared with other Rhodes scholars, for McLean had been educated at the Webb School, Vanderbilt, and Southwestern. McLean went on to earn an M.D. at Johns Hopkins but was prevented from practicing medicine by a long losing battle with tuberculosis. Ray Loomis Lange (1887–1966) practiced law in Birmingham, Alabama, from 1913 until his death.

2. Piano Sonata, Number 2, Opus 35, in B-flat minor.

3. William M. Rogers (1890–1951), like McLean a graduate of Southwestern University (now Southwestern at Memphis), practiced law in Birmingham from 1915 to 1945, except for service as a major in France in 1917–19.

To John James Ransom

December 28, 1912

Dear Father:

I have had a very pleasant Christmas in this place. I hope that all at home enjoyed the holidays. This was my third Christmas away from home, and was probably as grand a Christmas as I could wish under the circumstances.

Christmas day, as long as the daylight lasted, we spent playing golf on the Hawarden links, with the exception of about an hour and a half in the middle of the day when we were otherwise occupied. The Warden provided us with a fine turkey and appropriate trimmings. Christmas night I had the rare pleasure of beating the Warden a game of chess, winding up a good day in a very agreeable way.

I have done no work this week, but begin again to-morrow. I did two weeks' very good work here before Christmas. I read Plato's *Republic* in Greek, with more or less careful study; I expect to spend the rest of the vacation reading Kant's *Critique of Pure Reason* in the German. I am taking a holiday for the time being from my Greek History. My Philosophy work interests me much more than the History, and if I teach again I would like to teach Philosophy in some college.

The Library was almost deserted for Christmas but it is filling up again rapidly now. The fourth of our party is to come this week, Bland, of Ohio. He was President of the American Club last term and, with the President of the Colonial Club, is being entertained now by Lord Grey, who has just returned to England from his position as Governor-General of Canada.

Our amusements here are walking, biking and golf. This is a pretty country and the roads are very fine; Chester and Liverpool are not far away. I am very much interested in golf and had not had any idea that it was such a fine game. It can be made as strenuous as you please and furnishes the finest sort of exercise. Christmas day we played so much that my movements are still very much restricted. I am sorry there are not more golf-courses at home; but I suppose they will come in time, like the tennis-courts. The game requires a good deal of territory, there being either nine or eighteen "holes" anywhere from one hundred to five hundred yards apart. Most Tennessee towns could easily support a golf-club and I think it would do a great deal of good. In England the period from luncheon to tea, with all people having any leisure at all, is sacred for walking, riding or playing something, bathing and dressing for tea. It is almost impossible to live properly in this climate without using that arrangement, though of course health is a much easier matter to secure in the Southern states.

I hope Mama is well and strong. I would like to have eaten some of her plum pudding with thick sauce. Love to Annie and Ellene.

Aff'ly, your son,
John C. Ransom

To John James Ransom

February 2, 1913

Dear Father:

Your letter written just after your return from the visit to Florida turned up a few days ago. Am glad to hear that you had a pleasant trip, and that Dick and Lucile and the baby are doing so well. News from home is more welcome with me than ever as the end of my Oxford days comes on. I am getting quite anxious to get back and pick up the broken strings again.

I have not found any tempting posts for next year at my disposal as yet. But I am awaiting replies from several places. I have a good friend and Oxford graduate at the University of Alabama, in one W. R. Cooper. He has strong family connections with educational institutions in Alabama, I believe, and so I have written him to look me up something good. Am also making a strong attack on the U. of Georgia, where I once lost a debate, one of the most pleasant places I have ever visited. Mr. Wylie, Sec. of the Rhodes Trust here, is well acquainted with the Professor of Greek and writes in my interest; and E. W. Moise, of that university and Christ Church, writes to the same effect to the head of the Latin department, who is a special friend.[1] Another friend has written for me to Groton College, a wealthy institution out of Boston; and still another to Amherst. I wrote, too, to Max Souby at Murfreesboro, inquiring if there was another $1500.00 position to be filled in the Normal. I would prefer higher work, it is true, but would be quite content for a year or two with a position worth that much so near home. I shall write at once to Bishop Denny in hope that he knows of a good college position.[2]

Mr. Summar wrote that he is leaving Lewisburg this year, as the question of the school ownership is somewhat unsettled and conditions unsatisfactory; there is rumor, I believe, that it is to be made into a County High School. He wants me to start with him a new "Ransom and Summar School" anywhere I like. But that is of course not the kind of work I like. Am sure there would be a good future in prep. work, or even public school work, but I prefer work that leaves me leisure for studying and writing.

I have been favored with two house-party invitations for next summer; very agreeable, as it shows that my omissions as a member of society through absence are not entirely irretrievable. One was from a Miss Williams of Hopkinsville, who used to visit in Nashville; and the other from little Sara Bailey, of Chapel Hill, a former member of my First Latin Class at Lewisburg. She was fourteen then, and extremely pretty; now she has sent me her picture, which shows her still pretty, but a great big girl; and I am afraid she now adds an *h* to her first name, so that she is quite grown-up.

Annie may as well prepare for a good many sessions at the piano, and I hope the violinists won't discontinue their visits when I return.

I don't know just when I can leave Oxford for home; perhaps as early as the middle of July, but certainly not earlier. Examinations begin the first of June, and I will apply for an early *viva voce* which ought to come early in July; then it will be a question of whether Mr. Wylie consents for me to "go down" before Degree Day and take my B.A. *in absentia*. Of course I shall make every effort to hasten the day.

I have been having a very pleasant line of work of late. My tutors are fairly encouraging, but the Oxford standards are so indefinite that [it] is hard for one to tell his comparative merit. Style and method count a great deal, perhaps as much as ideas. Furthermore, there are tutors and tutors, and some are biassed towards certain views and other towards different ones. The chief bias that obtains at Oxford in Philosophy is toward the historical point of view, the accepted method of treating any subject being to state the successive historical views of it, and accept one of them with modifications, rather than start from the beginning with an independent analysis of the situation. Because of this weakness for historical criticism, I rather think the English are handicapped for the progress of philosophy; they will doubtless be always learned and sound, but less original, it would seem, than the Americans, who are not very sound, and than the Germans, who are both. Pragmatism, for instance, has too little historical standing to meet with the minimum of fair treatment at Oxford. Personally, I think that Pragmatism will change the map of philosophy in a generation or so, though it is such a wide term that few people can endorse all the doctrine which has been put forward under it. Dewey's *Studies in Logical Theory* (1905: Chicago Press) seems to me the most suggestive modern philosophical work that I know; and there are many fine men in the American universities working along the same lines now.

Lately I have been working in Moral Philosophy and am gradually formulating some views on that subject. In addition to several other subjects I have set aside for future treatment, I want now to write an attempt at the analysis of morality, and later a lighter affair on the restatement and the relative importance, under the theory, of the conventional virtues.

Our literary club meets regularly once a week and I usually write something on short notice to present for my contribution. I enclose a rather extravagant little story I wrote yesterday afternoon for this purpose. Please don't send it anywhere, as I am seeing whether the magazines want it.

I hope Mother's health is good and that Ellene still keeps up her strength at the university.

With love to all.

Affectionately, your son,
John C. Ransom

P.S. Held over a day or two in order to get my story back from the typist's. JCR

1. E. W. Moise was a year behind Ransom at Christ Church.

2. Collins Denny had taught Ransom philosophy at Vanderbilt before becoming a bishop in the Methodist church.

To Sara Ella Crowe Ransom

February 16, 1913

Dear Mother:

A long letter from Father came last night while I was at the American Club weekly meeting. I was sorry to hear that you had not been so well. Hope the Bishop's visit came off in due order.

Have had a very pleasant week in many ways. Hahn, a former German undergraduate and friend at Christ Church, has "come up" again for the remainder of Term, and I have exchanged a good many visits with him. He is very enthusiastic over the Literary Club which he assisted in founding before he "went down". It has grown and prospered beyond all recognition and is indeed a fine organization now. "The best thing in Oxford," he says. We meet weekly with the greatest enthusiasm. This term we have been writing, in addition to regular individual contributions, a joint serial; but that hasn't been very successful as a work of art, though very amusing.

Prof. Josiah Royce, of the chair of Philosophy at Harvard, is giving a series of lectures in Oxford this Term on "Human Nature and Christian Doctrine," or some such subject. He is a great Phi Beta Kappa, of course, and we listened to a Phi Beta Kappa address from him last Wednesday night. He speaks to the American Club next Saturday night, and just previous to the meeting we are giving him a dinner at the Randolph Hotel. I suppose he is the most prominent of the American philosophers since William James' death.

McLean and I had the Misses Murray in to tea early in the week; and along with them two of Sir James' grandchildren, Madeline and Sonny, twins, of South Africa. They are very nice little kids and we had a merry tea.

Yesterday afternoon I had the pleasure of hearing Mme. Melba sing at last. Two years ago I got a ticket and couldn't use it, having to "row a course" in final preparations for Torpids. Now, I am sorry to say, she seems to be beginning to lose her voice, as her high notes are not as true as I had expected from her. I don't think she is equal to little Miss Felice Lyne, who sang with Hammerstein's Opera in London last season, and hails from Kansas City. A baritone and a pianist and a flutist were along with Mme. Melba and we had quite a variegated performance. Oxford musical audiences seem quite partial to the piano above all other modes of music, and I am beginning to take that point of view. There are certainly many fine pianists who come to Oxford. Yesterday's pianist was a young girl, a Miss Una Bourne.

I have out a number of letters inquiring about vacancies in college faculties, but have gotten no replies as yet. I am canvassing the Southern State universities first, as it seems to me that is the best field for a young man in the Classics. I should like very much to get located at Athens, Ga., if possible. I haven't got all the testimonials I should like, and am writing to Bro. Ragsdale for something of a general nature. Shall be obliged if you will address the enclosed letter properly, as I never received the last list of Conference Appointments. Would like to know Bro. Hinkle's address, too.

I hope you are all well. Please take care of the peach crop this year.

With love to all.

Aff'ly, your son,
John C. Ransom

To Sara Ella Crowe Ransom

February 26, 1913

Dear Mother,

Life is pretty busy with me these last few months at Oxford, and I know I am not writing home often enough but my intentions are much better than my performances.

I don't think I have had any letters from home since I wrote last. I was glad to hear that Ellene had been doing so well at school, and only hope she hasn't been exerting herself too severely. Am sure it is a good thing that Annie has taken up piano solo work again; at any rate, it will be an agreeable thing for me when I am at home in the summer, for now I like the piano, I think, better than the violin or any other instrument.

The *Christian Advocate* comes regularly now and I have been much interested in reading of the Vanderbilt case.[1] I did not know the Church had such a strong case, as I had never heard much from that side. I noticed in this week's number that the Bishop spent the day at Arlington, as appointed, but the paper did not comment on the table fare which was provided him under your direction, though I know he had no complaint to make.

I have had two replies from my applications, and in both cases prospects look dubious. The U. of Georgia professes to be "much impressed" by my qualifications, but has no immediate vacancies; but Moise of that Univ. thinks from the tone of the answer that they may make a vacancy for my benefit. Then I heard rather favorably from Groton School, Mass., and I am told by Harvard men here that the pay is exceptionally good and that there is great opportunity for profitable tutorships and European travels in the vacation; but I also learn that it is modelled on the English public schools, that it is distinctly for wealthy boys, and that every effort is made to "Anglicize" them, so that in general it is the last word in snobbishness for American schools. Naturally I hesitate to go into an enterprise like that, and shall certainly leave it for a last resort.

A great event in the history of the Rhodes Scholarships has just occurred in the election of W. J. Bland, Ohio and Lincoln of my year, to the Presidency of the Union. The Union is Oxford's debating club, in which all the colleges take part, and, so far as I know, is much the greatest institution of its kind in existence. It has its own elaborate buildings, including numerous assembly rooms, club conveniences and a very fine and large library; and most of the statesmen of modern England, such as Gladstone and Asquith, have been members, even, as in the cases mentioned, Presidents. Bland is the first foreigner to hold that office. He is a very fine man and justly popular on all hands, though not the most fluent debater in Oxford by any means. This is the highest honor to be secured by an Oxford undergraduate, without any question, and the best performance that a Rhodes Scholar has yet given.

Last Saturday I had the superintendence of a very pleasant dinner given by ten or twelve of us to Dr. Royce, Professor of Philosophy at Harvard, and this term delivering the Hibbert Lectures at Manchester College. Then we proceeded to the American Club, where he gave us all a very fine address on "Loyalty and Provincialism." He impressed me very favorably, as contrasted with most of the Oxford philosophers, for being very kind and human.

We have been having two or three fine spring-like days, and it has turned the thoughts of all of us towards the summer at home. My dates are entirely unsettled as yet, but I shan't lose any time in effecting my return. I hope the fruit crop won't suffer any damage before its time. I am sadly behind in my correspondences, with the home people, but I shall immediately set to work to catch up, so as to make my peace before it is too late with all parties.

With love to all,

Aff'ly, your son,
John C. Ransom

1. Chancellor James H. Kirkland and some members of his faculty were resisting attempts of the Methodist Church, South, to become active participants in the administration of Vanderbilt University. Vanderbilt's association with the church was finally dissolved by court action.

To John James Ransom

Rosebank, Boar's Hill, March 28, 1913

Dear Father:

Mother's letter came two or three days ago, preceded by a note from Mr. Anderson, of the Pub. House, and a number of the *Bulletin.* He wishes me to write him an article on Wesleyan Education. I am writing him that I am now hard at work for Schools, and shall be until that event is over; and asking if I may wait until June to take up the task. I really can't afford the time now for outside things, as this is such a critical period with my regular work. I am glad to be enrolled in the Methodist Bureau, as my unaided efforts haven't met with conspicuous success up to the present in finding openings for next year. But a good friend of mine wrote for me to Phillips Exeter Academy, New Hampshire, which is possibly the finest boy's school in America, as you know; and to-day I have a favorable letter from them, promising an early opening if my qualifications prove satisfactory; and for the present (i.e. the coming) year they would like to refrigerate me at the Hotchkiss School, Connecticut, which is of very high rank and is after a temporary Latin man to take the place of the head of that department while he is on vacation. Both these places are of such prominence that I think a few years might not be wasted there from the point of view of a career, and of such excellent organization that the ordinary drudgery of preparatory school teaching doesn't apply, there being large faculties in each department and sufficient leisure to each teacher for study and self-culture. Another friend at Oxford a short time ago was showing me letters from the Hotchkiss School (unless I am badly mistaken) where he is about to take a position in Physics, which stated that they had ten men whom they were paying $2500 or more in addition to providing homes.

But of course I had rather find work nearer home. I should like to live in New England a year or two, but not at present, as I have been on the wing long enough for the time being. I still have several southern places to hear from, in addition to anything the Methodist Bureau can direct me to, before I shall consider my efforts entirely a failure in my own part of the country.

The thing troubling me just now is that my testimonials don't flow in fast enough. I have one or two good ones from tutors here, and Chancellor Kirkland sent me one that ought to be very valuable; but Bp. Denny, Dr. Dudley, Dr. Tolman, Dr. Steele and Prof. Summar haven't accepted my urgent invitation to contribute to the cause.[1]

My letters home have been very irregular for the last month or two. I am working very hard, and leading a very quiet and retired life, so I never have anything of particular interest to tell. My health is splendid, better, I think, than it ever was, and that is saying a good deal. Golf keeps me in very good trim, and when that fails, tennis. There are quite a number of Rhodes Scholars here on Boar's Hill this vacation. Bland and I have the best "digs," I think, and things are very pleasant. A number of us are keen golfers and have some good competitions. The Frilford links, of course, are among the best in England.

McLean and I have had several visitors from Oxford out to tea on various days. Sir James Murray's two daughters, and two grand-twins who live in South Africa but are in Oxford this year, came out one day and seemed to enjoy the country very much. The twins are a boy and a girl, eleven years old, and very nice and pretty.

Another visitor was Mr. John Murray, my Philosophy tutor, and no relation of Sir James's. He "stayed up" correcting examinations for two weeks. He is a young Scotchman, and the pick of the five tutors I have had at various times in my estimation. I have been about with him a good deal.

Yesterday there arrived a very fine fruit cake, about eighteen inches in diameter (including the hole at the center), from Miss Hefley of Tennessee. We expressed ourselves so forcibly on the lack of proper nourishment in England that she called upon her missionary enterprise and sent relief. She cooked it herself and I must say she is an artist. It has had a very enthusiastic reception and is the marvel of the English housewives who have been favored with a taste of it. It has more ingredients in the way of nuts, figs, raisins, etc. than two ordinary fruit cakes, and they are compounded in exactly the proper proportions.

The postman has just appeared over the hill and I must drop a very pleasant subject too hastily.

Love to Mother, Annie, Ellene and Dick, Lucile and Ella Crowe.

Aff'ly, your son,
John C. Ransom

1. All of these men, excepting M. M. Summar, taught Ransom at Vanderbilt; and all of them, including Summar, wrote excellent letters of recommendation for him. Copies of these letters are in the Ellene Ransom Papers at the Tennessee State Library and Archives.

To John James Ransom

May 10, 1913

Dear Father:

I have been very slack about writing home the past few months. But of course I am very busy now, and have little of interest to tell. I had your letter a day or two ago, and had a good one from Mother a day or so before my birth-day, and appreciated both.

I have accepted a position finally, the one for which I applied at Hotchkiss. They gave me the salary I wanted, which was $1500 and "home," the latter including room, board and incidentals like laundry. I hope you will not think I was hasty in closing with them before hearing further from Dr. Chappell, whose interest in my case, I am grateful for. But the Hotchkiss opening was an exceptionally good one, both financially and otherwise, and I thought I had better take it while I had the chance. I got the cable giving the offer last night and had to take it or leave it at once. It is true my preference was for college work where I might have leisure for study, but Hotchkiss offers considerable leisure, too, I believe, because the faculty is large and the discipline light. I suppose I am to teach Virgil and Caesar, judging from Dr. Buehler's questions as to my experience. The position is for a year only, while the head of the Latin Department of three men (who is a Ph.D.) is away on vacation; I suppose I am the Ph.D. while he is gone. After a year I imagine I can go into Phillips Exeter School, the best in America, if I wish to stay in boys'-school work; or into some college position, as at Yale, for which a mastership at a school like Hotchkiss is said to be considered an excellent recommendation.

The Hotchkiss School is at Lakeville, Connecticut, 800 ft. above the sea, and in very beautiful hill-country, according to the pictures and what I can hear. The foundation is worth $800,000 and the equipment includes all the essentials of a good boys' school. In sports they have golf, tennis, swimming the year round, a lake for boating in the warm seasons, a gymnasium, etc. The attendance is limited to 200. I am writing Dr. Buehler to send you a catalogue. I have seen it from Taber, of R.I., who has contracted to teach Physics there next year. He is a good friend of mine and it will be pleasant to have him there. He hasn't had any experience teaching and isn't to get quite as good a salary as I get.

After all, finances was the main point I was looking out for at present, and my position is very satisfactory on that point. Two or three years at that or a better rate ought to recuperate the family fortunes.

Please thank Dr. Chappell for me and any others who have used their influence for me. I shall write at once to Dr. Anderson about my engagement.

I am sorry you have not been so well the past few months. Hope all the others are well and strong. I still can't tell when I can get home, but fear it will have to be in August. Hotchkiss opens about the 16th or 17th of September, I believe, so I will get at least a month at home and possibly six weeks. That will be very fine after three years abroad, winding up with such a strenuous experience as Schools.

Bland and I will go out to Boar's Hill again about the middle of this week to stay the remaining two weeks till Schools. The climate and the quietness are the chief recommendations for preferring that place. Oxford is too distracting now with the prospect of Eights Week beginning this Thursday.

Please don't send any more letters to the *Advocate* as I haven't time to write them properly for publication, and they are much too intimate to go in as they are. I was considerably shocked to find a letter in the last *Advocate*.

Suppose spring has set in for good with you. We have had copious rain over here and things are much delayed.

Love to all.

Affectionately, your son,
John C. Ransom

To Sara Ella Crowe Ransom

June 8, 1913

Dear Mother:

Schools are over at last, and I hope I am not too sleepy and muddle-headed to write a letter home. It is strange how "fit" one feels during the excitement of the examinations, and how useless one becomes two or three days later when it wears off. I am scarcely able to read anything of any connected sense now; I drop off to sleep before five minutes is up.

The examinations went off fairly well, and the papers were quite fair on the whole. But I am not at all satisfied with myself. Am afraid I turned in a long series of very mediocre papers. I don't think I'll get my First. But just at present I am not worrying about that. I am very pleased to get my three years' work done, and that is satisfaction enough for the time being.

My *viva voce* examination is a long time off—the 20th of July. Degree Day is just a week later, the 2nd of August. And sailing day is the following Tuesday, the 5th of August. I have booked passage on the good ship Laconia (Cunard Line), Liverpool to Boston. I shan't delay my journey home beyond the minimum expected of tourists. A day in Boston and Hotchkiss, a day in New York, a few hours in Washington, and a day or so with my friend Jeb Stuart in Abingdon, Va. His health broke down a year ago and he has been mountaineering in E. Tennessee and Virginia this year. He is an old Emory and Henry and U. of Va. man, one of my best friends, and insists on my stopping over a day or so to give him the latest Oxford news. He "comes up" again next year. This brief itinerary will occupy me, I fear, till Saturday or Sunday, Aug. the 16th or 17th; and on one of those days I hope to be reinstated in the family circle. I certainly hope that Dick and Lucile and Ella Crowe will be on hand then. I have only four weeks to stay, I am sorry to say, before leaving for Hotchkiss. Please don't forget to tell me the way home because I only know the way as far as Union Station, Nashville.

In the meantime, while waiting for my *viva*, I shall be having a most delightful rest, so far as that is possible on the eve of going home, in Scotland. Hahn wants me to visit him at his place there. He is almost an invalid now, having just undergone a serious operation, but I believe is rapidly recovering, and he would be fine company in any case. He has a beautiful country home of his own, where he "baches," just East of Inverness, which is pretty far North. McLean has visited him there and I have been often invited. He is a very talented literary man and wants to read me some manuscript.

I have just had Papa's letter of May the 29th, in which he says you all were expecting Dick and family. I was delighted to get Dick's post-card pictures of the baby a few weeks ago. Dr. McLean thinks she is a very fine specimen for ten months, and I thought I could detect frequent indications that she would considerably outdo her father in the matter of good looks.

Ellene is doubtless in the throes of exams now, and she has my sympathy. She seems to have had a very fine year.

Am sorry that Father is not feeling stronger.

Tell Annie to be prepared, please, with the *Jägerlied* and with Chopin Op. 39.

With love for all.

Aff'ly, your son,
John C. Ransom

To John James Ransom

July 31, 1913

Dear Father:

I was sorry to have to cable such disagreeable news about the results of my Schools. I just missed my First, and that is about all there is to say. It is the first time I have ever failed at a critical point and it will be a good lesson for me. I consider it a moral defeat rather than intellectual; bad enough, but still one that can be remedied. I left too many loose ends dangling; did a good deal of excellent work, but was not quite methodical and thorough enough; and they exposed my weaknesses in a very long and severe *viva voce*, an hour and a half. As it was, two examiners wanted to give me a first, but three opposed. They left my case open till the results went to press, and they consider me the best of the Seconds. Of course this information is for private consumption only, as I don't want to publish any excuses.

I have had very pleasant days to conclude my experience of British life. I came from Glenernil Cottage last Wednesday, the 23rd, to do some work for my *viva*, and stayed in the meantime with my friend, John Murray. Then I went for a week-end to Southampton to cruise about on the river Salent. Commander Cumming of the Navy, whose wife visited at Glenernil Cottage, has been given an old man-o'-war, in honor of certain brave exploits. He keeps it moored on the Salent and they run down for week-ends there. Southampton waters are full of house-boats and pleasure craft of all kinds, and it is a delightful life to lead. The Commander has an ample supply of row-boats, sailing-yachts and motor-boats, and we had an almost continual cruise while I was there. Some-times we were accompanied by two charming young ladies from a neighbouring house-boat.

Oxford is very lovely now, though rather deserted, and I shall take away a fine taste of English life in my mouth. The river is especially fine just now, with ripe wheat along the banks.

This will be my last letter, I imagine, from this side. I sail next Tuesday, the 5th, and hope to be at home Saturday or Sunday, the 16th or 17th. I am getting very anxious to be at home again after such a long time.

With love to all.

Aff'ly, your son,
John C. Ransom

To John James Ransom

Lakeville, Conn., November 3, 1913

Dear Father,

I was very much taken with your letter of Oct. 24 in which you objected to my statement that life in Tennessee was incomplete on its artistic and dramatic side. You give a number of instances from Tennessee experience which go to illustrate the dramatic possibilities of country life.

I am still inclined to hold on to my point. My claim was that country conditions operate to produce in country people the qualities of stolidity, conformity, mental and spiritual inertia, callousness, monotony. That is first a question of psychological observation and I imagine that a few casual glances at familiar country types are enough to confirm my view. But if you are not sceptical of *a priori* reasoning, it will be easy to establish it in that way, too. The country community is very small; very native or *in*-bred and therefore very homogeneous; and very well fortified against the intrusion of ideas from without. Its ideal [of] humanity is very fixed and definite—and very narrow, because it is little more than the tabulation of its individual specimens. Because the country community is so homogeneous, no member of it is required to undergo any tremendous intellectual exertions in constructing the prevailing type; because he measures so nearly to this standard already, he has little trouble in attaining it. His ideals have such a slight elevation that he can reach them without great discomfiture. Instead of a star, he hitches his wagon to the placid, family mule, and feels very virtuous and deserving if he can attain a comfortable jog-trot.

Contrasts and surprises are the insuperable lacks of the country, and in their absence the country must always fail to attain a very high degree of morality. Your letter tries to make out a case for these very features, to show that they are not lacking in country life. To make out that case you take advantage of the historian's perspective: you look back over a considerable stretch of years, and choose for your purposes the outstanding incidents. Is it not a perfect answer to this sort of summary of the events of years, to point to the *dailiness* of the daily papers of big cities? Any issue of any daily paper of New York City records a greater number of dramatic incidents than your selections from many years. The historian of a single week of Chicago or New York or London would find more and better material for art and drama than the historian of a decade of Tennessee—perhaps without even eliminating Nashville and Memphis, which are given to advertising their own selves as cities of some sort. The artist in the big city doesn't have to wait for the accumulations of years.

I seem to use artist and moralist interchangeably, and that is not altogether carelessness, for I believe they have the same field. The artist (poet, painter, novelist, play-wright) is pre-eminently a man to play upon the strings of human nature; he is interested in humanity, its vivid passions, its subtle refinements, its slow fires; he communicates the fascination of the study and thereby becomes a moral preceptor. Of course this involves my definition of morality. On this point I would say, that whatever morality may be, to my way of thinking there is one thing which it is not: it cannot consist in a man's reading off his own narrow, special brand of humanity as the standard of all human excellence. There is surely little credit to be assigned the usual practice of the country community, wherein it formulates its own homogeneous character, and announces, without a trace of humor: That is the goal of humanity; attain that type and you are moral, good and perfect. To me morality means fidelity to type—and the moral struggle does not become excruciating nor worthy of much respect until that type is conceived as something that is "writ large" in some tremendous sweep of human nature: an aggregate hard for the intellect to comprehend and reduce, and the hard-won promulgation of the intellect harder still for the heart to obey. The Platonic magnification of a man's foibles, peculiarities, "individuality," stultifies itself as a formulation of moral law. Morality, if it has any meaning at all, means the subjection of the natural man with its animal cravings into conformity to some ideal standard that is different from the natural man. When it is identical, it ceases to be a moral standard at all, there is no moral ideal and no moral struggle. This follows from the consideration that it is not possible to measure, judge, estimate, value a thing by its own self. Yet the morality of the country community approximates this absolute zero of Platonism pretty closely upon occasions.

It is the city's incessant rubbing of elbows that keeps alive and quickens the moral impulse. Surprises and contacts come thick and fast, the moral nerves are kept a-tingle. A man can no more put his soul to sleep in the eloquent atmosphere of a big city than he can lay his body down to sun in the midst of Broadway. Sensibility is developed, and without the sensitive spirit there is surely little that marks us off from our friends of the stable and pasture. The dweller in the city can not easily become fixed in the ruts that his country cousin calls "principles." The evidence is too overwhelming to be summed up in a leisurely breath, and as a moral creature, he does not have the option of ignoring it. He gets a daily gymnastic in the art of shifting his spiritual center of gravity, overcoming his intellectual inertia. Deliver us from the man who has fixed principles, forever beyond the reach of fresh evidence or new argument. My citizen-hero (he is of Hellenic mould) possesses adaptability, mobility of heart and head, sympathy, a wide angle of vision and a proper intolerance of his own twenty-four peculiarities.

Of course I have overstated the case and I am not scornful of Tennessee. I don't know any land more delightful for climate or landscape or people or cooking. My whole contention is that no single community on this earth is complete and sufficient for itself—even though its name be Boston or Charleston. No fraction of humanity can escape the indispensable obligation, to look to the rest of its kind. My objection with Tennesseans is their continual praise of Tennessee, their indifference to the wide world. True, they are coming out of it now. The old oratorical conceits about the "proudest commonwealth," the "Volunteer State," have given place now to fisticuffs and gun-play and really serious discussion over vital constitutional points touching the rights of organized society. And of course there are plenty of cultivated people who inform themselves systematically, through the art and literature of the ages, of the nature of their universal humanity. Another healthy sign is the extension of the yellow press. The yellow journals do a missionary work, very crude and rough, like the methods of the Salvation Army, but equally effective: as the higher forms of art present their message in a more refined way, the sensational press, with abundance of lurid lights, brings to minds of coarser grain the irrefragable conclusion that the world is bigger and more variegated than the country community into which its issues have strayed. I think that Tennessee fills a very respectable and important place on the chart of humanity: but my advice to Annie as a Tennessean is, to beware of Tennessee myopia; to keep the eye of the soul open and clear; to maintain a consistent outlook upon the widest possible expanse of this humanity whereof we all are members.

Since starting this (Sunday to Tuesday) I have had a round of very busy hours. The second quarter of the fall term ended Saturday and I have been occupied with very arduous clerical duties. Now I am free again. Annie's letter came yesterday. I thought it sensible and fine. Glad to hear of Ella Crowe.

Thanks to you for opening this little controversy. It gave me opportunity to thunder on my favorite subject. Here at Hotchkiss I have no audience—or am just acquiring one.[1]

We had quite a cold snap last week. And think the paper said it came from Tennessee.

Love to all. Will write more sensibly next Saturday or Sunday.

Aff'ly, your son,
John C. Ransom

1. Ransom had begun his association with Samuel C. Chew, who had just completed his Ph.D. at Johns Hopkins and come to teach English at Hotchkiss.

To John James Ransom

December 8, 1913

Dear Father:

A card came from Annie today, telling about the Bazaar for which she was at work; otherwise I believe I haven't heard from home since your letter in regard to our joint note. I hope my reply arrived in time and was satisfactory.

All of last week was warm much beyond the usual December thermometer, but last night it turned suddenly cold and all to-day has alternated between cold snaps and snow flurries. The snow is about four inches deep now, and required good pushing before I got back from a little walk down to the village. The wind is dancing and howling and it is not hard to imagine that there are real winter possibilities in this latitude. I haven't seen a good winter in four years now and I am inclined to like the prospect. I have a pleasant room and some leisure for books and sociabilities, which seem to taste better when the storm is performing outside. In this case the cold is very potent at suggesting Christmas, and it has turned me, along with a lot of good people, to thinking of home. I have had no Christmas at home since four years ago. I think I am even more anxious to get home for this occasion than I was to see home when I sailed from Liverpool last August. I am looking forward to a fine celebration at Arlington Parsonage. I think home is less homelike in the summer time when everybody is out of doors and the parental hearthstone is only a figure of speech. It is a pity that Dick and Lucile and the baby can't join us for the holidays, but that is a luxury, of course, that the exigencies of the family strong-box temporarily deny. I picture some fine scenes on the Murfreesboro pike. I will undertake to brew the tea towards the dark of the day. Then we should have some games and some literary amusements. I think we ought to read some more-than-usually good book, you being reader-in-chief. Of course we shall have to call upon the distinguished musicians of the locality for their services. But I am continually congratulating myself upon belonging to the Ransom family, and don't see the necessity of going very far from home for entertainment. The great exception is Jim Crowe. I would like extremely much to have him up from Memphis for two or three days as one of the homefolks. I wouldn't think of giving him anything better than I was accustomed to having, and never did such a thing, and don't see why I should do that for anybody. So he wouldn't be much trouble for Mother. Please ask her to express herself, as he ought to be written to soon if I can manage to get him away from his work at all. He is a charming fellow, or used to be, and I think we would all like to have him.

Please don't think of returning the Meredith letters. I think they are too fine to be lost to the family library, and don't know any letters their equal. Besides, they were not so frightfully expensive ($4.00, to be exact). As to the anthropologies, please replenish your library with my compliments through Annie's account with G. E. Steckert.[1] Ask her to mention my name and he will do the rest. I am hardly in a position to lay claim to any great affluence, but I am very strongly of the opinion that a hundred dollars or so is no excessive proportion of the budget to go to books for the home. I undertake to spend no more for books than I make beyond my regular salary by tutoring. I'm now taking several boys and will have made about $40.00 by Christmas (at $2.00 per hour). Have been thinking of getting for the two of us Westermarck's *Origin and Development of Moral Ideas*, of which I have made some study at Oxford, and which is the most interesting and monumental attempt to reconstruct the origins of human society.[2] It is a 2-volume affair. Unless you have strong preferences elsewhere, will order that by Christmas time: meantime please order anything else that you like. I feel diffident about selecting Annie's books and of course cannot always tell what you would like. Have you seen Marett's (another Oxford acquaintance) Anthropology of the Home University Series?[3] I have it and will bring it along next week unless you write that you already have it.

I believe that my last letter was so brief that I didn't mention my Thanksgiving. I had a very good one. An Oxford class-mate, [E. H.] Eckel of Missouri, had asked me down to New York to see him, where he is studying in General Theological Seminary. But I had such limited time, and such plentiful opportunity elsewhere for the disposal of my cash, that I stayed here at Lakeville. We had a very fine dinner, and a chapel service without a sermon. Very pleasant, but not equal to last year's, when I had the pleasure of Miss Hefley's company at Thanksgiving dinner. The lady-folk about here are mostly married.

Saturday night the Forum and the Agora, our two societies, held a joint literary contest of 5 events; Declamation, Essay, Oration, Unwritten Speech and Extemporaneous Speech. While the judges were deliberating, the boys called upon the new masters for speeches, according to ancient custom. My effort was well received, the most successful of my career, I believe.

My time schedule is something like this. To New York Wednesday the 17th, out of N.Y. Thursday at 6 p.m., and in Nashville, by a wonderful succession of trains just made possible, at 8 p.m. Friday. I hope to get out home that identical night, if it can be managed. I must be back here Tuesday, the 6th. So I have something over two weeks at home.

Love to all,

Aff'ly, your son,
John C. Ransom

---

1. G. E. Steckert & Company was the New York affiliate of the publishing firm of Heitz and Mundel headquartered in Strasburg, France.

2. Edward Alexander Westermarck (1862–1939) published *Origin and Development of Moral Ideas* (2 vols., London: Macmillan, 1912).

3. Robert R. Marett (ed.), *Anthropology and the Classics: Six Lectures Delivered Before the University of Oxford* (Oxford: Clarendon Press, 1908).

To John James Ransom

February 4, 1914

Dear Father,

I had a letter from you about five days ago, if a hasty count is correct. Glad to know that Mother is well again after her strenuous Christmas "holidays."

Am leading a quiet existence and doing some pretty fair work. Am as unsettled as ever about my position here next year. Dr. Buehler has just sent me a note asking me to call at his office, which I can hardly do now till tomorrow. I am very much of the opinion that he has found another man to his taste for the English department next year, and wants to break the news gently to me. In that case I shall go elsewhere, as there is no other open position in the school which I would accept. Of course my present position I am occupying only temporarily during the absence of Mr. Barss. But I shall know better what to expect to-morrow. If I teach in preparatory school work again, I think it will be in New England because elsewhere I believe the work is not organized sufficiently to offer much leisure time for study to the teacher. I shall very probably apply for something at Vanderbilt without much hope of succeeding. Please let me hear as soon as the lawsuit is decided, and that will enable me to make application more intelligently.[1]

My private interests, as far as scholarship is concerned, are in very peculiar shape. I find myself working in three or four different directions at once, and it is hard to know where to put the most of my energies. Since Christmas I have done no advance work on my ethical theory, thinking it best to let it simmer a month or so and carry on some close disciplinary-study meantime. Have read carefully the greater part of Bergson, with much taking of notes, and am determined first of all to write one to two articles on the tendency of his philosophy, to show that it is a false lead he is giving us. He is not concerned with ethics primarily, but with the metaphysics of knowledge. He is an original genius and has a fascinating doctrine.

In the meantime still other interests have come up. In many argumentative tilts with Dr. Chew I have developed some idea on the critical canons of the novel with special reference to Meredith and Hardy. Could expand these into some articles or even (with enough pains) a book on the theory of the novel.

Most of all, I have lately conceived a new theory of poetics which Dr. Chew thinks I ought to advertise. Here it is briefly.[2] I recognize a good translation of Virgil with no difficulty, and I like it because even the translation is poetry. Yet it lacks meter. Everybody knows that poetry (in its complete form, at least) employs meter; but what *else* poetry contains no one has yet satisfactorily formulated. The place to study the question is in a Virgil class, or wherever we get poetical translations of the poetry of another language: for we no longer have the meter; and all we have saved is those less tangible elements that are not mechanical. The question then is How does the translation, that satisfies good taste, differ from correct and formal prose? What is unique in the good translation, as a result of this comparison, will be *x*, the unknown quality of poetry.

A little analysis discovers *x*. What the susceptible translator avoids like the plague is the smoothing out of the obscurities in the original. Though it reads strangely out of the artificial atmosphere of rhythm, the good translation preserves the discontinuities, ellipses, the failing to attain preciseness and perfect connection. It deliberately prefers, at times, the words that are not the most appropriate, those which mean the given thing yet involve it in accidental associations that provoke the imagination and enrich the logical process of following up the point, yet come perilously near to leading the mind altogether astray. This kind of selection in words and phrases, coupled with a proper disdain for fulness of expression and for the clear statement of logical connectives (like the obvious adverbial endings, like the perfect and passive verbal auxiliaries, like all classificatory endings of nouns)—this procedure means, with malice aforethought, to induce the mode of thought that is *imaginative* rather than logical or scientific. It does not stick so strictly to the point: it bridges chasms and doesn't tell what its bridges are made of; it deals in terms that are enveloped with a wealth of color, rather than those that pin the attention to the point, and it is not averse to running riot in this color at its own sweet will. So dreams, the extremity of the imaginative process, differ from scientific argumentation.

So much seems plausible when I try to analyse a tasteful translation of Virgil. But the convincing stroke is delivered when I reflect on the nature of meter and find *a priori* that the imaginative rather than the logical mode is precisely what the exigencies of meter might have been calculated to induce. Words have a double nature: they stand for things and are associated inseparably with thought; they also have definite sound-values, like the notes of a piano. Ordinary speaking prose (and perhaps ordinary writing prose) is unconscious of the sounds of its words. Poetry is invented when men see this double nature. Poetry presents first a musical arrangement of words: and second, fits into it what meaning it can. But, given the musical requirements, the choice of words to convey the ideas is vastly limited. On a more refined scale, the great poet is only the school boy using his rhyming dictionary, and choosing from six words there when he might have had five hundred in prose. And so the poet *has* to use words (even if he did not wish to) which fail of precision and introduce extraneous color and distract the attention and suggest beautiful enterprises to the imagination. His meter requires him, too, to throw away his connections at many points, to abbreviate his verbal expressions, to pass from object to object over zig-zag trajectories that no steed but Pegasus can follow. Finally the poet acquires the sure touch for his art, so that he no longer accepts the conscious dictation of his mechanical standard, but welcomes these aerial ventures for themselves and guides his steed as much as he is guided.

And so my theory of poetics aims to show an inevitable union between poetic form and what is called the poetic imagination. The practical question is, what to do with it. I have three alternatives [:] articles in the *Atlantic* (with their consent, of course); a text-book on Virgil, which I could do very well in six months in a way that has never been done before, but which I think is next to imperative for any guarantee of intelligent study of Latin poetry; or, best of all, but surely least profitable, a larger book of poetics, with exhaustive illustrations from English poets. I might even do all three.

But what will become of my *opus magnum* while this goes on?[3] I feel very certain that my idea there is worth saying. Certainly the best idea I have ever had. I have not fully stated it to you, I fear. I could easily set it down in style of a popular work on ethics and political theory, but I fear it would have no lasting value; and to do it properly will certainly require some time. Yet since I am aiming at an English department, and since publications on that subject are lighter, easier, and more profitable, I think I had better neglect the philosophy for the present. What do you think?

I haven't heard from Annie this week, I believe, but suppose she is well. Will write to Ellene next time I write home. She seems to have made a fine grade in Greek, better than mine, I think.

Love to Mama and Ellene,

Aff'ly, your son,
John C. Ransom

Think you had better not count on me financially; but I will try to help anyway. I mean the renewal of the $250 note. Thanks for your check for $2.00, balance of Christmas exchanges between us. JCR
I enclose some Castner-Knott stamps that have been in my pocket some time. With my compliments to Mrs. Ransom. JCR

---

1. Ransom refers to the suit between the Methodist Church, South, and Vanderbilt University.

2. This is the first extensive statement in which Ransom outlines his theories of the nature and function of poetic discourse, theories that would occupy much of his creative energy for the remainder of his life. That he was reading Henri Bergson (1859–1941), who wrote *Laughter* (1900), *Time and Free Will* (1889), *Creative Evolution* (1907), and other works of philosophy is significant.

3. The proposed book on ethics was not written.

To John James Ransom

April 9, 1914

Dear Father:

I have not heard from home in quite a long time, nearly a month, I imagine. Hope you are all well, Ellene back at work and relieved of her eye trouble, a fine brood of young chicks coming off every week or two, spring weather in the air, and a good peach crop in sight.

Have been particularly anxious to hear from you in regard to your views on my best course for next year. Am still undecided and have no immediate hurry to make up my mind. The Phillips-Exeter Trustees have post-poned their meeting till April 25, and I needn't give them a final answer till that date. They may vote additional money which would make the salary for the position open there at least as good as I am now getting. A very fine school. But the position is in Latin. To-day Dr. Buehler sent for me again, though I had thought all negotiations were off between us. He says that he wanted me for the head of his English department, but found it would have caused some ill-feeling, inasmuch as two older men are already in the department and I am not only young but quite new to English work. However he thinks of calling himself head of the department, giving lecture courses (it used to be his work) and getting a fourth man for "assistant." This position he thinks he can offer me, and it will pay about $1,650 and living—my present salary plus regular increase. That is another opening. I like this school, and I should like the English department above all others. The third prospect is concerned with university work. I think I can secure some sort of position at Harvard, at a bare living wage. Have had some correspondence with them. This is the finest of our universities, I think, and I would be associated with some of the best men in the English field: but in a very humble capacity. The last thing I am considering is a fellowship at Princeton. My application is on file there, backed up by some good testimonials. The fellowship I have applied for would pay about $1200, and my time would be all my own for specialized work. This is an ideal place every way but financially. I could make my living easily enough, but probably little more. I have applied for a position in a summer tutoring school at Roxbury, Conn., where I would work about six weeks and make five or six hundred dollars. This would be of some help. But I have not heard about that yet. The worst of the Princeton affair is that I get no news of my fate till May 1.

The chances are, unless you advise to the contrary, that I shall take this position at Hotchkiss if it is offered: otherwise that I shall count on the Princeton position. Finances are a primary consideration now; though my own debts are not pressing, they are not pleasant to think about; and I am anxious to help you with yours as well. Would like, too, to be in a position to help out Dick if he needs it. I have done a good deal of outside work here, and can do it next year, so that I would not be getting in a hopeless rut; though the company is not very exciting intellectually.

I have done a lot of work the last six weeks on my theory of poetics and at last have it nearly ready to send to the typist, thence to the *North American Review* or *Yale Review* (a fine new magazine of literature and philosophy). Will send you a copy when the typist returns it. It will be an article of about 7,000 words, I believe. If it meets with any special success, I may spend the summer expanding it for book form. I have a good deal still to say on the subject, especially in the way of illustrating the value of my theory by discussions of Whitman and other poets on the ragged edge of conventional meter, and then of some of the drawing-room poets like Tennyson and Swinburne, and then some of the prose poets like Carlyle.

Since starting this two days ago, have had a long letter from home, half of it from yourself and half from Mama. Glad to hear indirectly from Dick, and glad you all are well.

Must hurry this off on the afternoon mail. Love to all.

Aff'ly, your son,
John C. Ransom

To John James Ransom

April 24, 1914

Dear Father,

I have just returned from a two-days trip to Boston and Exeter, where I went to consult about a position for next year.

Neither position that I am offered is wholly satisfactory. I had a pleasant interview with Prof. Greenough, head of the English Department at Harvard. He offers me an assistantship in English A, a course in English composition, my duties being to correct and supervise the themes of 60 men. The only pleasing feature of the work is in reading with the class. Much prose reading is assigned, and no doubt it might be the occasion for a thorough working over of the subject of English prose on the part of the teacher. Of course the great benefit of this position is that it would serve as a debut to the best school of English in the country. And I could carry on graduate studies. But the re-imbursement is only $600, and that is almost prohibitive. However, he says for me to hold on to the offer as long as I like, even till late in the summer, for he has a large waiting list and can provide a substitute at any time. I must say Boston and Harvard are very attractive institutions, about as much so as Oxford.

I had an equally pleasant experience at Exeter. It is a better school than Hotchkiss, larger, with more mature boys, and a more liberal atmosphere. I imagine there is none better. They want me in Latin, but can't pay much money. They think they can pay me more than they paid the man who is going, a Ph.D. The trustees meet on Saturday, the 25th, and they will then make me the best offer they can. Presumably it won't be quite as much as I am getting here.

My friend, Dr. Chew, has had unofficial information through a friend to whom he wrote that I am not successful in my candidacy for the Princeton fellowship. Too many and too good men of their own. And Dr. Buehler is still uncertain about whether he can offer me the position here for next year—probably not. His trustees want him to get hold of an experienced and married man. The department has had too many changes in late years, and they want to make a permanent arrangement.

I can hardly re-open the Loomis matter, as you suggest. We closed negotiations because I did not feel content with the prospect of permanent work in [the] school, not because I did not like the salary offered. I am hardly the man for a new school that wants all of the interest and attention of its teachers.

I think Annie will be coming home after the 7th of May. I advised her to wait till Harlin could start out with her on that date. I suppose I have a letter from her now up at school postoffice.

A lot of work has piled up for me in my absence, and I had better start at it. We are having lovely spring weather now, grass getting green and trees budding visibly. But there is still a long way to go before summer.

Hope all are well. Was glad to get a long letter from you a few days ago. Love to all.

Aff'ly, your son,
John C. Ransom

To John James Ransom

May 13, 1914

Dear Father,

I had a card from Annie, written in Union Station last Saturday morning, saying she had had a pleasant trip and was safely landed, expecting you within a few minutes.

I think she must have enjoyed her four months in New York, though she must be glad to get home again.[1] She made fine use of her musical opportunities, and I think she had a fine teacher. She is a good financial manager, too. I wish she could have stayed longer, though possibly a study as close as music comes better in fairly short doses.

Have declined the Exeter position, my own inclination for Harvard being reinforced by your handsome letter written on my birthday. It is true I am sadly in debt. But another birthday made me think about the bad economy of spending year after year in uncongenial fields. I think I might be able to do something worth while in English, perhaps in literature as well as in criticism. I undoubtedly can get a good start in the latter at Harvard.

I am sending my article for your consideration. Don't trouble to return it, I have several copies. I don't know whether the magazines will take it or not.

Very cold without a fire to-night, and I think I had better get to bed. Love to all. Wish I could have gotten home with Annie.

Aff'ly, your son,
John C. Ransom

1. Ransom had provided money for Annie to study piano for four months at the von Ende School in New York City, called by *Etude* magazine the "foremost musical institution in America."

To John James Ransom

May 27, 1914

Dear Father:

Yours and mother's letter came to hand one day last week, and your enclosure of my manuscript with corrections.

Many thanks for your criticisms and emendations. I am taking them all to heart. But I wanted a general criticism which you did not offer. What did you think of the merits of my theory? It isn't of course in any final form, but I had hoped it said a thing worth saying and heretofore unsaid. So much so that I should like to work it out more fully and try to have it published from Harvard next year. I am returning Mss. to you, after noting all corrections so that Dick may take a look at it, and give me his ripe reflection.

Quite true that I have not been enterprising enough in the way of trying to burst into print. Shall try to improve in that respect, and make it a means of adding a modest supplement to my income next year. Other means is tutoring. My friend Sheer, of Harvard and Hotchkiss, who returns there next year, says that any amount of that may be had by a good man.

Yesterday's mail brought my *Poetics* back from *N.A. Review*. Am now sending it to *Yale Review*. If it doesn't catch on there, I shall conclude it is deficient somewhere: that is the best scholarly magazine we have, equal to the *Hibbert Journal*. Aside from the merits of the article, which are dubious, it is very technical for the *N.A. Review*, which is pretty popular nowadays.

The mail also gave me word from Harvard that I was officially appointed to a section of English A at Harvard and a similar section at Radcliffe. The latter is a great surprise, as I had not bargained for any dealings with the new woman. But it will give variety and possibly an insight into the unsearchable processes of the feminine mind. The lecture courses consist of two hours weekly with each section. The greater part of the work will be correction of themes.[1]

Suppose Dick, Lucile and Ella Crowe are with you now. Look forward to seeing them. What of Dick's prospects next year? I suppose Ella Crowe is a highly-cultivated young lady by this time.

I am planning another article now on *Nature in Literature*, very general and light. But Nature herself not very encouraging now for such operations. The weather for two weeks has been torrid and I haven't much spirit left after a very hard spring's work.

Please tell Annie that I have just found her letter to the Piano Co. in my pocket-book. I failed to attend to it, but will do so at once.

Saturday is Decoration Day and a holiday. I hope to spend it quietly at something literary. Three weeks from Saturday I hope to be at home, engaged in a dispassionate discussion with you on the subject of *Style* or something else, where we don't wholly agree.

With love to all,

Aff'ly, your son,
John C. Ransom

---

1. Ransom did not accept the position at Harvard because when he visited Vanderbilt in the summer of 1914 he was offered an instructorship in the department of English. He accepted and taught there until he went to Officers' Training Camp at Fort Oglethorpe, Georgia, on May 12, 1917.

To John James Ransom

Chattanooga, May 20, 1917

Dear Father:

Have just come down the Incline from Lookout Mountain, where I spent the day with the Sloans, Harlin's family-in-law. Had a fine dinner up there and enjoyed the change from camp. Mr. Sloan Jr. took me up this morning in his auto, and it was a very fine drive.

I also had a big feed last night. Had a wire from Mr. John Henry Smith yesterday morning saying that he would be at this hotel [Patten] that night and this morning. I met him immediately after getting in to town about five yesterday afternoon, and was set up to a grand dinner. The post is very handsome, well-laid out, with plenty of pretty officers'-quarters, and ranks among the best in the country. One feature is a whole lot of German prisoners, sailors from the Eitel Friedrich. They seem well-fed and idle, and I don't see why the government has not put them to work on the strenuous construction program just started to accommodate the regiments soon to arrive.

As to the selection made for the Officers' Training Camp from Nashville. Have heard many stories, but this one seems to me the correct version. Major Hughes of Nashville was extremely slow getting on the job as recruiting officer at Nashville, slow in doing the work when he got on it, and slow in sending in the papers when the work was done. So other cities got in well ahead of Nashville in order of recruiting. The committee of selection, which had to pick 2500 out of about 4000, took up the papers as they came to them, and found the full number of satisfactory candidates, which they marked *A*, before they had gone through the whole list. So a stack of Nashville papers was never touched.

About a dozen Nashville men have been preferred and entered the last week taking places vacated for one cause or another.

I don't take oath to the truth of this version of it.

Love to all,
John

To John James Ransom

U.S.S. St. Paul, September 22, 1917

Dear Father,

This is from somewhere on the ocean, and without going into particulars I am glad to tell you that we will soon complete a successful voyage. Uncle Sam has attended to the submarine question, and our passage has been quite free from excitement.

It has also been a smooth passage and therefore quite pleasant. I hear that our crowd broke all the records for consistent attendance at meals and almost caused embarrassment in the pantry. Next time the stewards will probably pray for a bit of weather.

I still am unable to give you my unit of the American Expeditionary Force as an address, since we have not yet been assigned to duty. But I have just thought of a great scheme, wonder it didn't occur to me before. I'll just use my old Oxford college for the time being as my address, and get them to forward anything that comes. If the cable rates are not too unreasonable, I'm cabling you on landing to that effect.

I am going to cable you some money early in the month. For two or three months about all my savings will have to go to settling my notes and bills. After that I hope to help you somewhat. In October I have to meet the following obligations: (1) Remainder of the late note $25.00; (2) remainder of Am[erican] Nat'l note (Mr. Scales security), $50.00 about Oct. 15; and (3) as much as possible of an insurance note of $111.00 with Mr. J. H. Smith on Oct. 15. Probably I'd better cable money separately to Am. Nat'l, but no doubt you will be good enough to attend to the other matters for me. This letter should reach you about Oct. 10 at latest, and I'll try to arrange to cable at that time.

I hope Annie got off in good style. Nobody wrote me as to whether Dr. Bowers settled that matter in full with Ellene, but I have felt pretty confident he did. Am sure Annie was all right if that is so. She will enjoy teaching again, I am sure.

I suppose Conference will be coming on soon, and I hope the Bishop and the P. E.'s do a good part by you. What else have you heard about the Brazilian Commission?

Intended to subscribe for you to a New York paper, but three weeks at my own expense on the road and in New York was so flattening to my roll that I couldn't quite make it.

With much love to Mother and Ellene.

Aff'ly, your son,
John C. Ransom

To Christopher Morley

West of Suez, [Fall, 1917]

Dear Kit:

Here we are, about to effect a perfectly serene landing and bring to a close the most uneventful journey that ever was done.

Can't send you my address yet, but suggest that if you know anything startling, you write me in care of Christ Church Oxford and the good souls there will forward it as soon as I'm able to give them an address. Wonder I didn't think of it before.

Awfully anxious to hear whether they exempted you. They should have, all right. Drop me a line at once, won't you?

I wrote to *Independent*, to *Seven Arts*, and to Curry of Vanderbilt, serving due notice of my intentions on each and every one.[1]

In case the old Mss. is languishing idle, *won't you please pack up the following and send to* YALE REVIEW, with whom I have had some correspondence about my efforts previously: *The Christian, Wrestling, Prayer, Friendship, By the Riverside, Sickness*. They will surely want some of these, unless I am badly mistaken. But if there is any hope of a book, of course it wouldn't do to fool with them.[2]

Best regards to Helen and Junior. Fine visits I had out at your place, and a nice afternoon jaunting with you just before I sailed.

Yours ever,
John C. Ransom

1. Ransom refers to Walter Clyde Curry, a distinguished medievalist and Renaissance scholar. He would become a member of the Fugitives and would succeed Edwin Mims as chairman of the Vanderbilt English department.

2. Ransom alludes to the manuscript that would become *Poems about God*.

To Christopher Morley

F.A. School of Instruction, A.E.F., *via* New York, October 7, 1917

Dear Christoph:

For fear some of my several notes haven't carried, I'll just point you again to my address as above.

I enclose a little effort I've had in mind some time, and just arrived at today. Do you think it will do?

Often wondering what the Exemption Board did for you.

Haven't had a scrap of mail as yet, that's the only drawback to my present *modus vivendi*, which is otherwise great fun. The most delightful French cooking so far. Mustn't go into the military particulars.

Best regards to Helen and Junior.

Yours ever
John C Ransom

To Sara Ella Crowe Ransom

November 27, 1917

Dear Mother:

Glad I didn't write my weekly letter Sunday (the 25th), since Papa's letter written from Conference at Gallatin has come in the meantime. I am still writing you at Goodlettsville, though I know the chances are against that as the home address now. Will be mightily glad when I get a letter written after Conference.

My own address will change pretty soon now, as the course at the Artillery School will soon be over. We get all sorts of rumors about what is coming next, but nobody knows. Our training is still far from complete and my own prediction is that we will be sent to another school. Anyhow, it seems to be pretty well agreed that we will get a few days leave for Christmas. My French instructor, who is a Southerner from Gascony, advises us by all means to spend the time on a trip to southern France. Travel is cheaper for us now than it ever was before being at only one-fourth the regular rate (for soldiers only), and it really is a fine chance to go touring. Would like to see Nice and Marseilles, and it might be possible to take a little flier over to Florence.

Thanksgiving is almost on us, and means a holiday for all of Uncle Sam's men. There has been much agitation in favor of turkeys and cranberry sauce and according to the Paris–New York *Herald*, enough were shipped from home to take care of all the soldiers over here. But it is extremely doubtful whether they will get this far. We are officers and have to provide our own ration. We have a contract with a French caterer, and the whole business is rather complicated, so I don't really think I'll have to answer light or dark meat this time.

Tell Papa his diagnosis of my situation was a little in error. I haven't been stationed at Oxford at all and so haven't had a chance to get married to my English affinity. That is one point, and another is that this is the first I've ever heard of such a person. Have never had any matrimonial designs on England, either in general or in particular. So tell the girls back at home not to get discouraged about me yet a while.

Dinner (7 p.m.) bell is ringing and I must be punctual as becomes a military man. There really isn't a bit of news so far as I am aware. Health never so good in my life, work interesting, war still far short of what Gen. Sherman claimed for it. Please tell them all to write to me whenever they have time, as letters from home are the best things in a soldier's schedule.

Much love to all.

Aff'ly, your son,
John C. Ransom

To Christopher Morley

December 26, 1917

Dear Christopher:

Had your letter the other day. I think I have not missed any of your letters—at least I have had several.

I fear you will take the vicissitudes of P[oems]. about G[od]. more seriously than I do. Have become very distrustful about the merits of them myself, and am not a bit sore at the poor publishers who don't see them. Just let them wait a while, my dear Chris. At present I have no chance at composition—next to none, that is. Can't even consider the matter. I'd really prefer to let the things alone a while; maybe at my new station I can do something. I have about three things nearly done, but can't get a chance to finish them off properly. Never mind. Harcourt will reconsider [manuscript].

Am leaving the F.A. School on Friday, the 28th, with orders to report to the First Brigade. Whether as an active officer or only attached, I don't know. In any case, I am hoping for a little more freedom and responsibility than we have found here as thoroughly-supervised students.

Best of all, I will spend this week-end in Paris. With that sort of thing possible, war will never be what Gen. Sherman claimed for it.

Had great fun this morning, getting "gassed" by way of practice.

Am with many fine fellows, and improving my disposition every day. But I had no idea France was so cold in the winter. It's been well below freezing almost the whole of this month.

Much love to the family. Must hurry up now and get some packing done.

Yours ever,
John C. Ransom

To John James Ransom

March 7, [1918]

Dear Father,

Have had two or three new letters since my last, the latest of them being from Mother and dated New Year's. Mighty glad to find that everybody is feeling fine, if a little cold. That was a good testimonial the Doctor gave you when he examined you.

Was mighty sorry to learn that you had been taking my private letters and putting them into the paper. I sincerely hoped and thought you wouldn't do that, especially since I had expressed my own wishes on the matter so clearly. I don't think you have the right to publish private correspondence that way. However that may be, I am afraid now to say anything in my letters home that might stand the remotest chance of being considered worthy of the paper. It's a pleasure to write private letters thinking they are for very particular consumption, but not to make every letter an essay for the paper.

Am doing well and feeling fine. Heard from Annie and Ella Crowe.

Much love to all.

Aff'ly, your son,
John C. Ransom

To Christopher Morley

April 29, 1918

Dear Christopher:

Another cheerful letter from you turned up a few days ago.

In the meantime you'll be interested to know that I've been sent back as indicated above to be an Instructor in artillery. That is both good and bad. I had just had a taste of battle on two fronts, and such was the situation that I felt a little ashamed to be running off to the rear to a position of comparative luxury. On the other hand, I must admit that I love the comforts of this world, and here I have them in plenty. I am reminded of my former existence as a college instructor. I have a freedom and ease that I didn't think obtainable in the army.

Possibly I can woo the Muse a little more assiduously over a desk than over a caisson. At any rate, I've just turned in and finished off a couple of efforts that had been in the back of my head some few weeks, and here they are.

I'm not the kind to be discouraged by editors, as long as my bread doesn't issue from them. Too thick of skin, I suppose. I kept right on with my illusions as if they really amounted. But I find myself hoping that in the early summer you may think it well to make another attack on H. Holt, after I can make a few revisions and additions.

Love to Helen and the young Morley.

Yours ever,
JC Ransom
1ST LT APO 718 AEF

To Sara Ella Crowe Ransom

May 12, 1918

Dear Mother,

Gen. Pershing has given notice that he expects all his soldiers to do their duty this Mother's Day; but the reminder wasn't necessary in this particular case. Somehow I failed to write last Sunday, the second week I have done so in France, I believe; kept putting it off till the next Sunday was so near it was no use. But I suppose you have my letter written immediately after I arrived here, and stating that I now have a new position as Instructor of Artillery.

Yesterday the mail-man put me on his books again, and I got letters from you (April 1), Father (March 29), Miss Edna, Roberta Dillon Lyne, and Miss Edna—maybe others—and about three weeks of back numbers of the *London Times*. So I have had a fine time of it ever since.

I've felt rather badly about writing such poor letters home the past few months, as if I didn't appreciate the many good letters that you and Father, Ellene and Annie were constantly writing. But I hated so much the sort of advertising one gets by being put into the paper, even though it is meant in a kindly way. I know from many conversations that it is quite embarrassing to the soldiers over here to hear of the heroics that take shape in their honor in the home-towns. I read every one of the American papers published in Paris (the N.Y. *Herald* and *Chicago Tribune*); and am very much depressed by their terrific way of headlining the slightest manoeuver the "Sammies" make, while in the next column hundreds of thousands of Frenchmen and Britishers are doing their duty without any fuss. Besides the general principle of the thing, too, it is always embarrassing to think that you can say perfectly suitable things in a private letter which become indiscretions if they are published. For instance, I was mortified to read in *The Alumnus* my letter to Dr. Mims, which contained purely private matters for one thing, and sentiments almost unpatriotic for another.[1] Of course I won't write to him any more.

I'm positively ashamed to be so well situated and so comfortable as I am here. I believe I can go into details about the place now as I couldn't last fall. Since the school is now officially called the Saumur Artillery School, you will infer that it is located at Saumur, a town of 12,000 population, far to the west of Paris, on the Loire, and near the city of Tours. The buildings which serve as headquarters (they are rather outgrown by the enormous school the Americans are developing here) are those which were formerly the French Cavalry School, where the finest riders in the world were turned out, and where our own army got all its theory of horsemanship. This is beautiful country and peaceful.

As an instructor I have few restrictions to contend with and much independence. I rent (at a very low figure) a comfortable apartment in town, consisting of three well-furnished rooms on the ground floor. And that at the best hotel in the city, at the same rate that I formerly paid for mess in the students' hall. While I have to eat black bread and there are no signs of hotel service nowadays, I am faring a little better than I ever did in my life except at home itself. Even in wartime a French hotel is somewhat better than American hotels in peace-time. I have assigned to me the best horse I have ever ridden, named Hola. My work will consist of instructing a section of twenty officers, or candidates (I don't know which), on the 155 gun; but as my class doesn't arrive till June 1 I have only review work going on now. So you see that on the whole I am not entitled to any sympathy, for I am in rather more comfortable circumstances than I am accustomed to. I don't even lack cigars (you may be sorry to learn this); for we have a Commissary here well stocked with American cigars (and candies too) at prices a good deal below what they are paying at home. It is nice to be thought a hero and having a hard time, but the truth must be told.

All the same I shall be glad when my six months (at most) are up here and I take to the field again. I didn't come to France to continue my pedagogical career.

Have been wondering what sort of garden the parsonage had, and whether Father is still keen about tending garden, or whether his enthusiasm has withered, something like the way you claim mine did. From this distance at any rate, I think I shouldn't mind a little fatigue-duty in the furrows, since for the present it is not to be the trenches.

Am going to write Annie a long letter soon, and Dick and Ella Crowe.

Am far behind with my correspondence. That reminds me, Miss Edna wrote me an exceptionally nice letter which is in the latest arrivals.

With much love to all.

Affectionately, your son,
John C. Ransom
1ST. LIEUT. APO 718 AEF

1. Edwin Mims, chairman of the Vanderbilt English department from 1912 to 1942, was a Victorian scholar who was a prolific editor and author. An advocate of the New South, he often thwarted Ransom and other Fugitives and Agrarians.

To Christopher Morley

May 13, 1918

Dear Old Man:

Here he comes again, you'll say, but I've got perfectly shameless about it now.

The old book is clean done, I think now. That is, it's big enough as far as volume goes, and I've outgrown it till it's getting a bit artificial with me. Hence my desire to wind it up if possible.[1]

I'm counting on your intercession with H. Holt as you know. Somehow I feel it is good enough for them now.

Before that, here's some more work for your bedraggled typist—an introduction, a new poem, and some substitutions. Please let her make the whole thing fairly presentable as for looks. I hope you like the introduction, and the new poetry. Besides the present substitutions, I realize there's a vast number of small changes to be made which can best take place at the proof-sheet stage if God prospers us to that point. I do hope that may be before I leave this present haven, where I would have leisure to do a decent job.

I can't help feeling a bit lonely and conscience-smitten living here in comfort, though the Lord knows it's not my fault I'm here. The poor fellows at the front have it very differently. I have here an independent apartment in the town of Saumur, *pension* arrangements with the hotel, which boasts an excellent cuisine, a horse of my own, and only a moderate amount of work. (I am assuming that you got my letter of two weeks ago telling that I am now an instructor in the Saumur School of Artillery.)

Which reminds me, if in the page of *Contents* I send (in order to show the order I should like) you find a title you don't recognize, be sure to let me know, as I may have sent you something that didn't arrive.

Enough now of the poet and warrior.

To-day at the Y.M.C.A. I had the good luck and the bad luck to start two different stories of yours in *Collier's* only to find that all but the first page of each was missing from the magazines. I liked what I read about the Balliol youth immensely—but beware of those puns! None of these quibble-springs between Midwives.

What of Kathleen? Hope she has found home and happiness by this date.

My love to the family, and the same plus everlasting gratitude to yourself, from

Yours ever
John C Ransom

---

1. *Poems about God.*

To Sara Ella Crowe Ransom

Saumur, June 10, 1918

Dear Mother,

Have spent today in rather more official employment than any day for over a month now. My section came at last and I've launched out again as an instructor. Up to this time I've been mostly marking time here, though the dozen or so of us left without sections have been going through the motions of holding practice classes, "lecturing" each other by turns, and doing review work.

I shall like my class very well I think. They are not officers, all candidates, and fresh from the states. I believe none of them is from Tennessee, though. I've had no time to go over their papers carefully and find out about them. Most of them have been to college more or less—one to Princeton, one to Columbia, etc. They seem quite "keen" to get to work, and quite impressed by the possibilities of the 155 gun, which is a perfect stranger to them all.

I don't know of a bit of news outside of that, unless that I've changed my arrangements a little, and now dine at the new officers' mess instead of the hotel. The mess is very fine now, and in fact is run by the same management that runs the hotel. The food is much the same, except that I now get ham and eggs for breakfast, butter twice a day, unlimited bread, and meat every day of the week. The service is not quite so fastidious as at the hotel; but now that I'm busy it's quite satisfactory to be rushed along at meals instead of nibbling along at a more ladylike speed.

Haven't had any mail for ten days, so I expect to have a whole armful of it any day now.

Hope everybody flourishes—best love to all—

Aff'ly, your son,
John C. Ransom

To John James Ransom

June 17, 1918

Dear Father,

Two letters from home the other day, one from you and one from Mother, both dated about May 15, as well as I remember (they are at home and I'm at the Y just now). Till then I'd had no mail for over two weeks.

By this time I imagine Ellene is out of school, and Annie is home again. Hope you are having as fine June weather as we get over here. Though the gardens hereabouts do need a rain.

My section of artillery students (and candidates for commission) seem to be hard at work and profiting more or less by my frequent attentions. They work much more than I do, I must say. My schedule for each of my first two weeks has called for about 22 hours of class work. The necessary preparation has been considerably less, thanks to the review I've had of late while waiting for my class. So I have plenty of time to ride my horse Hola (a frisky French one), and to read and write, and now and then to play a little tennis. Nothing warlike about me.

Read "Martin Chuzzlewit" the other day, a Y.M.C.A. book. It's terrific on the subject of America, I didn't know Dickens had it in him to get so excited. Today a Mrs. Magruder, whose husband is in Am. diplomatic service and who is living here to see her brother (of Harvard) now a candidate in the school, gave me some others—Swinburne's poems, for one—which will come in handily.

Thanks for attending to the insurance for me—didn't know you had written out a check in my favor. Glad it didn't have to be cashed. Much love to everybody.

Aff'ly, your son,
John C. Ransom

To Christopher Morley

November 12, 1918

Dear Christopher:

Yesterday the armistice was signed, and the war is over, except that we will be engaged for a while in giving it a decent burial. I know you and Helen rejoiced. My own feelings seem entirely too pale when I think of what my old mother and father will be feeling; and when I see the incredible happiness of the poor French and Belgians.

I managed to get a two-days *permission* to Paris Saturday and Sunday, but the inconsiderate Boches refused to sign till Monday morning, and I was cheated out of the sight of Paris *en fête.* Nobody but a strong man could have deliberately taken his train from the capital at 8 p.m. Sunday as I did. The crowds were enormous, and Paris for the first time in four years looked worthy of herself; last night she must have outdone herself.

The gratitude of the French is touching. America outdistances England many kilometers in their hearts. It is most embarrassing to an *ambusquer* (that's *argot* and I can't find the correct spelling) like myself. Even in little Saumur the people almost went mad. I was adjutant at retreat last night, and I must confess the formation wasn't conducted according to Hoyle, such was the excitement.

The school work goes on. How long, no one hereabouts can say. I am just completing a course, and was making ready to "go up" again, but now I don't know.

Among many things I have been thinking about, the proudest one is the white record of Wilson. Just lately many have been carping at his magnanimity—perhaps around the peace board he will be scorned for leniency. It happened to Lincoln. I can't forget my many misguided brave German friends. When all fear of a terrible enemy is gone, it is time for hatred to stop and generosity to begin. This "Wilson peace" that now seems to some so feeble is the one that seemed to all so bold when it first was proposed: the same peace of justice. I hope you publicists will not allow it to be forgotten that no sooner had Lloyd-George got the dirty words out of his mouth, "Our engagements in the east are now at an end since Russia has betrayed us," than Wilson said: "Our program in the east is the same as it always has been." That was the greatest word of the war.

My peace-thoughts have gone to such a length, today I wrote two letters on civil topics. One to the Nashville *Tennessean*, which I have written a certain number of editorials for in the past, asking about an editorial job after the war; the other to Prof Cross, of Yale, asking about a position in the Yale faculty of English with special reference to the subject of Advanced Composition. I have fallen into a nest of Californians here of late and am also planning a similar letter to U. of Cal. at Berkeley. Furthermore, I'm counting on making Philadelphia my first stop on the way homeward, where I will solicit your sage advice about the future. I'm open-minded; that means, I haven't got a job and want one. Vanderbilt isn't quite big enough for my peculiar tastes.

I hope Kathleen is soon to take the boards and become illustrious forever.

I haven't seen the proof of my book. Not long ago 8,000 bags of AEF mail were lost, and I'm apprehensive that my book was in one of the bags. If I don't hear from it within ten days more, I'm going to send you a list of revisions I've made in my text—though it isn't complete. Then will you be so kind as to enter them on a proof-sheet?

Must now prepare a lesson on High Air Bursts. So more anon. Much love to Helen and Junior.

Yours as ever,
(Lt) John C Ransom
APO 718 AEF

To Christopher Morley

Nancy, March 17, 1919

Dear Christopher:

I've no doubt you must have written to me, but my mail has gone sadly astray during my many wanderings since Saumur.

I'm in clover now, as you will assume from my new office number above. I'm a student in a good French university, dabbling in letters, reading and writing (r. French and wr. English) and doing nothing of a military complexion. To-day for example it was too snowy for my idea of a March day, and I've stayed by the fire in an exceptionally easy chair, what time I was not discussing a particularly fine French *menu* for my luncheon. This is almost my normal life back again, if the geography of the case could be shifted a little.

I'll be here till the end of June. After that I hope for an early release from the army, and the pleasure of an early reunion at Philadelphia. I'll probably teach again—that's probably my normal existence. I've put out some feelers at Yale and Brown, I still have some standing probably at Vanderbilt. I'm interested mainly in Advanced Composition, mostly around the Literary Club idea, with which I had some success at Vanderbilt. Do you think there's anything at Haverford?[1]

Yesterday I picked up an *Atlantic* for March, in the local Y. Was immediately confronted with H. Holt's page of announcements, and my own name over your rash indorsement. Will you never stop this reckless kindness? This was the first news from the front since November, I think. I never saw the proof—didn't want to, except for the decent reason of conserving your candle-power. I presumed my letter reached you with the revisions I favored. Naturally I'd like to see my poor child, and hope to do so in time.

I've been sonneteering a good deal of late. I've got a whole book in my head—a lot of sonnets in a lot of sequences with the same characters and history. But I am absolutely destitute of critics. That's why I don't know whether I'm well-advised. Here's one of a lighter tinkle I submit.

I never managed to meet Helen's brother. I do hope you've all had a happy armistice and will allow me to week-end with you again.

Much love,
John C Ransom
IST LIEUT FA

Minerva had no pride of pedigree,
And so they shot her, bent of a broken leg,
Without a grief: then they looked butcheringly
On the unprovided babe she left to beg.

But who came coursing, like the tall corn slanting,
Beautiful, proud, and furious with anger?
It was the farmer's slender daughter, panting,
And pitiful to orphans in their danger.

You flew your ribbon from his yellow head,
Managed his bottle over many a meal,
Now he is big, and tramps the flower-bed,
And still nobody dares pronounce him veal.
But I make little marvel of this calf,
Being not the whole of history, not half.[2]

---

1. Morley was a graduate of Haverford College.

2. An unpublished poem.

To Christopher Morley

June 17, 1919

Dear Christopher:

Not that there's any news worth writing. But I'm just celebrating the recent announcement that, with other officers formerly of the Army of Occupation but now students, I'm to report to Brest the first of July for transportation to America. This means that I'll see you before the month is out. D.v.

Do you know of a job anywhere for an earnest young man, Christopher? C'est moi. I'm just hesitating as to whether to return to Vanderbilt. I'd rather live in the East if I can get something.

If I have any time in New York on arrival, I'll stop at Hotel Bretton Hall, 86th and B'way, if that tavern is still doing business. Anyhow, I'll call there for my mail, and maybe you will drop me a line to that address along about the middle of the month.

My youngest sister Ellene is to be in New York for a year, beginning next month, studying English at Columbia. She is a nice little parson's daughter, a graduate of Vanderbilt, and quite an intellectuelle in her way. Another reason for my wanting to settle in New York.

My warmest regards to Helen. I'll surely descend upon you soon!

Yours
John C Ransom
1ST LIEUT FA

To Christopher Morley

Nashville, August 27, 1919

Dear Christopher:

You will see from the address that I've reneged, reverted, and fallen flat. Yes, I shall be at Vanderbilt again this year, as Assistant Professor in English. That's mainly because I find my mother and father getting old and somewhat lonely, and thought best to spend this year with them.

In New York I had some interviews, though I could get no word from either Holliday or Harcourt. Was particularly well treated by Anderson, of Putnam's, who was most encouraging: the best he had himself was a "25-or-30-a-week job" learning the business.

I also interviewed Aydelotte at Boston, and the gentlemen of Columbia, along more academic lines. They too were encouraging and I fully expected when I left New York to return thither in short order. And by the way, the reason I didn't come by Phila. was the one-cent-a-mile consideration: my ticket bought at that rate permitted no stop-over.

Your book is delightful, I mean "Rocking Horse"—of course one must specify in your case. Have shown it to many people who are charmed with one accord. On the south-bound train a most devastating journey was lightened by my discovery of an old college-chum, a beautiful girl whose little 3-year old boy died a few months ago. She read your book and turned in with characteristic energy to write a poem herself in your honor. It was successful, rather sad in tone, and I wish I could lay my hand on it to send you. Your poems are by no means of the nursery-rhyme genre, as advertised: you have too much of the salt of sophistication.

Please give my heartiest regards to Helen and the youngsters. Wish I could have seen 'em! Perhaps I'll get up that way Christmas. I'm surely going east next year!

Do you recall which of that first batch of sonnets ("Frail Flowers") you may have used in the column? I'm on the point of patronizing the government's stamp factory.

Yours
John CR

1921–1929

HILE HE WAS at Oxford, William Y. Elliott showed Robert Graves Ransom's *Poems about God* and some of the poems being read at the Fugitive meetings. When the first issue of the *Fugitive* appeared in April, 1922, Elliott gave Graves a copy. Graves liked Ransom's poetry and wrote that he would like to find Ransom an English publisher. Ransom's response indicates that he had already repudiated *Poems about God* and was writing poems in a different mode. (He had written "Necrological" and other poems in what the critics would call his mature manner: an ironic tone, a dramatic framework, a dualistic theme, a juxtaposition of archaic and modern elements, formal and informal language.) Rather than republishing *Poems about God*, Ransom wrote Graves, why not bring out a volume that would include some of his "recent stuff"? These initial letters developed into a lively correspondence between the two poets, with the result that Graves, assisted by T. S. Eliot, persuaded the Hogarth Press to bring out *Grace after Meat* (1924). The volume was about equally divided between poems from *Poems about God* and those of more recent composition. After *Grace* appeared, the correspondence between the two poets diminished and had almost ceased by the late 1920s, when Ransom asked Graves to support his application for a Guggenheim fellowship.

In the meantime Christopher Morley had convinced Alfred A. Knopf to publish *Chills and Fever* (1924), which appeared a few months before *Grace after Meat* was released. With the publication of *Two Gentlemen in Bonds* in 1927, also by Knopf, Ransom's reputation as one of the most important poets of his generation was securely established. Most of his poetry had already been written, and he was returning to his first love, literary criticism. Some of his most illuminating ideas on the nature and function of poetry can be followed almost step by step as they developed in the lengthy correspondence with Allen Tate from 1922 to 1926 before they appeared in the critical essays of the 1930s and 1940s. The most significant of these letters, perhaps, is that of September 5, 1926, in which Ransom outlined in detail the basic plan of the book-length manuscript on which he was working and would continue to work for the next two or three years. This manuscript, which he always referred to as "The Third Moment," was finally destroyed because Ransom decided it was "hopelessly abstract." Although many of the basic principles Ransom was concerned with are carried forward to *The World's Body*, the details of the theory he was developing in the mid-1920s can be reconstructed only from these letters.

The letters to Tate of this period also include a subject on which Ransom and his former student could never agree and one which in 1923 would develop into a public controversy that almost dissolved the relationship between the two men before it could develop into friendship. *The Waste Land*, Ransom wrote Tate, on December 17, 1922, "doesn't satisfy me though it is amazing." Because T. S. Eliot, despite his arguments in such essays as

"Tradition and Individual Talent," had no sense of literary form, his poem, Ransom was convinced, had no "proper continuity and singleness." Ransom's comparison of Eliot to Vachel Lindsay displeased Tate, and when later Ransom reviewed *The Waste Land*, accusing Eliot of "expository discontinuity" and arguing that one responsibility of the artist is an imaginative fusion of disparate elements, Tate responded in a letter to the *Literary Review* (in which Ransom's article had appeared) that Ransom had condemned Eliot's poetry because of his philosophic pluralism. The debate was prevented from developing into an open feud only by the intervention of Donald Davidson, who was able to soothe the ruffled feelings of both men and bring them together again.

The two poets then began to exchange poems again and to request candid critical reactions. (Most of the poems came from Tate because Ransom was writing little poetry.) Tate reviewed Ransom's *Two Gentlemen in Bonds* (1927), and Ransom responded that "you have done me the honor of more inward examination than I have yet secured from any source." Ransom commented on Tate's "Poetry and the Absolute" and complimented him on the style of the piece but pointed out that "it is two years behind your present thinking."

The Dayton "anti-evolution" trial of 1924, Donald Davidson wrote in 1957, broke in on the literary concerns of him and some of his friends, including Ransom, "like a midnight alarm." A little later—Tate thinks it was in 1926—Tate wrote Ransom a letter far different from the ones he and his friend had been exchanging. "I told him," Tate wrote in 1942, "that we must do something about . . . the culture of the South." Ransom apparently had written a similar letter to Tate at approximately the same time, for the two letters crossed in the mail. The nature of the letters exchanged between the two friends was drastically and immediately altered because the activities that would result in *I'll Take My Stand* (1930) were already under way.

To Robert Graves

Nashville, July 11, [1922]

Dear Mr. Graves:

Our friend William Elliott,[1] of Balliol, tells me that you wrote me a letter in care of my publishers, Henry Holt and Co.[2] That letter, I'm sorry to say, has never turned up—unless it may be they put an envelope around it which made it appear like a catalogue of school-books, and I pitched it into the wastebasket.

I shall go ahead anyway, and write to thank you for the kind words you have been saying about my *Poems about God*. Of course you know they didn't do much over here, and the fact is, they are very juvenile in spots. I'm enclosing some recent stuff I have done. I shall submit another manuscript to the publishers this summer, though of course I don't know whether they'll want it.

I like your theory about the poetic origins, as your apostle Elliott propounds it. When a poet does something he likes, I'm sure it is usually because he has turned on one of his subliminal selves and let him do most of the work. (This may be objectionable to you as terminology.) But I had not thought of the matter in the light of a Katharsis, of life-and-death importance to the subject. Of course, if you take grotesquerie for instance, the poet feels quite happy to ease himself of it; but it doesn't seem so urgent. Possibly there are in the great poets deeper wells which have to find release.

By the way, I thought you might be interested in the poem "Philomela," which I send.[3] The substance of it is that my fellow-countrymen seem to be without the faculty for song—the nightingale doesn't inhabit here. I'm thinking of naming my book after that poem. Also, I may as well confess, of dedicating it to you, because you represent as I see it the best tendency extant in modern poetry.

This brings me to "Pier-Glass," which Elliott showed me. It is lovely. I think you are absolutely on the right road—both the sophisticated man and the lyrist can follow you there. Not your stories nor your prosody take on the hard lines of a demonstration—they are both beautifully casual and inspired. Our great trouble over here is, we are *nouveaux philosophes*—we try to hit off the cosmos every time. Expository and laborious.

I'd give a lot to meet you and join in your debates—if not kicked out. Perhaps I may have this pleasure after a year or so, as I am prospecting a six-months stop in England about then.[4] Meanwhile, haven't you had under advisement at all one of those poetical tours of this country which have now been thoroughly standardized by your compatriots?

John C. Ransom.

---

1. William Yandell Elliott, a graduate of Vanderbilt, studied at Balliol College, Oxford, as a Rhodes scholar from 1920 to 1923.

2. *Poems about God* (New York: Henry Holt and Company, 1919) was Ransom's first book of poems.

3. First published in the *Fugitive*, II (February–March, 1923), 8–9.

4. Ransom did not return to England until September, 1931.

To Robert Graves

August 31, 1922

My dear Graves:

I was delighted with your peachy letter, and the photo. Shall send you ours when we get one.

You have my permission to use anything of mine anywhere, and at any time. And to re-entitle anything, or edit it as you please.

I am having a *Poems about God* sent. Or rather, I'm sending for a fresh stock from the publisher, so that I may put my name in it before forwarding to you. This ought to start in your direction within a week. I'm sending at once copies of the two numbers previously issued of *The Fugitive*. The third number will be out this month, and you shall get one promptly. More presently about this.

What is much more appalling for you, I'm sending by registered post a MS. entitled "Philomela," being a compilation from *God* and my later stuff.[1] This on the assumption that you will show it to the right publisher, for publication as early as possible, as you suggested. Your letter arrived here at about the same time with a note from H. Holt, my former publisher, to the effect that he was returning my MS. with thanks, etc. He did not raise the question of merit so much as that of market: "in view of the continued low state of the demand for poetry," etc. Most of our publishers are disgustingly like that: they place their bets on "sure things" if they can. I would have hopes of landing Harcourt, Brace, and Co., or Knopf, or Doran, however; but in view of the possibility of an English appearance I think I prefer to waive that, and take my chances on a later entry *via* the Trans-Atlantic route.

My book as I have sent it contains 46 poems and a hundred pages or so. It can be chopped up to fit the format, it will hardly need expansion, though I have many left-overs. I used a little over half of *Poems about G.* I have arranged them in the chronological order largely; which order shows a regular progress in technique, I suppose. I made slight revisions in the early ones. I had to leave out many as being too theological or too raw (Grace—the sun-stroke thing).[2] Make any further changes you see fit. Lop off the Dedication, down to your name only, if it's out of place; I have a rather elaborate dedicatory word that is a kind of confession of faith. In short, do what you please with it.

No time for more right at present—must take my wife off to Baseball. Shall write you later about what an interesting group of youngbloods we have here writing the *Fugitive*.

I'll be eternally grateful—

Yours,
John Crowe Ransom

---

1. This manuscript became *Grace after Meat* (London: Hogarth Press, 1924).

2. Ransom objected to this poem, which appeared in *Poems about God* and *Grace after Meat*, owing to its subject. A hired hand dies soon after he returns to the field following a hearty midday meal. Ransom tried to persuade Graves not to include the poem in *Grace after Meat*, but Graves liked it so well he made it the title poem of the volume.

To Robert Graves

October 22, [1922]

Dear Robert Graves:

Do send us some poetry for the *Fugitive*.[1] I have meant all this autumn to write and ask you. We are all very anxious to get it. We announced in the October number that the Christmas number would have visitors' poetry: well, you are our first choice. From this side we have been promised or have already received poetry from Witter Bynner, Percy, McClure, and some others.[2] No doubt Bill [Elliott] has already seen you about this. Of course anything already published in England would serve our purposes, though we should prefer something not yet in book form. If you will do this within a week or so after getting this I'll be awfully grateful.

I am assuming that you know all about the *Fugitive*. For fear you haven't seen our late numbers I'm sending them a second time. We are having good sport, and gradually penetrating the sancta of some of our toploftical critics. Really I think there are some good poets in our crowd, all young. Tate, Davidson, and [Merrill] Moore (who's only eighteen years old) are extremely gifted and fairly prolific. I have an idea we can keep up indefinitely unless for some reason the group breaks up.

I want to enter a couple of corrections to my book MS. I sent you a short time ago. My typewriter made some stupid slips, I see from looking it over: (1) On p. 91, "Adventure This Side of Pluralism," penultimate quatrain, third line, the word *endless* should be *endlessly*; (2) on p. 92, same poem, last quatrain, third line, the word *respective* should be *invective*.

Have lately got hold of *Fairies and Fusiliers* (of which I was familiar with scattering single poems) and read with much interest. It astonishes me what a similarity of tone and technique too there is between your first book and my first book. Since then we have branched off with somewhat of an angle between us perhaps. You are much further along than I in technique. I find myself hampered and tortured in looking for a *form* to carry my themes; have given every chance to modern irregular forms affected over here by some clever people, but am definitely against them now. In philosophy I cannot (I mean in my poems) be anything but honest; which means that I am usually a rebel and a poor admirer of our beloved cosmos. Whether this is an abnormally persistent juvenile strain, I can't say. Finally, I must say I am more and more devoted to poetry (though I wrote nothing in my honeymoon year) and seem to be rather accelerating if anything the rate of my production. All this is tiresomely personal stuff, I guess. I find myself putting it down here as to a poetical psychologist. One finds it useless to pretend that one is utterly spontaneous and not frequently introspective and wary and foresighted as a poet.

Robb (Mrs. JCR) and I are trying to get us a beautiful little Spanish cottage built, and will surely insist on getting you and your wife and babies over to see us in it.[3] Tennessee is physically a lovely spot, not very tidy perhaps.

Yours sincerely,
John C. Ransom

1. Graves published three poems in the *Fugitive*: "On the Poet's Birth" and "A Valentine," I (December, 1922), 103, 112; and "The Corner-Knot," V (December, 1925), 124.

2. The December, 1922, issue of the *Fugitive* had poems by Witter Bynner, Robert Graves, David Morton, and William Alexander Percy but not John McClure.

3. This house was not built.

To Allen Tate

December 17, [1922]

Dear Allan:

I've been really teetering on the edge of a letter for quite a few weeks. Perhaps the deciding force is the handsome dedication I find in the December FUGITIVE under the masterpiece. I liked the compliment immensely.[1]

Your new poems offered last night under Don's sponsorship created a good deal of comment. The party lines were drawn about as usual, Whip Johnson and Whip Ransom polling their full party strengths. But we had one accession of importance to our side—Stevenson. After publishing *Nuptials* and after his stout defenses of the modern point of view last night I am inclined to declare a half-holiday and celebrate a sinner saved.

What do you think of the new FUGITIVE? I think mechanically it's much the most attractive one yet. But I do beg to differ with one committee on the selections in some cases. My quarrel would be on the Moore selections and on the place of honor given to A CERTAIN MAN and on any place given to RONDEAU FOR AUTUMN. (I don't quarrel any more about *Nebrismus*.[2] Life is short. Kismet Selah.)

It strikes me that the great poem of the number (after NUPTIALS always) is Percy's.[3] I do like his tone—it's like a rare old violin, I suppose, mellow. I think all art should be like that.

Ridley [Wills]'s criticism was based on good foundations. I agree with you, only his vocabulary didn't enable him to make his point. I get quite sick of continuous detail work in composition; I think the most of us (not often you) are like jeweller's apprentices; we invent nothing, we hardly see the whole, but we are good at cutting the individual stones. Our patterns that we make out of all our treasures are either nil or they are perfectly standard: WHAT WE LACK IS ESSENTIALLY ARTISTIC TASTE. Would it be painter's parlance to say that we can paint but we can't compose?

But going far beneath that, let us speak to the old and eternal question. WASTE LANDS doesn't satisfy me though it is amazing. Do you recall that chapter in his prose book where he laments the absence of a form, from which void comes all this waste of the modern spirit unable to use its strength? Well, in poem after poem he is surely trying for the form; but hasn't got it. The reason he hasn't got it I take to be chiefly because the form has got to be a philosophy and no less. Here are some scattering (if not glittering) generalities about a work of art: The art-thing sounds like the first immediate transcript of reality, but it isn't; it's a long way from the event. It isn't the raw stuff of experience. The passion in it has mellowed down—emotion recollected in TRANQUILLITY, etc., etc. Above all things else, the core of experience in the record has been taken up into the sum total of things and its relations there discovered are given in the work of art.[4] That is why the marginal meanings, the associations, the interlinear element of a poem are all-important. The most delicate piece of work that a poet has to do is to avoid a misleading connection in his phrasing. There must not be a trace of the expository philosophical method, but nevertheless the substance of the philosophical conclusion must be there for the intelligent reader. The artist can't stay off this necessity—can't hold aloof, be the impartial spectator, the colorless medium of information, the carrier of a perfectly undirected passion, the Know-Nothing from Missouri. I can't help believing more and more (it must be the trace that the classical pedagogy has left on me) that the work of art must be perfectly serious, ripe, rational, mature—full of heart, but with enough head there to govern heart. The young man (I don't mean as measured by his teeth) Aristotle said was incapable of moral philosophy; I don't know about that, but I feel sure he is not up to poetry. ——— Back to T. S. E. again, he has the gift of tongues but thinks he must keep the hemispheres out of it. Hasn't it struck you as amazing that he shows so much wisdom in his prose while he favors a poetic vernacular that is utterly irrationalized? And isn't it pure pretense (unconscious pretense I will say) to write as if wisdom were not and pure blank tracts of experience—waste lands—were all there is? There's no such thing either as pure blank irony—that's artificial, and passes inevitably into tragic irony or pity or something with a solid substance of dogma even, or else sterilizes the artistic impulse back of it.

This is hopeless dull stuff I've been getting off. I should have condensed it and made your pain shorter. Here's another thing about Eliot that has struck me: (1) NUPTIALS antedated WASTE LANDS and contained most of its effective devices—only it has a proper continuity and singleness that W L has not. Notably NUPTIALS has little bits of refrains from proverbs and the vernacular of the day that I imagine the world never saw till W L came to its attention,—never saw used that way, I mean. And (2) have you been struck with any resemblance between Vachel Lindsay (of all people) and Eliot? The latter is a kind of burlesque or reductio ad absurdum of the former, carries three or four times as many tunes forward at one time, and repeats with unholy mock-unction things that Vachel gets out of his system with revival fervor. Funny.

I send my two last efforts. Have done little good this term, but now that Curry gets back onto his job and I am going to move with my wife and baby to where I can cultivate a rather less complicated domestic life (it's on 17th Ave. S. near Ward Belmont), I'll have a better chance. Note last night's exhibit, the long one; it's in blank verse; rimes and jingles were getting intolerable; and if little Max seems any good I'll do some more about him.[5] Please give me a long criticism about them; some faults I see plain, but I want to see the others.

About time I was acknowledging your former criticisms. They were just right—your exceptions to my metrical vagaries in the short one well taken. As to the other one, HERE LIES A LADY, your compliments far too handsome, but the LITERARY REVIEW OF THE EVENING POST snapped it up all the same.

I enclose a fulmination from the latter journal bearing on the previous discussion.[6] I could swallow it whole if it were not so sadly in the best manner of a little pedagod.

We all hope you are coming for the big Christmas meeting. At that time I am going to launch my insurrection about next year's *Fugitive*.

I'm tired of waiting on the English proposition and the other day sent off a MS. to Harcourt's.[7] Harcourt handled my stuff before when he was with Henry Holt, and I think has a mild prepossession in my favor. Anyway, it's a better MS. than the one Holt returned [to] me early in the summer.

Why don't you collect your choicest wares and offer them to a publisher? Don and I think you have enough stuff to go big in volume form.

Ever yours,
John Crowe Ransom

---

1. Tate's poem "Nuptials," which appeared in the *Fugitive* for December, 1922, was dedicated to Ransom.

2. A poem by Sidney Mttron Hirsch, which appeared in the same number of the *Fugitive*. Tate and Davidson argued against the inclusion of this poem; but Ransom, Davidson believed, did not argue strongly enough against its publication.

3. In the *Fugitive* for December, 1922, W. A. Percy published "Safe Secrets."

4. This is an early statement of Ransom's poetic theory that he later called "The Third Moment."

5. "First Travels of Max," *Fugitive*, II (June–July, 1923), 86–87.

6. "Waste Lands," *Literary Review*, III (July 14, 1923), 825–26.

7. An early version of *Chills and Fever*, published by Knopf in 1924.

To Robert Graves

January 4, 1923

My dear Graves:

I've just written *Who's Who in A.* that I'm publishing "Vaunting Oak" in England.[1] Not that this fact matters a damn—it's routine stuff, they send out circulars and you put the items down. I'd just as soon be in error in that tome. But it came a little hard to write "Grace after Meat"—it emphasizes a poem I don't like.

I return the contract with notations which I hope do not impair any validity. I am not the kind of best seller for publishing houses to "law" over.

You're taking a wonderful meticulous interest in this project. Yours be the title at least! If I were certain you would use "Grace" I wouldn't have been insubordinate as above.

Ransom

1. One of the titles Ransom suggested for *Grace after Meat.*

To Robert Graves

February 1, 1923

Dear Graves:

I don't know whether I've written yet to thank you for your poems for the *Fugitive.* We used "The Poet's Birth" and "Valentine," and are saving the other two—unless you want them more immediately?[1]

We are awfully grateful for your help—and will appreciate anything you send us.

I must apologize for some publicity that my friend Christopher Morley, in his column on the N.Y. *Evening Post*, gave to some innocent words of yours contained in a private letter to me. Recently I sent him my Ms. (which includes many that you have and a good many later ones, and goes under the title "Chills and Fevers") to look over and possibly handle with the publishers for me; I am very intimate with him, having been up together with him at Oxford, and I quoted a sentence of unguarded approval of my stuff contained in a letter you wrote me last year; I was quite mortified and astonished to see Morley quoting the same in his column a day or two later. My deepest apologies for giving away a private sentiment! The sentence was to the effect that you thought "Poems about God" a very important thing in recent American poetry.

Morley meant entirely well, he thinks highly of us both. He writes me asking me to present his best compliments. He has sponsored your "On English Poetry" without any reservations. Writes: "It is delicious to discover that poetry is a sort of police-court report of a brawl among the Ideas!" As to my own work, he is extremely enthusiastic over my later stuff, and guarantees to get me a publisher at once.

My best to Old Bill.

Yours,
John C. Ransom

P.S. Never mind about my MS that you have. I dare say your publishers are as canny as ours. If any of them are nibbling, make any revisions, excisions, changes you want to.

---

1. The "other two" were never used in the *Fugitive*, unless one of them was "The Corner-Knot," which appeared in the issue for December, 1925.

To Allen Tate

[February, 1923]

Dear Allen,

Note my steady progress. This note I believe has been owing only about a couple of weeks.

As to the storm-bird Pegasus, you doubtless know by this time that in deference to your and Don's objections the committee removed him from the line-up. You were so much more strenuous in opposition than we could possibly be in support.[1] But my conscience has been smarting all the same—especially since the worthy author took his medicine like a man at our Saturday meeting.

I have a wicked suspicion that you and I do not differ so widely in critical ideas except when you erect a wilful smoke-screen of Prejudice to interfere with your vision of the delicate charms of a hated rival's masterpiece! Seriously, I approach the old Frank's efforts with, if anything, a certain prepossession in his favor, because I like him much as a man, and I like his unusual modesty as an author. He was really fine the other night; read a piece considerably better than Pegasus, and invited all sorts of mutilations upon it.

About Pegasus, however. There were many errors which the committee wrote out of the thing. At that stage I considered it (still consider it) quite innocuous, and favored using it as a friendly overture from Sinister to Dexter. It was certainly about a couple of centuries late in coming; but was quaint rather than vicious, and consistent in its tone if pedantic, and not a bit pretentious: much preferable therefore to Sidney [Hirsch]'s things, which are hugely ambitious and solemn as the tomb and in the event therefore ridiculous.

But have no fears, my dear good man. Henceforth the Committee will judge by a standard a little higher than to pass the Pegasuses. We had a full and free discussion at meeting, received a vote of confidence as a committee, and were instructed not to heed any principle of representation in our selections. Our party in other words is firmly in the saddle; and it behooves us to be generous where we can safely do so. Personally, it would seem to me far more obscene (the idea gives me a nausea) to smash things up in a temper, than to print anything imaginable in our joint magazine. We are reputed to be gentlemen and sportsmen rather than ladies in the village choir. We *are* a group, and presumably committed to individual sacrifices. Least of all would it become you or me, us two, to weep and rage. There is as you know a wide disapproval of our stuffs, and yet we have been most handsomely awarded with space.

In short, I am tremendously pleased with our present working arrangement. I might add that I have found the other members of the committee thoroughly reasonable.

You are hitting a great stride these days. I return Yellow River with pensive annotations.[2] Almost thou persuadest me to be a Christian—but I am a tough heathen. Still I am unable to see the art-thing in the heterogeny. I require for the satisfaction of my peculiar complex something more coherent than is offered in the mere cross-section of a brain at a given instant. You are attempting an art of the sub-rational. To me that seems as unnecessary and as limiting as is the hackneyed American formula for the short-story: Everything in dramatic situation, no comments, no author's personality. We know what that produces. Or pure Imagism, in poetry. Isn't it an assumption that the poetic is antithetical to the rational?

As usual, I toss you the laurel scenery for the speed and felicity of your phrasing.

As ever yours,
John C. Ransom

On reading this sounds to me perhaps a trifle like an "elder brother." I recant—wherever you may get the same idea. Not meant so. JCR

---

1. A poem by James M. Frank, to which both Davidson and Tate objected. Tate wrote Davidson on January 16, 1923: "I will withdraw from The Fugitive if the poem in question goes in the next or any issue."

2. Never published.

To Allen Tate

Denver, Colorado, July 30, [1923]

Dear Tate:

Your carbon copy of letter to Editor of *Lit Review* was a sock-dolager.[1] Don't misunderstand me—I don't mean your arguments—but the tone.

You shouldn't do those things. Your duplicity is charming from an intellectual point of view, but there's also a sentimental one. It was a regular bolt from the blue, being so amazingly at variance with previous talks and pretending to such a toploftical state of erudition! But I won't get started, I have taken it all out in the enclosed paper which I have just this moment done and without a typewriter.

Yours about the make-up came today, with further jovial reference to yours-to-the-Review, convincing me that you didn't see it really in the light that showed it to me. Enough said.

But what's all this about Don as Editor and you as Associate Editor? Are you going to be with us next year? Well, I'm dead against it. Every member knows we have no Editor in the ordinary dictionary sense of that term: then we have no business publishing on a false basis.

Yours still,
John C. Ransom

[Copy of a letter sent to the editor of the Literary Review *(August 11, 1923)]*

Sir,

With your permission I would supplement Mr. Allen Tate's letter, not by questioning if it does justice to the tone of my article, but by asserting that it by no means does justice to the state of his own mind. One might gather from this letter that it was written by an enemy bent on demolishing such scant reputation for scholarship as I might have laboriously constructed, when as a matter of fact the author and I have enjoyed a long and peaceable acquaintance, and it is himself who sends me a copy of his letter with certain waggish additions for my private benefit. The truth is, Tate has for two years suffered the damning experience of being a pupil in my classes, and I take it his letter is but a proper sign of his final emancipation, composed upon his accession to the ripe age of twenty-three. I am confident that our official relations have been mutually profitable. For instance, when I borrowed the lone volume which constituted his library of Remy de Gourmont; and when I reciprocated by lending him my lone volume of [F. H.] Bradley, and by commending him to an examination of the Kantian System. (I have returned his Remy, but he still keeps my Bradley.) With his researches into the genetic criticism since Wundt,[2] and into the Freudian emphasis, I am obliged to confess I had nothing to do. I always gave him due credit on the grade books for having a brilliant mind, though I was not in possession of the magic formula for putting it to work. I applaud the rate at which his mind travels—taking its text undoubtedly from the view it entertains of T. S. Eliot himself, of whom it is spoken, "He must shift all the time." I do not know a better illustration of this quality than Tate's reference to my "superannuated" theories of art; having as I do the most definite recollections which enable me to say that this superannuation, so far as Tate is concerned, has entirely taken place these last three months.

To the point of his letter, I have only one thing to say seriously. I am at a loss when he ascribes to my paper an admiration for the coherent quality of Mr. Eliot's prose, inasmuch as the paper contains no treatment whatsoever of this subject. But speaking my impression of a prose which I have not seen for a year, I would say that in my opinion Mr. Eliot's critical prose is vitiated by precisely the same quality that marks in a greater degree the prose of Mr. Tate's letter and the work of a whole sodality of younger critics—it abhors the academic (*i.e.*, the honest and thoroughgoing) method, and is only specious, using its glittering scraps of comment and citations without any convincing assurance that the subject has been really digested.

J.C.R.

---

1. Tate wrote in part: "Ransom's article . . . violates so thoroughly the principle of free critical inquiry and at the same time does such scant justice to the school of so-called philosophical criticism . . . that it may be of interest to your readers to consider the possible fallacy of his method and a few of the errors into which it leads him." The errors include a "thorough-going schematism of the origin and process of artistic creation," a failure to account for the "psychological origins of art as a standard of aesthetics," a failure to see the form of the poem, and a confusion of parody and irony (*Literary Review* of the New York *Evening Post*, August 4, 1923).

2. Wilhelm Wundt (1832–1920), German philosopher and psychologist.

To Donald Davidson

August 21, [1923]

Dear Friend Don:

Am this a.m. in receipt of a long letter from Jesse [Wills], with an outline of our new mast-head, and of a carbon copy of your modest and manly letter "To The Fugitives" dated Aug. 14. A former letter from some Fugitives also contained a cryptic reference to "Don's book" which I have not seen fully explicated as yet; but I feel that I have basis enough for forthwith extending to you my heart-felt congratulations upon the occasion of a publisher for your poems, and to all Fugitives my felicitations upon securing you to run our affairs for another year.[1]

At the same time, I am not satisfied with our mast-head, and must declare my intention of agitating for a change as soon as I can attend a next meeting; but in doing so, I cheerfully engage to abhor "strife and recrimination," to conserve my weak arsenal of "tomahawks and war-whoops" against a more appropriate occasion, and to approach the question "with a feeling of good will."

I think our leader's title should be "Managing Editor," with the utmost deference to the happy selection of the person that has just been made. In a previous letter to the group, by way of casting my vote, I said the same thing, but too briefly out of a lack of time.

The new mast-head, if Jesse has furnished me an accurate draft, is to show a list of thirteen "Editors." Beneath that appears the name of an "Editor of the Fugitive." I fail to see an accurate distinction there. It occurs to me that with thirteen "Editors," the only additional Editor must be either, (1) an Editor-in-Chief, or (2) a Managing Editor. I consider that the former is not the correct designation of the office whose duties were so closely defined in the Resolutions, since those duties do not include what to the world and in the dictionary are the chiefest editorial functions, namely, a responsibility for the contents. The latter title I would think falls exactly into the place, but has the disadvantage of being somewhat the less of a worldly honor, and therefore may not appeal to an incumbent or worth the onerous burdens of the office; that is a perfectly fair question which the incumbent would have the perfect right to settle for himself.

If that is not a strong argument, it is at least reinforced by the fact that we have advertised extensively that we have no chief. Personally, I have written three editorials, some by command, and two personal letters, these I believe both by request and voluntarily, to make this point. More recently the official pronouncement was conveyed to Digby,[2] who last week inserted in his column a notice concluding: "It seems that the Fugitive has no Editor, and is never likely to have, but is published by some thirteen Editors of whom one has as much say as the other—" (or words to that effect). So much display surely involves a certain responsibility.

In stating my personal and selfish attitude, I mean to pose only as an example of what I had heretofore conceived was the universal (or nearly so) Fugitive opinion. From the professional point of view, we all (with the possible exception of Curry) regard poetry as a potential source of profit. As an associate professor specializing in composition, I know that the *Fugitive* is of direct professional importance to me. It is for that reason that I resent (if one can resent without feeling a personal grievance) a misrepresentation of the facts which permits the assumption that my own part in the magazine is of less importance than that of some other.

This is about as systematic a statement as I can make in a hurry and in the absence of my typewriter. Don't forget that there is no animus whatever in my position, and that I had rather have you in the position in question than the joint efforts of any other two men rolled into one.

Have had a busy summer, but school closes this week. I can certainly use a rest. Hope you have had the vacation that has long been overdue.

Yours as ever,
John C Ransom

---

1. Davidson's *An Outland Piper* had been accepted by Houghton, Mifflin and would appear the next year.

2. A pseudonym of Christopher Morley.

To Louis Untermeyer

Nashville, November 12, 1923

Dear Mr. Untermeyer:[1]

Again I acknowledge a kind letter—one received now some six weeks ago. I've delayed my reply because I was expecting from day to day news of my volume that I thought might make an interesting communication for you.[2]

I grieve to say that Harcourt was unable to "see" my poems; an incapacity which most readers share, and which I would lay to my own blame if it were not for the shining example of a few superior critics like yourself who do catch my point and are not repelled by some nameless and unaccustomed manner of my presentation!

But I am able since yesterday to say that Knopf is "extremely enthusiastic" about my volume and offers to publish it; no earlier than "early autumn of 1924," however.

We have felt very grateful for your commendation of our *Fugitive*, and hope that you received duly at your Vienna address the October number, and have been able to continue your sympathetic attitude. We now have a publisher-patron who relieves us of all the financial chores,[3] and an Editor (Davidson) who is willing to attend strictly to the necessary office work, so that I feel we will at any rate not suffer any immediate disintegration. By the way, perhaps you have seen old Braithwaite's annual Poetry Revue in the *Transcript* of October 6, in which he singles out our magazine as having displayed "more character and originality" than any in this country, and awards us 18 or 20 places among the poems of his current *Anthology*—including your *Tangential.*[4]

And this leads me to say that we all would appreciate at any time the favor of a contribution from your own pen, though aware of the insufficient public that we can offer to a writer. But it may be that your present occupation with fiction leaves you no time for your customary devotions to the other art.

Some day I hope to make your acquaintance and that of Mrs. Untermeyer in person. I am in fact sending out a feeler or two towards the Eastern colleges and expect eventually to locate myself in that section.

Sincerely yours,
John C. Ransom

---

1. Louis Untermeyer (1885–1977), a poet and editor chiefly known for his anthologies of poetry.

2. *Chills and Fever* (New York: Knopf, 1924).

3. Jacques Back, manager of a Nashville advertising agency, served as business director of the *Fugitive* from October, 1923, through December, 1924.

4. Since 1913 William S. Braithwaite had published a yearbook of what he deemed "the best magazine verse."

To Robert Graves

November 19, [1923]

Dear Graves:

I am overjoyed to hear about my election to British publicity through Hogarth Press.[1] I know very well to whom I am indebted to, and feel immensely grateful, but won't dwell on that side of it as I know you will not require nor want my testimony there. I say you take a sporting interest in my small cause!

You'll be glad to hear too that I am just signing up with your American publisher, Alfred Knopf, to bring out "Chills and Fever" early next autumn. I have an idea H. P. will exhibit me first, in which case I may look forward to some advance interest on this side in my forthcoming volume, always provided I do not disappoint your reckless faith in the reception I get from your British public.

You are a plenipotentiary in handling my English book. I have more confidence, naturally, in your knowledge of the situation than in my own ignorance. I now raise (pretty hastily) a few points you mention, by way of suggestions only.

Title. I've consulted a Latinist and a naturalist, and am distressed to learn that *Ilex Priscus* is Latinically sound, but can mean only a holm-oak, which is evergreen, and useless for my peculiarly devastating intentions. I fear it will have to be: *Quercus Prisca.* This falls a little short on the score of melopoïea. Would you prefer "Old Oak"? Which wouldn't be very "snappy" as a book-title, but which I'll resort to on this side for entitling the poem. Do what seems best, even to retaining the old title as a sort of Americanism and characteristic piece of bad scholarship.

The line in *Parting at Dawn*—"Till they are as the barren Cenobite,"—is intentionally thus. I have—lately—a horror of over-strained, overdone effects, and the present form represents an older—"Till these be as the barren Cenobite." I wanted my climax in the sestet, without too much local excitement in the octet. Of course "are" means "will be," and I believe is good English in that sense. But again, it shall be just as you prefer.

The line—"Ye harping the springe that catches the dove"—is also intentional. "Ye" is a vocative, going with "Musicians." But if it's obscure, I think I should revise to "that are harping the, *etc.*"

And so forth. I'm sure there are errors. I'd be delighted, though I shudder at the imposition of it, if you'll handle my proof. I too prefer the simpler words of dedication—the other was a lame statement in bad form.

Your selection of the poems shall stand. Personally, I'd say "Grace" is an artistic offense, and I'd rather pose for an artist than exhibit my history. But if you'd like to have written it, my judgment is wrong. Besides, it may strike British readers, who are more used to red meat and regular liquor than ours.

I watch for *The Owl* with great interest.

I enclose my prize poem to settle the vast doubts you have entertained about its hundred-dollar quality.[2]

Some day (of about 72 hours) we'll thresh out the poetic principle. I expect to come in for some of the threshing myself. But my ideas are forming and I grow in conviction if not in absolute rightness.

Yours to command
John C. Ransom

P.S. Here's another item for editorial consideration. In the local version of my *Winter Remembered* I have but five stanzas, those beginning (in this order)—

Two evils—
Think not—
Better to walk forth—
And where I went—
Dear love—.

In the *Winter Owl* version appeared (in 2nd place I think) another stanza which I have cast off. I think it does not harmonize thoroughly with the others, and is inferior. Besides, the poem's long enough. Originally I had two or three sonnets in a series of which this is the remains. Will you consider this point!

John C. Ransom

---

1. Ransom is referring to *Grace after Meat*'s acceptance by the Hogarth Press, owned by Virginia and Leonard Woolf. A young poet could not reasonably expect a greater compliment than having his work published by this house, which was among the leading English publishers.

2. Ransom's "Armageddon" won first prize ($100) for the best poem submitted to the Poetry Society of South Carolina in 1923.

To Robert Graves

November 20, [1923]

Dear Graves:

Some second thoughts here.

More and more I like your selections. Am reconciled to them all. I hope, however, that you will use the MS as a copy for those poems which I revised from the "Poems about God" volume and sent you. "Cloak Model" and "Resurrection" in particular seem to need this revision.

That pestilential title again. I feel that *Ilex* must go; it's a glaring inaccuracy which an Englishman like yourself, and therefore a Latinist, ought not to have smiled upon! And as to *Quercus*, that's unfortunately a feminine and won't do for my particular oak.

How about running your eye over this lot of suggestions? "Under the Locusts"—(I like you for liking that, which I think is about the best thing in the volume)—or to set them down where the visibility will be higher, here they are:

Under the Locusts;
*Lean Locust Branches;
Great Oak;
American Oak;
*Throes of Oak;
Mortal Oak;
*Vaunting Oak;
or Any Title Poem.[1]

And if none of these seems to work, I guess once more it's up to you to straighten me out and denominate me [better] than I can do.

I like Hogarth Press. I saw their booklist which came with "Featherbed."[2] They get distinguished books—or have hitherto. They are somewhat analogous to Knopf over here, evidently. I wonder if "Featherbed" is an average piece of bookmaking for them, or something very special as it truly seems to be.

You and Morley (who did for P. about G. what you are doing for this one) are birds of a feather and a credit to ornithology.

Ever thine,
John C. Ransom

---

1. Ransom starred the suggested titles which he preferred. Graves, of course, accepted none of them.

2. "Featherbed" is a narrative poem published July 20, 1923, with an introductory letter to Ransom.

To Robert Graves

December 30, [1923]

My dear Robert Graves:

I don't believe I shall try to prosecute my grievances against the *Grace* poem over your magnanimous protests—I don't feel I would be convincing in that rôle. I'll wait till it's somebody else's poem that offends.

Was delighted with your letter. You are too considerate in offering to try to get proofs to me. I don't care a hang about them, *provided* you can stand the strain of correcting them for me. If there's to be time, I'd gladly do this office of course.

No, I can't honestly applaud your selection of title: *Grace after Meat.* Is that a snappy title? I don't believe, aside from the poem it refers to, it has too much relevance to the whole. The title under which I have printed my oak poem in the *Fugitive* is *Vaunting Oak*. Do you fancy that? You are the judge and jury and sheriff too. I realize the cogency of your judgments in these matters and most gladly give you a free hand. I daresay I'll like the title you mention after I get familiar with it.

I must thank you for the noble company and beautiful mechanical setting in which I found myself upon receipt of *Winter Owl*.[1] A very very choice morsel of bookmaking I thought. My friends have preened me much on this great appearance. Please accept my profoundest obeisance as an editor. As to contents, I liked everything. Present company excepted, I liked best Hardy's funny poem and Guedalla's fine prose.[2] Garnett's story was fine too.[3] (By the way, I think *Lady into Fox* an immortal if anything contemporary is.[4]) That Indian philosopher writes well—I've never however been able to follow their dialectic which is so annihilating to all the edge, point, shape, and individuality of Anglo-Saxon concepts—I'm racially incapable of doing a Buddha. Old W. H. Davies appeared in a new rôle—distinctly literary and 17th Century—makes me think that as a vagabond and a natural (the pose I've assigned him always—he's a fakir).[5] The art department intrigued me though I'm rankly outside when it comes to that. A thing like Nicholson's "Shire Horse" of course anybody must fall for.

I enclose one I've just done for *Fugitive* amusement. The brethren didn't seem to cotton to it I must say. Is it any good?

Yours
John C Ransom

P.S. The enclosed referred to is *Captain Carpenter*. I also enclose *Old Mansion* which I piously hope you will like. I do. JCR

---

1. *Winter Owl* was a British periodical in which Graves published three poems and an article in the November, 1923, issue.
2. Philip Guedalla (1889–1944), a historian.
3. David Garnett (b. 1892), an editor and fictionist.
4. *Lady into Fox* by Garnett is a short novel that won the Hawthornden and Tait-Black prizes for 1923.
5. W. H. Davies (1871–1940) was a minor English poet.

To Robert Graves

January 28, [1924]

Dear Robert:

Please overlook this typescript—the machine is handy while the intimate stylus is not.

Your letter came yesterday, and has caused me much grief: purely because it makes me think I have been extremely inconsiderate in bothering you about that title. You are a good fellow not to rail on me, after the extremity of kindness which you have manifested. I bow to your judgment entirely, and I wish to say that the title you liked (and which I feel sure that Woolf decided upon) will not "spoil the book" for me; I see the point that you make; we must have a caption with a handle to it, and nothing vague and pious. Therefore forget my pestiferous cavils.

I am happy to think that my booklet is already with the printers.

Robb and I have no picture now; but we are getting some snapshots done which will include at least my little girl Helen (two years old, whose greatest delight is rhyming) if not my little boy of four months. Robb, by the way, is a Wyoming girl who can ride, shoot, and fish better than her husband and who is the best woman golfer in this town (150,000 souls, including the blacks, who are now generally accredited with coming under that category though the point was long debated). If we come to England year after next, as seems likely or at least possible, I have designs on Frilford Heath Golf Club, whose hospitality I used to abuse.

I send a couple of my latest, and conclude in haste.

Yours sincerely,
John Crowe Ransom

To Allen Tate

April 15, [1924]

Dear Tate:

Was quite glad to get such a fine letter. It is a good thing there are a few choice spirits—not all departed—to cultivate the real epistolary amenities: I will say this, you are well-nigh the last surviving member of your fine species!

Since the appearance of the April *Fugitive* about four days ago, have perused your prose article with considerable care and some frequency, and finally elicited from it some of the fine ideas which you have so precariously and prodigally therein hinted at.[1] But speaking of the "rational exposition" which would appear to be J. C. R.'s desideration,[2] you evidently realize that you haven't qualified—you don't care and why should you?

Now how do we differ in free verse? For the life of me I can't see that exactly. You say, free verse is O.K. for a man whose stuff is good enough to go down in one way or another—see Sandburg. I agree. But you say, *only* for such a man will it do. Then you turn to poetry as an "art having to do with verse-forms and kindred paraphernalia"—you imply that the art in itself (notwithstanding the exceptional Sandburg) has to do by definition with these paraphernalia. On the third page you show how necessary they are.

And how about this? (You plead guilty to Sophist, and now Socrates would question you.) Admitting that you define the function of the paraphernalia one way, and I another, still you too regard them as necessary; and how then will you escape my dualism? How can a man "casually" use these paraphernalia when he knows he must? Since you picture me as putting the premium on an "antic capacity" for virtuosity, can't I return the compliment? In either system the poet must (a) make sense and (b) with the same words make meter. . . . "Their stanza . . . is a pattern erected only to be broken down . . . rime, a device for artificial emphasis or dramatic suspense. . . ." Do you then figure that this higher sort of rime, that is so felicitous, "comes natural"? So far as you use my paraphernalia, my dear man, you will have to pay the same price that I do.

Or do you want Polyphonic prose: Of course you are aware that so-called rimes (i.e., correspondences) recur momentarily in all prose speech quite casually? But the minute they come where they are required—e.g. at line-ends—they become rimes proper; and there is "art" in this.

"They erect sound-patterns only to break them down again for a greater illusion of freedom."[3] This is very ingenious, but have you really considered if it is true? In the first place, do you think you can substantiate it among the poets of the tradition as you saucily imply? Waiving "inviolable"—since nobody but Pope regarded the ruler as inviolable, and not even Pope for that matter—didn't every one of them look on rime and stanzas as a pretty definite, determinate pattern, and one just about as much so as another? Give us some cases! And in the second place, here's what your theory would involve: a stanza, rigid and nonsensical and extreme, followed by a series of non-stanzas, elastic and free and spontaneous; a horrible example first of the evils of slavery, and then the labor of love that is free and good; an argument for freedom by the device of contrast. Now do we have that in modern poems? Surely not. A good poem is homogeneous. I would imagine this is the truer (if tamer) psychology: the poet hates his bondage—the patterns; but he knows it is the condition of his art; and so he takes just as much liberty as he can: if experimentally minded, he goes pretty far, testing (1) whether he will conform sufficiently to remain in his art, or failing that, (2) whether he may not be a Sandburg, and have stuff good enough to stand in any shape, art or no art.

As to the "rational exposition" question, I don't assume that either poetry or prose is exclusively confined to it. But if on the contrary you assume, as one might think you do, that the "pure presentation of ideas and sensations" is the business of poetry, somebody will ask you: "Suppose it's done in prose—free verse—is it then poetry?" It will be embarrassing.

But though I have trouble with your pp. 1 and 3, your p. 2 seems to me as good a thing as you've ever done—or anybody else in that field. And I admire many other bits here and there. But honestly I question if the whole is worth the immense labor of working it out that falls upon the reader.

Well, there it is! Doubtless you detect the pedagogical flavor in what I say. I've been thinking of your admirable reviews in Don's page:[4] it's clear you are cultivating "rational exposition" on the sly, and I for one like it, up to a certain point.

Your poem was read in the original form at the last meeting 8 days ago.[5] Your revision is an enormous improvement. Much criticism was indulged on the original version and a good time was had by all. I endeavored to make two points. First, it is remarkable in your poetry for a great development of the discursive reason; you have an admirable fulness and flexibility of style. Second, in theme it is antipractical; I contending (against Curry *et al.*) that its theme is that of a young man whose science, or naturalism, or rationalism, unfits him, to his own sorrow, for the romantic attitude even where he is challenged by a very inviting situation. In the revision, however, this anti-romanticism seems to me a little mitigated. It's certainly an able performance, any way you take it. As a substitute member of the Selection Committee (in Jesse's place) I might say it was declined for the April number on the ground that the prose piece of the same author's was already pretty esoteric, and more of the same might have tended to excess.

Will we see you with us this summer? And what's the news from Yale?

Many thanks for your kind words about *Poet Laureate*.[6] The old Chancellor has taken quite a fancy to my prose stuff, is still "off" my poetry.

Yours,
John C. R.

P.S. (On another reading):
1. "The older song is in a very real sense more traditional than any other mode practiced by poets at the present time."[7] What does it mean?
2. "Baudelaire's Theory of Correspondences is at once the backbone of Modern poetic diction and the character which distinguishes it from both the English Tradition and free verse (an escape from the dilemma)." Considering your title, this is the backbone of your article. But strikes me as one of the most fantastic dogmas you ever could tie to. Shakespeare has a lot of correspondences: I daresay the Imagists have; if they (Vers Librists, Imagists) don't, suppose they should—would they then be Vers Librists or moderns? And chiefly, don't you imagine that I can cite you scores of modern poems, wholly acceptable as such, which haven't a scrap of correspondences about them? This is really a most nonsensical differentia, my fine Allen!! Can't see how I forgot to mention it above—struck me as something fierce.

J. C. R.

---

1. "One Escape from the Dilemma."
2. "The Future of Poetry," *Fugitive*, III (February, 1924), 2–4.
3. Ransom is not quoting Tate exactly. Tate's sentence reads: "Their stanza, or any metrical scheme, is a pattern erected only to be broken down for an increased illusion of freedom."
4. From February 4, 1924, to November 30, 1930, Donald Davidson edited a book page for the Nashville *Tennessean*.
5. Probably "Prothesis for Marriage,"

which appeared in the *Double Dealer*, VI (August–September, 1924), 214.

6. Ransom's "The Poet Laureate" appeared in the *Literary Review*, IV (March 29, 1924), 625–26.

7. Again Ransom's quotation is inexact. Tate wrote: "For the older song has assumed a variation—as I believe, a development, and is in a very real sense more traditional than any other mode practiced by poets at the present time."

To Allen Tate

April 22, [1924]

Dear Allen:

I reply instantly to your latest, just arrived, though it will involve a certain reduction from the fine proportions of the letter that you are entitled to, and that I should write if I had more than these 30 minutes at my disposal just this afternoon.

It is evident that my letter went forth and stands convicted of the serious charge (for a rational expositor) of not having said what it intended. I am staggered at the monument of discourtesy which I have erected. I wasn't at all consciously in any belittling attitude as I surveyed your article and tried to collect my fugitive thoughts. I particularly deplore my having raised the question whether it was worth the reader's time to work out your system; that, I suppose, was another of the overstatements which are pedagogically sound (receiving their justification from Plato himself) but damnable between friends. The difficulty of making you fully out was extreme: that was about all I had a right to say. And furthermore: My attention in the letter was occupied mostly with points in the negative sense, and I failed to specify the many things that were admirable. And I should have noted, too, what I saw from the start, that you had undertaken a subject of which the inherent difficulty made a full exposition impossible in the limits assigned you.

Your most recent letter clears up some other confusions that existed in my mind. For example, I see that you are specifically thinking of a certain school of poets whose differentia *is* in the correspondences. (And by the by, I used the word in my letter in two senses, and I understood the sense in which your article had used it.) Now I guess I am excessively dogmatic, in spite of a vast disrespect for dogma that I entertain, but I wouldn't undertake to deny the existence of such a school. My errors and lapses are far too violent for me to waive the good old alibi of plain ignorance. And here was what threw me off: It seemed to me that you were defining the school at the moment by the metrical test; you seemed to locate them along a line of which one extreme was the tradition and the other was free verse; and I therefore raised the question whether you would find that the school you discovered by the metrical differentia would turn out to be the very same school that you might discover by a totally unrelated other differentia.

This topic would stand considerable expansion and expatiation still, but I forbear at this writing. After all, I believe it is a fact that you are the only available victim for me, when it comes to giving my aesthetic theories an airing; and it is possible (though I do not wish to flatter myself) that I am one of the most accessible responses you yourself can find when you are similarly engaged.

I would much like to see some aesthetics done at great and fitting length on your part.

Last night's meeting of the Fugitives was a good one, as things are going. Jesse read by long odds the best poem of considerable length (150 lines) that a Fugitive had yet perpetrated.[1] Your sonnet was read, admired, and condemned in the most standard manner. Your word of explanation is illuminating; especially as I thought you had in the octette given to the bridegroom such a perversion of his customary role that you exposed yourself to a certain ridicule [I] think is extremely good. It is especially good for your purpose, of which Don has told me. I am sure you have enough stuff to go to the publishers with, and wish I could see a copy of the whole thing some time while you are waiting to hear your fate.

Morley wrote me the most effusive letter of praises I ever had, about my manuscript, and then spilled a little of it in his column in the POST. He says: "Have no fear: beyond the possible probable shadow of doubt I will get you a good publisher for your really glorious farrago." Good words, mates: By the way, my title is CHILLS AND FEVERS.

Write me when you think I deserve it. Curry is coming for a call directly and I'll close while I may.

Yours ever,
John

---

1. Ransom is referring to Jesse Wills's poem "Eden," *Fugitive*, III (June, 1924), 72–75.

To Allen Tate

May 6, [1924]

Dear Allen:

I wish you could have listened in on our meeting of last evening. In the first place, you would have been able to renew your slipping confidence that you had cast in your lot among friends. I believe a letter is in process of getting itself written to express to you more formally the sense of the group as deeply appreciative of your labors and loyalty on behalf of the common cause,—l. and l. which have never seemed to waver despite the fact that you so obviously were in the position of an extremely attenuated minority. We all, as a matter of fact, despite the naturally tyrannous tendencies of any overwhelming majority, feel thoroughly disposed to render you full credit for the value of your services and to give you the most ample representation in any exhibit of the work of the group. Of course in the long run, there is no estimating the value of any highly differentiated departure on the part of an individual—who knows which of the individual men may ultimately become the cornerstone of the edifice? Caution at least would prompt us against any exclusions.

Except in the case of the peculiar individualities of Messrs Frank and Hirsch. And you would have been amused and edified to note how, in the course of a long and rather quiet discussion of the verities of group procedure, last night, we frankly took the position that the dear magazine was open to any sort of performance that could style itself Modern; not to the antique, Oriental, or Semitic modes. The victims assented very handsomely. The point was made, and assented to, that such policy had indeed produced its results: had reached the critical audience it was aimed at; and no departure is contemplated or petitioned for. So though you may be a minority, your inalienable rights are secured to you in perpetuity; whereas there is another minority party which can never rejoice in those blessings.

More and more, at each meeting, there develops a great disinclination to abandon the Fugitive. We are now committed to finishing the year on the present basis, with Back as goat; and with the expectation of going on ourselves indefinitely, the ways and means to be later determined. So I really believe there's life in the old carcass yet.

About criticism again. To enlarge on a point I had already made and you had already seemed to approve. Instead of naming two differentiae as defining your Twentieth Century model, you named three: the formal, the philosophical, and the rhetorical (if I may so denominate the matter of the Correspondences). My own article dealt almost wholly with the formal, and I was led by the common fallacy of protection of my own interests into thinking that you were dealing primarily with the formal in your article; whence I was at a loss to know how your Modern group, defined by formal marks, could also be a group capable of definition by still other marks. In other words, I thought your performance was dialectical and *a priori*; you wanted to establish a mode of compromise which would escape an ugly dilemma. But in fact, it seems rather from what you say that you had in mind an actual group which did actually present several distinguishing marks. Personally, my own disquietude is wholly over the formal difficulties; I would take it for granted that the other differentia will attend any good performance, whatever the form may be; so it has been in the past. The traditional poets generally have defined themselves sharply but under a common conception of form; but it is this form that is broken down now. Philosophies and rhetorical modes may come and go, but the matter of the form is with us now and forever. An art defines itself as an adventure in a given form.

Now we are each probably in error in taking a very limited statement of the other's and inferring that it represents the sum of the other's understanding. I am now quite ready to believe that your resources are more extensive than your actual show in the small context. On the other hand, I beg you to believe that I am aware of a good many difficulties in my way though I may seem to deal very hurriedly with them.

I do feel entitled to impeach your treatment as exposition. I feel that you are in contact with red-hot truth, for you continually drop glowing and impressive sparks whenever you wax critical. But you tend to rely successively on the sparks, when we want a continuous blaze. In other words, you get hold of a beautiful intuition and immediately antagonize your followers by founding a Church thereon; when the probability is, you have stopped considerably short of the core of truth and are naming some accidental relation or other as THE FUNDAMENTALS. I should think you ought to get your own consent to a little subordination among your (seemingly) perfectly insubordinate ideas. It is poetic, Modern, and pluralistic to exalt each in turn to the pinnacle; but the net result is confusion, which I feel is not really your purpose in prose, at any rate. Why are you not more provisional, tentative, qualified, disparaging, as you contemplate the Stream of your Ideas? It may be my expectation is quite commonplace and pedagogical, but I have been expecting all these years to find from you a piece of critical prose that has a single leading idea, one that lends itself to rather plain statement, and treated at a length which will allow for about a thousand brilliant excursions hither and yon, but with so much resolution that from every one of these excursions you can effect your safe return? In the end, I think you probably have no conception how powerful would be the single impression of an idea so leading and so dominating, that is, if you have ever thought of impressing the academic mind.

As an example of the sort of thesis with which I have no confidence whatever that you could deal with safely, I cite: The Impossibility of Aristotelian Classicism in Modern Poetry. There is a subject which would call out all your worst vices.

As you see, I am taking you at your word about the belligerent attitude between friendly critics.

About some criticism of your own, for which I am much obliged,—you have confirmed my judgment but not my secret wish about Religio Medici Kentuckiensis.[1] I have consigned it to oblivion. Yet I was tempted, because Steve [Alec B. Stevenson] chose to praise it as a masterpiece; one can agree with any absurdity that is in one's favor. The example in point was merely a very dull dramatic monologue. About "Ada Ruel" I don't believe I can agree with you entirely; I have kept it, with some change of title.[2] I wonder if it can be that it offends you in some detail or other only? It seems to me quite tolerable stuff, but not calculated to make the great ones totter on their thrones.

About my recent stuff generally: Religio Medici is more than a year old. I never even typed it till lately, as I didn't think much of it. My recent poems, in reverse order as nearly as I can recollect, are: Miss Euphemia; Tom, Tom, the Piper's Son; Ada Ruel; Bells for John Whiteside's Daughter; Prometheus; Captain Carpenter. Somehow I can't appropriate a value as I should like from your criticism here, and your explanation as found in my supposititious dualism. I feel on the contrary that the formal difficulty of late has somewhat receded for me; and that in general my method of composition is not peculiar to myself. Really, I doubt if one without the advantage of such self-commmittal as I may have made publicly in my article would find a formal criticism there.[3] Incidentally, I quite agree that the form is organic with the matter, and so in effect I urged in my article: it is the formal preoccupation that destroys art, which must not appear meditated; nor *be* meditated, for that matter.

About my former criticism of your sonnet, in which I did not make myself clear. I meant that your treatment of the *theme* (rather than the *title*) laid you open, rather, to ridicule from your enemies; after all, wouldn't it strike the average Philistine as the most incredible pose to hear the bridegroom introducing himself to the bride in the terms you use? Of course it isn't a pose; but most artists in your situation would prefer to defend themselves by putting wit into the premises, for wit is the best sign of a man's capacity for self-defense. Compare your Epithalamion with any other that is on record: it is a most marvelous betrayal of a rôle![4]

And so forth, and so forth. Now to school after this nonsense.

As usual,
John

May 9

P.S. These 3 days I have fought off an urge to dismiss this screed to Rockport, W.Va.—but that Freudian entity the Censor kept inhibiting me till now I find from Don that *Lumberport* is more accurate. I feel that your residence in the state has been so brief as yet that you will pardon me for assuming that your name alone, irrespective of the address, would furnish a sufficient identification on a piece of mail.

As to Monday's meeting: I find again that my tones seem rather cold. As a matter of fact, you are *persona gratissima* in our eyes—a priceless value to a dull stodgy group. Even in absence you have inspired us to rededicate ourselves to *honest criticism* of our weekly stints: now each reading is followed by criticism from *each member in turn*, and the author is at least assured of having reactions to go by. But once more, we miss you sadly;

parliaments are sleepy affairs when they are suddenly deprived of the obstructions, jibes, and provocations of their Left. We all hope you can be with us again this summer.

Do you remember—did I tell you—that when I quizzed Knopf about the possibility of changes in the MS which they had accepted, they agreed, on the proviso that I consult with Morley about the final form of it? Well, I sent it off to him last week, and learn today that *Religio Medici* (one of the lot of extras I sent him as in my judgment unworthy) has been inserted and so therefore committed to posterity instead of oblivion.

But that will be enough about this bad poem—or you'll be committing it to memory, and prostituting a noble intellect.

John

P.S. 2. (Terrible Afterthought)
Look at this prose affair and give me a criticism if it inspires any. It's come back to me from whither I had sent it. And could you return it pretty soon?

JCR

---

1. This poem was never published.
2. Appeared as "Ada Ruel" in the *Fugitive*, III (April, 1924), 39; the title was changed to "The Tall Girl" in *Chills and Fever* (1924).
3. "The Future of Poetry," *Fugitive*, III (February, 1924), 2–4.
4. Ransom is apparently referring to "Prothesis for Marriage."

To Louis Untermeyer

June 14, [1924]

Dear Mr. Untermeyer:

Have been most extraordinarily busy since your acceptable letter arrived about 10 or 12 days ago—doing a bit of moving and packing and starting some courses in Peabody Teachers' College here, Summer School. Perhaps Davidson's letter, in which I asked him to indicate that mine was forthcoming and that I entertained your proposition most favorably, has turned up before now; he wrote primarily to thank you for the poem you sent the *Fugitive*.[1]

To reply first to the second part of your letter: I am delighted to join the American Miscellany.[2] Naturally, I could hardly fail to avail myself of an opportunity to move in such fast company. And I think the general idea a good one, too; was already familiar with the last volume published. I presume I shall make use of the whole 20 pages allotted me, but can hardly say at this time. Having just turned in the MS for "Chills and Fever," my stock at this moment is cleaned out—shelf empty, barrel dry. But I hope I may have some creative powers left for the future.

And now about my works, which you wish to examine with a view to possible use for your anthology: The London volume, sad to say, is not out yet; it was postponed from spring to "early autumn" for reasons I do not know.[3] And the publisher is not "Beaumont Press"—I wonder if by a slip of the pen I may have given you that name—but "Hogarth Press," run by Leonard and Virginia Woolf. I shall not permit you to buy a copy when it comes out, anyway, but am writing them (as I had always intended) to send it and credit to my allowance of author's copies. I'm sorry I shan't have a chance to write my compliments into the copy.

The name of this book is "Grace after Meat," a title for which Robert Graves is responsible, as giving rather the flavor of my peculiar performance, and taking its rise also from an execrable poem, "Grace," which appeared in "Poems about God," and which Graves would not hear of omitting from the present volume. It will be a small book, composed of 10 poems about God, and 10 more recent. No poem there which is not in my two American books; though some of the earlier ones will show revision. There will be an introduction by Graves, I believe. So on the whole, it will not be worth much for your purposes.

"Chills and Fever" will be out in early fall too, defined in this case as between August 25 and October 25.

As I see from the address on your poem that you are returning to America in July, I think, I'd better wait before sending an address to my English publisher.

Yours sincerely,
John Crowe Ransom

---

1. Louis Untermeyer's "Schubert at Hoeldrichsmuehle" was published in the *Fugitive*, III (August, 1924), 102.

2. Ransom's sonnet sequence, "Two Gentlemen in Bonds," was published in the *Miscellany of American Poetry*, edited by Louis Untermeyer (New York: Harcourt, Brace, 1925), 145–64.

3. *Grace after Meat.*

To Robert Graves

July 4, [1924]

Dear Robert,

I will favor you with my typewriter for the sake of your own convenience—have heard that some hands are legible but illiterate while others are illegible though literate—in either case I am suspicious of mine.

I am greatly excited by your *Mock Beggar Hall*, which by the by for some reason was slow in transit, only reaching me yesterday. A tremendous variety and contrariety of thoughts and images are stirred up within me.

As a modern poet you are unique—you have an advantage that almost none other has, that indeed most others in these dogdays call an impediment—you have a content, a philosophy, a system of ideas that you can hold with passion, and your new book is convincing evidence of its mass and scope and of the extent to which it has taken hold of you. You have the makings of a "school" (I mean in the vulgar sense in which history records that the Lake School flourished about 1800 and 50 A.D.)—one, I need not remind you, that bases on principles far from occidental in tone, and to which following and patronage will come slowly in your and my benighted communities. Personally, I am prepared to go to the absolute limit in accepting everything that you say. I accept thoroughly your gospel of diabolism—if you won't object to that name. The devils are indeed in us and about us at every single step we make and it is the place of the poet to discover them—peculiarly his place to confound the historian and scientist and practitioner. I love your social passion which gives unity and body to all your exhibit and supplies that emotional overtone I find essential to poetry. Personally, I had no such experience as you did in the War, but other experience and perhaps sympathy and imagination help to supply me with the background to understand and to want to commit myself. And by the way, did Mallik fight in the War? or is it the superior philosophy and self-dispossessive faculty of his race that gives him insight?[1] I have been feeling rather the lack of a positive in my own work; feeling, that is, that I was only partially expressing myself, and along satirical and negative lines mostly when I was sure that I was capable of a doctrine, a dogma more or less inspired, anything to give the heathen after trying to destroy their feeble superstitions. It may be that I'll matriculate with you—if Responsions are not too hard. (More seriously, it won't be quite as easy as that for me; I'm a hard case.) I am sure that a certain stage of poetics is now past for me, and there'll be a Religion in whatever I put forth next.

Pardon the personal intrusion into which my last paragraph lapsed. I was going on to say that your themes are all admirable: Mock Beggar Hall is an exquisite occasion for you; so are Antinomies and Antigonus,[2] and Mallik's piece which you admirably point for the purpose. Your prologue is very funny and cunning. No piece at all, so far as I recall, is beside the point in a volume of overwhelming unity. Full Moon is perfectly superb; it has for me, among other meanings, an alarming one; seems to celebrate the passing of Love (which is Romantic Poetry, the prepossession of our flower-lyrical China) when the mermaids *tailed* and *finned* swim the rarefied seas of philosophy in which we are reduced to icebergs. I'm not wholly ready to put the Muses into the church yet. This is just a notion personal, of course.

I have a criticism of your book which I frankly base on *a priori* grounds. It's half discursive with reason and half focussed into poetry. The prose intermissions signify a kind of ratiocination that frequently comes in verse too. I guess that this is a sort of inaugural book—you are aware of the gentle stupid reader, who could never in the world be trusted to make the application of a strict poem, and accordingly here, seeing that your matter is strange and fresh for the old lady, you oblige her with annotation and footnote. In other words I define art as the last nakedness and precision of image, and I find much of your volume cluttered with otherness. Your poems stand somewhere, as a rule, between Full Moon, the poem, and Interchange of Selves, the prose. As I recall "La Boxe," that was strictly a poem. You may not agree with such dogmatic differentiation as I make here, and I am aware I am arbitrary in a preference; or on the other hand you mean the volume as conciliatory and you think it needful (as assuredly it is) to pronounce and then expound the parable. I cannot believe that you are not an Artist as well as a Prophet, nor that you would for a moment deny that the categories are quite separate. I met you first as Artist, and if I discover your other character too, I will not see your first phase corrupted without a protest.

And I will say that I feel after looking over all the above that I will seem anything but an adept to you in my power of apprehending a novelty. I shall have to take more time to it. The whole impact of the thing is fresh on me and I dare say I haven't ruminated sufficiently to attempt a review of the performance as yet.

I have this day declined an offer to go to Dallas, Texas, to teach in Southern Methodist University. The idea would strike you as quaint in the first place. Dallas connotes bigness—capital of the biggest State, which is three-fourths as big as Germany was—or so I've been told.[3] The Ku Klux Klan make very merry down there, and the sun shines hot. The Methodists are in fine feather, it's a most suitable habitat. So I turned down an extra five hundred dollars—my hesitating hand supported by my loyal and more resolute wife—and will remain longer in what is really an abode of great freedom. The pinch of poverty however is upon me.

I have felt quite melancholy—a damned unworthy sort of it, too—in reading proof of "Chills and Fever," which is to appear [the] latter part of August. I liked the looks of the book, in fact felt weakly tender over it. Then I thought of what the public would think; or rather, how they wouldn't be able to think anything, it would be for them a hopelessly hard nut to crack. For odd as it may seem to you, I can assure you that my simple strains will not find in Nashville, not even among fond relatives, nor well-wishers more frequent than I deserve, more than two persons who will guess what I am after (I make loyal exception to my Fugitive brethren of course); and in the whole United States I should imagine that [there] are not fifty who *could* read with sympathy, not over ten who *will*. It makes one feel outcast indeed to think how he can shed blood and sweat for such inessential causes. I have recovered from this lowness of spirits, however, and feel the more shamed when I contemplate your own case—how you have actually known popular acceptance, and could reassure yourself of it on the quickest notice, and now as you must well understand are to sacrifice that pretty completely in the interest of what you will hear is a mere idiosyncrasy. I honor you.

I don't know when we may get together. But Robb and I are sanguine of disposition. Perhaps next year or the year after we'll go over for six months. In the meantime we'll have to write to each other.

Yours,
John Crowe Ransom

1. Basanta Mallik, a Bengali intellectual, was sent to Oxford by the Maharajah of Nepal to take courses in "British political psychology." *Mock Beggar Hall* (London: Hogarth Press, 1924) contains fifteen new poems by Graves and a "re-Englishing" of an "actionless drama for three actors and a moving background" by Mallik. Mallik led Graves into metaphysical studies.

2. "Antinomies" and "Antigonus" are poems in *Mock Beggar Hall.*

3. Dallas was not the capital of Texas in 1924; Ransom is referring to the city as a financial and industrial center.

To Robert Graves

July 6, [1924]

Dear Robert:

I wrote you on yesterday, after first perusal of *Mock Beggar Hall*: today I've been doing a further reading, strengthened by a better variety of Manila Hemp for smoking, to this effect:

I hereby recall my doubts about the art-form of your book, as carried in yesterday's deliverance. M.B.H. is not a group of lyrics in the usual sense, true enough; and the pre-possessed reader looks vainly and amazedly to find his stubborn expectations of a given art realized. Let that be. You have an intricate content here, as new and brilliant as anything I've seen; and your presentation satisfies. I suppose to ask for anything different is an impertinence. Your subject-matter is very delicate, and difficult to pin down; your success is overwhelming.

You have written a chapter in the history of the spirit. It will stand to your credit.

One sees you are disgusted with the simple-mindedness of what over here we call the English poetic tradition,—the antinomies, the hyperboles, the simplifications that fill poets' heads. I've long felt that, and so have many of us. To me it has presented itself as an alternative with which we are confronted of electing to write poetry or electing to write prose. You show superior qualities when you go straight to your mark and realize yourself so easily in a form which is both and neither.

I know I'm rather talking "balls" in dilating so much on the formal question.

Of course I find myself in Antigonus in the person of carping James: you have anticipated the objection.

And now to your thesis. You are aware that the occidental mind has almost always proved constitutionally incapable of the point of view represented by The Other in your title-poem, by John in Antigonus. The utmost reach of this mind is to solve the conflict by faith and the leap-in-the-dark which is the Western view of Christianity—"I acted as my Saviour approves action." The "What would Jesus do" question is one that babes rather than philosophers pronounce—a form of the Romantic urge as irrational as any that has yet been entertained. But that doesn't satisfy you—you demand full and perfect understanding, that's the first requirement. But as to your next step I am far from clear—I don't even know whether you mean me to grasp it by logic. You appear to resort to a Providence to settle the conflict finally, and ask the participants just to stop dead still and wait for it to happen. Perhaps at times you are in favor of taking sides—just a little—and again you will sit on a cloud above the conflict and wait. The orientals take a step here I believe which is clearer to them than to me. In Antigonus John after a certain point invokes Providence to patch things up while he goes off to write his eclogue. In M.B.H. (poem, not volume) the poet attains to a certain level of thought, a high one, and there leaves the problem, properly confident that to have attained even so far is a triumph.

Your analysis is exquisite, but the question will be raised as what after all is the nature of your solution; particularly, how your solution differs from that of the Christian religion, and whether it does not approach a neo-Hegelian absolutism which is the western equivalent of orientalism but which is in practice vanity and annihilation. To the lay mind something beyond the "absentee's profession" seems called for under the circumstances; our hopes have been raised, and to what end? Or is the philosophy of this occasion mystic and ineffable?

It interests me more than any book I've seen come off the press.

I might put it this way: As a sceptical mind you are engaged in a mighty wrestling with the toils—Jacob with the angel. Scepticism does actually produce, or at least is consistent with, the finest sympathy, the most delicate sensitivity; it destroys dogma and faces truth gladly, and cannot be unprofitable. But it is left negative in the end though it may grope for a positive. Where is its motor power? Your next step will be a religion of some kind; I feel that your position still stops short. But what you are trying is a huge thing.

Thoughts recorded on the Underwood have a way of looking not only cold and desolate, as these do, but even stupid. One thinks that one's mind is really better and more understanding than one's marks on the paper.

Could it be held that tolerance, which is negative, is a complete gospel? Tolerance of devils I admit is a rare fruit of the spirit.

John Crowe Ransom

To Robert Graves

June 12, 1925

Dear Robert:

These hot days of school-teaching in Tennessee—for I have developed a damnable habit of teaching now the year round—prompt me to wishing vainly I could be summering in England for a change. I am in fact making several sly plans, any one of which might land me there next year or the year after. I do surely feel that I need it—I grow necessarily a bit stale in my present unrelieved monotony. But I don't mean to go into that—just to say that I'm thinking about you, and still hopefully intending to get over to see you.

Robb—who's Mrs. J. C. R.—is so sanguine that she's read a number of travel books about England. We think we'd do a lot of cycling, tramping, boating, and golfing. We're both anxious to try country life and take things quietly, once we get there. I feel that Oxford would necessarily be our headquarters.

I've given a lot of thought—mostly of an unsystematic, recurrent kind—to the poetic problem these last few months. I have noticed that you and I don't entirely speak the same language in aesthetic discussion—and I realize the profit in handling the thing by means of new terms; which is a great—probably a controlling reason—why I must get to England and talk with you. On the other hand, I put the problem in a form (generally) of which I have not seen you take any notice. I'm beginning just now on some very severe writing on these matters; I already have a virtual promise of publication from Harcourt, one of our best publishers. Do you know Eliot's (T. S.) "Homage to John Dryden"? He confirms many of my own ideas—or in fact "beats me to them" though I didn't see the pamphlet till the other day. I don't like the 19th century or juvenility in poetry. I'm convinced that it is hopeless for poetry to flout science—and that the highest poetry is superficially & technically scientific, in style and thought, while at heart it's full of life and emotional significance. The point is, How scientific may poetry become—and I mean by this how disillusioned of the ordinary easy romanticism, how exact and fearless of statement—before it becomes non-poetry? I've observed many poets (like Allen Tate) castigate their own poetry with science till poetry was quite intimidated, and committed suicide—so I know the dangers of cerebration in poetry. The best poetry (for me) is the most perilous—it's poetry on-the-way-to-becoming science.

I read with pleasure and a feeling of almost entire agreement your book "On the Meaning of Dreams." I reviewed it (rather stodgily though quite admiringly) for the local sheet.[1] The one objection I take to the book is your rather disparaging references to Freud. To my mind he's a revolutionary of the first order, a very great name in the history of thought, though I know his excesses. Of course you know his "Beyond the Pleasure Principle," which is as great an adventure and as modest a one, in speculation as we would care to see. Or his "Group Psychology," somewhat less so.

I am sending you by this mail a MS. of Laura Riding Gottschalk's.[2] She is anxious for you to see a substantial piece of her work, since you have several times referred very kindly to her. She is a remarkable person in my opinion, and of tremendous promise. Just now I think she is tired and strained—and she has several volumes out before the publishers, with probably only a slight chance of success. Don't return this work; but maybe you will favor her with a criticism, or it is just possible you may consider that it merits a word with some English publisher. If you care to communicate with her, I will forward any mail, or convey any messages. She's now with her sister in California.

I'm sure you read the *Saturday Review* (American)—since you publish with them. Then did you read Edwin Muir's English letter, treating among other topics my book?[3] It was much the most philosophic statement of my position that I have seen, though not the most favorable. I am led to wonder which of us (Muir and me) occupies the later position—whether he is at a stage where he cannot remain, or whether I am yet to reach that stage as a final goal—if I am so lucky.

Your own "Mock Beggar Hall" I dare say has not yet had a competent handling. All the thews and sinews of reading and criticism became unbraced in the 19th Century, and the readers and critics of our generation are correspondingly soft. Both prose and poetry have degenerated and been diluted.

Your own general success, however, both antedates and surpasses mine: this fact permits me to feel gratification because our work has much in common and irritation because the facilities of communication do not permit it to have more.

By the way, you won't mind my saying to you what I would by no means publish to the general: I barely missed winning the Pulitzer Prize ($1,000) for 1924, being defeated in favor of Robinson (who had already won it in 1922) because my work was offensive to one elderly committeeman who wouldn't budge to suit the others' wish, and who had his way because the decision had to be unanimous.

Yours,
John Crowe Ransom

---

1. *The Meaning of Dreams* was published in Great Britain in September, 1924, and in the United States in May, 1925. Ransom's review appeared in the Nashville *Tennessean* for May 31, 1925.

2. Laura Riding Gottschalk (b. 1901), now Laura Riding Jackson, a poet and critic, would later collaborate with Graves on such works as *A Survey of Modernist Poetry* (1927).

3. Muir's review was published in the *Saturday Review of Literature*, I (June 6, 1925), 807.

To Robert Graves

September 23, [1925]

Dear Robert:

I was quite anxious to learn whether it was to be this year or a later year in America for you—that was what I was waiting to learn before writing—in fact I wasn't sure but what you might be over here already.

It will be splendid if you can get Laura Riding Gottschalk's book published. She is writing me now that she has had another rejection, this time by Alfred Knopf, and of her choicest MS. And by the way, there is probably a much better volume of hers possible (as compared with the one you have) if you want to see the MS as she arranged it for Knopf's inspection. But if Hogarth Press will do only a small book, and you feel that you are perfectly satisfied with what material you have got, let's let it go at that. So I will put it this way: Please write me a line at once if you care to examine a fuller MS of her poetry for Hogarth's choice. I will write her that I have written you to this effect; she wrote to me showing concern as to whether you had a best selection, and anxious to appear in England in the best light possible, since she appears to have no American career in sight. She doesn't know yet that you will probably succeed in publishing her.[1] She is a brilliant young woman, much more so in her prose and conversation even than in her verse. She was recently divorced from her husband, a Louisville college professor. She has had a remarkable career—up from the slums, I think, much battered about as a kid, and foreign (perhaps Polish Jew?) by birth. English is not native to her, nor is the English tradition, greatly to her mortification. As a poet, she cannot to save her life, as a general thing, achieve her customary distinction in the regular verse forms. And she tries perhaps to put more into poetry than it will bear. With these misgivings I will go as far as you or anybody in her praise. She is now in New York trying to make a living doing hack literary work. She is very fine personally, but very intense for company.

So much for her—and I'm awfully glad she has picked up such a good friend in you.

About young me: I have in mind a year in England, contingent to a considerable degree. If things look right I'm going to try to get a Guggenheim Fellowship for the school year 1926–27.[2] That is like the Rhodes Scholarship a little, but much better in terms, and quite elastic in purpose. The Board invites you to submit your subject & plan of study; you must be specific, and they decide whether your thesis is a valuable-looking one and whether you are the man who could work it out. They profess to give special consideration to those who practice the creative arts. Probably I could get one; I know some of the Board. But I'll need to have (a) a good plan of work and (b) some strong letters about my capacity. If your conscience doesn't titillate too readily I'm wondering if you might do me one of the latter. I'm sure you could help me with the former.

Now as to (a), I'd want to go to Oxford with Robb and the babies, and work there. Not the least of my advantages would be getting you to join in my speculations. I feel that I could produce a book, which is the *desideratum* of the Board; and I wonder also if I might not accomplish some kind of degree at the same time. Bill Elliott, who came through here this summer en route from California to Harvard, thought I could do a D.Litt. at Oxford—the notion astonished me. Is that likely? I'm sure I could do a Ph.D. at Paris—and without any French residence to speak of, too.[3]

I must define my subject. A lot of my hobbies you know—Mixed Modes, Poetic Irony, Nature in Poetry; these would stand a lot of treatment. Most of my mind at this time is on what I am calling (for the present) the Gothic principle in English poetry, with special reference to Milton, or to Shakespeare. I'll send you a copy of an article on it within a few days. Gothic is another opposition for Classic—but it means emphasis on the detail (and hence on the homely and even the obscene) rather than on the whole; it means formlessness and local excitement; it implies Roman Catholicism and fundamentalism rather than Greek philosophy or science; it's a vanishing principle in English literature, but is racially very appealing to us. But I shouldn't attempt in a few words to give my idea. Tell me any ideas you have as to which of these subjects strikes you as important; especially when I've sent you a piece stating my Gothic principle.[4] And tell me if you would want to back me up with a strong letter of endorsement; be honest.

So much for that. If I think after some prying around that I shouldn't get one of the Fellowships, I won't try. But if I tried & succeeded, I'd have a very fine year in England, in great part I hope with you.

Your book "Poetic Unreason" delighted me greatly. In the current *Fugitive* I indicate very hurriedly how much.[5] You bring some new vitality to literary criticism. I am so much in agreement with your principal argument that it seems captious to take an exception at a few places; but this I do rather heartily to your passage on Milton and (I think) your passage on Aristotle. I examined the Phoenix "insert" very carefully and am bound to think that (a) it is not really a novelty in the Miltonic rhyme-schemes, and (b) it is not extraneous but essential to the sense of the context, and (c) there is practically no piracy in the thing. It's really no more an "insert" than hundreds of passages obviously constructed upon a couple of rhyme words. I'll argue this matter with you later. And by the way, the "Captain or Colonel" sonnet is usually (as by Masson[6]) and (I think) most sensibly taken as a bit of pedantic fooling and not a piteous plea for mercy. It looks incredible that Milton could have meant it for what it seems to be—or that you, whose usual practice is to look underneath the lines, should in this one instance insist on looking only at the top of them. Do you think the evidence is that Milton was a coward? or a pretty polemical and hard-headed fighter?

This too deserves argument; but I notice that you confess to a bias and don't really put forward the coward-thesis *in propria persona* as the latest edition of the individual who wrote the book.

I've got to go to a literary tea given by some lady writers.

I'm anxious to see your new book of poems.

The Guggenheim application would have to go in with all the papers in December.

Yours ever
John Ransom

---

1. The Hogarth Press published Laura Riding's *The Close Chaplet* the next year, 1926.

2. Ransom did not receive this fellowship.

3. During this period Ransom often expressed his conviction that, despite his three years at Oxford, his lack of an advanced degree would impede his academic career.

4. Ransom was working out the fundamental principles of his theory of the nature and function of poetry.

5. Graves's *Poetic Unreason* (London: Cecil Palmer, 1925) provided Ransom with the occasion for an editorial review, "A Doctrine of Relativity," *Fugitive*, IV (September, 1925), 93–94.

6. Ransom alludes to David Masson (1822–1907), author of the seven-volume *Life of John Milton* (1859–94).

To Robert Graves

December 2, [1925]

My dear Robert Graves:

Your several letters all came and were affectionately greeted, though this is perforce a sort of blanket acknowledgement. I want to thank you for your letter written but not sent during last spring, enclosing a small but highly regarded royalty check from Hogarth and your statement about family sickness while my sister was in London[1]—a state of things which I had long ago taken for granted, that or some other set of circumstances; you are most punctilious. Then I want to thank you for the book, *Welchman's Hose*:[2] a fine work after *Mock-beggar Hall*, which was much too caviar to the general; I love *M. H.* as something unclassified, a great *document*, but perhaps as I have very gradually and very reluctantly come to believe, far more truth than poetry. I feel that there you strained the function of poetry, to which now you have grandly returned. Especially in the post-bellum *Sport* piece, which is surely a great poem. Last of all, but not least, as you shall presently see, my best bow for your sporting offer to perjure yourself in my interest as I go in for a Guggenheim Fellowship. And more of that now.

The reason I haven't written sooner is I've been driving my mind towards the definition and delimitation of my thesis. I enclose a draught of a Preface which I shall surely have to offer to convince the honorable committee of selection that I am indeed up to something tangible. With it I shall enclose at least a statement of my projected chapter-heads, and in some cases a rough indication of their contents. I'll be sending that to you as I work it out. And I herewith enclose a circular about the Fellowship: you will see its elastic terms and requirements. The Committee is a rather doubtful quantity as to personnel; but at least it has Aydelotte, B.Litt. in English Literature from Oxford, and also a good classicist on its list of names.[3] You will read their expectations as to the form of an application. Your letter will be of immense help. I shall ask you to write it at your leisure; as a matter of fact, one is supposed to give merely the names as references, and let the Secretary solicit the gentlemen for confidential letters; but seeing the distance and time involved in your case, I know it will be helpful if you don't wait to be invited by the Secretary, but *send it on to him* as soon as you get ready. You may or may not care to wait till you see my Table of Contents which I am preparing—either way is all right. And you handsomely mention the possibility of getting a letter also from Lawrence, and (though this would be too good to hope for) from the Merton Professor of English. (Is that Gordon?)[4] Well, either will be of untold value; especially if you could communicate to them the subject I am interested in, and get them to express themselves as to its value; but of value in any event. I have precious few academic authorities to cite in my behalf. It doesn't matter about the degree; I'd hope to get a B.Litt. from Oxford, or maybe a Ph.D. from Paris, if it didn't involve too much extra and wasteful work; but with the Guggenheim Trust as I understand it, publication is the desideratum, and it is also mine as well.

I have been particularly anxious to get my subject before you, and yet it is a trying undertaking—I could talk quite a few days with you without coming to the bottom of it, it has developed to such an extent in my head. Generally it is expected that the applicant shall have already done some publication in his subject, which he can present as an earnest of good faith and of the value of his work. I have nothing—beyond a few samples of my prose style, and a poetic record which I shall not hesitate to bring forward. Therefore where I can get a word about my thesis put in with the Committee, to convince them that I know what I am about and that I am about something worth the doing—by all means I want that word to go in. Hence the long enclosure in this letter.

It is, I feel, a thesis after your own heart—touches your own interest at many many points. But it is especially timely for an American to do; our need is greater than your need. With us, our whole education, our culture, is a euphemism—it's directed against the uncouth pioneer instincts that linger in us, and ought to linger so far as literature is concerned. Hence the enormous weight of social responsibility, falsely conceived, that rests upon the shoulders of our writers. For I shall have a chapter on The Nature of Genius; and I understand that to be essentially the kind of mind that has access to the solid inherited folk-stratum underneath his conscious accumulation of culture; or in figurative language, it's the mind of the low man, like Chaucer and Shakespeare, who got themselves into society, wrote in the fine style like their betters for a while, and after they found it quite too easy to speak that language, developed the idea of giving vent simultaneously to their low natures, to the great enlivenment of the impoverished literary forms of society. And I have a chapter on Shakespeare called Thinking in Gothic: there I propose to analyse a huge number of specimen passages to show his theory of poetry; it consists in smooth classical coherence only up to a certain point, where he lets out a tremendously unexpected crude misfit phrase, which miraculously gives all the vitality to the passage. (This is the very point that you made, with a most ignominious examplar of the thing in your case, about my habit of "periodically detonating a most unlikely and most effective phrase"—in your review of me in the Saturday Review.[5]) And a very fine chapter, I think, on Religion and Gothic, in which I show that all religions that are vital are a folk product first, and contain sensational and obscene features in plenty: but get themselves taken up by the higher critics, theologians, and Liberals, who try to emasculate them of their Gothic quality—whereas they cannot survive this process if they are to stay the religions of the whole society.[6] And a chapter on science as anti-Gothic, which makes this point: The scientists are exactly like Plato; they would deny the poets a place in the state, because the poets deal with imitations; the true reality is the Idea, in Platonic language, or the type and generality, in scientific language, and the concrete persons and things are only imitations. The whole interest of science is to classify and generalize, and it has no patience with human personality or even the stubborn familiar thinghood of things; and art and religion between them save this sense of existence to the people. My hardest chapter will be on the relation of Gothic and classical; and undoubtedly it will come to this: Classical is more intellectualized, more philosophical; both are comprehensive and fair statements of the whole of life; Gothic gives *undigested* facts, concrete reality in all its stubborn identity, while classical presents these facts as already on the way to being integrated into a system, as already half-abstracted; and the usefulness of Gothic (which racially evidently suits us) is to resist the too-easily philosophising process and hold us to the fact. In other words, classical is all right when it is genuine, when it implies a philosophy which has proceeded out of authentic experience of suffering; but it is dangerous when it is the product of the mind that generalises before it has experienced; and Gothic is on the whole safer.

All the previous paragraph seems terribly bald and cold—you can't do all that in a paragraph. But I will add that most of my chapters will be historical—they will present English literature with the interpretation that my thesis calls for. I would pay my particular attention perhaps to the shortcomings of the nineteenth Century.

So much for all that. Now let me say that it will be great if you land that Cairo position, and you would be a shining ornament to the position. I hope, however, if you will permit the familiarity, that the Trustees are not too familiar with your Mock-Beggar Hall—or they might fear for your imperialism, might think you confounded your colors too easily. Let me hear what about that.

I'll have to rush this hasty letter off.

Yours ever,
John Crowe Ransom

---

1. Annie Ransom visited England during the summer of 1925.

2. *Welchman's Hose* is a book-length poem by Graves first published in September, 1925 (London: The Fleuron).

3. Frank Aydelotte, president of Swarthmore College and American secretary of the Rhodes trustees, chaired the Guggenheim selection committee from 1925 to 1950.

4. T. E. Lawrence, author of *Seven Pillars of Wisdom* (1926), was now a fellow at Jesus College, Oxford; George Stuart Gordon was Merton Professor of English at Oxford from 1922 to 1928.

5. Graves reviewed *Chills and Fever* for the *Saturday Review of Literature*, I (December 27, 1924), 412.

6. The ideas outlined in this paragraph are developed in *God without Thunder* (1930) and *The World's Body* (1938).

To Allen Tate

Memphis, June 18, [1926]

Dear Allen:

You have probably thought by this time that your letter of May would meet with the same discourteous treatment as others you have sent, but not so. I have had little chance to answer till now; a little spell of illness and the business of packing my family off to Denver, completing my Vanderbilt year and getting myself off and established here on a six weeks teaching course.

The unfortunate Laura [Riding] letter has not only misrepresented you but myself too, and I must get that straight. She is a deep and mischievous person as doubtless you well know. The thing that really mattered in her late escapade, I felt, was her attributing to me a sort of jealous and malignant tone towards you which I did not have; and it matters more than ever now, since I learn from your letter that she sent you a carbon of her manuscript, and led you (very naturally) to conclude that I had been publishing abroad my own unfavorable and certainly meddlesome opinions of your person, character, and mentality. I on the other hand, in wondering where she could have got that impression of my state of mind, could think of no other source than yourself; I thought you must have (doubtless unconsciously) communicated to her such an impression as to my general state of mind, and she applied this working hypothesis to the details in hand and made out her case. The other origin which occurred to me as also possible was this: she found me, mistakenly or otherwise, such a complete prig that she conceived my priggishness could issue in only one opinion as to your life in New York, your work, and your relations with her; but, while all things are doubtless possible, I cannot think that this piece of thinking reflects credit on her intelligence, and therefore I reject it. I now lean most to the idea that she was simply up to mischief.

I do not know whether she brought to your attention a little piece of work she did last summer. She sent to the *Saturday Review* a very long letter replying to your letter which concerned a recent article by Maxwell Bodenheim;[1] in her letter she fetched far and dragged me in for some eulogistic words, as possessing somehow (I forget the details, which were rather absurd) a point of view in offset to yours. The periodical very naturally rejected it, and she then sent it to me as a possible contribution to the FUGITIVE; and failing that event, she specified that I was to send it on to you for your reading.

She is, or was at any rate, such a complete child of fortune, and in such obvious search of a protector and master, that I think I have a sort of formula to explain these two actions. In looking over the Fugitives, who were as it happened then her nearest and dearest, she seized upon the idea that you and I were the two leaders of the opposing parties, and that it would be a thrill to have us fighting for the prize, which was none other than Laura. I don't mean for these terms to be applied too grossly. I was Agamemnon and you were Achilles, and she, it follows, was the fair Briseïs (have I got the lady's name correctly?). Is there a Briseïs complex?[2] Her business was to provoke our mutual distrust and antagonism; she was first rather on my side in a tentative way, if you will pardon my assumption of such a magnificent role; then decidedly on your side; probably permanently in your camp, and yet committed like a natural woman to a profession of intrigue and coquetry all the same. It is because you and I are men capable of making up our minds for ourselves that I resent her attempt to embroil us, and in this letter I am putting in my resistance. I hate to abuse a small woman, but I won't accept the role she has thrust upon me.

Of all the states of mind I can now conceive, the one I should feel as most shameful for me would be just that state of jealousy towards you which she ascribes to me. In our printed altercation, for which I have most sincerely blushed, there was the look of just such a thing;[3] and I undertake there shall never come from me another such exhibition, nor do I believe it is in me to furnish the makings for so exhibiting.

Therefore I wish to say plainly: I have never entertained any opinions about your life nor hers in New York; that impertinence did not even begin in my mind, much less come to the surface in any expression, oral or written, to any person whatsoever. Furthermore: I have been most scrupulous in every possible public expression that I ever made about you. I have possibly made unfavorable comments about you to a very few intimate friends, which I know have never gone any further. Laura probably has heard comments from me in Fugitive meetings upon your offered work; so have you; and these were never unfriendly. I talked with her privately as the minimum courtesy I could do her on her visit last fall, for perhaps an hour; I believe we discussed all the Fugitives, including yourself, in the literary sense strictly; my sense of innocence is such that I do not remember anything specific that was said. Her impression that I was busy offering disparagements at your expense, whether to her or anybody else, is manufactured out of the virgin cloth of her mind.

I must go even further, in order to get myself accurately into the record. I have great respect for your work; my personal feeling is warm and friendly; I greatly admire the uncompromising purity of your literary intention, and the quality of its recent output; I find a great deal of heroism in the course you have set yourself; and I share fully most of your philosophical ideas, as reflected in your current reviews and articles.

The effect of these feelings on my part is vitiated, I know, by my lamentable shortcomings as a correspondent, for which I apologize unreservedly. Your feeling of being disesteemed and injured, as indicated at the close of your late letter, is a perfectly natural one, and therefore I ask the liberty of disregarding it and attempting herewith to overcome it. As a graceless correspondent I am Lloyd's best bet. Yet I have written you two or three letters which, upon re-reading, I have consigned to the wastebasket. I always feel especial reluctance, here of late, to write to intelligent people, because in such exchanges one is required to put his impressions of art and things to the last analysis, and this is painful and laborious; I say to myself, we can get together sometime and talk it out; I hate to put my half-baked ideas to the paper.

I had already replied to Laura's letter, as mildly as I could bring myself to do; I wish I had waited till I had cooled off still further. The thing has distinctly its comic side—though I suggest this rather in disrespect to the serious Eighteenth-Century tone in which you concluded your letter. Undoubtedly we were rather absurd in the way we received Laura at Nashville—prim, formidable, and stiff. What she came for was human companionship of the most bare-soul description; she had neither birth, subsistence, place, reputation, nor friends, and was a very poor little woman indeed. She got only a rather formal welcome, though she is mistaken in assuming that we burned with suppressed libidinous desires, whether with her or others as the object. We quite missed the point. She on her side did not realize that we had already established our respective personal relationships on satisfactory and rather final bases, and that we were open to literary relationships but not to personal. I realize there is a sort of mean-ness in such an admission. So she left us, and I have greatly honored you for sharing with her your mind (at least to some extent) and certainly your material goods. You saved her self-respect and her whole future career; and then when you had done about all you could (as you intimate, and as Don had already told me) along comes Robert Graves and saves her some more. She is lucky. I certainly wish her well and I predict for her a substantial and deserved literary reputation, but I hope she will not meddle again with me.

I have a delicious prospect in the offing. From here I go to Colorado, teach for three weeks out there in August, and then have four months to please myself. I have got a term's leave of absence from Vanderbilt on the ground of doing some "study"; which means, I want to put together my scraps of aesthetical doctrine and whip a book into shape. I am sure you would consent to the main body of my ideas, which are for that matter not particularly revolutionary; I'd love to talk them over with you. Our plan is (Robb's and mine) to park the babies with the grandparents and go down about Santa Fe, where we will rent us some kind of shack in the mountains for the whole four months.

I presume to send you a little poem just done for such comment as your leisure and inclination can afford.[4] Frankly, I expect to discount your criticism; I do not see with you when it comes to poetry; I accept almost every specific criticism, without having in the least the same scale of comparative values. Yet I need criticism, and profit by it; especially when it is honest, and therefore uncommon; and when it is reasoned, and therefore extremely rare.

I should greatly like to meet your charming family.

I'm here till July 13, and the office at Vanderbilt always has my address.

Sincerely yours,
John C. Ransom.

---

1. Maxwell Bodenheim (1892–1954) was a poet, novelist, and playwright associated with bohemian circles in Chicago and New York.

2. Briseïs was Achilles' slave-concubine, who was taken by Agamemnon but later restored to him.

3. The "Waste Lands" affair. Ransom was attempting to prevent the recurrence of a breach between him and Tate.

4. This poem is probably "Ghosts," which first appeared in *Harper's Magazine*, CXIV (December, 1920), 50, and was included in *Two Gentlemen in Bonds* (1927) as the second part of "Hilda."

To Donald Davidson

Denver, August 8, [1926]

Good old-friend Don:

Let's see now if I get in all the acknowledgments: I wish to thank you for several letters: the one containing kind words about my fumbling review; the one that had the Library book list, which was most admirable; the ones that sent me a couple of Sunday pages, which I greatly enjoyed (not excluding my own piece therein); even the one enclosing the plaintive entreaties of the would-be and harshly-mishandled contributors to the deceased *Fugitive*; and the one that enclosed for my vote the new plan of resurrection of that body.

As to this last: I o.k. the enterprise without official reservations of any sort. But, I've got misgivings, which are for you privately. These concern mostly our vanishing personnel. I'm just afraid I may be a non-contributor, to start with the least first; I get my MS in to Knopf for the printer next week, and then I'm in for a season of prose, which may quite envelop my quick spirits.[1] And Red [Warren]—can you rely on anything from him? And Allen—I've seen some fine things from him which he has just sent me but they destroy any illusion that we are a "school" of poets with unity. And Jesse [Wills]—but I know he has already some fine stuff. And Merrill [Moore]—I suppose we can always draw on his old storehouse. And Laura—I feel quite repelled against her as a Fugitive, and so does Allen, I know—she is a little politician that plays dirty tricks, I'm afraid, and her work is far more radical than anything we want to show. I'm wondering about the volume, quality, and uniformity of any 64-page display we might make. The editors must be courageous, and must judge always with this recourse in the back of their heads, that we issue no book at all.[2] You are obviously the editor—no other plan is possible—and I'll cheerfully lend what little moral support I possibly can, to the point of writing Untermeyer or anybody with respect to finding a publisher. But it ought to be a *damned good* volume or it will fall flat, even if published by a good house—it ought to have snap, sparkle, and substance and unity all at once. It can't be the usual miscellany or anthology thing. It's got to be as consistent and formidable as the early Imagist volumes. Since when there has been nothing like what we propose. These are apprehensions and desires only, and I don't lift my voice up once to limit my own co-operation and loyalty to whatever performance the crowd commits itself.

A fine letter from Bill Elliott the other day, showing some better verses than usual, and enclosing also his Mussolini reprint from *Pol. Science Quar.* He finds Harvard quite a strain—too much limelight, speed, and competition to be comfortable. So he says. But I judge he is quite equal to keeping up the pace.

I'm at a hotel in Greeley writing this, and I've run out of paper and must double back on the trail. Hope you find this continuation.

Next week, the 26th, I'm through here and my vacation proper begins. My wife and I, I think, will get us a summer cottage (the one that's chinked up the best against the winds) up in the foothills above Denver—there are a lot of them there, on the bus-lines, and accessible to the grandparents living in the city. Rent cheap. Fine mountain air and scenery.

I do believe I've got some good doctrines to work into shape. Have reinforced myself with a lot of philosophy books which seem to give me moral support. All I crave now is expert consultants; I'll have to work the whole thing out and submit the results to you and Curry at New Year's.[3]

We had the finest trip imaginable in between Memphis and Greeley—I mean the M. and G. periods of slavery. I went straight from M. to join Mrs. R. at Rock Springs, Wyo., where her brother lives. He took us in his car clear around the state; the feature was 3 days in Yellowstone Park. Never neglect to go there if your brother-in-law invites you. It far exceeds expectations, and even advertisement.

I spent a week-end with the English faculty at the U. of Colorado, up at Boulder, too; read from my new poems, and was much pic-nicked and entertained.

I've learned a lot about the non-Shakespearean Elizabethan dramas here at Greeley. Also about the 19th C. Romantics, especially Keats and Byron. I never before got quite the right hold on them.

If you don't send me some carbons of your poetry I'll take it personally. Mightily interested in the Belmont-Fire and Indian-Legend work.[4] It's very similar in intention to Allen Tate's new work, but I think is poetic in a positive way in which his is not. Or have you had more illness in the family and no time for poetry? God forbid.

Yours ever,
John C. Ransom

---

1. *Two Gentlemen in Bonds.*

2. Ransom is reacting to Davidson's suggestion that the Fugitives bring out a yearly anthology of their verse. One was published, *Fugitives: An Anthology of Verse* (New York: Harcourt, Brace, 1928).

3. Ransom was working on "The Third Moment."

4. Davidson's *The Tall Men* (New York: Houghton, Mifflin, 1927).

To Allen Tate

Indian Hills, Denver, September 5, [1926]

Dear Allen:

My reply to your recent favors will fall into two parts; this is the first one, and is a little further elaboration of my aesthetical ideas, in which my interest is now, since I have official status with my Authorities as a Composer *in absentia*, professional. This gives me a certain feeling of pretentiousness.

The second part will be more personal, and devoted mostly to an opinion on the poems you were good enough to send me. My excuse for the order of the parts is, I am doing the easier one first.

I will call my study, unless I am subsequently disillusioned by unforeseen developments,

THE THIRD MOMENT.

The three moments in the historical order of experience are as follows:

I. First Moment. Bear in mind that the moments as I shall describe them are immensely simplified and ideal. The first moment is the original experience—pure of all intellectual content, unreflective, concrete, and singular; there are no distinctions, and the subject is identical with the Whole. *Infancy—Pure Experience.*

II. Second Moment. The moment after. This moment is specific for human experience as distinguished from the ideally animal experience. Biologically man is peculiar in that he must record and use his successive experiences; the beasts are not under this necessity; with them the experience is the end in itself, and takes care of itself. In the second moment cognition takes place; never mind the fact that cognition is always recognition, and presupposes *two* moments,—for we can say that the First Moment must be *repeated* before the time arrives for the (qualitatively) second moment. *Youth—Science.* The feature of the second moment is, it is now that the record must be taken of the first moment that has just transpired. This record proceeds inevitably by way of *concepts* discovered in cognition. It is the beginning of science. Its ends are practical; but its means are *abstractions*; and these, it must be insisted, are subtractions from the whole. Now what becomes of the whole in this operation? A feature, or several features, are taken up and spread upon the record; let us say, they are written down on lasting tablets; at the least, they go into that Ready Memory where items of knowledge are constantly in use, and constantly available. The rest goes somewhere and is preserved, else we could never miss it; it goes, according to Bergson, into Pure Memory; according to the modern school of psychologists, into the Unconscious, where it is far from idle, and whence it somewhere, sometime, will come up again. So experience becomes History, conceptualized knowledge, in respect to a part, and Unconscious Knowledge, lost knowledge, in respect to the vast residue of the unconceptual. So also is generated the cognitive or scientific habit; which is that which disposes us to shorten the subsequent First moments of our experience to the minimum, to dwell upon our subsequent fresh experiences only long enough to reduce them as here; and which is so powerful when formed that many of us unquestionably spend most of our waking lives in entertaining or arriving at concepts.

III. Third Moment. We become aware of the deficiency of the record. Most of experience is quite missing from it. All our concepts and all our histories put together cannot add up into the wholeness with which we started out. Philosophical syntheses do no good—the Absolutists are quaint when they try to put Humpty-Dumpty together again by logic—they only give us a Whole which, as Kant would say, is obtained by *comprehensio log-*

ica and not by *comprehensio aesthetica*—a Whole which it is only necessary to say fails to give us satisfaction. *Maturity—Aesthetic and Reconciliation.* The world of science and knowledge which we have laboriously constructed is a world of illusion; not one of its items can be intuited; we suddenly appear to ourselves as monsters, as unnatural members of humanity; and we move to right ourselves again. (The scientific world, as seen on these terms, quite clearly appears as an artificial or *phenomenal* world, and so our objection is quite regular and eclectic.) How can we get back to that first moment? There is only one answer: By images. The Imagination is the faculty of Pure Memory, or unconscious mind; it brings out the original experiences from the dark storeroom, where we dwell upon them with a joy proportionate to our previous despair. And therefore, when we make images, we are regressive; we are trying to reconstitute an experience which we once had, only to handle and mutilate. Only, we cannot quite reconstitute them. Association is too strong for us; the habit of cognition is too strong. The images come out much mixed and adulterated with concepts. Experience without concepts is advocated by some systems, and has some healing power, but it is not an adult mode; it cannot really produce images without concepts, but only an imageless and conceptless state; as in the Dionysian state of Nietzsche or the Orientalism of Schopenhauer. What we really get, therefore, by this deliberate recourse to images, is a mixed world composed of both images and concepts; or a sort of practicable reconciliation of the two worlds. Therefore we are not really opposed to science, except as it monopolises and warps us; we are perfectly content to dwell in the phenomenal world for much of our time; this is to be specifically human; we would not be babes nor beasts; we require merely the fulness of life, which is existence in the midst of all our faculties. And our Aesthetic can never deny science wholly, which would be wildly romantic, and not reasonable, if not quite suicidal. Science is a kind of blindness, but necessary and useful; exactly as the typical successful mercenary appears blind to the poet, but still is indispensable. An important detail is, to show why, with our formed cognitive habit or apparatus, we cannot have *fresh experience* of first moments; because they disintegrate as fast as they come. And this corollary: In Nature as compared with Art, our sense of Wholeness is extremely vague and unsatisfactory; the artistic contemplation of nature is better, a very advanced state, in which we are conscious of the scene as we might have conceptualized it, and at the same time of the scene as we actually do persist in intuiting it. But this is quite like Art: a Mixture. (This leads us to a distinction between *Romantic or Pure* tendencies and *Gothic or Mixed* which is like the distinction between the *East* and the *West.*)

My next head will be:

WORKS OF THE THIRD MOMENT

There seem to be five different states, or operations, in which we try to reconstitute the fugitive first moment; and the order of presentation which we choose will be that in which conscious intention is exhibited from lowest to highest.

1. Dreams. These are compensatory regressions not intended.
2. Fancies, or day-dreams. In which at least *consent* is present.
3. Religion. Where we are almost conscious of the significance of the state.
4. Morals. Where we wilfully, and with a certain sophistication, induce that sort of obscurantism which ignores cognition and calculation; which would be mere instinct except that we know what we are doing. Thoroughly Romantic and anti-Scientific. With a minimum of image. Except where it associates itself with 3.
5. Art. Attended with pretty complete purpose and sophistication. And equipped with technique.

But naturally I do not propose on short notice (i.e., in my book) to give a complete or even schematic statement of all the arts; I proceed without more ado to

POETRY

And here my treatment will be as suggested by the general method of my approach, which gives us, I think, some novelties as compared with the worn doctrines now in vogue. Essentially: Poetry is always the exhibit of Opposition and at the same time Reconciliation between the Conceptual or Formal and the Individual or Concrete. An obvious case of the Formal is meter; which nevertheless does not seem to impair the life and effectiveness of the Concrete Experience. They coexist. This obvious fact was what started me off, years ago, into this whole way of reasoning.

But I pause to make this Remark: I appreciate the enormous psychological difficulties in the way of stating myself. I have often wondered how aesthetes, logicians, metaphysicists ever had the courage to propound anything, in view of the slippery psychological entities they have to handle; but my effort seems to involve no more than anybody-else's.—Yours for the first instalment,

John C. Ransom

To Allen Tate

September 13, [1926]

Dear Allen:

Here comes the rest of my letter—a week late. In the meantime I have been scribbling as you will see from the inclosure.

We are very nicely settled out here about 45 minutes from Denver. It is the nearest mountains we could find from that base; and having the kids with us (the youngest, Reavill, is 3 years old tomorrow) we were afraid to venture further. Our altitude is about 7000 feet, and has its effect possibly in the unfortunate transcendental note which appears in my written stuff. We are in a tight cabin, fit for all weather at least, and best of all, just a hundred yards above the grocery store. First we meditated parking the children with either pair of grandparents; but I'm glad we didn't, as the little cusses are pretty good company, and I have a sanctum in which they can't enter when I sport my oak. We are here till Christmas, I suppose. A letter from Dr. Mims says they will manage somehow in my absence—which after all was no more than could be expected of such a leading institution as your Alma Mater.

I have read the poems you sent me many times; each time seeing more fine turns in them; but never, I will have to say frankly, finding perfect satisfaction. For that matter, I haven't found it in your poetry for several years; but cheerfully acknowledge that I merely am not in sympathy with your intention, which after all is not a matter for debate. I too like your amended Causerie II the best of all; and in fact liked it even in its original state the most.[1] I have scribbled a few comments here and there on the poems. Here I will just say, Don't you overdo your idea of perfect contemporaneity? Incidentally, I found a lot of meat in your remarks on the subject a propos of my first little statement of my creed, which I had sent, very prematurely, I think; and intend to keep them in mind. Now, even an old codger like Kant said that the first quality of the artist must be originality, and as an academe I must of course agree. But isn't the quality of being contemporary an accidental one—rather, a spontaneous one? You speak of trying out a new means of expression to fit your subject; but does this mean that you cannot find it in the language of the day? Which, after all, is pretty syntactical, pretty much like the older styles—the Modernism creeps in accidentally and slightly. I have felt that your new language is Futurism; is your guess as to the turn speech will ultimately take; in which case you would not be contemporary, but consciously ahead of the times, which would be as bad as being archaic, in the sense that spontaneous creation would be hampered as much. The course I have marked out for myself as the safest is simply that of not letting the question of the old and new get into my mind at all, of keeping up a certain heat of composition in the faith that the imagery will be sufficient unto the day and unto the nature of my subject;—but I merely mention this to illustrate my point of view.

I also call in question the idea which comes into many of your poems, if not most of them—that we are fallen upon evil days. Not merely as a subject for poetry; here I know that the *Ubi sunt* motif is one of the main sources of poetry; but it is generally a note of individual homesickness, not a philosophy of the age; as the latter it produces a very broad canvas, perhaps broader than a poem can manage, I feel; which would apply to the scattering effect of your first Causerie, and to the total effect of the series.

But with regard to the merits of the thesis in itself: I don't believe you are justified. I doubt if these times have even the distinction of being located near the nadir of human history. I think the fundamental life-history of individuals is about the same in all the periods; or at least it may be. It certainly may be for us individually, for any of us. The poetical subjects to me are peculiarly individual interests, which I cannot see as particularly different for any reasons of time and space. But here again I have to acknowledge a personal bias: of late years (it was beginning during your latter days in Nashville) I have become somewhat soft and easy in my assessments of human nature; I am particularly taken, on the positive side, with the idea that provincial life is the best; this was my idea before Spengler reinforced me;[2] certainly in the provinces the personal themes for drama and poetry are the same as ever; life is just as prolific as ever of the cases; and only in the city, where for the most part the disaffected go, do you find that scorn for the Main Streeters which seems must now [be] such a blemish on our productive literary arts. In other words, in questioning this feature of your poetry, I am raising a doubt as to whether it is the perfect poetic state; for the poet as much as the philosopher is under obligation to find his positive experience; and the merely critical state, in which he refuses to find it (very properly) in the ordinary anti-poetic scene which must always abound, is just a halfway house, just the approach, to the creative work of art. *I.e.*, the general background to your work might seem to be a truculent or *moral* state rather than a philosophical or *aesthetic* one. Joyce Hawley is just like a tame version of Juvenal;[3] but after all is Juvenal our goal as poets? And haven't Joyce Hawleys bathed in the nude in nearly all times, certainly in many times whose poets were finding their usual provender without doing her the honor of paying her any attention?

These are cautions and fears—I don't put them very positively. I feel very reluctant to pass a judgment on your poetry at all; and admit that your present work may be the necessary preparation for work which will transcend us all. I will say this much in the opposite sense: there is an almost unfailing brilliance in what you write; your images and relations have such a quality of daring and unexpectedness; though to me they seem wasted by an intention which is held to with anything but spontaneity and freedom.

I had a letter from Laura [Riding] two or three weeks ago. She and Graves are up at London, where they find they can work better without the distractions of the family upon them. She wrote only in a slightly injured tone, which surprises me. I have not replied; but if I do, I will tell her that my affection is even more parlous than when I wrote, seeing I did not know then that she was sending you the copy of the letter she wrote me.

Graves sent me his Hogarth pamphlet, "Another Future of Poetry," which I send along.[4] Will you send it to Davidson when you are done with it? It is pretty good, but has not much philosophy behind it.

I am ashamed to confess that I could not find Books in all the Denver bookstores. Not knowing which number to order, I wonder if you will be good enough to let me see your copy? Which will be promptly returned.

My opinion of your critical faculties is a very doubtful favor, you will say on seeing the bulk of this letter, of which nine-tenths are my stuff calling for your opinion. Take your time, and say as little or as much as the spirit moves you.

Yours sincerely,
John

1. First published in *Transition*, III (June, 1927), 139–42.

2. Oswald Spengler (1880–1936), a German philosopher, who wrote *Decline of the West* (1918–22).

3. As a headnote to his poem "Causerie" Tate quoted an unascribed story from the New York *Times*: "Party on the stage of the Earl Carroll Theater on Feb. 23. At this party Joyce Hawley, a chorus-girl, bathed in the nude in a bathtub filled with alleged wine."

4. *Another Future for Poetry* (London: Hogarth Press, 1926).

To Allen Tate

Nashville, February 20, 1927

Dear Allen:

I was intensely pleased by *your beautiful* (equal emphasis on the *your* and the *beautiful*) review of my book.[1] I had not expected that you would entertain these sentiments. Even now I feel like wondering whether your remarks are: (1) your habitual honest reflections, or (2) the fruit of your generosity as a friend. In either case I find pleasure, and perhaps would as soon have it one way as the other. (Note for proofing: The "English publication" was "Grace *after* Meat," not "G. before M." Graves' title, by the way. JCR)

I should add, that you have done me the honor of more inward examination than I have yet secured from any source. You will unquestionably agree that the critics don't usually come anywhere near the heart of the matter—ironically enough, I haven't "got" your own work, and I confess it with some shame. I am obliged to see that in rationalism and Noblesse Oblige you have picked out two cues that penetrate very deep into my stuff—and I rather like, too, the more synthetic concept of the Old South under which you put them. George Bond has just reviewed me in the Dallas paper along the usual lines: my Southernism is suspect, it is far less than 100 per cent; whereas the Southernism he has in mind is a recent feminized (or, as you say, sentimentalized) vulgarism that presents a terrible declension if I know anything about the values. Anyhow, I don't write consciously as a Southerner or a non-Southerner. It is perhaps for that reason that I am not willing as yet to confess that I shall not write any more poetry, or that when

I do it will be a redundancy along the old lines. If I am not mistaken, I shall be compelled to keep on writing poetry for the very consideration that makes me believe that that way lies health and sanity; but I have a notion that it will become more and more radical and fundamental and less and less local.

I hope you meet John Gould Fletcher as he stops East on his way back to England. He is a very fine old-fashioned Southern aristocrat, with a mind that is not much poetically, I am afraid, but yet is absolutely independent and considerably active, and a personality that is about as decent and fine as any I've met in a long time. He was here this week and Don and I were delighted with him. He's going to Boston to see [Conrad] Aiken and Bill Elliott, both apparently his warm friends. He remarked in his lecture, by the way, that the Ironists (a group which for him includes Eliot, Aiken, and the Fugitives) are peculiarly a Southern set; Eliot being the northernmost, and hailing from St. Louis; this bunch, he says, particularly in the case of Eliot of course, are the only American poets who are having any influence on young Englishmen.

It happens that I wrote you a letter last week on the occasion of your New Republic article[2]—this letter is still hanging fire, waiting to be fixed up for a properer detonation. I'll let it stay where it is, and fire a fresher blast herewith. Your article I considered not only the best thing on the subject that I had encountered, but the best piece of exposition of a difficult thesis that I had found of yours anywhere. I admire it extravagantly.

I raise two queries only. Do you not, like [I. A.] Richards, stake everything on the chance of recovering some cosmological values out of the debris? That seems to me the source of your unhopefulness. I agree with you that you have to reject Richards' device of suspended belief—you can't write poetry with your fingers crossed, you can't tell truth by means of lies. My own solution is just this: The poets are through with cosmologies and Magical Views. In the place of these vulgarisms, these obsessions with pure magnitude, they will simply exhibit the infinite of quality that is in every situation anywhere, anytime. The poet, again, will simply refer concept to image, with the intention and with the effect of showing how the concept, the poor thin thing, is drowned in the image, how the determinate is drowned in the contingent, and how, ultimately, this world can neither be understood nor possessed. In the poet's art we will have to see, if we are willing to look at all, the objectivity of the world; this is a dreadful, an appalling, a religious, and a humble attitude to which we will come perforce after the conceited Subjectivism into which we have been persuaded by the practical and the scientific life alike. The issue will take place on its most emotional and poignant plane, of course, when the concepts referred back to reality are the dearest concepts; in the degree that poetry approaches to this plane, it approaches tragedy, and I think that serious poetry always approaches tragedy. In tragedy we admit to the impertinence of the whole possessive attitude, to the failure of our effort to grasp and to dominate the world. But in tragedy also we return to another very fundamental and very healing attitude which is the attitude of Respect. Such is our native dualism. We should alternate these affections doubtless—there are obviously two extremes in which we follow a unilateral principle,—we can be 100 per cent Occidentals and sacrifice all quality, or we can be pure Orientals and sacrifice all quantitative calculation and practice. Poetry and tragedy arise under neither one of these exclusive principles; poetry is the sense of the dualism. If you have no dear concepts, to which you have given everything in your time, your images are children's images and without meaning and substance. But if you still cherish your concepts without a suspicion—well, just look round at us and see us doing that very thing in these days!

It is in this sense—which I am expressing much too briefly—that I seem to myself to be much more radical than you yourself. I simply renounce Cosmology and Magic.

Second query: Do you not attach too much importance to the principle of a community between the poet and his public? Very fine thing if possible. But poets can't wait on that. To some extent they are not merely the expression, they are also the prophets and teachers of their compatriots. Poetry comes out spontaneously, not after looking to see if the times are ripe. Too much fine poetry has had to wait on its public to come after it, and the values in it have been posthumous. Poetry is individual first, it is social second. It is not so important that Dante's public believed in the Trinity; more important that Dante did.

My view is that we must, as critics, not only define the fictions of science for what they are, but also the fictions of philosophy. Philosophy of the usual or "constructive" sort, and not of the Kantian or critical sort, is an attempt to formulate in a more sophisticated way, but still, to formulate, the reality which science has quite obviously failed to grasp. So are religious systems. Their formulas must be questioned. They particularly are under illusions of grandeur and magnitudes. The State, the Soul, God, the World, the Cosmos (with a capital)—these are types of the scientific fiction put together by reason and quite exceeding the scenes: Supersensibles. They have in this condition no aesthetic quality, no reality. But religion, art (of the old order), and philosophy have more or less slily, more or less flagrantly, tried to animate them, to give them quality and life. Hence religious art, and hence such philosophical formulas as Purposiveness (Kant), The Idea (Hegel), God (Wordsworth), Will (Schopenhauer), Personality (Lipps), Organism (Whitehead), and Freedom (Sanborn).[3] Actually these constructions are analogies and fictions: supersensibly made to resemble the Sensibles. What we require always is to return simply to the senses; and this means, not that there is any superior *certainty* attaching to sensibles, (seeing that everything is certain according to the New Realists, including the very thin qualitative essences of the scientific concepts,) but that every Sensible is a source of inexhaustible sensation, and carries its own infinity with it at every movement, in a way that Supersensibles cannot possibly do. Reality means simply inexhaustible quality. It is only by retreating from the Sensibles, as we generally do in some fraction of the first second after the encounter, that we have our strange delusion of power and possession; and it is inevitably by returning to the Sensibles for an honest look that we disabuse ourselves of this delusion. The artist is the man who keeps his eyes open and is not afraid to look. Hardy's world of reals is just outside his door. It is quite a quaint idea that we are to find this world out there somewhere transcending sense. And there are no formulas. The formulas are the specific delusions.

Does this sound to you like plain bull? I never sent you the real meat of my study; the first chapters were introductory and eclectic. I have a lot of eclecticism in my stuff, and some novelty, too. That consideration doesn't matter.

I've been mulling things over and talking, where I could get the chance, these two months. My 200 pages of MS done in Colorado I must rehandle to get my approaches, accents, and climaxes effective as possible. It's a big job, doubtless in fact too big a job, that I'm tackling. I will start rewriting at once now, and by summer, or certainly by the end of summer, I think I will have it in a sort of shape.

Yours ever,
John

1. Review of *Two Gentlemen in Bonds*, *Nation*, CXXIV (March 30, 1927), 346.

2. "The Revolt Against Literature," *New Republic*, XLIX (February 9, 1927), 329–30.

3. Theodor Lipps (1815–1914), a German philosopher. Herbert Sanborn had been chairman of the Vanderbilt philosophy department for many years.

To Allen Tate

[Spring, 1927]

Dear Allen:

To begin with the last of your three letters first.

The ars aesthetica is so bulgy that I can't begin to get myself down in the mere dimensions of a letter—something more cosmic is necessary.[1] I'll have to wait till two or three of those chapters get re-done and ship them along. It is needless to say, I see that you for your part have done some ruminating too, and I would like to see a more extended version of your own ripest conclusions. Letters don't express either of us very far. I must say that I admire the rigor with which you attack the subjects which I throw out very vaguely—you are nothing if not thoroughgoing. With this apologetic as preliminary I resume the discussion.

Two admissions: First, I find concept the necessary ingredient of the dualistic pudding that you find it. That is the quantitative side of it as you rightly say. It is just that which I understood you to take exception to some months ago; when I wrote (in a chapter sent you) that in poetry we at last come to a reconciliation between the two principles, I understood that you refused to be reconciled, and said that was where we had to part company,—which was a grief to me. Now it appears that we have swapped places, or seemed to have done so; you are writing now that I can't deny quantity and concepts and the rational though I seemed to; whereas I reply that I don't, and didn't, but that I thought you did, and had.

Surely that amounts to something like this. The Orientals and the Mystics (of some varieties) may want a universe that is pure quality; the Occidentals and Scientists may want one that is pure quantity, or at least only the fraction of one percent impure; but neither party can produce the likeness of this World in any recognizable form, and certainly neither can produce an art. The Orientals have no values—values being in my sense elements of experience that have quantitative importance or availability for repetition, elements that are persisting cores of experience, or in other words ultimately Familiar Universals. The arts of Orientals, so far as they are Oriental, lack the emotional tensions that cluster round the "dear concepts." The arts of the Occidentals, on the other hand, so far as they are Occidental, lack the suggestion of substantial or qualitative content, they are logical or thin. Put it still another way: Orientalism is the attempt to confront the pure Objectivity of the world, while Occidentalism is the attempt to subjectify and possess the world. The one is mere Nihilism which, as Elmer Davis[2] says, will curl up and quit without even trying; the other is pure Will and Rotarian Optimism which does not admit defeat, does not recognize tragedy, and fools itself like a kid with its toys when it contemplates its apparent successes. What we require as intelligences is the conflict of the two principles. We have to be devoted and even scarred in a cause, and yet even then admit the presumptuousness of it. We have to have a sense of the poetry of the miscellaneous which is practically an irrelevance because it is the distracting and dangerous admission of the Great Uncompassable Objectivity; a sense of humor, which applies the sense of this helplessness to our own little careers; and the sense of tragedy which is the sum and climax of all the little moments of detachment and impotence issuing in their final drama. Aestheticism and Moralism would be good names for Orientalism and Occidentalism,—neither one of them good for anything, unless as stadia in the pursuit of wisdom.

This is surely obvious, but I put it down to get myself straight.

Second admission: When I said I seemed more radical than you, I was certainly referring to my critical or philosophical views, not to my poetical practises. More on this presently. But now that you challenge me on the point of our respective poetries, I don't know but what my proud claim may hold there. I am perhaps more radical in this respect: Having thrown over cosmologies, mythologies, and all the quantitative Infinites as the subject of poetry, I do a kind of stuff that is simple beyond all your power of condescension; and this was why I was amazed (and awfully pleased) at your kind words for the *Nation*. You on the other hand create a poetry which has a Mythology (miraculous and Infinite), or else the tragic complaint that your Mythology has broken down, or else the querulous note (underscored and emphasized and repeated) that you are seeking in a dark despair for a Mythology that doesn't yet appear.

And a note: My view of the New Realists is far from being grounded on a comprehensive study of the exhibits. I know Perry only by hearsay; the book I know is Spaulding's.[3] If I am not mistaken, it is that book which you have in mind and which supplies the terms in which you describe this school. What struck me in Spaulding was the extreme hospitality of his Realism; everything is a Real for him, though some things are Subsistents rather than Existents. That is a fine point of departure for an aesthetic. As poets we should have nothing to do with the Subsistents. Nowhere does Spaulding examine the vast and obvious difference that lies between the two kinds of Reals. For that matter, nowhere does the word art occur in his pages, or at least nowhere pointedly enough to supply one of the terms listed among the more than 500 that make up his Index; and the term aesthetic supplies only a single entry among the many thousands of passages cited in that Index. (These figures are according to my recollection.)

And now about the Cosmologies and Mythologies. I am a desperate Positivist, Nominalist, Philistine, Sensationalist, and Sceptic. I enclose bits of a chapter done last fall, and much needing to be done over; but on the whole I stand by it. May I say this much here: *I believe in universals*, and I see that there is no perception, no image which words can reconstitute, that is not full of recognition and concept and universal. But I object to universals which are constructed and not found. In other words, I object to those universals which are supersensible, which are mathematically infinite and grasped by reason rather than sense. Why should art bother with them? To use them at all art has to *imagine* them, which is to put with them the contingency and quality that are not there. These supersensibles are the totalities which we construct by mathematics in our number and space-time continua. They are elegant as fictions, and result in bridges and other sensibles ultimately; but should be held strictly as fictions all the same, as entities which cannot be perceived and have no aesthetic quality. The reason we have to reject them aesthetically is that, when we try to use them aesthetically, we tell lies and fall into disrepute and lose even our own self-respect. Yvor Winters, who is clearly a very fine man and whose indirect introduction to me in your letter I greatly relished, seems to agree with me here.

Furthermore. Here is a point which I believe you haven't considered, and which I am afraid must prove fatal to your hopes. You have been treating poetry in perfect isolation from the other arts. You have arrived at a view of poetry which makes it depend for its life on the reconstitution of cosmologies and supersensibles. Now I think the way of treating poetry separately from the other arts exposes us to almost any sort of error; hardly any error is too extravagant to look likely under this method. But isn't that a poor view of an art which cannot be applied, *mutatis mutandis*, to the other arts? And how can you possibly show more than the most incidental relation between St. Thomas and the history of painting or music or architecture? And how can you possibly maintain that these arts are knocked out if the Copernican or Darwinian heresy prove true? You don't write of a crisis in the arts generally, more than the possible difficulty of finding arts and patrons of art in a scientific age; and what right have you to conclude that poetry is a particularly perishable art, which is now about to die because of what has been going on in science and philosophy? To me this consideration seems to show that your view is not robustious and hardy enough; nor radical enough.

I am returning Winters' letter. It's great.

I was amazed to find in your letter No. 2 of this series, and apropos of nothing particularly, your apostrophe to Memory, Nostalgia, and Home; and your beautiful poem Ignis Fatuus.[4] Amazed because it seems to me quite imperative to try to do a big chapter on a hitherto unexplored subject, The Nostalgia of Art; has seemed to me so for some time. I have a very nice scheme for a chapter on The Strange in juxtaposition with this one on Nostalgia; these two features of reality, attended to for their own sake and indulged rather fully, are sure signs of the aesthetic attitude and introduce us into an exquisite series of psychological considerations.

The Fugitives met last night. The more I think about it, the more I am convinced of the excellence and the enduring vitality of our common cause. Here at Vanderbilt, which draws a lot of Old South talent, we have a very workable mine of young poets and fresh minds; always some one or two or more just clamoring for the right food and drink and society. We've got to keep on working that field; we have some perpetuals for the carry-over, like Don and me; and our cause is, we all have sensed this at about the same moment, the Old South. Lytle wrote me the other day from Yale, for instance, on the poor quality of the men up there. I like my own people, or rather I respect them intensely. I also walk a great deal and throw fits over the physical beauty of this place. Our fight is for survival; and it's got to be waged not so much against the Yankees as against the exponents of the New South. I see clearly that you are as unreconstructed and unmodernized as any of us, if not more so. We must think about this business and take some very long calculations ahead. More about this some time soon.

I'll return the poems in a few days. These hit me pretty hard; the first time I've felt this in some while on reading your poetry. I don't fix the blame on you; on the other hand, I don't know that I'm ready to give you a hundred percent indorsement, if I should review some of the other recent ones, and I suppose you don't particularly need it. I'll comment when I return the poems. Incidentally, I don't figure myself much of a critic; criticism is quite presumptuous, and I give it more and more reluctantly; I don't think it's quite a good man's business to do too much of it because it results in one of two ways: He commits gross injustices, or he is drawn too much out of his own bias and nature by the effort of understanding and sympathy.

Yours,
John

1. Ransom was attempting to complete the manuscript "The Third Moment," in which he outlined his theories of art.

2. Elmer Holmes Davis, the journalist and news analyst who had been a Rhodes scholar when Ransom was at Christ Church, Oxford.

3. Ralph Barton Perry (1876–1957) and Edward Gleason Spaulding (1873–1940), both philosophers, collaborated on *The New Realists* (1912).

4. First published in *Fugitives: An Anthology of Verse.*

To Allen Tate

[Spring, 1927]

Dear Allen:

Here's another little blast, delivered in haste without too precise an aim.

I. About value again. Value, as my remark in yesterday's would suggest, is quantitative. Perry[1] is right: Value is the supposed responsiveness and manageability of the world under your own heroic dictatorship. Value in the object is its capacity to serve your own purpose. Therefore, valuation is pretty obviously, pretty cheaply, your *subjectification* of the world, and an escape from the obligation to respect its objectivity. Of course one may say that there are Objective Values as well as Subjective Values—but then one is not speaking Coolidge English. It seems better, simpler, to say that the World has its value- or service-side for us, but that ultimately it is quite appallingly independent of us, and that in realizing this we exhibit our sense of beauty, sense of humor, sense of tragedy, and religiosity. . . .[2] And as for religion, we observe the continuous degeneration of every faith. By a universal & melancholy law of its nature, apparently. In this way: Religion begins pure; it is—cf. Schleiermacher[3]—our sense of impotence before a greater [Power?] than we, our humble confession of impotence, our philosophy of Objectivity; and then very soon it becomes a desperate frightened effort to *placate* this Objectivity and make it amenable after all; whether you call it at this stage magic or whether you call it Faith in God or whether even you call it a philosophical embrace of the Absolute. Its end becomes then practical after all: "What I could not gain by Science & Will I can gain by insight and renunciation—I win after all." Religion begins by abandoning Valuation, and then proceeds to pick it up again on a little different elevation where the dishonesty is not so apparent. The inevitable tendency of religion is to slide downhill. And I'm thinking that the only recourse is, frankly, to consider the aesthetic feature of religion as cardinal, and to demand—as we do it in art—that it take a fresh new form each time. The same logic which rejects the trite in art must right the systematic & formulary in religion. Actually—for you and me and the elite whom I know—art is the true religion and no other is needed. And for me—if not for you and others of the elite—this art must beware of cosmologies and the "fixed points of reference" or it will sincerely become a merely systematic religion and scheme of valuation.

II. About Rationalism & *noblesse oblige*. You do me the honor to let me be a mouthpiece for a very noble historic culture.[4] But this is the accidental and perhaps the questionable feature of your interpretation, and certainly the less important feature. What is important in your witness was that my stuff presents the dualistic philosophy of an assertive element *versus* an element of withdrawal and Respect. Your terms *Rationalism* and *noblesse oblige* are nearly as ultimate and pure as could be stated in discourse. If you are right, I am happy—I've put unconsciously into my creative work the philosophy which independently I have argued out discursively. I write this in no arrogance, of course—understanding well that the aesthetic quality is always a specific quality and is not guaranteed by the philosophy under it—a matter of practice, not theory. But what rather astonishes me is that having given me such a gorgeous Dichotomy of interest, you now seem to take it all back by saying that I rest on a couple of specific concepts (viewed now in your sentence as not a Dichotomy at all, merely two chance concepts out of many) (casual, local little things?) and exhibit a fairly simple and coherent (and special?) coherence. If your original diagnosis was right, then I raise the dualistic issue which is fundamental and not special; I do a variety of what we all must do. And as for the simplicity of my product, you know I have always been offensive in talking about maturity and seeming to make it a personal advantage of my own that I have achieved maturity by comparison with "others who might be mentioned." Well, frankly, and no offense intended, I have found it mighty hard to get to my simplicity—have had to fight off a lot of counter tendencies—simplicity is not to be regarded as a beginning but a goal—it's a purification and abnegation. What I miss nearly everywhere in poetry is this simplicity. I haven't really got it yet. The mind with its defensive apparatus sets up a thousand false goals & objectives to keep us from simplicity; all of them meant to disguise the fact that we don't really want to face the music and confront the Pure Fact which is in the aesthetic situation. My objects as a poet might be something like the following, though I won't promise to stick by my analysis: (1) I want to find the Experience that is in the common actuals; (2) I want this experience to carry (by association of course) the dearest possible values to which we have attached ourselves; (3) I want to face the disintegration or nullification of these values as calmly and religiously as possible. That's a simple program hard to realize.

III. I've used the word Dichotomy. Another version of my present view (and I know it's largely yours): Art is our refusal to yield to the blandishments of "constructive" philosophy and permit the poignant & actual Dichotomy to be dissipated in a Trichotomy; our rejection of Third Terms; our denial of Hegel's right to solve a pair of contradictions with a Triad. And here's a slogan: Give us Dualism, or we'll give you no Art. This slogan is counter to philosophy; we have a fight to make there as well as the simpler fight we make on science.

Yours,
John

1. Ransom may be referring to Ralph Barton Perry.

2. Ransom often used ellipses to indicate a shift of subject.

3. Friedrich Ernst Daniel Schleiermacher (1768–1834), German theologian and philosopher.

4. Ransom is referring to Tate's review of *Two Gentlemen in Bonds.*

To Allen Tate

April 3 and 13, 1927

Dear Allen:

Am several large letters behindhand.

To take them up in order: I've got more and more interested in Hart Crane's book and have been meaning to write you, and perhaps do a little critical article he eminently inspires.[1] I am about agreed with you that he is doing the "most important" work done in these days here. And I suspect you and I after all would rate its importance by the same consideration: Crane is by long odds the free-est mind in contemporary history—maybe since Blake. I mean, most free from abstraction, from quantification, from Fernandez' "judgment," from conceptualism;[2] can work most inwardly with his material; has got a cortex with fewest deep ruts and main lines and readiest switching facilities; a stock of experience the most viable, a set of communications the most complete. Another man has a lot of this & that is Merrill Moore, but with this important difference: Crane shuttles back & forth among nuclei that are of major, massive, adult importance, while Moore traces (sometimes) just as surprising & swift a pattern but the materials are apt to be trifling & juvenile.

So that I am not ready to say that Crane is the finest poet and artist—though I'm just as humble as I can be in my definitions, here, I don't want to rape the Muses, just look at them in their traditional aspect—these haughty & beautiful ladies are very old, you know. I note some reservations in your Foreword to Crane, and I wonder if they would not be even more accented if you wrote the piece today: since then you have abandoned a position of All-Quality and no compromise with Quantity, and come to insist on (substantially) my own Dualism, and even gone me one or two better in requiring for a "major poet" a grand quantitative system of fixed values in which to seek the play of quality. In your Foreword you find that his "subject" is not always suited to his "vision." Doesn't this mean that you find a certain deficiency (it may be wilful & experimental) in judgment, a gorgeous excess in vision?

Technically, Crane's peculiarity today is his total addiction to the literal *metaphor* as opposed to the simile. Or would you say *synecdoche*? He's got the poetic convictions and in a most unparalleled way the courage of them. The general poet keeps his logical subject intact while mentioning and correlating all the alternative subjects; Crane actually leaves the logical subject and commits himself with great rapidity to its alternates; the most complete Proteus I've ever encountered in verse. The conviction with which he makes these committals is staggering, silencing, and—inspiring.

In an age when conceptualism is easier and commoner than qualitative thinking, Crane is of the magnitude & importance you have marked. I wish I knew him; I'd like particularly to know how far he realizes that he is a voice crying in the wilderness, an extremist, and a John the Baptist; can it be that his Dionysianism (cf. Nietzsche) is wholly spontaneous? Or is it partly a deep didactic to purge the spirits of men, his own and the others too? Is this type of thinking to be his last or is it his preparation? I have not liked his Faustus & Helena for the same reason that I have objected to some of your own work since the early Fugitive days: it is too tractarian; it is aesthetics first and poetry second—as dangerous a combination as if it were ordinary Methodism first and poetry second. In his poems generally there is so much variety in the values, such a lack of reiteration & emphasis, that it is mighty hard to assign him any common, healthy, human "principles" as the basis of life. It looks as if he might have a grand passion for the sea, towards the close of his book, that would direct & therefore save his vast talent, attach it to something & humanize it.

But I don't minimize his greatness as a man whose capacity for vision, mobility of mind, deliverance from the fixed tracks of contemporary thinking, must be a mortification to all the other living poets. He is the man best for these times.

Or putting it more tamely but more tangibly. Poetry is (or has been, if you prefer) an art or "technique" in this sense, among possible other senses: It must do more than one thing at the same time; its basis is a prose or logical substrate, but that must consist with a rhythmical development of sounded words, and with one or more, often many, secondary and "associational" meanings which may be systematic as in an allegory, but must at least have a very high frequency, and a great displacement-value when considered as a nervous principle on the behavioristic hypothesis. Poetry is more than prose, but it must first be prose: that is my thesis. Crane has the largest "more than" extant, but has he the prose? And does he need it? These are the critical questions he raises.

Another letter. I liked tremendously your Poetic Absolute.[3] I criticize it chiefly on the ground that you laid much more weight on my own slight note than it could bear—it was merely your point of departure.[4] I admire your style here more than anywhere else. I think you emphasize exactly the right point for us—just as Crane emphasizes it. At the same time I can see that it is two years behind your present thinking. You can't make your formula out of an unqualified Absolute—your recent formulas have been dualistic. And even in your article you quote Donne's poem to show how readily his items link up with the conceptual world, but proceed straightway to claim that in spite of its origin it is an Absolute, and out of all relations. Of course it doesn't stop being related; and for that matter, you know very well that in its capacity of being an Absolute it never shows a single quality that is strictly internal & absolute, but each quality is a relation; the unpredictable & absolute property of the thing being simply that it can never be confined to a *single* relation or group of relations but always has novel relations to give out if you will look at it. And I think your insistence that we mustn't psychologize the finished poem, but treat it as ultimate, finished, absolute is a species of idolatry; the poem is hot not cold, living not dead, a source of constant fresh experience not a page that has been turned. I don't insist on a genetic account of the poem at all, merely on an account of it which considers it as a human experience, whether for the poet or for the reader. Call it an unpredictable source of energy; but this energy is of two components: the container, which is the relative & quantitative, and the movement, which is free and contingent and qualitative. As fast as you define poetry as the Absolute, you must amend it by saying what kind of Absolute; and that is, namely, an Absolute which consists in infinite relativity.

Third One. Thanks again for your review in the Nation. It's good they dropped the last paragraph: that was very handsome of you but quite gratuitous & supernumerary and it was good editing to drop it. I'm glad you wrote it and glad they dropped it.

Fourth: Winters has written me a nice note with some enclosures. Your final statement—final in that controversy,—which was one enclosure, I liked very much and thought was final indeed—from every standpoint. I mean its first part, the main core thesis. But I agree with him in thinking that you magnify the dangers of the present predicament of poetry. So does Richards. I again make an objection to which you have not replied: No theory of poetry will do which will not apply, *mutatis mutandis*, to the other arts. Now painting, music, architecture, & sculpture have no particular relation to the validity of current religious & philosophical beliefs; they go their way regardless. It does not matter what they behold when they look at the world, that thing beheld is capable of furnishing two separate experiences: a quantitative, systematic, subjective experience; and a qualitative, "absolute," objectified experience. No situation lacks either of these capacities. So with poetry. The act of aesthetizing a material is generally regarded as easy & spontaneous; it is, in this sense, that genius accomplishes it with comparative ease. But whether genius or just common talent is at work, its process eventually is one of attention, of hard looking, of dwelling on the material as an objectivity which we have not yet exhausted rather than on the material as an aspect which we take hold of exclusively, and pass from quickly. (The obligation to be aesthetic is the obligation to open our eyes very wide. Little pig-eyes can't do this—they focus too tightly: there is a physical property which we can actually apprehend here, an eye which definitely looks capable of vision, and a good chapter could base on just such an eye & develop most of the laws of aesthetics.) Aesthetic experience of course requires will & effort, but the will to stand still and get out of oneself, not the will to hurry on & to impose oneself. Here again we get back to first psychological principles, and to Kant's several exclusions by which the beautiful is not the desirable, not the possessible, not the good, the useful, etc. My point here is simply that poetry, like all the arts, is simply a necessary variety of thinking, and will take place everywhere & at all times indifferently.

Fifth. Your cry for a new & vast quantitative scheme to work in is the last infirmity of a noble mind. That requirement must take care of itself, and will, in the case of poets who are firmly constituted on the pure intellectual side. The vision, as a matter of fact, doesn't amount to much unless it handles *values*, i.e., quantitative terms, or terms which count in practical & ethical life by daily repetition. The exquisite pain & joy of art depends on exhibiting & then surrendering these values. All beauty is capable of reduction to tragedy, so is all humor; it's not free & full unless it hints of just this possibility. Tragedy is the logical end of all art, and implied in all art. Nostalgia is another name for it: the destruction of dear & familiar values. Poe's theory of poetry—a very pure application of this principle—the lovely woman seen dead, etc. Now you will agree at once that tragedy involves quantity, and if you will admit that tragedy is merely an implicit feature of all works of art, you will agree to my general principle.

Sixth. Major & Minor. Potency in art is a function of the quantitative or dimensional properties in the situation. See a lot of Merrill Moore nonsense—where the values are trifling, the poetry is silly, we get no kick out of it. The experience is not fundamental & perilous. So major poetry will stay with us as long as poetry does. But it is a mechanical principle which requires the major character of poetry to be indexed by the spatial or temporal or cosmic (both spatial & temporal) scale explicitly formulated. Majorness is a psychological principle & not an external. Its index is the amount of turnover produced in our gray stuff. The size of the values depends on how much we use them, govern our practical lives by them; on schemes & desires & passions which have dominated us & will do it again.

And Sixth, more specifically. We don't have to copy Milton & Dante to get major poetry. The Odyssey is as major as the Iliad. The major strain in Milton may be construed as depending only on a relation to a cold set of scientific beliefs systematized as theology; in my view, however, it depends on his ability to read the reigning values of our common life into nearly all his situations, even when they look slight, for these values are more major, more important, integral, central for us than the mere intellectual beliefs. It is academic to say the majors are the references to the beliefs alone. Poetry on that principle would always be cold and formal. And what about Shakespeare? Is he major? And the novel? Dramatic & narrative poetry may be major in two senses; it constantly handles matters of import; and it extends actually to dimensions that are considerable—to long poems, in fact.

Seventh. I send along an Oxford tract by a philosopher which is astonishingly good—infinitely better than has come from any academic seat in this country. Yet it is Crocean,[5] and it has substantially the same limitations as your Absolute. It emphasizes Individuality in the work of art, as counter to Universality, the reigning principle of philosophy, ethics, & the sciences. But actually this individuality is half of the dualism. Art is the meeting-place of the individual & the universal, the absolute & the relative. The Crocean emphasis, I do not deny, is what England & America have needed, however—in these races the nineteenth century witnessed the entire encroachment of didacticism, philosophy, & purpose upon the pure aesthetic vision.

Eighth. I am delighted with your idea of a book on the Old South, but have had little time to think closely upon it—our difficulty is just this: There's so little in Southern literature to point the principle. I subordinate always art to the aesthetic of life; its function is to initiate us into the aesthetic life, it is not for us the final end. In the Old South the life aesthetic was actually realized, and there are the fewer object-lessons in its specific art. The old bird in the bluejeans sitting on the stump with the hound-dog at his feet knew this aesthetic, even. Our symposium of authors would be more concerned, seems to me, with making this principle clear than with exhibiting the Southern artists, who were frequently quite inferior to their Southern public in real aesthetic capacity. But there are performances, surely, to which we can point with pride, if you believe the book should be one mainly of literary criticism.

Ninth. I've got out an article somewhat in this field, though rather emulsified into pap for popular consumption.[6] I enclose a copy, which please return along with the Oxford tract when you are done.

Tenth. Use any poems of mine you want in your anthology. I enclose copies of the ones you wanted. But I must mention, Knopf will make you pay for them—$10 each, I think; that is not fatal to a Houghton Mifflin publication?

Eleventh. I enclose my annual Easter poem.[7] Don't return it unless with some marginal notes, which I humbly solicit.

Twelfth. You are a damned good man and I respect you more & more.

Yours,
John Crowe Ransom

---

1. *White Buildings: Poems by Hart Crane* (New York: Liveright, 1926), for which Tate wrote the foreword.

2. Probably a reference to Macedonio Fernández (1884–1952), an Argentinian philosopher, poet, and short-story writer who believed in transcendental subjectivism.

3. "Poetry and the Absolute," *Sewanee Review*, XXXV (January, 1927), 41–52.

4. "Thoughts on the Poetic Discontent," *Fugitive*, IV (June, 1925), 63–64; reprinted in *Calendar of Modern Letters*, I (August, 1925), 460–63.

5. An allusion to Benedetto Croce (1866–1952), an Italian philosopher and critic.

6. Ransom may be referring to "The South—Old or New?" *Sewanee Review*, XXXVI (April, 1928), 139–47.

7. Apparently never published.

To Allen Tate

Memphis, June 25, [1927]

Dear Allen:

Winding up the matter of my representation in our Anthology, ahead of your "lead line" of July 1:—[1]

On Don[ald Davidson]'s authority I assume that my quota of poems will stand about as now, though the Knopfs will require some fee for reprinting. If I am in error that will be O.K. with me—it is for the Fugitives to decide without me. My final choice of poems to make this quota is a bit different from the collection you now have, as follows: I would take out Good Ships, Philomela, and Number Five. In place of the last I would put in What Ducks Require, which is not subject to fee, and which represents me at this writing as a late piece and (as my poems go) a most adequate one. For "Good Ships" and "Philomela" I would substitute something from my last volume, not now represented in the collection: Equilibrists first of all; and if there is still room after that long one is introduced, "Our Two Worthies." Am perfectly prepared to drop the last in respect to the proper limitation of my space. I enclose careful copies of the three new poems I name.

I think the order of my poems should be as follows: The Lover, Under the Locusts, Necrological, Bells for John W's Daughter, Judith of Bethulia, Captain Carpenter, Our Two Worthies (if it gets in), Equilibrists, and Ducks.

When I hear from you definitely that this selection is O.K., or what part is O.K., I shall write to Mrs. Knopf and ask for her bill,—to come to you or to Stevenson.

I am glad to hear you are going to the country. I'm going to do that myself one of these days; we shall buy a little place somewhere out of Nashville to live, I suppose, perpetually. Have this June got my professorship at Vanderbilt; I suppose I can now make a decent living; and I am quite happy to live on, where and how I have been living these ten years and more.

About our joint Southernism: Two considerations occur to me as bearing on the hopefulness of the cause. One is yourself, and many other men who exhibit the same stubbornness of temperament and habit; men of my acquaintance born and bred in the South who go North and cannot bring themselves to surrender to an alien mode of life; this fact, many times repeated within my own knowledge, argues something ineradicable in Southern culture. The other one: Croce (with one or two others) appears to have inspired a geniune and powerful revival of Italianism (in a most advanced aesthetic sense) among the younger generation of Italians. Why can't we? Look at the Vanderbilt crowd; the Candidates are always there, just waiting to be shown what their cause is. The same thing in half a dozen other Southern universities. This is where ideas are communicated, even in the midst of the general confusion, and all the better if the ideas are clear and self-sufficient.

I took the essay I sent you (Pioneering on Principle), reduced & compressed it to a rather provocative belligerent form, and sent it to Mark Van Doren, under the title: The South—Old or New? He wrote very nicely about it, but his Managing Editor (some other Van Doren) returned it saying that everybody had read it, but I had not convinced a certain member that the South ever *had* an antique culture, nor the members in general that this reputed antique culture stood any chance of survival. Does a writer have to convert the editors before he can get a hearing? Of course there is bad abolitionist blood in the Nation personnel; but I had aimed at them just for this reason.

I couldn't keep from jumping on Edmund Wilson for his Muses out of Work;[2] he was frightfully impertinent, I think, though rather decent to me personally. I wish he had not cut off the latter third of my letter, which was very much to the general point about the precarious position of critics. I mention this because you will have been surprised at my Positivistic heresies if you noticed my letter in this week's New Republic; and frankly I think of you as a rather absolute critic too; I used to be but have long since repented in sackcloth.

Drop me a meditation occasionally if you are willing to risk my irresponsible habits of communication.

Yours
John C. R.

P.S. Back in Nashville to stay after July 19.

1. *Fugitives: An Anthology of Verse.*

2. Wilson's review of *Fugitives: An Anthology of Verse* was generally favorable, but he angered Davidson by referring to him as David Donaldson.

To Allen Tate

Nashville, October 25, [1927]

Dear Allen:

Your letter to the *Criterion* seems to me a good one which I return for you to do with as you wish.[1] You refer it to me, I suppose, because I was the Fugitive specifically mentioned; while you wrote it, I am sure, because all the Fugitives collectively were indicted. As for myself, I do not intend to write a word to the *C* though I shall write to Graves. I have been accused before of "deriving" or "borrowing" from several poets such as Eliot, Williams, Stevens, Graves, Frost, and Robinson; and have never thought it worth while to reply. Especially so—*a fortiori*—where the accusation is in a mere letter which is concerned chiefly with other fish than me. Do as you like about your letter. I remark, however, that the upshot of it is to magnify the relation between Laura [Riding] and the Fugitives, whereas Graves' letter (inspired perhaps largely by Laura herself) does all it can to minify them. The affair seems to me too trifling to notice. Certainly I don't think it gives us new ground to move against Laura, because after all it is Graves who writes the letter.

Graves is clearly a madman. But I think Fletcher's criticism was mighty poor. The last thing to say about Laura is that she is a borrower, or anything but *sui generis*: fortunately for humanity. I think really, and regretfully, that F[letcher] himself is a borrower. I notice, in his prose, things he has borrowed from you. I notice, in his poem about crossing the Atlantic, several "influences," to put it mildly; he asked me to write him a criticism of it, but I hate to do it.

Yours ever
John

1. The letter by Tate was not published.

To T. S. Eliot

February 5, 1928

My dear Mr. Eliot:

Allen Tate suggests that you may be interested in the enclosed MS, "Pictures and Things." It is a chapter of a book which I have had under way for two or three years now dealing with the general aesthetic problem; in this case with the painter's problem. It takes Stein's recent book, "The A.B.C. of Aesthetics," as a point of departure but constitutes in no sense a review.

This sort of thing is far too stiff and formidable for our American periodicals, I am afraid. After one unsuccessful trial I have left off the attempt to find a home-market for it and try it on you. Perhaps if you do not find it the thing for your own publication, you will nevertheless be good enough to drop me a few lines to let me know what you think of it. I feel that there is a dire need of an adequate Aesthetic—I would like to think that I have one.[1]

Anyway, I remain,

Yours sincerely,
John Crowe Ransom

1. This essay was not published. Ransom did not publish anything in the *Criterion*.

To Allen Tate

April 3, [1928]

Dear Allen:

Have been wanting to write my congratulations—they are belated but fervent. I refer to your successes in: landing the Guggenheim; publishing the Stonewall Jackson; getting acceptance of your volume of verse;[1] and getting [Edmund] Wilson's remarks on your work in connection with his recent *Fugitive* review, the most adequate remarks on you I have yet seen in print.

As for Guggenheim, it is my judgement that the Committee should get the congratulations. You are the most deserving candidate they have had the opportunity to honor, and a credit to American letters.

Indeed, you are riding now & henceforth on the crest. You have amply justified your highly-original and non-gregarious policy of discipline and study these past five years.

I feel sure you will be getting down this way before you sail, which according to Don will be in September. I hope you get here before June 6, for I leave about then for a summer in State Teachers' College, Greeley, Colo.

Many things remain for definitive treatment, pending our get-together. For example, the problem of whether the difficulties experienced by the creative writer today are peculiar to him and not experienced by the artist anywhere.

The opus of mine advances.[2] It is about thought-out now, and largely written (indeed re-written), and I hope can be finished this summer. But those matters won't stand rushing. I'll send you two or three chapters soon to give you my drift.

Yours
John Crowe Ransom.

---

1. *Stonewall Jackson, the Good Soldier* (New York: Minton, Balch, 1928) and *Mr. Pope and Other Poems* (New York: Minton, Balch, 1928).

2. Ransom was still working on "The Third Moment."

To James H. Kirkland

October 1, 1928

Dear Mr. Chancellor:

The other day you again very kindly enquired about the progress of my book, and also told me of a similar inquiry from Aydelotte. I venture to think that you may be interested if I answer the question a little more fully and formally than I have done in talking with you, and so I write this letter.

I might say, too, that for some time I have felt that I owed you at regular intervals and officially a communication about the status of my project. Two years ago you were so good as to grant me a term's leave of absence to get this project going. I appreciated that favor, and feel only too glad to give an account of the work which it enabled me to undertake. I have failed to do so mainly for the reason that, every time I started to write to you, I have thought that the completed work would soon be forthcoming and the letter was unnecessary. I again labor under the impression—possibly under the delusion—that "it won't be long now"; but considering the previous record I will at least make sure that I get in a report during this season.

The thesis which I am putting forward in my book has weighed upon my mind ever since more than two years ago. I have devoted to it about all the spare time I have had for thinking, with the exception of some time on certain problems which have occurred to me in my graduate Milton course. And now I not only am more interested in it than ever, but feel more assured of its justice and worth.

I could not in a few words define this thesis, and I suppose you will not care to be added to the list of victims on whom I have tried out my doctrines in advance of publication. Briefly, I am concerned with the antipathy between art and science, and the affiliations between art, religion, and philosophy. These last three I call "post-scientific," in the sense that I believe them to be adult experiences which come after science, and are critical and corrective of science. When I say art, I wish to mean all the specific fine arts indifferently, but of course my testimony is principally in the field of literature. Probably my title will be, "Studies in the Post-scientific Function," unless such a title seems too severe to offer to the publishers and the public.

During this month, or at least during the fall, I shall have an article appearing in the *Saturday Review* which is a condensation of some of my arguments, and I shall take the opportunity to send you a copy.[1]

In such a speculative field as this, I am now very glad that I did not rush my views too quickly into book form. They have profited by the fact that I have spent time trying to locate them within the general field of aesthetic ideas, and to write them out supplied with the background and references which a good work requires. I have been obliged to do a great deal of reading and also a great deal of re-writing.

My manuscript is now so far advanced that I hope to have it finished during this school year. At any rate, I feel safe in undertaking to have it finished not later than the end of next summer.

Sincerely yours,
John Crowe Ransom

1. "Classical and Romantic," *Saturday Review of Literature*, VI (September 14, 1929), 125–27.

To Allen Tate

July 4, 1929

Dear Allen:

I have nothing but admiration for your "Fallacy of Humanism."[1] First, I think you have mastered your weapon of style; the first exhibit of yours that absolutely convinced me. I don't mean to sound insulting; your weapon in this case is a big one, like Ulysses' bow, not to be mastered in a day. This is a beautiful piece of dialectic, of the last coherency and cogency.

(I think I'll venture to interpolate here a thought that I have been gratefully entertaining, even at the risk of sounding insulting again: Your ease of style in prose is bound to affect your poetic manner in the direction that I for my part have desired for you. It will be impossible, I think—and surely it is undesirable—to maintain two styles, one for Saturday and one for Sunday, or one for the field and one for the parlor: It is my feeling that your eventual poetic character will be very far from anything we have seen from you. Excuse the avuncular digression.)

I congratulate myself that between your view and my view there is absolutely no serious interval; only here and a variation of vocabulary, or a difference of respective degrees of intensity and scales as one of us has stayed longer within certain groups of items in the whole.

Your first two sections are entirely effective. You are far more *au courant* than I ever will be—I couldn't write these sections for the lack of patience to master the subject. I have never (for several years) read Babbitt without applying my general thesis, which is somewhat (not very articulately) what yours is. I have said, "He's a 100% schoolmaster, talking about Check & Restraint"—which is analogous to your calling him eclectic.[2] I have never found him making any effective appeal to such a public as the collegiates; his doctrine hasn't any blood in it, & is bound to go down against any competing doctrine. I have seen that he had no reason, no authority, for his position, though he referred much to Aristotle. (He uses Aristotelian authority exactly as Dr. Mims, with the minor difference that he has actually read his Ethics; he hasn't read between the lines, we may be sure.) I have been aware of the talk of late about a Humanistic revival, but have not followed it or believed in it; it's like spinsters advocating culture & decorum. So I welcome, envy and admire your full and damaging exposition—if indeed I should not call it exposé.

Your third section has more in it than anything on the subject, in a comparable length, that I have ever found. My hat is off and my head ducked low. You use a sort of Bergsonian terminology with great novelty & charm. There are some verbal questions I would like to discuss with you; I am sure that we agree perfectly on the facts.

Your snake is very seductive.

It is just as you say: Religion is fundamental and prior to intelligent (or human) conduct on any plane. I had this in mind even in so secular a paper as my Southern one; but of course didn't venture to press the point there. Religion is the only effective defense against Progress, & our very vicious economic system; against empire and against socialism, or any other political foolishness.[3] It is our only guarantee of security and—an item that seems to me to carry a good deal of persuasive power—the enjoyment of life. The fear of the Lord is the beginning of wisdom; a big beginning, but only a beginning of which the end is the love of the Lord. Substitute nature for the Lord and he won't feel aggrieved. The Jews knew all about that in their Old Testament; the New Testament was a temptation which the soft-headed Western World couldn't resist; in the N.T. it seems (to the soft-headed W. W.) that the love of the Lord is the beginning of wisdom, and it's the kind of love a world bears to a faithful slave population, or public service that never sleeps; better, the kind a scientist bears to the gentle, tractable elements in his test-tubes, which so gladly yield him of their secrets, and work for him. The N.T. has been a failure & a backset as a religious myth; not its own fault, as I think, but nevertheless a failure; it's hurt us.[4]

Since last February I've been writing a hot & hasty book on religion which I hope to complete this summer—an interlude in my aesthetic interests, and far from being disconnected with them,—it can't possibly be a really finished & permanent book under the circumstances, but nevertheless it's a sincere book and one that somebody ought to write. It will be called *Giants for Gods*, I think. The point is that so many myth-systems (doubtless all of them) have contained myths (*many* in the Greek system) of giants, or earth-born (super-man in Nietzsche's myth), who were not Gods but only demi-Gods, yet *thought* they were Gods and behaved themselves accordingly. Prometheus, for example, whom the Greeks with all their intellectualism could not quite endorse. (Please read, if you haven't already, S. T. Coleridge's paper on *Prometheus Bound*; the most philosophical piece of literary criticism an Englishman has ever uttered.) Shelley's *Prometheus* is quite innocent of anything Greek in its spirit; he accepts the Giant. Satan is the Hebrew Prometheus and so conceived in Milton's P.L.—he is *Lucifer* the spirit of the Renaissance, the Zeitgeist of Milton's own age of science, very *boldly* displayed and only rejected after a proper hesitation. But then *Jesus is Lucifer* again; all the Saviors in the myths are Giants, *and the problem is in what sense they can save, and for what purpose they are to be worshipped.* Of course they are all earth-born, or half-human and half-god; the whole matter of the myth is to ask & determine the question, what is *man's* destiny, what is his proper relation to the God of nature? The function of Jesus in setting up as a Giant was to *decline* to set up as a God. But he may have wavered in his purpose; or the myth-makers in theirs, if you prefer. So the Western world raised this Giant to God, better than *HOMOI-OUSION*, in fact *HOMO-OUSION*;[5] little by little the God of the Jews has been whittled down into the Spirit of Science, or the Spirit of Love, or the Spirit of Rotary; *and now religion is not religion at all, but a purely secular experience, like Y.M.C.A. and Boy Scouts.* Humanism in religion means pretending that Man is God.

I am getting started here but will spare you; I hereby subside. I only wish I could talk with you a couple of days, and perhaps read to you some of my chapters.

But I'll hold this letter two or three days in order to get hold of a paper of mine in the aesthetic field which bears on the relation of tragedy to religion, among other things; and propounds a view of romanticism on the *positive* or *loving* side of religious experience; the paper is "Classical and Romantic" *and is an abridgement of some very central chapters in my aesthetic system.*[6] Canby has had it about 8 months, but told me in March that he had to wait till summer, the dull book season, to print it; it being mighty long by his standards.[7] I would relish a comment of yours.

I'll also send you some pages from the July *Sewanee Review*, when it appears: "Flux and Blur in Contemporary Art."[8] It is an examination of Wyndham Lewis' Time-book;[9] not very good, but perhaps sound in the main. *It relates to the time and space distinctions. I note that you put religion on the side of the Time-Sense*, as Bergsonians would do, and you ask Lewis to do the same—or at least to put the devil on the side of the Space-sense. But Lewis' prejudice in favor of space over time is interesting; and Spengler in Vol II very sharply puts religion under the Space-sense, and I should say very favorably. It is my own opinion that the issue is not between Space & Time, but between Contingency, Indeterminateness, Evil, Chaos, etc. in Space *and* in Time—the aspect in which science & knowledge fail to know events in Space and in Time—and on the other hand Necessity, Determinateness, Good (or Control), Cosmos, etc etc. The God of a genuine religion will always look to the soft humanist like the God of Evil; and so he is in the sense that he is *not* committed to humane purposes. The God of a Quasi-religion on the other hand will necessarily look to the stern religionist (the realistic religionist) like a humanitarian but impotent Giant. More specifically, I try to show that Lewis does not really object to time in the arts, but to *flux* in the temporal arts; and in the spatial arts (which he is obliged sometimes to mention, but always foolishly when he attempts to apply his time-thesis), to *blur* or inter-penetration. In either case he objects to contingency. He is simply a critic who prefers his universals to his particulars; a version of the moralist-pedagogue-critic.

Thank you for liking my Southern article and for seeing some traces of the "profound" in it; it was only as profound as I dared to make it. By the way, my own title for it was "Reconstructed but Unregenerate";[10] but that was too stiff for the editors, who gave it an ante-bellum title in the tone I detested and tried to avoid.[11] In May I wrote to the English editor of the "Today and Tomorrow Series" (Dutton publishes it, doesn't he?)—this Editor a nameless gentleman to me—enclosing a proof copy of my article and offering to write a booklet for the series which would be an elaboration of the article, and which would be entitled: "Dixie: The Future of the South."[12] Would not this performance serve the cause? I had a receipt of arrival for the article but so far no letter of disposal. If you think the project worthy and happen to be in a position to approach the editor with a favorable word on its behalf, my blessing on you.

I might have said earlier in my letter what seems to be an invariable feature of my correspondence with you:—that I had long meant to write you, etc etc. This letter has a fulness, I observe, which will probably appall you somewhat. Let it serve as amends, in part, for my previous omissions, rather than as a provocation to any epistolary debauch on your part which may not fit in with your schedule.

I have been hearing of you from several sources; was greatly interested in a long letter to Don, for example, last spring. I read with gratitude your article in the January *Bookman*.[13] I confess I don't know of your prospective movements and plans. Andrew Lytle says you are thinking of retiring to Virginia. I wish you would make it Tennessee. Some day I am going to kick out of teaching and become a writer and surprise everybody. I seem to myself to be making progress with all the speed of a snail. But for fear my uncouth epistolary manners may sometime be misconstrued—though I don't fear that very keenly—I want to say that you have always my entire confidence, esteem, and affection and I wish we were allocated by the Inscrutable God to a common neighborhood where we might talk occasionally.

Yours ever
John Crowe Ransom

---

1. "The Fallacy of Humanism," *Criterion*, VIII (July, 1929), 661–68.

2. Irving Babbitt (1865–1933), author of *Rousseau and Romanticism* (1919) and other works and leader of the New Humanist movement.

3. "The South—Old or New?"

4. The germ of *God without Thunder* (1930) is apparent in these statements, especially in the next paragraph. While he was writing the book, he referred to it as "Giants for Gods."

5. Of like substance; of the same substance.

6. "Classical and Romantic."

7. Henry Seidel Canby (1878–1961), Yale literary historian and author of *Turn West, Turn East* (1951) and other books, was then editor of the *Saturday Review*.

8. "Flux and Blur in Contemporary Art," *Sewanee Review*, XXXVII (July, 1929), 353–66.

9. Percy Wyndham Lewis (1884–1957), painter, novelist, and editor; Ransom refers to *Time and Western Man* (1927).

10. Ransom subsequently used that title for his essay in *I'll Take My Stand* (1930).

11. "The South—Old or New?"

12. This essay was never published.

13. "American Poetry Since 1920," *Bookman*, LXVIII (January, 1929), 503–508.

1930–1939

N THE EARLY 1930s Ransom was heavily involved in the publication of the Agrarian manifesto *I'll Take My Stand* (1930) and the series of public debates that followed the appearance of the book. His letters reveal the extent of his involvement in these two projects. Together with Tate and Davidson he was responsible for securing the contributors and assigning the topics for the individual essays. Both versions of the introduction to *I'll Take My Stand*—"Articles of an Agrarian Reform" and "A Statement of Principles"—were written by Ransom; he also contributed the leading essay in the collection; and he appeared in four public debates, including two with Stringfellow Barr and one each with William S. Knickerbocker, editor of the *Sewanee Review*, and William D. Anderson, president of the Bibb Manufacturing Company of Macon, Georgia.

Ransom spent the academic year of 1931–1932 in Exeter, England, on a Guggenheim fellowship, and his letters of this year are filled with his reactions to England after an absence of more than fifteen years. Much of his creative energy during this year was spent in composing a defense of Agrarianism under the working title "Land!" Although he completed two different versions of this manuscript and published two articles from it, the project was finally abandoned after the book was refused by three publishers.

In January, 1931, Ransom wrote Donald Davidson that he was eager to complete the Agrarian book ("Land!") because he had begun "to feel active on the inside again" and wanted to get back to some "creative writing." It was not poetry, however, that was arousing Ransom's creative imagination; instead he was beginning to think seriously of the book that would be published as *The World's Body* (1938). Early in the spring of 1932 he wrote a "longish essay on Milton," which he published the next year as two essays and which, with some revisions, would form the two opening chapters of the book. He wrote a rough sketch entitled "Poetry: A Note in Ontology," one of his most illuminating statements on the nature and function of poetry, which would appear as a chapter in *The World's Body*.

During the mid-1930s the Agrarians were able to form a journalistic relationship with Seward Collins' *American Review* such as they had attempted to establish since the publication of *I'll Take My Stand*. Not only did Ransom publish many of his essays in the *Review*, but, like the other Agrarians, he tended to view the journal as an official and essential organ of the movement. Many of his letters of the period, therefore, are concerned with such questions as who in the group will review W. T. Couch's *Culture in the South* or Aubrey Starke's *Sidney Lanier*. When Starke reacted violently against Warren's "The Blind Poet: Sidney Lanier," Ransom responded in the same issue.

He and Tate continued to exchange critical essays, and Tate sent his poetry, but Ransom was writing little poetry of his own. One can well understand Ransom's statement in the preface to *The World's Body* that he and

Tate "have been in close communication" and that he shares Tate's "views of poetry" with "fewest and slightest reservations." After reading Tate's "Three Types of Poetry," for example, Ransom wrote Tate in 1934: "I have just re-read it, after a week on an essay of my own, and will put down a few of my reflections. It is a very important essay, the best in the field. My own will not be contradictory—couldn't be, for I endorse about everything in yours. Just another set of terms, a slightly different angle of approach." The reader of Ransom's "Poetry: A Note in Ontology," the essay to which he refers in this comment, will be impressed by how accurately Ransom points up the differences between the two essays and will understand better Ransom's assertion in *The World's Body*: "Between us, when the talk was at a certain temperature, I have seen observations come to the surface in a manner to illustrate the theory of anonymous or communal authorship."

In his review of Tate's *The Mediterranean and Other Poems*, to which Ransom refers in a letter of September 17, 1936, he says that Tate's poetry is being adversely affected by his overt advocacy of Agrarian doctrine: "What is true in part for you (though a part that is ominously increasing) is true nearly in full for me: *patriotism* has nearly eaten me up, and I've got to get out of it." Thus the way was opening for Ransom to move away from his support of Agrarianism to a period in which more and more of his time and energy would be expended in attempting to define the nature and function of poetic discourse. His movement away from Agrarianism made his decision to leave Vanderbilt and his friends and associates there much easier. His moving to Kenyon, as Tate later wrote, was a *felix culpa* or a *felix crimen*, for almost immediately upon his arrival there he became involved in a series of events that profoundly affected the course of modern American letters.

To Allen Tate

Nashville, January 5, 1930

Dear Allen:

I am mighty glad to hear you are getting back today to these shores, and not for your own pleasure's sake either. Don says he has already written a welcome letter to solicit your counsels for the New Confederacy. But before I go to that, I want to say that I admire more and more the way your career is shaping, and nothing would give me more pleasure than to talk at great length personally with you,—not only on the Cause but on literary and religious matters, which ultimately are about the only interests I have.

I hope the family is well, and you are pleasantly located.

I probably owe you a couple of letters, which is as usual. Don shows me letters from you, with whose opinions I nearly always agree.

Don, Andrew and I have been doing recently a great deal of confabbing. By the way, Andrew has more drive and courage (of the practical kind) than any of us, and I think we would be much mistaken in leaving him out of our joint volume (supposing it is a sort of initial bow to the public) unless his offering was definitely not presentable. He has a fine thesis for his contribution and can put it in good shape, I think. We have done a little proselyting, which does not seem immensely difficult. We will have plenty of friends. But we ought to be ourselves a group of eight or ten, so that we could dispense with the immediate friends if necessary. It is my idea that our book ought to contain that many articles, from that many charter members, so to speak.

Now, how to make sure that so many writers are properly indoctrinated. Here is a chance to kill three or four distinct birds at one throw. You long ago proposed that we issue a Manifesto. Suppose we don't wait for the doctrines to ripen fully, but go on record now with them. In other words, put it into the book as our tentative Articles of Faith. It might have these advantages: (1) It would give all the writers something to look at in shaping their contributions, and increase the unity and force of the book as a whole; (2) It would (even before 1) serve as a test of faith for the writers, and start us all out committed equally to a Cause; (3) It might be used independently of the book to this extent:—Suppose the book is for early fall: then in late spring wouldn't the *New Republic* print the manifesto, if worded generally enough to be intelligible by itself; which would put a little money in the war chest and serve as a preliminary ad. for the book.

Anyway, Don and Andrew and I agreed to write separate manifestoes for comparison.[1] Up to date, I seem to be the only one who has finished one: and mine doesn't quite suit me yet. I enclose it. It isn't a very pretty copy. Don and Andrew agree to all my doctrines, but there may be issues of expediency to consider. There are some hard strategic questions to answer. It is probably my tendency, and probably yours also, to be rather abstract and philosophical about such matters, and that might easily be overdone.

After the book.[2] The next thing is clearly to get us a press and go to hammering. There is one way to do it which is more practical than another, and that is to acquire a Tennessee county newspaper. We are actually pricing one, through Jim Campbell our recruit from Franklin.[3] The paper would make the living of one or two of us; and it might be you, or Don, or me. I warn you that I am in earnest about this. Both Don and I are very discouraged about the good of academic employment on the ground stated in my Article 9—the one that is most personal of them all to myself.[4] I would gladly get out at a little sacrifice; so would Don if his wife would let him.

In running a county weekly there would be some chance, but not much, to fight for the Cause. The point is that with the press available we could issue tracts and a periodical for Southern and national circulation. I am sure that our group would offer not less but *more* than enough of polemical articles, and that we would command a great hearing, and might even make a commercial success.

We may very well get us a good county paper by (1) buying on credit, or (2) having the backing of some local patriots, successfully recruited, or (3) getting most of the purchase money out of the proceeds from our book.

This is the way our minds are running. But we all hope you will be able to come down here yourself and live right in the movement—and you shall have the pick of the financial plans if there are any. *At the very least* we hope you can get down here very early for a good thorough set of conversations. In a conference many of your apprehensions I think will disappear. And on the other hand, your advices are wanted orally.

Possibly we are all about to make fools of ourselves. But it isn't fatal—I've done it before. And on the other hand, I can't imagine anything appearing on the American scene as more of a novelty and an occasion for respect and even awe than a sizable group of young literary men (who have already won their spurs, mostly) manifesting themselves in the capacity of a Cause, about which they have convictions. If only we can follow up that book with a furious stream of publications! The New Confederacy *vs* the New Republic!

Yours ever,
John Crowe Ransom

---

1. Only Ransom wrote the manifesto.
2. *I'll Take My Stand: The South and the Agrarian Tradition* (New York: Harper, 1930).
3. James Campbell, an attorney practicing in Franklin, Tennessee, near Nashville. The Agrarians never acquired a newspaper.
4. Article 9 of the original manifesto reads in part: "The evil with which we are concerned does not lie in this physical distress, but in the spiritual poverty that marks the age of machines."

To Robert Penn Warren

January 20, 1930

Dear Red:

I am indebted to you for (1) your good note of last fall, (2) your sending of Richards' little book,[1] and (3) recently your gift of the magnificent John Brown himself.[2] And Robb and I had the felicity of receiving your betrothal announcement.

In order. I was a little appalled to learn that you had passed around my *Ghosts*—not that I didn't like the flattering gesture, but that edition of the thing was a sort of first one in which I have had to make considerable changes, and am still making them.[3] There was one bad error of terminology in the mathematical section. But the ideas are still substantially as advanced, and if anybody approves them I am glad. Among the changes up to date is the addition of a longish section on the Holy Ghost as Paraclete, with a good deal more about the New Testament and Occidentalism and the Roman Church, the topic barely indicated in the close of the version that you have. I don't entirely believe in Romanism as Tate and other friends do,—by the way, I think it is impossible to find Romanism or its influence in our Old South; what we had there was pure Calvinism, and that had all the essential elements of a great religion in it, except possibly some aesthetic ones.

Richards I already knew, but am glad to get the book. I reviewed it for Don several seasons ago, and remember to have made this comment: Richards has no theory of art, but only a theory of poetry. What he says about poetry could not possibly be translated for the benefit of the other arts. Whereas what we want is a theory of poetry that is also a theory of all the arts; and the test of all arts. This carries the criticism of Richards' specific theory of poetry, as a matter of implication perhaps, that the state of theological belief in an age is not necessarily fatal to poetry; except as it is a general index to the spiritual climate, and therefore to the possibility of the arts in general. Shakespeare certainly had not a theology yet was an artist. The novel as a form of art rests on no particular theology. I admit that Milton could hardly have been Milton without his orthodoxy, and that orthodoxy is important. But he has (I mean, Richards has) made too much of modern scepticism. To make this point well I would need to launch forth into the true theory of art, i.e., *Ransom's* theory, but this is hardly the occasion. I shall victimize you sufficiently in the future, it is to be hoped. In general, it seems to me that Richards is just right as far as he goes, and he is certainly on my side, but he doesn't go nearly far enough, and he is a good example of a common kind of aesthetic theorist who makes all his generalizations on one art, which may or may not prove to be of importance to the arts in general.

John Brown is a beautiful piece of work, as I can see from having only so far browsed rather extensively in it. Shortly I mean to give it a sober and prayerful reading. I can say already that you are a stylist; that is, you commit yourself to a style and do not change your mind throughout 120,000 words; scarcely any young writer could make that boast. Furthermore, I can say that you understand composition; that is, the art of composing in very large units. As to the sentimental background, you know that I shared that from the start. My hat is off to you.

What is immediately on my mind is to say: Now is the time for all good men to come to the aid of the party. Don, Andew Lytle, Tate, and I have got things cooked up to the point where they can't be stopped.[4] I refer to the Old South movement, about which we had a few flying words last summer. Our project is immediate to this extent:—We must at once get out that symposium of essays on the South old and new, and aim for early fall publication. Several publishers, all who have heard of it, want the thing. We mean to make it more pointed and unified and provocative by including in the book by way of a poem a statement of faith to which all the contributors subscribe,—indicating that we are already a group, and have thought the

To Allen Tate

January 25, 1930

Dear Allen:

Your second letter, with the notes and additions about the manifesto, came this morning.

I think your points are well taken, and promise that we shall all give them a very thorough study. I believe you are right in your suggestion of the omission of one of my Articles. I think the two or three additional Articles are good. My impression just at the moment is that the two that deal with Humanism ought to be one; and possibly that it ought to be incorporated into the one I have about the helplessness of the educational institution or the cultural programs to accomplish anything; I had Humanism in mind there without calling its name. Its name should be called, and its deficiency stated in hard terms. The Article you give dealing with the two spirits in recent Southern letters is excellent and timely. But just now I am giving only my first impressions. More later. We will speed this manifesto business up as you suggest.[1]

You have asked us for more information about the county paper program. Well, we mean to get that information for you and ourselves too. We will speed Campbell in Franklin to complete his inquiries. We will feel out the prospects in some other towns. It is my strong feeling that we must start this paper next fall. Naturally, before any one of us is committed to it we must have the most definite kind of information that is available. We have some already, but it is general and not local. We are going to have a conference right away to get this matter going faster. The book by itself is scarcely worth doing if we don't follow it up, and if, in short, we don't get a press and put it to work. The sooner we make the arrangements, the easier thing out. Several of us were going to prepare alternative statements, but I with my ingenuous spirit seem to have been the only one to offer so far. I send along a copy of my creed, which is provisional, and subject to the General Will, and really just a man of straw for the other brethren to knock down.

Our project is a little more extensive to this degree:—We are now planning to buy (mostly on credit) a county paper, say at Franklin, Tennessee. From this enterprise one or more of us could make a living. There wouldn't be much fight or importance in a county paper of course. But it would provide our group with a press, with which we could issue pamphlets and particularly a periodical, for circulation Southern and country-wide. We need to write furiously, and we will have the stuff to write. There are some men of affairs in our crowd, notably Andrew Lytle and Jim Campbell of Franklin; they mean business, and we are in earnest. This is a warning. Allen Tate writes now from New York that if this is carried out he will move down here—though he waives the obligation and privilege of the county paper editorship. All this so far of course is strictly confidential. We are getting an option on one or more Tennessee papers. I think we will put this thing over.

Of course we have been counting on you as one of the faithful. I don't mean to mortgage your career, but only for the time being to get your article and your signature. Haven't you a burning message on the subject of ruralism as the salvation of the negro? or this, that, or the other? Don and I think that you are such a force that we don't need even to indicate to you your subject. Won't you state it and work it up? Limited to 12,000 or 15,000 words ordinarily. Then later we can organize and pursue our more ultimate projects if we will.

We have a very fine Britisher staying with us at Vanderbilt now, thanks to the Carnegie Endowment for International Peace. He is J. Y. T. Greig, a Scotsman, now teaching at Durham University.[5] He sat in at our discussion the other evening and seemed thoroughly converted. He remarks that Europeans very commonly have our view about industrialism, which they call Americanism, and that we would have unlimited sympathy there. Suggests also that we ought to get a capable and famous Britisher to write us an article, and accept him into the company as a friend and adviser. Seems to

we will find them to make. I am not sure whether Don is available for running a county paper. I am sure that I am if I don't have to make too much of a financial sacrifice; that I can't do, since I have not only my acquired family, but my original one, that is, my parents, in part to look after. But I will make some sacrifice anyway. As far as that is concerned, a county paper couldn't furnish much less of a living than does a minor professorship in a college. My wife and I are quite ready to take a chance if it doesn't look too much like suicide. But I don't mean to assume that I am essential to this scheme. There is Andy [Lytle]; possibly there will be Red Warren; and in fact some less capable men of ideas that we might easily proselyte might be the very ones to run the county paper for us. That is a move that I feel pretty sure we can work out, and that I am determined we shall work out without unnecessary delay.

I enclose an article (i.e. copy) which I am sending to the *Bookman*. It deals with Shafer and Humanism. I would like to make it more outright, but refrain for fear of competing with Shafer on his own ground.[2] I hope you approve it. I know from Don's and Andy's letters from you that you have been on the point of calling on Shafer in person. I sympathize with your feelings and wish you well. At the same time I hope you may have got your own consent to let the matter lie. Shafer is the man most injured by the Shafer article.

Yours,
John

1. Tate is reacting to a draft entitled "Articles of an Agrarian Reform," an early version of "The Statement of Principles" with which *I'll Take My Stand* opens.

2. This essay apparently was never published. But Tate published "The Same Fallacy of Humanism: A Reply to Mr. Robert Shafer," *Bookman*, LXXI (March, 1930), 31–36. Shafer was associated with the New Humanists.

To Allen Tate

February 22, [1930]

Dear Allen:

The Harper's vs. Macmillan situation is amusing.[1] If Don had not been Hamlet he would not have written his indefinite letter of last Sunday or Monday to Macmillan; and still less would he have written after receiving your telegram to extend to Titterton further hopes of getting into our plan.[2] He could have retired with ease and honor from his Macmillan commitments at either time, and he could do so now. He's just not built that way; or at least he's gone downhill from the manner in which God first constructed him. He's been steadily losing his power of productivity. Last summer, at some sacrifice, he went away to Yaddo to write a book; but after a month the book hadn't come, nor begun to come. That impaired his morale, I think; it was a tragic experience. I don't fuss with him, but rather jolly him along. I hope he can come to life again, and maybe your coming will be the thing to bring that about.

Don't weaken on the Harper's proposition. I haven't expressed myself particularly & don't intend to. Don likes to think he's managing. But I would say, and will say if we have to act as a group, that Macmillan had better just be let down as gently but firmly as possible, and we have no more time to worry about it.

Here's one thing I am just a little bit worried about. Don suggests, as if jokingly, that the advance money will come in handy for summer expenses of the individual contributors.[3] I think he is planning, without knowing it, to break up the idea of acquiring a paper, to which project the profits of the volume should go, as I have often said without meeting with opposition. I think Don is secretly scared about that venture, and all the decisions it will involve. So I'll have to oppose the division of the spoils now, or after the volume has been on sale. Unless I find myself in a minority of one. By the way, Owsley is strong for the paper; so there's at least you, Andrew, Owsley and I.

Here's a matter that embarrasses me a little, in view of my strong moral stand of the last paragraph. You mention the prospect of *Harper's Magazine* using some of the articles. What will become of the pay for them? If I should use my old article as the nucleus of my contributions, *Harper's* will have already used that, and paid me $200, which I couldn't possibly now turn over.[4] If I should use an article I'm now writing and thinking independently of submitting to *Harper's*, I'd hate to turn over the money I might get for that. (Probably a needless worry, as it isn't in line with the policy of their editors, who wrote me recently: "We think you are too hard on science." They meant: "on industrialism.") I'll follow the group's will in this, if it should affect my pocketbook, or if it shouldn't. But I wonder if any article that is placed independently ought not to be the property of the writer till turned over for book publication; and if any article that is used by the *Magazine* because it is shortly to be printed by the House ought not to be the property of the group?

You know Young, and you are the one to deal with him.[5] But it is my feeling that we ought to get the benefit of his name if it doesn't sacrifice our principles—and of the beautiful English of his contribution.

Will dash off to the last mail with this.

Yours ever,
John C. Ransom

1. Allen Tate had secured a contract from Harper to publish *I'll Take My Stand.* His contract was issued on February 8, 1930; Donald Davidson received a contract for the same project from Macmillan that was dated February 21, 1930.

2. Lewis Titterton, associate editor at Macmillan.

3. Harper had paid an advance on royalties of $300; the contract provided for 10 percent on the first 2,500 copies sold, 12.5 percent on the next 2,500, and 15 percent on copies sold over 5,000.

4. "The South Defends Its Heritage," *Harper's Magazine*, CLIX (June, 1929), 108–18.

5. The group was planning an appropriate invitation to Stark Young, a novelist and critic, who responded by contributing an essay to the symposium.

To Allen Tate

February 25, 1930

Dear Allen:

We had a group meeting and this is to say confidentially what may or may not appear definitely in Don's letter: *We authorize you.*[1] Don takes things hard and makes difficulties at every turn. But he is not consciously of an ugly spirit, and we all met in good humor. His error was in not letting Titterton down the moment he got your telegram about the contract. He has got himself into the position which he refers to as "discredited." The only graceful way out that he can imagine, I think, would be not to give the contract to *either* publisher. He thinks you acted "hastily" which from a man of his recent temperament is a compliment. Please continue to act that way.

In haste,
John C. R.

P.S. He will grieve about this a long time, without ever drawing the moral that is obvious. The amount of time which he can *kill* by grieving and reflecting is immense. I would be indignant if it were not Don.

JCR

1. To sign the contract with Harper for *I'll Take My Stand.*

To Allen Tate

[March 15, 1930]

Dear Allen:

We had a critical—if not fatal—meeting of the local group last night: Davidson, Lytle, Lanier, Owsley, Wade (who has at last come in), and myself.

We discussed a revised edition of the Manifesto at considerable length. With every discussion this work becomes more formidable and its dimensions increase. I think it was the common opinion, or at least feeling, that something is wrong with it. As a Manifesto it is too bulky and too difficult and too various in its topics. At the least, it needs a good deal of work before it is ready to submit for publication. I forgot to say what is the chief of its faults: it is rather too dogmatic, and not sufficiently tentative in its tone; not that exactly, but brash, personal—I think we don't want to say what *we* will do.

Anyhow. It was agreed that it needed more attention and work. Hence, delay. The next step was to decide that we had just as well wait on the Symposium in general. That is, our ideas might clarify better in time; and besides, once we had got to that point, it seemed that everybody wanted to wait anyway on the score of urgent previous commitments that would make it hard to get articles done in time for fall publication. Wade and Owsley seem definitely to be too engaged for the present; Lytle also very busy with his book; Lanier chronically busy; even Don doubting if he could get his piece done; leaving me as the only single one that did not want more time. So it was decided almost unanimously, though without any formal vote, to aim at publication in 1931, and abandon the project for the moment. I offered no opposition: I was dumbfounded; I went home and told my wife it was all off for the present, and she thought even more than I that we had been very feeble.

This morning, however, on my talking it over with Don, I find that he is inclined to agree with me, and we have called the crowd together again, to meet one hour from now. I will add in a postscript anything which may be decided contrary to the proposals I am making to you here.

I might add that the one redeeming feature of last night's meeting was the reading of the first draft of Nixon's article, and also fiery letters from him. His article will be magnificent when it is ready finally. And he has fighting spirit.

I am going to try to make the crowd reconsider, and I believe Don wants that too. My position is that we are beginning a campaign, not a battle, and we are taking this opening battle far too seriously. I have never in my life been more deeply impressed with the dilatoriness and indecision of the academic mind. I am obliged to reflect that even if we had that press, about which we have talked for years, and the chance of a periodical all our own, the articles for it would come in at the rate of about one per annum per man—the pains of production seem to be like the pains of female labor. I feel like giving up the group idea up entirely and going it alone if our project—such an easy one, and under discussion now for some two years—is to fall through like this. I also feel that we have been betraying you and Nixon and Warren in trying to interest you in such a group and even urging you personally to come down here and cast in your physical lot with us.

Here is what I propose. Let's get an offer from a publisher for fall publication. Then let's publish even if we have to leave out some of our best men; they can come in later when we do other books. Here are the certainties in the way of contributions: yourself, Don, Lytle, myself, Lanier, Nixon, Barr; 7 there. Then let us immediately close with some other contributors from the following list: Warren (whom we are waiting to hear from), Wade and Owsley (who *might* make the sacrifice of their prior projects and write for us), Young (even if we have to consider him just about half a loyal member), and J. G. Fletcher.[1] I think we ought to land three of them, making 10 in all, and enough for a book. Then let us recast the Symposium as a statement of principles, rather miscellaneous but more full and leisurely than in their present form, and get the signatures of all, even the non-contributors, to it. If one of several essays of mine already written will do as my stint, I'd gladly get that part of it in shape. For the immediate present we might waive the idea of printing the Articles separately, and come back to it for decision a little later. I think this general scheme will be agreed to, as the brethren are very amiable, just lackadaisical.

Would you then undertake something like this? First, to get Fletcher at once to come in; we need him, and I think he is one of the best critical minds writing English today. Second, to see if a publisher is willing to close with us on some such terms as this: A symposium by 8 or 10 men, for fall publication, if the manuscript must be submitted by April 30; or a symposium by 10 or 12 men if it may be submitted as late as July 1 or 15. Of course, for the present we can not quite name the contributors; but I think we could do so in three weeks time. Once the trade was completed there would be no backing out, and everybody would fall to. As to the publisher, you have named Harper's; I would add also the possibility of Coward-McCann,—I have thought before to write and ask you to see Jesse Carmack, a Tennessean (Harvard) with them, very well up on things, and very anxious to get a manuscript from this section; he is a responsible man with Coward-McCann, and I understand from him that they propose to *sell books*: I should think they are as good people as the publishers of the Humanist book. Don says also that you should see Macmillan; they have been after us for a long time for something; and Doubleday-Doran, where there is Munson, ditto.[2] If these moves meet with your approval, and if you feel that you have enough assurance on our part to enable you to approach publishers, I hope you will do it.

About that county paper. I begin to feel that this is peculiarly Lytle's project and mine,—I hear nothing from the others in regard to it. But Lytle is in earnest; he remarks that if his crops are good, we will be able to make a down payment next fall and start off. So I am not giving up that idea; only warning you that the state of the group mind does not seem after all to be as heroic as I may have judged.

On the matter of subjects for articles. Several more were developed last night, in addition to the standing untaken ones of Education, and Religion, and Race in the South. We need an essay defining an agrarian society, in terms of economic distinctions; and indicating the place in it of cities, professions, and industries. Also one on the place of woman in an agrarian society. There isn't a doubt that the women have revolted from the farm and that the old-fashioned farm wasn't meant for them, and the new agrarianism must be improved for their benefit; otherwise the women are invariably our enemies, and frankly I am afraid of them. Another article of great value would be a simple but full one on how the actual countryman's life ought to be made livable again; Andrew knows all about that, and it is just possible that is his true article; he sees that the farmer now lives out of a paper sack, and that farms are getting industrialized just like factories, etc., etc.

This is about all I can write for the present. I'll write more fully later.

Yours
John

P.S. The meeting was a great success—the brethren once more in line—Don professing uncertainty however—he is developing into Hamlet, discontented but unproductive—it's rather serious—I fear all of us pedagogical Humanists are doing likewise—now it seems that Wade & Owsley can do us articles within two or three months anyway, by a great effort—I really think we are saved.

JCR

P.S. We can safely leave the composition of the articles to the brethren, I think. If there develops a piece of duplication we can consult & edit then; it isn't likely, I believe. Your idea of cross-references & Don's of an editorial final resume both mighty fine, especially yours. Let's put confidence in our men and turn them loose. This probably necessary in view of shortness of time.

---

1. All of the men named contributed essays to *I'll Take My Stand*, excepting Stringfellow Barr.

2. Gorham B. Munson, a literary hodman who founded and edited the magazine *Secession* and was associated with the Lost Generation before this time.

To Allen Tate

October 28, [1930]

Dear Allen—

Thanks for your magnificent reinforcements.

I believe the letter had better wait a little. The fact is, I have letters now from both Milton and Knickerbocker, both expressing great concern.[1] I'll save them to show you. Milton asks me whether to kill the article, send it back to the author for revision, or print my letter conspicuously beside the article. I am replying that this is for him to decide; that I don't mind the review provided my letter appears beside it.

Knickerbocker writes that he isn't conscious of any wrongdoing. And will I please note in pencil the offending passages in order that they may be modified? I am answering him as per the enclosed carbon.

I guess I have done myself out of a big ad, for I feel that Milton and K. between them are now going to kill the thing. In a way I am sorry, but then when the matter was brought to me in advance I was bound to make the protest I did, or I would have been making myself an accessory.

And just think, Knickerbocker is a Doctor of Philosophy and a Bachelor not only of Arts but of Divinity!

I'll let you know what happens, and in the meantime—I thank you heartily.

I had wondered if Andy was not with you. Please tell him that I have a God without Thunder for him if he will do me the honor, and the reason I haven't sent it was that I didn't know his address; but that now I have no wrapping paper, and will just hold it till he comes by.

I'm glad you are going to Virginia, and we'll talk it all over, battlefields, vehicles, strategy, and everything, when you and Carolyn come Saturday.[2]

Mr. Finney discovers and hands Don the strangest exhibit:[3] Barr has reversed himself and stolen our thunder in the review of Odum's book.[4] I enclose it. But save it: it may prove highly useful in a rebuttal. Or is it possible, after all, that Barr is converted and is going to crawl out of the debate? He writes me rather lovingly about getting the Harper proofs and liking the stuff. Probably I flatter ourselves, however, in thinking of anything so desperate as his reneging.

Yours ever,
John

I'm sorry I made such an unprofitable comment on the *Virgil*. The article shows up grand.[5]

---

1. George Fort Milton, editor of the Chattanooga *News*, and W. S. Knickerbocker. The article for the *News*, written by W. B. Hesseltine, professor of history at the University of Chattanooga, was generally critical of the Agrarians: the author stated that the promise that a life on the soil would enrich the arts "has no basis in fact." Knickerbocker's generally favorable review appeared in the *Saturday Review of Literature*, VII (December 20, 1930), 467. He called *I'll Take My Stand* the "most audacious book ever written by Southerners."

2. Caroline Gordon Tate.

3. James I. Finney (1877–1930) was editor and part-owner of the Columbia *Daily Herald* from 1907 to 1926 and was then editor of the Nashville *Tennessean* until his death.

4. Stringfellow Barr, then at the University of Virginia, had agreed to engage the Agrarians in public debate. Seeking ways to present their views to the public, Ransom was eager to debate almost anyone. Barr did debate Ransom before approximately 3,500 persons in Richmond, Virginia, on November 14, 1930. Here he refers to Barr's review of Howard W. Odum's *American Epoch: Southern Portraiture in the National Picture* (*Books*, October 26, 1930, p. 2). Odum (1884–1954), a sociologist, taught at the University of North Carolina and was a leader of the Chapel Hill regionalists.

5. "The Bi-Millennium of Virgil," *New Republic*, LXIV (October 29, 1930), 296–98.

To Allen Tate

[December, 1930]

Dear Allen:

Here's a quick draught of my ideas, for you to go on and elaborate if you like, or use in any way that it seems to have a use. It's clear from my statement that we have a brand-new economic idea to spring; that it might appeal even to industrialists (industry for industrialists, back to the farm with the farmers); that we are no longer negative but positive; that our sectionalism is honest and even helpful.

My idea in the *Signatories* section is to claim briefly for the group (1) a literary & journalistic competence, (2) acquaintance with the farm problem, and (3) general responsibility. Perhaps some generalizations to that effect followed by a list of signatories with specific professional status, books, etc. The seven are Tate, Lytle, Davidson, Lanier, Owsley (who tells us to sign *anything* for him), Wade, and Ransom.

But stop! Davidson is extremely recalcitrant; not to say ugly. He's got conscientious objections, which get stronger every morning. He reminds us of his article against Yankee philanthropies. He says: "I'd prefer our support from a group of Southern backers." I say: "Who'll get them?" He says, "It will take time." I would say it's his genius (passion) for killing time that is at the bottom of this. I'll show him what I've written and maybe he'll sign.

H. A. Moe is in Atlanta Dec. 10 and (if necessary) Dec. 11, in care of E. W. Moise, Citizens & Southern Bank Bldg.[1] He's due in Chicago morning of Dec. 13. If you want to wire him, Lanier will meet him here and drive him to Clarksville: maybe Don will go. Even if he only leaves Atlanta night of Dec. 11, he'll be here at 7 Friday morning, and have about 12 hours till the Dixie Flier passes Guthrie that p.m. I wish I could join in this movement. If you want to reach me—it's hardly likely of course—I'm in care Dr. John M. Fletcher, Tulane University, N.O., from evening of Dec. 12 to morning Dec. 16.

Allons! mes enfants terribles, mes petits pauvres, mes frêres.

John

In haste.

P.S. If Don says he'll break with us before signing for a Guggenheim I'm in favor nevertheless of signing. You have my proxy.

P.S. Here's Saturday's Chattanooga *News*. A fine spread. Hesseltine I think does as well as anybody could do to answer an unanswerable position. Save this or return to Don or Lanier, please.

---

1. Henry Allen Moe was executive director of the Guggenheim Foundation.

To Allen Tate

December 5, 1930

Dear Allen:

The note of yesterday didn't get mailed, and since then I have had your exciting communication which would indicate that the Armies of the Lower-Cumberland will be fully occupied next week without going on foreign excursions.

Yes, Knickerbocker is my opponent, and he came in the office here Wednesday, after first asking if I had a gun. He is as cheery, friendly, bright, and foolish as ever but I do not find it in my unmilitary nature to continue to feel sore at him. Perhaps I'll have a reversion about the 15th inst. We discussed the debate and decided that he would lead off on the ground that *he attacked our book*; and I would defend. Ten-minute rebuttals. I expect to enjoy this bout, having outgrown I hope my first greenness. I expect even more to enjoy New Orleans and Louisiana and will bring you and Gen. Lytle the fullest reports.

I will talk the Moe prospectus fully with Gens. Lanier and Davidson and will assure you of spirited reinforcements from this section so far as my influence avails anything. As I must move my force at dawn of the 11th, it will not be possible for me to join in your movement. But I consider it the largest operation in which any of the patriot troops have yet participated and extend my heartiest good wishes.

Davidson and I called on Gen. Owsley. He leaves tomorrow for Florida to fish, swim, and live in the sun. His spirits are far from broken, and he promises to keep in closest touch with us.

You'll be hearing from us very shortly.

Yours,
John

P.S. The Republican General [George Fort] Milton keeps writing to the effect that he thinks Gen. Lytle has written well in answer to the traitor Hesseltine.

P.S. II. You never heard such gloom as Don emanates on the Moe skirmish. It's loss of honor, suicide, and mayhem. But he consents to talk for an hour with Lanier & me this evening. I'll do my best. I rely on Gen. Lanier's military intuition.

To Louis Untermeyer

July 7, 1931

Dear Louis:

While I am in Europe this following year, I shall see if I can't run over to Dr. Freud's clinic and get my correspondence-inhibition analyzed and cured. I start most of my letters by apologizing for my sins as a correspondent. I am easily the world's best non-correspondent. I am especially at fault with you, considering how sincerely grateful I am for your several extreme favors, and how constant and affectionate my feelings towards you and Jean after your little visit of last year to Nashville. So there's that. Bear with an erring brother.

Won't you folks be in England some time or other between October 1, 1931, and September 10, 1932?[1] If so, let's plan at once to communize: I think we are going to take the family Ford; it will certainly be a comfort, and we are putting up the alibi that it will also be an economy. It's our idea to stay mostly in Britain, and, in the winter at least, to find a quiet nest somewhere in Devon or Cornwall. We're going to go till we get lodgings some place that is just right. I've no idea of playing the literary circles, or doing anything except getting an eyeful of British country landscape and leading a life as easy and comfortable as possible on a fairly impecunious base. I shan't try particularly to work but will see if I've lost the art of loafing, and will hope that some poetry will want to come out eventually. Robb likes golf, the kids like ponies and bathing and fresh air, and I like 'em all. I'm going to play the po're schoolmaster on a holiday. But we'll all get a little homesick and therefore I hope you and Jean will come along. We could do a beautiful month together, whether at golf, bridge, walking, talking, or lettering. We'll probably run over to Brittany or the Loire for a spell next spring, and we're going to try to train the children to be left alone when we want to leave them.

The reason I've just cancelled passage on the Britannic August 1, and asked for reservations on the same boat Sept. 26, is that I've got a little book to finish before we go. It's called "Capitalism and the Land."[2] I'm not so hot for capitalism as an abstract proposition, but the fact is that I debated and discussed and even wrote that topic all last winter, and now figure that I might as well "capitalize" my efforts into a book and get it behind me. Your estimable house now has a 20,000-word sample under consideration and I expect to hear every day whether they want to sign me a contract for the whole. I'm now in the 5th week of a 6-weeks course at Memphis—West Tennessee Teachers College—where I'm repeating myself sadly in some lectures I've done here now for 4 or 5 years. After next week I return to Nashville to work hard about 8 weeks and get that book in shape. Any chance of your making Tennessee this summer? I've an impression you're dispensing light and poetry over the Union impartially just now—weren't you out at Greeley the other day? Come on to Nashville and help me with my lay ideas on the economic situation.

I used the 4th Edition in my course on Modern Literature at Vanderbilt in the spring, and am using it here now.[3] It stands up fine. However, I have two posers for you: (1) Didn't Robinson say that Reuben Bright "tore down *to* the slaughter house"? I think he ought to have said that, anyhow. And (2) is Robert Frost's "Fire and Ice" a deep and philosophical poem, rather than just a pleasant conceit? When he says "Ice is great," that's an easy little colloquialism that seems to me decisive as to the tone and intention of the piece.

These are minor cavillings. My prose class wants me to prove to them today that the best poems in the language are not Walter Malone's "Opportunity" and Kipling's "If." I've already proved that Kilmer's "Trees" wasn't. So you see what an elementary sort of service I'm having to perform. At the Nineteenth Century Club (well named) last week I read my "Captain Carpenter," and am told that some of the elder sisters felt contaminated by some of the language and went home to read "Idylls of the King" for purification.

My family is in Denver and Wyoming—a set of grand-parents lives there. I'm lonesome. But, with much love to you and Jean, I'm

Ever yours,
John Crowe Ransom

---

1. Ransom and his family spent the academic year 1931–32 and most of the summer of 1932 in England.
2. Never published.
3. Ransom is referring to Untermeyer's *Modern American and British Poetry* (New York: Harcourt, Brace, 1928).

To Allen Tate

Starcross, Devon, November 23, [1931]

Dear Allen:

Though we are as well situated as possible, sometimes we get a bit homesick—if not to be under the Star Spangled Banner, at least under the Stars and Bars. This evening while the wind howls I'd like to discuss a few matters with you, Sister Caroline, and Brother Andrew, and Brother Don.

But speaking of Brothers Andrew, Don, et al, what-in-hell is *Ol Brer Ransom and His Friends*?[1] I see that for a title of something in the contents of the Fall number, *Hound & Horn*. Sounds like the indefatigable Knickerbocker to me.

Your note on Milton is a grand piece of critical work—the best thing written in years on Milton.[2] Better than that, of course, inasmuch as *nothing* critical has been written on Milton in my time. I would like to talk with you, however, on a couple of your points. In the first place, do I understand you as going over to Richards' view that any private myth will serve the poet, if only he can sustain it? Is then the poet only a novelist? And what about the social sanction behind the myth; in other words, what about his use of a myth which happens to be *the Myth*, the religious credo of his society! You and I perhaps rather take to Milton's myth as our myth already; what about the heathen who find it alien and obnoxious? It would be my policy as an expounder of Milton, I think, to try to make the said heathen believe in his myth after all, as a perfectly reasonable one; while it seems to be your policy rather to say, don't bother to believe it but just see how consistently he uses it, how coherent he makes it, and what an excellent body it gives to his work. Perhaps I exaggerate our difference here. I feel it the more because I suppose I am rather indebted to you for the point that behind the major poet is not only a bit of a myth but *the Myth*—his and his society's as well. I used to think that dramatic poetry, or narrative poetry, about our sort of fictitious material would do for major poetry; I thought of Elizabethan drama as a proof. But for some years I've been changed, and have felt that religion must inform poetry, or at any rate great poetry: witness the Greek drama and all epic. As for Milton, I think that his passion and solemnity flow from his conviction that he is a prophet expounding orthodoxy; not from his use of a story invented for the occasion.

The other point is about excitement in Milton's diction and style. He may lack the extremely local & violent excitements of the metaphysical poets. He has extraordinary excitement all the same. There is hardly a predictable phrase in Milton—he avoided it like the devil. He was in his style what Yeats is in his—always putting a quirk, a twist, upon his language; sometimes a matter of the phrase, sometimes a matter of the versification. Compare him with Spenser and see how much he has added. Spenser is the poet who is all smoothness; Milton is his master, who never does routine work and keeps his mind always laboring. His facility, or rather felicity, rests on top of the character or energy of his lines and makes them look right and easy, but the veneer is deceptive. It takes an active eye and an active ear to get Milton. In Shakespeare, again, you find a lot of pure Spenserian melody without much intellectual activity—speeches of kings, lovers, conventional stage characters; and you find also passages where the incongruities are piled up thick, creating the most intense excitement. The latter are pure genius, of course, but not necessarily the highest art. Milton is always an artist, the most subtle one, I have rather thought, in classical English.

You will see what point is in these criticisms of mine. I have not time to state them more precisely. I trust your aesthetic sense very firmly. You saw these points all the time, I dare say, and I am only quarreling with an emphasis you put on other points in a short article.

We are settled very nicely on the Devon coast, 10 mi. from Exeter. The beach is very fine; so is the country; the food is excellent and we are comfortable. The golf course has gorse and heather and sea, the perfect combination.

One very important feature in our situation is an arrangement with the Principal of University College at Exeter (my old Philosophy Don of Oxford days) whereby I go in three mornings a week, do a bit of college work, and get on the payroll to the amount of about £200 for the year. (The year is 3 terms of 10 weeks each, with a month at Christmas and a month at Easter for vacation). I hope this is perfectly ethical for a Guggenheim Fellow—I haven't referred it to the powers, however. It has given us all the personal acquaintance we could desire, and it's a fine set of people too. The extra tidbit is helpful, as you may imagine. While on that subject, let me say that our lodgings, inclusive, cost us £5–14–0 per week, which is now well under $25.00 in good hard American money.

I have made so bold as to add a little to your literary burdens and to my obligations to your kindness. In this way. I sent Harper's 25,000 words of my book manuscript; with instructions to send it to you if they didn't want it.[3] I offered to furnish the whole manuscript, 65,000 words, by Jan 15. I wanted $500 advance in royalty. If you get it within a few days, will you please serve it to another publisher for me. Harcourt, & Scribner, have declined it.

Again: I sent an article on England (*A Lion in Distress*) to *Harper's Magazine*, with similar instructions.[4] I am nothing if not flattering as to your generosity. This article, by the way, is sound, but not so hot in some ways. I have been at too great pains to talk kindly of England while prophesying doom. (As a member of the College Staff here, etc.)

I should greatly relish some personal news. It has been borne in upon me that I am not due any until I take the initiative, so I start with you. How is landed life? To me it seems more and more the only life possible to sensitive people. Eliot, by the way, has some remarks again to that effect in the October *Criterion*, which I suppose you have seen; a nice piece of dialectic.[5]

I have made no effort to crash the literary gates but have met a few interesting people. Christopher Dawson lives two miles away from me, and has called, but we were out. I shall meet him in a day or so.[6]

Robb says it's bedtime. She's just been reading in the *Times* the complaint of the Hon. Sec. of the Anti-Grey-Squirrel Campaign who says: "Why have not English birds as good a right to our trees as American tree rats?" She picks up all such references and has quite a collection. I got used to them when she was a little girl in school.

Love to Caroline and all the faithful.

Yours ever,
John C. R.

---

1. Ransom is referring to W. S. Knickerbocker's "Mr. Ransom and the Old South," *Sewanee Review*, XXXIX (April, 1931), 222–39.

2. In "A Note on Donne," *New Republic*, LXX (April 16, 1932), 212–13, Tate argues that Milton's "settled belief in the relation be-

tween a fixed human nature and a perfect divine order . . . makes Milton's mythology possible."

3. "Land!" was a manuscript that Ransom worked on for two years but did not publish.

4. Never published.

5. T. S. Eliot, "A Commentary," *Criterion*, XL (October, 1931), 65–72.

6. Christopher Dawson (1889–1970), philosopher and cultural historian, was a lecturer at University College at Exeter during 1930–36.

To Allen Tate

May, 19 [1932]

Dear Allen:

Regretfully, I must admit defeat in my Egyptian tutorship project. That's pretty definite now. The Principal, my former Greats tutor, is apparently very anxious to have you semi-officially attached to his staff, and unwilling to promise any remunerative labors in particular, and unlikely, I fear, to have any for you. But I must do him the courtesy of extending his warm invitation to you to come and make your home here and fraternize with his faculty.

The project would have gone through if at the critical moment the Carnegie Foundation for International Peace (!), who sent Greig to Vanderbilt, had not notified the Principal they were sending to him next year Dr. Donald Macmurrey, historian, and, as it happens, an old friend of mine who started teaching at Vanderbilt with me, and who is the son of the late esteemed Professor Macmurrey of Peabody.[1] Though the Principal understands that you are a better man than Macmurrey, Macmurrey is a gift, and you are expensive. The budget here has had to be slashed this year and may be due for more slashing, and the Principal is too doubtful of his power to divert English pounds in the direction of American men of letters without meeting with complaint, Etc etc. The upshot of it is that the project is simply a dud and I do not see the slightest hope of its working to your interest. I am sorry.

Again I raise the whisper, To Mexico! But I whisper discreetly—this is your party. I find, and I think everybody else who comes to Europe on a family scale must find, that it is sure to cost more than you think, and if you are not very well guaranteed you are going to suffer from the feeling that you are a long way from home.

Since May 1, or before, we have been living on a nice old Devon farm out on the moors or highlands—real agrarianism. We get good air, infinite pleasure, much food, pleasant service; it's a place of which the address is worth having, and superior to our former place where we stayed the six months; though no place for winter, for the temperature is at least 10 degrees above that of the coast. However, we pay now 7 1/2 guineas per week, which is £7–17–6, which is $25 or a little to [the] rise of that; whereas we paid at the other place about £6 or £6–10–0, figuring it on an inclusive basis. That last is a minimum figure, I am sure, for board and lodging; the other is more the usual thing. You can do somewhat better if you take rooms and attendance, which means that you buy your own food, or at least have the landlady buy it and itemize it for you. That's really better for the other reason that you can feel more free to ask for what you like. You can also rent a cottage, at about £2 or £2–10–0, hire a servant, and live as you please; better living, but more trouble, and scarcely money-saving unless you skimp.

I don't know anything at the moment about France. Robb and I hope to run over for a week in Paris, but haven't as yet. In fact, we've lived like mice when they are quiet, but during the summer we'll do a little whirlwinding about these parts, probably leaving the children on the farm where they can do no damage.

Sorry especially I have kept you waiting so long to get this unsatisfactory information. I'm anxious to see what you decide on, and to know if we shan't get to meet somewhere this summer.

A letter yesterday from Harcourt turns down my "Land!" for the second time, which makes it pretty conclusive. And I find they've notified you that they have it ready to send wherever you may advise. Again I impose on you. But this time I think it's really better to withdraw it from circulation for the moment, if not for good. I had wanted you to see it in its present form, which, I am sure, is much better than its earlier; and I would have suggested that Macmillan might be interested. But this is too faraway a point to negotiate from, and the economic subject matter shifts so rapidly that an utterance becomes an anachronism before it can get to print. Don't peddle it any further, therefore. It may be that in the fall I can take it up again profitably. But it may be, on the other hand, that my kind of economics won't do, and that I'd better stick to poetry and aesthetics. I've learned a lot of economics lately, too! But I must confess I haven't the economist's air, flair, style, method, or whatnot. I may wait till we have an organ of our own to land my stuff in when it is my turn to be editor.

And I think another article probably came to you from *Harper's*—a sort of travel story, innocents-abroad, etc.—Harper's man, Allen, thought the *Atlantic Monthly* might like it—that he himself was notoriously hard to please, etc. Just hold that piece too, please: I'm going to harden it, touch it up, cutting out all but the part about speechmaking before Rotary Clubs.

The article on the land will appear in the July *Harper's*, I believe.[2] It is slightly but not offensively cut from what it was.

English spring is delightful, they say, though it hasn't appeared hereabouts this season. Much rain & cold; the leaves are not halfway out yet. But every day seems a little more promising. And we are all well and enjoying life. Everybody remarks that Reavill is much improved in color, spirits, and (somewhat) weight.

I've got a lot of observations on poetry to get off my chest. But not at this writing, as I've got to prepare two public speeches. Walter de la Mare made a keen address—i.e. read a keen paper—on poetic technique some two weeks ago, and I go on in a few days with "Poetry & Happiness."[3] Perhaps I'll send it to you to see if, as Southern Editor, you can use it or recommend it for *Hound & Horn*. It won't be as sappy as the title sounds, and in fact I'll give it another title.

Best regards to Sister Caroline.

Yours ever,
John

1. Donald LeCrone Macmurrey (b. 1890), an author and economic historian.

2. The essay "Land! An Answer to the Unemployment Problem," did appear in *Harper's Magazine*, CLXV (July, 1932), 216–24.

3. Apparently this essay was never published.

To Allen Tate

Nashville, October 25, [1932]

Dear Allen:

Affectionate regards from the Ransoms to Sister Caroline and Nancy and yourself. We like being back home, but we miss you.

We were mighty sorry to miss the reunion in Paris. We were in London all that time, wishing it was Paris, though glad that if it wasn't Paris it was really London. The children were homesick but managed to like London pretty well; Lyons' Corner House more than Westminster Abbey, and American movies more than Buckingham Palace. We hadn't had the heart to leave them at Meacombe Farm and maybe it was just as well. They are at Peabody again, and Reavill is O.K.—getting better all the time, and fully recovered in spirits. They didn't care at all for New York, where we stopped five days; Reavill asked when we were going back to America, which we did at length, and felt much better for it.

Don is gone for the year,[1] Red and Cinina are here, and Andrew spent three or four days amongst us recently. Don is on Wade's place at Marshallville, Ga., and writes Wade that his soul is finally at peace, or words to that effect. I saw him here just before school opened. He had tur'ble hard times last spring here, and is still one of the most intransigent spirits incarnated since Saul of Tarsus kicked against the pricks, but I believe he will pull through.[2] You know, our rebel doctrines are good for all [of] us but Don, and very doubtful there, because they are flames to his tinder.

Red is as good a head and heart as I've known and it's a pleasure to be with him. I haven't really passed time with him before since the Great Fugitive Days and doubtless never knew him as others of you did. He and C. have taken the foreman's cottage on the magnificent Dr. Burch place, East of the river—his rental consists in fixing up the house and living in it. It's an idyllic spot, a cabin in a bower.

Andrew is moving in the same direction I am, mentally. I hope you won't be too disgusted. He's prepared to accept *some* industrialization in the South to keep our farmers from feeding out of the hands of the Yankees; for they have to have commerce with *somebody* though that is not to be their prime object of existence. I guess I've gone off even further. In England last year I got so used to defending America that I forgot there were two or half a dozen Americas; I'm trying to see if we can't save the whole business, as Abraham tried to save all Sodom, though it was a wicked city. About Andrew, however: his finances are mighty bad; one of the in-laws of his Dad is trying to sell 'em out or something and a crisis is approaching. He's gone back there to be on the spot and butt-in wherever he can. He read me some scenes of a play which were magnificent: Southern character stuff, very broad, not quite farcical, obviously something that would be a revelation on Broadway because of its color and picturesque quality, if A. doesn't try to make a fine, subtle, consecutive play out of it. Comic, not tragic. I urged him to go ahead and be content to start with that, not to write the Great Southern Play the first time.[3]

Robb and I have gone semi-agrarian. We have a two-acre place out on Glendale Lane, a stone's throw from the John Trotwood Moore[4] place on Granny White. Our renter of last year is again a renter this year, and we're making a little money on the deal. But we won't stay there, we're going out still further in another year.

I should have written before this to tell you about my commission to do the Pound essay for Ford.[5] But I've been mighty rushed, and waited to see if my mind was really set the way it is. It is. I'm not the man to write one of the essays. I'm not a Pound man. I have not read the Cantos, but on the strength of the *Collected Poems* I see I'm hopeless. There's hardly a creative poem there if you except the satires on contemporary figures and custom. Marvellous translations from the heroic dead, in small fragments. If the poems were stories, I'd say he was a model historical romancer. But that's not enough to go on. He's a Humanist who thinks he's a modern. After I expressed these heresies, Red pointed me to the Pound-passages in *Time and Western Man*, which I had read and forgotten—unless they influenced me unconsciously. I wouldn't be savage about it, as Wyndham Lewis is, but I couldn't possibly gainsay his exposition, which is to the effect that Pound is an ultra-conservative and classicist who has advertised all his life as a Revolutionist. These are my sentiments. Please convey them with my fullest regrets, apologies, and thanks-for-the-honor to Ford; whose notion of doing honor to one neglected is grand.

My poor book is nearly a total loss—I don't like it. It would have been a passable book published a year ago.[6] Several publishers nearly took it. Within these next ten days I will have kicked it into the incinerator or else taken a grand new start and started over on a new outline altogether. The latter course would relieve my system, and I am getting a little bit gone on my new (hypothetical) approach. I've never thanked you sufficiently for your kindness & trouble.

Saturday evenings the Warrens, Laniers, and Ransoms sit about the Ransoms' green table; with possibly a bachelor or two on hand to furnish the sports of war. We speak reverently of you-all.

Your letter sounded like good tidings from what is commonly reputed here to be an evil land. Clearly there are two Frances, and you've chosen the better one. I hope you are all happy.

Yours,
John

P.S. Any errands? messages? odd jobs? I'll do any of them for you according to direction.

JCR

---

1. Donald Davidson was on leave for the academic year 1932–33 and had been replaced by Robert Penn Warren.

2. Ransom is referring to the destruction of Wesley Hall by fire; Davidson and his wife had an apartment there.

3. This play by Andrew Lytle was not published.

4. John Trotwood Moore (1858–1929), a minor southern writer who was the father of Merrill Moore.

5. Apparently Ford Madox Ford had invited Ransom to write an essay on Ezra Pound. Ransom later reviewed Pound's *Eleven New Cantos, Saturday Review of Literature*, XI (January 19, 1935), 434–35.

6. "Land!" (apparently Ransom destroyed this manuscript).

To Andrew Lytle

Albuquerque, N.M., July 15, 1933

Dear Andy:

I imagine you getting right down to the soil, extracting strength, flourishing like the bay tree, and living handsomely on—among other fine things—sorghum molasses. I hope the crops are panning out right. There are no crops in this country to speak of, the landscape is mostly useful to painters, and to Mexicans who can live on beans.

Haven't seen you since about early May—you weren't there for Fletcher's visit and the Fugitive meeting.[1] Fletcher wants us to do another book at once, he's a-rarin'. He's out here at Santa Fe, by the way, for the summer. He and I represented the South at the South Western regional conference, and I must say or shouldn't that we had much more of a program and an agreement on things than the local gentlemen had.

I enclose the poem I read at the Fugitive meeting.[2] Red apparently liked it, the others have been fairly non-committal.

McFadden's *Liberty* magazine has got our agrarian doctrine on its practical side. They are continually having both editorials and articles on getting the farmer out of the money markets, and getting the unemployed on the land. The movement seems to be so logical that anybody can see it now. But the long look ahead is not part of these pieces. They have no philosophy on the subject, just a line for immediate action; neither a political nor a moral philosophy.

My stay has been pleasant here, though the work has been rather heavy. It's hot in the daytime, but dry, and it's cool at nights. The country around, up in the hills, is grand, but being here without a car I haven't had much of a go at it. The Indian and Spanish interest makes this country, from the point of view of the white man. I'm keen on Spanish cooking, music, language, and general outlook, even though it's all rather debased as it's come down through the Mexicans; the average Spaniard here is mixed Indian and Spanish. But as far as that's concerned, the Indians here are not so bad. These Indians were not killers, they raised corn, had beautiful handicrafts, and built pretty good adobe cities; they still do, and have; and it's a pity they're going in for white man's radio and whiskey.

Am getting pretty homesick, though, after six weeks away from family and tribe. I'm through here the 29th and will get home about the 1st or 2nd. After that I'm pretty indefinite. I don't know what Sister Robb's ideas are, quite—I know she's been negotiating for a house for the year, probably a very rural sort of place well out of town. We may put in a little time closing a trade and then move in. I'd like for us to pay you a visit if you want us and it's positively convenient to you-all; don't know whether I can depend on you to tell me honest or not. Must tackle some writing as soon as I can get sort of settled again.

Best regards to Mr. Lytle,[3] and take care of yourself. Much to talk over with you.

Yours
John R.

1. John Gould Fletcher had spoken to the Centennial Club in Nashville during the previous year.

2. "Autumn Grief to Margaret," *Saturday Review of Literature*, XI (September 29, 1934), 137; later published as "To Margaret."

3. Andrew Lytle's father Robert.

To Allen Tate

Nashville, [Autumn 1934]

Dear Allen:

A wire yesterday from [Seward] Collins (which I would enclose but have left at home) asks, "Who should review the N.C. Symposium *Culture in the South*, evidently deserving serious considerations?"[1] I take it he addresses me as a member of the group. Don, Red, Andrew, and I think you are the man. I wired Collins to that effect today. He seems not yet to have a copy of the work, so I send by this mail Don's copy to you, and I told Collins in the wire to let you (or us) have another when he could: granting that he'll want to take a look at it himself when it arrives.

It's a huge, important and most various book, evidently. From a casual inspection I judge that your own book is mentioned by half of the writers at least, with all shades of approval or disapproval; that many of the present contributors are Agrarians (see, surprisingly, Clarence Poe), and that these are the most temperate and reasonable in their performance. I'm anxious to go through it all when there is time.

I judge that Collins would like it at once,—perhaps he's going to press about Monday week, the 15th as he says he's gradually moving up the lead-date. Maybe you can drop him a line to make sure that he holds a place for your review in the forthcoming number. Maybe on the other hand, of course, you find yourself too busy to fool with it; though I hope not, and Red and Andrew imagine that you have an open period, more or less, just now while waiting to start on your library work.

And there my responsibility ends. But not my interest. You will undoubtedly be read by every contributor to the volume, and that's a crowd of important people; add to it the other important Southerners who'll read the book and hear about your remarks, and you get the crowd that's run the South. Nobody can talk to them as you can. In the main, the enemy is coming reluctantly over to our side. I suggest that we be wise, fixed, but not repelling. But you know more about that than I do.

The week end at Benfolly was wonderful. I think liquoring-up at midday is the nicest way I've tried: you get the whole effect and don't have to waste some of the magic hours in sleep. We had a fine time.

I left my Eliot on your mantle, and Robb thinks she left a handkerchief. I don't need the Eliot now, having a library copy, and Robb has handkerchiefs even, so don't bother till you come to town, and then if you see them (and don't want the Eliot) bring them along.

Yours,
John

1. W. T. Couch (ed.), *Culture in the South* (Chapel Hill: University of North Carolina Press, 1933). Tate's review appeared in the *American Review*, II (February, 1934), 411–32.

To Allen Tate

[1934]

Dear Allen:

You are right of course about the poetry—unless there is an error about mine, which I am inclined to pardon. We will follow your plan.

I am sending the Essay to New York as directed.[1] Both Curry and Don read it, with applause. I have just re-read it, after a week on an essay of my own, and will put down a few of my reflections.[2] It is a very important essay, the best in the field. My own will not be contradictory—couldn't be, for I endorse about everything in yours. Just another set of terms, a slightly different angle of approach.

1) You do Spenser a little wrong. He's probably in the main not very allegorical, just loose and romantic in the Medieval Romance sense. (Sp.'s contemporaries were allegorizing Ariosto, for reasons of piety; there's hardly an ounce of allegory in him.) Sp. had his tongue in his cheek. His best things are digressions, stories with no bearing on the plan which he outlined for Raleigh. He couldn't bother with his plan really.

2) You don't notice a large tract of poetry—the "pure poetry" which George Moore talks about [in] an anthology is the poetry of things. That's, logically, the primary, the first poetry.

3) You hit the nail on the head when you say that the scientific canon of truth can't apply to poetry. You do up Richards beautifully. But is there *no sort of truth* that is applicable to poetry? Taste, harmony, etc? Must it contain scientific truth only accidentally? If so, under what law does the poet compose?

4) If the body of science is true only in the sense that it leads to successful action, that is another way of going *Pragmatic* as a philosopher.

5) "Creation" is a big loose word. Poetic objects, images, even ideas, I suppose, are what the poet creates. Out of what? And again, by what law?

6) The last few pages are not up to the rest, in condensation and force. And (see 5 above) it's a let down to be told about creative poetry, "There it is, look for yourself."

7) Your term Platonism is exact, and historically the only word. I am using it heavily; I think independently, but one can't be sure. I've been telling students for years where to find Platonism in our everyday life and especially on Sundays.

8) My division of the types is this: *A* Physical poetry, or poetry of things; *B* Platonic poetry, or poetry of ideas (allegory, Victorian verse, etc.); and *C* metaphysical poetry which-to-define gives me all the pain of this particular essay. My title is, however: "Poetry—a Note in Ontology." There are things (or perceptions), and there are ideas; then they (rarely) have a beautiful union, which is metaphysical poetry. But what does *metaphysical* mean? Dryden started the word in this application; and I think the context shows he used it in the popular sense, the only one he could have mastered, of "supernatural," "mythical." I am back at my God-without-Thunder thesis. The poets must *animate* the barren ideas and relations; but they have been intimidated. Cowley started the modern weakness; see *The Mistress*; blazing with scientific current concepts; but see his recantation, and his handsome tribute to Hobbes. Hobbes was the enemy, the Satan. Hobbes was of

the "commonsense" school strictly; a naturalist philosopher. After Hobbes their name is legion.

9) The poets are not bold any longer; nor quick and terse; no guts. See the prolixity of 19th c. stuff, which is timidity. The mere things strike them as a safe recourse. Shelley writes—"Thou Young Dawn, Turn all thy dew to Splendor." But dew is a thing and splendor is a Platonic idea. The early 17th c. would have said: Turn thy dew, which is water, into fire, and accomplish the transsubstantiation of the elements.

10) There are in metaphysical poetry large-scale effects, as in Par. Lost, and small-scale effects, as in metaphors and conceits. Dryden probably admitted to the former as eligible; he was afraid the latter were silly; he grudgingly testified in favor of Milton, as soon as he could see him a classic, a Virgil or Dante, treating a big and still fairly presentable myth in a good sober way.

I am all het up over this topic, and not yet entirely articulate, as you probably have decided.

Love to the ladies.

Yours,
John

---

1. Allen Tate, "Three Types of Poetry," *New Republic*, LXXVIII (March 14, 1934), 126–28; (March 28, 1934), 180–82; and (April 11, 1934), 237–40.

2. Ransom is outlining "Poetry: A Note in Ontology" which first appeared in the *American Review*, III (May, 1934), 172–200.

To Allen Tate

[1934]

Dear Allen:

I can hardly tell you how much I appreciate your rather instant disposition of my manuscript, as well as your substantial approval of its content.[1]

I have revised it a bit. See the Inserts 8A and 23A. As for 8a, the illustration of Platonic Poetry, I felt that the easiest and obviousest would be the best. As to the definition of conceit as "meant metaphor," I decided after all not to change. For it is not put forward exactly as a formal or sufficient definition; and it carries my sense in an easy popular way, *i.e.*, it probably does well enough, and certainly it "represents" me at this stage of my working with the general idea. I suppose every man feels limited to his own terms; I do; they are pretty pedestrian terms too as a rule.

But see also pp. 17 and 18, p. 18 being brand-new. I re-state the poetic devices, sharpen them; and especially no. 2; in the present form I have the idea it comprehends some of the force of your "creative" poetry. And dwells on the difficult subject of the *truth* of poetry, reflecting my tendency to maintain that poetry has it.

See also the last page or so, where I have made the conclusion a little more sharply and less hurriedly.

I enclose the poem which you invite.[2]

I'll be mightily obliged if you can get H & H to (a) accept the two pieces (not meaning any disparagement to the Southern Editor) and (b) pay for them upon acceptance. State of the exchequer, etc. The unspeakable Collins has not paid me yet for my *Farmers*.[3]

I'm writing now to Fletcher pretty sharply—that he mustn't talk to split this-here agrarian group; that if he attacks Tate he has to fight J. C. R. and also undoubtedly the others of us; that he must stop being childish; that he mustn't assume that I'm for him. He is just mad, I suppose (in the dictionary sense).

Yes, we must talk further about the poetic problem. I don't undertake to claim knowledge as my province for a while yet; I'm not sure about a good many slippery articles of doctrine.

Sorry you didn't get out to the Couchville Pike.[4] Better luck, I'm hoping, next time.

Yours,
John

---

1. "Poetry: A Note in Ontology."

2. "Prelude to an Evening." Tate had asked to see the poem in his capacity as southern editor of *Hound and Horn*. Despite Tate's recommendation the poem was refused—apparently because the editor of *Hound and Horn* received a negative reaction from R. P. Blackmur.

3. "Happy Farmers," *American Review*, I (October, 1933), 513–35. Seward Collins, editor of the *American Review*, was notorious for his erratic payment of contributors. Both "Poetry: A Note in Ontology" and "Prelude to an Evening" were first published in the *American Review*.

4. Where Ransom was then living.

To Allen Tate

September 17, 1936

Dear Allen:

It looks as if I can't make Monteagle, at least till after school starts. The exchequer is low after I've been off the payroll a summer; and many chores have turned up. Best regards to Caroline & Andrew.

I wanted you to see my Santayana piece, which I enclose.[1] It's on our old subject, where our tendencies slightly clash. You are looking, I believe, for something special in the aesthetic experience, whereas I can see only an ordinary scientific or animal core *plus* glittering contingency.

In Sunday's *Banner* you will see my review of *Mediterranean*, if you think it's worth a dime, which it hardly is.[2] Excuse the performance in view of the medium. However, it has started me on an exciting excursion of thought which I want to bring before you. I say there in one place that *patriotism* is eating at *lyricism*. What is true in part for you (though a part that is ominously increasing) is true nearly in full for me: *patriotism* has nearly eaten me up, and I've got to get out of it.

So what? I think we need an objective literary standard. (The Church was an objective standard for certain planes of experience; it took a big burden off the private man.) Let's have it in an *American Academy of Letters*. Properly founded, it would counteract the Agrarian-Distributist Movement in our minds, and incidentally be a very great service to American literature. I'm suggesting that you and I found it; or you at least, since I'm diffident as to whether my public position would justify my part in it. Here's a little outline of specifications as they occur to me at this stage.

AMERICAN ACADEMY OF LETTERS

I. *Purpose.* In view of the fact that contemporary literature offers too many technically brilliant performers who lack solidity, completeness, flexibility, and background, A. A. L. is intended to supply public recognition exclusively to those who are not lacking.

II. *Qualifications for Membership.*

1. *Dignity.* As exhibited in literary tone, of course.
2. *Productivity.* A sort of quantitative requirement, not mechanically measured.
3. *Scope.* The specialist who works exclusively in one field ought nevertheless to be able to bring his whole mind to bear on it; there should be implications of completeness in his work, or perhaps by explicit philosophy and criticism he can indicate his completeness. The purely literary workman who performs in several fields with distinction is highly eligible. But, even the philosopher, scholar, historian, theologian, or scientist, if he meets this requirement, and the others (including especially 5), ought to be eligible.
4. *Positive Traditionalism.* This eliminates artists who exploit a novelty, or a revolutionary device, and do not assimilate and use the literary tradition; and, for that matter, those whose output is contrary to the interests of patriotism.
5. *Style.* The symbol of personal individuation, which is the real object of the American tradition and of any literary tradition.

III. *Proceedings.* An annual meeting for the election and seating of members; perhaps after the beginning under the rule that not more than 2 members may be elected in any one year. Coronation of the best book by a nonmember, and honorable mentions; the book crowned to receive a money prize raised (if possible) by subscription of participating publishers. Official publicity only.

IV. *Inauguration.* A list can be prepared of not more than 25 names of writers who seem most eligible; and a statement of the aims and principles of the AAL. You and I, or you alone, or you and somebody else, can send the list and statement to those whose names appear on the list. Each one will be requested to signify his allegiance or otherwise, and if he joins to suggest names not on the list that he may recommend or to indicate objections to names on the list. And if a substantial vote favors a new name, or if there is substantial objection to a given name, it must be understood that the list will be revised accordingly, and the persons on the revised list will have a winter meeting to complete and announce the initial organization.

Of course I've figured a little on a list. Alphabetically:

1. Cabell, J B
2. Cather, Willa
3. Cram, Ralph
4. Dodd (historian)
5. Dreiser—with reluctance—
6. Fletcher, J G
7. Freeman, Douglas
8. Frost, Robt—we're almost obliged—
9. Glasgow, E
10. Krutch, J W
11. Lewis, S—after all, he'a a Nobelist
12. Lovett, Robert Morss
13. MacLeish, A
14. Moore, Marianne
15. More, P E
16. Pound, Ezra
17. Ransom—?
18. Santayana
19. Seldes, Gilbert
20. Tate—excuse the inadvertence: this name leads all the rest.
21. Van Doren, M
22. Wade, John
23. Wharton, Edith
24. Winters, Y
25. Young, Stark

A list of *nearly* qualified:

1. Agar, H
2. Aiken, C—but this one is too weak, I guess.
3. Davidson, D
4. Gordon, C
5. Lytle, A
6. Owsley, F
7. Warren, R P

and Adams, J T—? Brooks, V[an Wyck]—Mumford, L—? Allen, H[ervey]—?

It's hard to reject the brethren and sistren, but give them time. We couldn't let our list be confused with a Fugitive or Agrarian organization. I think Owsley is the strongest, or Agar, at the moment. Is it possible that old Ford is an American citizen? Of course my list is very hasty. You will naturally have a good many differences, and I am sure some names I haven't thought of.

What do you think?

I hope you'll be getting down here before long. But not next Monday or Tuesday, because they're opening days.

Yours,
John C. R.

P.S. An Academy has got to be pretty catholic; a lot of them will necessarily be strange bedfellows. If too many alien persons seem to go into any national list, our only alternative would be a Southern Academy. But that is too close to our peculiar variety of patriotism, it wouldn't do us any good. Nor would it be formidable enough to get anywhere. We can whip out the Southern writers too easily.

---

1. "Art and Mr. Santayana," *Virginia Quarterly Review*, XIII (Summer, 1937), 420–36; reprinted in *The World's Body* (New York: Scribners, 1938).

2. Ransom's review of Tate's *The Mediterranean and Other Poems* appeared in the Nashville *Banner* for September 20, 1936.

To Allen Tate

[September, 1936]

Dear Allen:

I came home late yesterday p.m. to see your letter. Thanks for the invitation. It was not possible to get away to Monteagle—jobs & engagements.

All your remarks duly considered. It would be fine to elevate literature through an American Academy but pitiful if we proved unable to do the job. About that you would know better than I. I'm inclined to think a third sponsor, a third and fourth, say Young and Van Doren, might help if we wanted to try it. Would it be worth while to consult Young by correspondence before abandoning the idea? But I guess he'a a minority influence, a little bit like the Fugitives.

I think I'd favor a select national organization over a Southern. For myself, I've been thinking of a lot of names. A *Senate*? An *Institute*? A *College of Letters*? Or a more descriptive title: *Institute of Poetry and Tradition; Inst. of Literary Autonomy and Tradition; Inst. of Independent Letters? Inst. of Living Tradition*?

I would revise my statement of qualifications in order to include the main thing which I omitted: the *purity, autonomy, anti-Platonism* of the poetry. This kind of poetry is necessary but does not at all refuse to go with a history or philosophy which is literary or assimilated, sound, and deep. *Pure and Applied Literature*. The fiction and the verse pure; the others applied. And as for the purpose of the organization there would be two ineptitudes to combat: (1) the kind of writing which is merely specialized and lacks implications and background; (2) the ostensible pure art which is hired out to causes. You, for example, would qualify under either category; but might wish to keep the categories quite separate. Our intentions would be two, and they would look contradictory: to have our literature created by persons of philosophical capacity; to have its pure forms without taint of explicit philosophy. You will be able to phrase that. It should have a statement to which the writers of our complexion would instantly assent when they saw it.

I'll think of it some more between now and Friday. It might be that we feel sure enough at that time to call the right brethren into conference. But as you say we must ask them to take it or leave it. We can't leave much of anything open to popular determinations.

Yours,
John

P.S. I wish E. Wilson had not gone haywire. And that Cabell had had a palsied arm fifteen years ago. And that Don & Red had produced more books.

P.S. Robb says you-all stay with us when you come Friday. *Be sure.*

To Allen Tate

March 11, 1937

Dear Allen:

Thanks for your two letters.

I have never let myself think badly of Agar: he didn't understand us, and that shows he was not *of* us as much we might have thought.[1] But you have to give a man time. His actions in New York were quite honorable, as he had made no commitments to us which he had to violate. I like the tone of his letter. I hope to see him when he is here with the teachers, and I feel that friendship between us, so far as I am concerned, is entirely unimpaired. I enclose the letter you sent, after showing it to Lyle [Lanier] and talking it to Don. They are not hostile to Agar, certainly Lyle is not, and Don not openly. They think there's nothing particularly to do about it, and that we all acted right in our decision, and they must be correct about that.

I am delighted with your refusal to go to Northwestern considering the grounds of it, though I shall miss your company.[2] I think Don is going. He was the second choice. But he has not said definitely that he has accepted.

Though I hope to be steadfast also in keeping to literature and its margins, I find myself lapsing occasionally. For example, to go to Northwestern, where gainful labor is the sole consideration with me; and, a more dangerous case, to write an article I am now engaged on, which I can't talk to you without many words, but which I shall send when I have finished it; it's a sort of postscript to agrarianism as far as I am in it; but a thing I had to get off my chest.[3]

Very bad news now: your answer about the Writers Conference was most heartening. But we failed in getting any of three desired speakers: Freeman, Young, De Voto.[4] Sickness or engagements. All want to be asked later. One or two other eminent Southern writers answered in the negative too. So that it seemed that we couldn't have the most brilliant show this spring, but might have it if we waited till next spring. That is now our plan. I must talk with you some time about the conception and conduct of a Writers Conference. I hope that you-all will find yourselves in Nashville anyway about that time or earlier, so that we can have a real writer's confab if not a public ceremony.

Caroline's book is very beautiful, but I mean to write her presently and say so.[5] The current *American Review* had a mighty nice word from Dorothea Brande, of all people, about it, and also the symposium on poetry, which is very handsome.

Affectionately,
John

1. Herbert Agar (1897–1980), longtime editor of the Louisville *Courier-Journal* and author of *The People's Choice* and other books, coedited the second Agrarian symposium, *Who Owns America?* (1936), with Allen Tate.

2. Ransom appeared on a panel held at Northwestern University that concerned Agrarianism. Tate refused the invitation because he was not offered a fee.

3. Ransom apparently is referring to "Criticism, Inc.," *Virginia Quarterly Review*, XIII (Autumn, 1937), 586–602. This essay shows the direction Ransom wants his career to take.

4. Douglas Southall Freeman (editor of the Richmond *News Leader*), Stark Young (drama critic for the *New Republic*), and Bernard De Voto (editor of the *Saturday Review*) were all practicing journalists and editors with considerable expertise in history and literature.

5. Scribners published two novels by Caroline Gordon in 1937: *None Shall Look Back* and *The Garden of Adonis*.

To Allen Tate

April 6, 1937

Dear Allen:

Delighted to hear of near-completion of negotiations on the Tate-Johnson Freshman Omnibus.[1]

Use anything you please of mine, without charge. This reply to your handsome proposal is based on (1) the fact that I'm delighted to appear in a work which will really have some distinction, if I can forecast it, and (2) the fact that you undoubtedly would do the same for me if our positions were reversed. In fact, I've given free permissions in one or two quarters where no old affections are involved at all. But I warn you that Knopf is a Jew and will charge you money for poetry re-prints of mine. I advise you in this connection that you might consider any of three pieces which postdate the day of the Knopf publication of my verse: *Painted Head* and *Prelude to an Evening*, both in Untermeyer; and *Autumn Grief of Margaret*, in the Sat. Review of Lit. about July 1936.[2] But I have no interest in mentioning them otherwise.

But wait. It occurs to me that maybe you have one of those Christian contracts under which the publisher pays for permissions; that's the kind it ought to be, but not the usual kind; if that is so, and you are sure it won't redound to the hurt of your prospect of placing the business with Oxford Press—for instance by increasing the permissions requirement to an impossible figure—then I'll take the money for the prose thing. *Strictly on the understanding that you pay none of it.* So I'll include two formal answers to your question and you throw one of them away. Good wishes.

Yes, Agar was here, made a magnificent speech, and we had a fine time. I ventured not to include Don in our dinner and after-dinner sessions. I never liked Herbert so well. In particular I felt convinced of his fundamental sincerity as well as intelligence.

I enclose a last act of patriotism; you see, I'm signing off but a little by degrees. Perhaps this one had better never been written, because it will seem to Don like treason and unfriendship.[3] It's been on my conscience a long time. I can imagine that it is a line you yourself might not care to take, feeling that our Agrarian position is stronger if we just urge it single and pure, without reference to politics. But I have felt uneasy a long time over that. I've sent it to Collins.

Yours ever,
John C R

P.S. Wasn't that a blow, the Winslow story in the papers? Mrs. W. bringing an injunction-suit against her daughter to keep her from selling the family heirlooms, etc. Must talk to you about this.

---

1. A. Theodore Johnson and Allen Tate (eds.), *America Through the Essay: An Anthology for English Courses* (New York: Oxford University Press, 1938).

2. "Autumn Grief of Margaret," *Saturday Review of Literature*, XI (September 29, 1934), 137.

3. This essay, apparently on an Agrarian theme, was not published.

To Edwin Mims

June 8, 1937

Dear Doctor Mims:

Thank you very much for your kind note of yesterday. I assure you that I am thinking very hard of all the considerations which you mention. Naturally I do not know whether any other offer will be made me here besides the one worked out by Dean Carmichael, and so I cannot discuss very intelligently the alternatives that I will know by Thursday, according to my appointment with Dean Carmichael.

I must tell you all of my thinking about the Kenyon offer. Since I first talked to you I have the formal offer in writing, and I have satisfied myself that it is gilt-edged, in a financial sense, and on the basis of a five-year arrangement. I have also now a long full letter from Chalmers, the new head there, sustaining in full every single construction which I had placed upon the offer.[1]

At Kenyon they propose a good living, which will not make me affluent, but will ease all my financial worries; that is all I want.[2] They also propose for me to continue my own writing, not write for the alumni publication; and they depend on me to share my work with the advanced students so far as possible. I shall have a fair load of teaching to do, less than here; much of it is in courses which they ask me to define, according to the interests I have. The difference between the Vanderbilt offer which I will receive and the Kenyon offer is therefore twofold: first, in the amount of salary; second, in the superior opportunity to work for myself. I have so many writing projects just at this stage of my life which fall through for the lack of time and strength to work at them that I am dismayed. Naturally, as time goes on, I feel my interest growing in the kind of writing which is peculiar or individual with me; I want very much to go on as far as possible with it.

It is true that, if this kind of writing were on regionalism or agrarianism, I would be going into foreign parts. But I have about contributed all I have to those movements, and I have of late gone almost entirely into pure literary work. My group does not need me; in fact, we are not an organized aggressive group anyway. Among the literary labors I would like to do are poems; but it takes more peace and contentedness to do them than seems possible at Vanderbilt, where I have found my obligations and natural extensions of interest increasing all the time of late years. At my time of life it seems legitimate for me to work at literature a little more single-mindedly than I have been doing.

As I told you, it is with no hard feelings that I contemplate the probability that Vanderbilt will not approximate the terms of the Kenyon offer. I said "cannot," I suppose, since you say I did, meaning that it looks humanly impossible at this moment for the university to overturn a system in my single honor; it would be brazen to expect it.[3] At the same time, I do not approve the system, and I remark that no business institution could flourish on such a rule. I find it very embarrassing to receive the publicity I have had the last two weeks, and I do not try to pass on the justice of the extravagant things that have been said about me, but at the same time I cannot but be grateful to the friends who have said them, nor unmindful of the general principle which they are making, and in which I think I would join them if I felt personally unconcerned.[4]

But this seems to be anticipating my answer of Thursday, and I can assure you that I have not yet made it up. There are countless reasons why I should like to remain at Vanderbilt. And I thank you for urging it.

Yours,
John Crowe Ransom

1. Gordon K. Chalmers, president designate of Kenyon College.

2. The Kenyon offer was $4,500 and a house; at Vanderbilt Ransom was earning $3,820 and paying $45 a month for rent. The teaching load at Kenyon was nine hours each semester. At Vanderbilt he regularly taught twelve—and often, when a colleague was on leave, fifteen. Chancellor Kirkland offered to raise Ransom's salary to $4,200; later Frank Rand offered a special supplement of $500. This last amount, however, apparently was never included in the official offer.

3. Kirkland had said that he could not raise Ransom's salary without increasing the salaries of other members of the faculty with equivalent qualifications.

4. The Nashville *Tennessean* had carried letters from Allen Tate, Chancellor Kirkland, Andrew Lytle, Randall Jarrell, George Marion O'Donnell, and others. The interest aroused by these letters had prompted the Associated Press to send out to its subscribers a summary statement of the controversy, and *Time* magazine had sent a correspondent from Atlanta to gather information for a story.

To Allen Tate

Gainesville, June 17, 1937

Dear Allen:

The big dinner left me in a melancholy state, and to tell the truth, mighty glad to get on the train and hurry away from the scene of so many friendships and acquaintances broken off.[1] I can't tell you how grateful I feel to the old guard, and especially to you, who must have worked prodigiously to produce such really magnificent effects. I hope you are now back to your real career, which most likely is a considerably more important one than any I have had or shall have. You are a fire horse, and when the smoke begins to smell you can't keep out of the harness. I guess there'll never be complete immunity for any good man from patriotism, and its forms will always be unpredictable when they come. In view of that necessity, I guess I'll amend what I was writing to you last fall to this effect: Let's keep out of a *repetitive* patriotism at least.

I was mighty sorry to postpone my visit to Benfolly, but the press of things rather had me down.[2] Later. Besides, going to Ohio isn't what it might once have been, though it is pretty bad; the trails are good, and we will expect you all to visit us. In fact, the institution will undoubtedly receive great profit from your visits, and it is actually an obligation to a Professor of Poetry to insist upon them.

I want to say this formally, too, before the subject is retired: I share fully in your notions about the principle involved in my relations to the University; at least, so far as I can be objective, I think I would have agitated with you if the hero had been somebody else than myself.

This is a strange place to a not-deep Southerner. A good place, rather like L.S.U. except that the youth of the state is more mixed, not quite such fine and vital stock as you see down there. But the air is hot and languid. I have a big but congenial job working on my Scribner's manuscript, and it is enough to keep me going ahead and forgetting about the weather.[3]

I enclose a letter which I inadvertently carried away from Nashville instead of turning over to you; the one from Lambert Davis, handsome enough.[4] No, on second thought, I guess you have finished with the exhibit, and I'll just send it to my mother, where you can get it if you should really need it. It was read out, and you are familiar with it.[5]

Love to everybody.
Yours,
John

1. Allen Tate had given a dinner in Ransom's honor, at which Ransom announced his decision to go to Kenyon. The dinner was attended by more than one hundred persons.

2. Tate's home, near Clarksville, Tennessee.

3. *The World's Body.*

4. Editor of the *Virginia Quarterly Review.*

5. Testimonial letters were read aloud at the dinner in Ransom's honor.

To Allen Tate

Gambier, Ohio, October 10, [1937]

Dear Allen:

Mighty fine to hear from you, especially when the letter had such a fine enclosure. The SELF-EXEGESIS is a keen thing, quite proportionate in fact to the work it handles.[1] The matter of publication involves problems of strategy perhaps, but not serious ones. We certainly need some close modern critical studies; I mean modern as based on some close modern work as object of study; and we rarely get it. The poet himself can do it better than anybody else, if he is articulate. Ergo, you ought to publish it. But you ought to make this condition—unnecessary if you are dealing with a smart editor—that the piece follow a reprinting of the poem itself. (The piece would become a companion-piece to a modern classic.) Then it is worth twice as much to the reader, therefore to the magazine. Your constructions of the poem in parts interested me but differed from the ones I had made; I take yours as official.

Not by way of emulation at all, I enclose my latest piece—the first fruits of the Kenyon dispensation. I've had this in mind a long time, but only now have put it together on paper.[2] Please comment. I'm sending it to Davis at Charlottesville. I spoke to [Cleanth] Brooks at your house about it, but I think did not commit myself; if Davis doesn't bite I'll certainly send it to Baton Rouge. I cannot but feel a little resentful of the paying end of their arrangements down there; they pay a little better than Davis but infinitely later. Let me have this copy back if you don't mind.

Can hardly tell you how much I miss my familiars and my known corners and places down in Tennessee. This is a pleasant place physically but without much character spiritually. So far I have not found many literary students; the faculty are much better, but evidently they don't expect much of their students. However, there are many new men here, so that maybe the place may be due for a change. (New professors, I mean.) It's handsome in physical equipment.

It has been pretty lonesome in our big house. After settling us, Robb went back to Tennessee and got the children started in school (Helen back in Peabody, Reavill at Webb) and played in one more golf tournament. Then last week while just on the point of turning homeward she was called to Denver, where her father is seriously ill. I don't know when we will be established again. Mr. Reavill was mighty weak and poorly last summer, and I fear the worst. Not much news about him yet. Robb of course took with her young Jack, whose pleasant company I miss.

Randall and Cal are pretty good company; both good fellows in extremely different ways.[3] Randall has gone physical and collegiate with a rush; tennis is the occasion; good for him. Cal is sawing wood and getting out to all his college engagements in businesslike if surly manner; taking Latin and Greek and philosophy and, of course, English; wants to be really educated; and personally is about as gentle and considerate a boy as I've ever dealt with. Cal is quite excited over the idea of seeing you Thanksgiving, as you suggest.

What about your coming up here to see me? Any time, the sooner the better. Absolutely nothing here physically but walks and cider. My suggestion is selfish entirely. But wait; you would do better after our housekeeping department is installed with Robb's return; unless you wanted to risk the small-town restaurant resources which I depend on now.

Yours,
John.

The Thanksgiving plan sounds fine. Let's wait a few weeks till I know more about Mr. Reavill before settling.

---

1. "Narcissus as Narcissus," *Virginia Quarterly Review*, XLV (Winter, 1938), 108–22.

2. "Shakespeare at Sonnets," *Southern Review*, III (Winter, 1938), 531–53; reprinted in *The World's Body*.

3. Randall Jarrell and Robert Lowell had followed Ransom to Kenyon and were living in his home.

To Allen Tate

October 18, [1937]

Dear Allen:

Mighty glad to hear so promptly from you about the Shakespeare piece.[1] Thanks for the remarks, and also the very important correction in the text of a poem; that error would have been disastrous. You are right in the remarks, I agree. I had in my first copy a section on the "good" romantic poems of Shakespeare, and really had picked out several, 6 or 8, which we couldn't do without though they are romantic; had to leave this part out for space. And as to the structure, I remember starting in to work out this question: whether Shakespeare, by doing it often, doesn't make a convention of his own in the matter of pretending to have the third quatrain co-ordinate, but really tying it in with the couplet to make a kind of sextet; if he means it, it's good; then I seem to have forgotten about finishing that study, or else felt too crowded with the rest of the material of the essay. I agree that it ought to be handled before abusing Shakespeare.

On the whole, I have the feeling that the sonnet is too little and too studied to permit variations of structure ad-libitum; it's the most structured of all the small forms; and there's always the actual Italian structure if you want to write that kind of sonnet. And by the way, I didn't read your omnibus review of summer poetry in Sou. Review till a few weeks ago, and I meant to congratulate you on it; it's the closest analysis (in the Blackmur part) of modern work I've seen, except for what you do in the SELF-EXEGESIS: mighty fine.[2] But the present point is that there I remember you reproach Blackmur for having an unstructured logic in a fast Shakespearean sonnet form. Never mind. I always feel that I have done violences when I get through a piece of criticism.

I have read the magnificent Selected Poems in Jarrell's copy.[3] Mine didn't come. But don't do anything about it. I am writing to Don to ask if he can trace a copy for me there. And come to think about it, I've been carrying round with me a notice of a book or parcel held for me in the Nashville U.S.

Postoffice; I'll check on that right away. And many thanks. I want to go through it closely. I didn't think Beatty's review, by the way, in a Sunday paper which Amy sent Jarrell, was too happy; but then think of the difficulties of doing anything in a Nashville paper.[4]

You take punishment so kindly, that please read the enclosed preface, and meditate strictly on my book-title.[5] I am very much puzzled about this; can always fall back on "Poets Without Laurels," as you suggested. Can I put over the new title? And is the tone of the preface too ambitious? Ambition is a tur'ble thing when you don't get away with it. I need your good literary judgment badly. Please do this for me as soon as convenient. I am now committed powerfully to getting in my book MS by Oct. 31. I have held it up in order to get in the Shakespeare piece.

Sister Robb will be back in about ten days; Mr. Reavill's improving.

We'll be mighty proud to see you in January when Caroline lectures, but maybe we can have you before that too.

John

1. "Shakespeare at Sonnets."

2. Tate's "R. P. Blackmur and Others," *Southern Review*, III (Summer, 1937), 183–98.

3. Tate, *Selected Poems* (New York: Scribners, 1937).

4. Richmond Croom Beatty's review of Tate's *Selected Poems* appeared in the Nashville *Tennessean* on October 10, 1937.

5. *The World's Body.*

To Allen Tate

October 29, [1937]

Dear Allen:

Many thanks for your letter and criticism. Your comments are so just and useful that I shall use them all. It's hard to get the objective view of your own stuff. At the moment, though, I see so many deficiencies in the essays that if I didn't have the contract in hand I'd probably not be wanting to republish the most of them. The fact is, I see so much future for critical studies that my own are just beginnings; it's the biggest field that could possibly be found for systematic study, almost a virgin field. I want to wade right into it.

A very interesting situation has come up. My president called me in yesterday to talk in the greatest privacy about a project which he feels sure he can put through, beginning next year: a fine *Review*, backed & financed by his Trustees. (These last seem to be in the hollow of his hand; they are rich, experimental, and trusting; I've never heard of such Trustees.) He thinks of its editing as a full-time one-man-job, aside from secretarial and business help. Doesn't want to withdraw me from all teaching, and proposes to go out and get another man to be a co-editor with me, both of us to teach half-time, (i.e., six hours). Wants to consider long and hard with me the choice of the man. Names a man or two I don't know and therefore suspect, is much impressed with the idea of Van Doren. I held my peace but instantly occupied my mind with the idea of: TATE. After Tate, Warren, of course.

There are two sides to my problem: selling Kenyon to Tate; and selling Tate to Kenyon.

Under the first head. The physical equipment here, as well as the landscape, is about perfect. It's much like Tennessee hill country, and the campus and buildings are charming. The faculty is most decent; fully up to the Vanderbilt average in culture and solid learning if not in aggressiveness; already supplemented by a lot of new blood, and the President picks them well. The Ohio human community, however, is nearly a dead loss: a flat characterless race. A great loss here for a man moving from the South. My only thought is, It's a good place to work; and it would be a better place for the Ransoms to live if the Tates were here; maybe in part you might work this *vice versa*. And I not only would covet having you in the human and the editorial functions, but in the teaching. I have an idea we could really found criticism if we got together on it. The boys here are a very mannerly pleasant lot, without much intellectual interest. But that will change, rather fast. I've already secured the promise of some very substantial Poetry Scholarships, perhaps half a dozen, with which I hope to go to some good places (Harvard, L.S.U., Vanderbilt, Chicago) and buy in that many good writers, of sound attitudes, of course, as sophomores and juniors, to leaven the lump as quickly as possible. And there's the understanding that we'll be able to keep the good ones for a fifth year, and give them an M.A. or something, if there's enough demand for it in English; which there will be. I wonder what Sister Caroline would think about this place; it would seem empty, I'm afraid. There's absolutely nothing anti-Southern here, the Southerners are liked; but at the same time there's nothing Southern. I might add, it's not a churchy place at all; perfect freedom of conduct, for boys as well as faculty; very much freer than Southwestern, for example.

And now in the second place. I've barely met the President's wife, who has been a little ill, and not receiving as yet. She has several degrees, including one from Oxford, and taught four years at Mt. Holyoke, where she met the President. She is the former Roberta Teale Schwartz, who used to send us poems and once, I think, got the $50.00 prize—or did she?[1] She has the chief influence on her husband; literary judgment, I am sure. She is personally very fine, unaffected, maybe deep; I haven't sounded her out. She and he are under the dominion of Robert Frost's achievement and I gather that they favor a dual editorship of literary men. Personally I don't so much mind the thought of political philosophy, religion, philosophy in general, having representations in the review if I (or you) have an editorial veto on the stuff in exercise of a *literary* control; and if it is understood that this inclusion at once enlarges the size and scale of the project and does not propose to reduce the pure literary exhibit. I'm writing Elliott at once, mentioning my plan to have you here; I think he'll support that, as it won't work against his other suggestions. (Chalmers quite agrees now that the political pieces must be really philosophical pieces; Elliott backed up that idea, and after all Elliott knows his philosophy though he's not a literary man.)

My problem is to indoctrinate Chalmers with an idea of what *real* distinction for a periodical is; then to put over the absolute necessity of associating you with it. I will feed him with my representations as fast as he can take them. I've just begun to fight. I wanted him to learn of the difficulty of getting a proper man, or think of it at least, before I propose the brilliant solution of Tate; and I think he's considering this favorably. Tomorrow Lambert Davis comes, and he will certainly reinforce my suggestion if I'm not entirely mistaken in him. I haven't heard from Perkins, but I didn't write till the weekend; it occurred to me I'd better wait till I could be sure you had written, and last week I didn't get to it (after Lowell reported that you had written).[2]

One of Chalmers' conferees, Odell Shepherd, apparently a warm admirer of mine, told him the quarterly must stand for *regionalism*. I have ventured to think not, much to C's relief; it ought not to stand for anything but good principles and finished techniques; it ought not to be pocketed.

About Greensboro. (I told C. that I had just had your letter about your virtual offer there, and had had the powerful immediate reaction of wanting to take Mr. Tate away from Greensboro, if as it seemed he was prepared to pull up stakes and leave his rural and philosophical habitation.) My conscience quirks a little bit because one of the Greensboro men wrote me last spring about wanting a man to work with the writers, and I pushed Frierson.[3] It didn't occur to me that you would be available. I've taught there, and I never taught in a less Southern atmosphere. It's a pretty awful place, at least if you were on the regular teaching schedule, as I was. Kenyon is infinitely preferable. By the way, I would like to see you here with reference to the teaching, only a little less than as an editor. For next year we go out and bring in about five first-rate college Sophomores, picked by MS. competition (ostensibly), given substantial money scholarships, and intended to be a literary leaven here. (I will do the picking.) That will be really interesting. Please hold off the Greensboro people a while.

I'm in Louisville (Rhodes Scholarship Committee) from next Friday evening at dinner (the 17th) to late afternoon of Saturday the 18th; and have to appear then at Indianapolis for dinner (I suppose) Sunday evening the 19th, preliminary to District Com. meeting all day Monday. I'm writing to the Seelbach for a room. There may be nothing worth while in it, but I would enjoy dinner and a long evening with you there the night of Saturday the 18th, and would most gladly be host; but hesitate to mention it because from a business point of view the long drive might not be worth your while.

(Dinner and hotel—this is a serious offer.) I feel sure I can get out of Louisville Sun. morning and make Indianapolis that evening; if I missed an Ind. dinner it wouldn't matter, provided I got in by, say, 8 p.m. By the way, if you *should* fancy this excursion, write me in care of Seelbach unless you write as early as Monday, for I leave here Wednesday a.m. for Columbus, where I am due for the Ohio Com.'s meeting. I'm a committeeman in a big way.

Yours,
J C R

1. Roberta Teale Swartz's "Do Not Say Our Love Can Go" won second place in the 1923 Ward-Belmont Contest sponsored by the *Fugitive*. She received special mention but no cash award.

2. Lambert Davis, at this time managing editor of the *Virginia Quarterly Review*, was subsequently an editor at Harcourt, Brace, and director of the University of North Carolina Press. Maxwell Perkins, editor at Scribners.

3. William Frierson, a minor member of the Fugitives.

To Allen Tate

[October 30, 1937]

Dear Allen:

Thanks for several letters.

I couldn't help on the *Poets v. Laurels* copy, as my proof though expected had not begun to arrive and I could find no other copy at all. Sorry.

The other day I had a long talk with Chalmers about the Review, and about you. (The first time I had proposed you.) I think the prospect is good. I wish he and the Trustees would approach the matter by saying: "Here is Ransom on the grounds and perhaps we might get both Ransom and Tate on the grounds, and they are such men of letters that their literary judgment will be in all respects better than our own, therefore we'll furnish the money and count on them to apply it where it will do the most good." I'm afraid that is not the situation exactly. Chalmers supposes I'm all right but his devotion doesn't go quite that far; you he doesn't know, and wants to know better; I've given him a list of people to write to for objective information. He knows both you and I are Agrarians and I think felt apprehensive over that (probably knowing nothing about it) until I told him that I would not like to see the Review pinned to any economic or political program.

He spent last week in New York and places East, and talked with many people. Munson was the only man who advised him to leave out politics, and saw a new quarterly as the successor to the old *Dial*. Bill Elliott, who has great influence with him, told him first of all that he must get a really eminent man to go in with me on terms of equality, that no half-baked youngster would do, etc.; told him also that the other man ought to have an eminence in political philosophy analogous to my (reputed) one in literature; thought and thought about the identity of the man and *could not think of one* who was good enough except Friedrich (?) at Harvard, who has been wanting a Review but could not be had from Harvard, and who might possibly supply most of the need by being an advisory editor *at* Harvard.[1] That is favorable, on the whole; it spiked effectually some pet names that Chalmers was mulling over, and seems to me to fit into a Review with what Frost has called the "clear school" of poetry. I scent a danger here. Chalmers has poked fun at Eliot a bit, once or twice, though his understanding of matters is not at all precise and he is, in the last resort, humble. (Chalmers is in no sense a meddler. The editors once selected will have free rein. He is the ideal President.) Unless you absolutely repudiate the whole idea, I propose to talk a great deal with them and indoctrinate them if possible. I am to invite Lambert Davis here to give us a lot of practical knowledge about *Review*-ing, and I shall make sure that he expresses himself about Mr. Tate as an editor and man of letters.

That's about all for the present. Consider this at your leisure, and quite privately for the time being, and let me hear from you.

I write this out of some distraction. A wire yesterday informed me of Mr. Reavill's death. It will be a big blow for Robb, whose standard for husbands, I think, has always been to measure them against her father as the pattern of men. He was an epical sort of man and as good a friend as I ever had. I feel sure that Mrs. Reavill will now come and make her home with us; I am sending a wire presently to insist on it.

Naturally I have no November plans at present. Lowell wants to drive down and see you if you will let him, and to take me, and Robb if she can go. He is a mighty fine boy, and applying himself prodigiously. I would like mightily to see you all, and will write you as soon as I can.

Affectionately,
John

P.S. Pipkin[2] came up for Chalmers' inauguration last week—a nice gesture. He was extremely amiable, his attitudes very good. He has no worries about the permanence of the *Review* at L.S.U.

If Caroline wants to drop a note to Robb, she is at 1765 York St., Denver. I imagine she'll be there two weeks or so.

This letter strikes me as a bit untactful. The reason I'll have to sell Tate to Kenyon is that he is far too good for the place and intellectually at the moment beyond its grasp. I have dwelt on this because I'll need a little cooperation. Some time before long I'll want to exhibit you—informally, of course, as my guest.

---

1. Carl Joachim Friedrich (b. 1901), a political economist and professor of government at Harvard, 1936–71, the author of several books on political theory.

2. Charles W. Pipkin, an editor of the *Southern Review*, with Cleanth Brooks and Robert Penn Warren, until his sudden death in 1941. Pipkin, a political scientist, who was dean of the Louisiana State University graduate school, was largely responsible for the founding of the *Southern Review*.

To Allen Tate

November 4, 1937

Dear Allen:

Very greatly cheered over your acceptance of Kenyon and the Review project. Of that there's nothing new to report, except that Davis writes encouragingly that he will come in December to talk with Chalmers and me; he is not at all distressed over a new Review, thinks a rather larger number of them might regularize or standardize a form of critical literature and all might help each other.

It seems to me that our cue would be to stick to literature entirely. There's no decent consistent group writing politics; if there is, it belongs to Collins; our own group will be less and less productive; and the pains of balancing righteousness against expediency, and the attitudes of Board members and faculties, make the whole job of doing a political quarterly cost more than it is worth. In the severe field of letters there is vocation enough for us: in criticism, in poetry, in fiction.

The *Southern Review*, by the way, is slipping unless I am greatly mistaken. They are at their high standard by the pure accident that there are now a good number of fine critics who have no where to market their wares. Their fiction could be greatly improved, and certainly their poetry; and even their criticism, though you and I have often contributed to that. A Review of half their size, all literary, and all of the highest contemporary excellence, would be a distinguished thing. (One with much more attention to the English writers, too.)

To bear on this point I enclose a letter from the two Associate Editors. The boys deal pretty pedantically with my poor paper, you will see;[1] I thought when I read it I must have mistakenly sent it to the *Yale Review* and got back an epistle from Miss Helen Macafee. I wrote them a pretty warm letter but after thinking over it withheld it and wrote another. I also revised the thing, adding a bit, taking account of points of theirs which seemed to me worth anything, generally improving it; I wanted to do this anyway. The thing is, I believe, that Cleanth is showing his limitations as a thinker with one thing on his mind at a time, and he is not providing for Red the suggestions and stimuli that Red requires. *Those boys are stale.* (I have said this frankly to them.) Think of an editorial letter in the style of this one, even conceding that it is written to a friend. I really stepped on their toes a little, come to think about it. For Red is a Shakespearean, and would not like my irresponsible knocks for the comfort of the Philistines; and Cleanth is an expert on metaphysical poetry, and thinks everybody ought to discuss the thing in his minute terms. They are a bit magisterial, or is it just my oversensitive imagination?

Robb writes that Mrs. Reavill is too dispirited at the moment to know just what she wants to do, and I suspect that Robb will be kept there for some time yet. I'll have a clearer idea before long. If she should stay into December, I think I would go down to Nashville Thanksgiving, and in fact I must go before long, to get our car, which Robb had to abandon there when she got the wire about her father. More about that as soon as I can manage it.

Affectionately,
John

1. "Shakespeare at Sonnets."

To Allen Tate

November 19, [1937]

Dear Allen:

We were sorry not to see you and Caroline the other day, and sorrier on account of the occasion that required your absence. Was very much shocked to hear about that fine girl's act. But it was not possible for us to tarry to see you later; I went to Nashville and came almost immediately back, and we had to hurry along.

This afternoon I am going in for a long talk with Chalmers and will bring up for the first time the matter of the other editor, and also the matter of writing to Scribner's. I had already mentioned the latter, and found him well impressed with the idea, and having no particular notions of his own. I think it will be best if you write Perkins first, strictly in confidence of course, and giving him to understand that I am about to write him also. If he cares to negotiate the matter of a Scribner's-Kenyon review, he will be prepared to say so; furthermore, if he cares to make any recommendations about the other editor, I will be sure to mention our general plan when I write him, and he can get in his word about Tate as an answer to that point. But of course he should reply to my letter without reference to any other correspondence. I am glad you like the idea, and think it may appeal to Scribner's. I think it ought to.

I have delayed having this out with Chalmers, thinking that he will see of his own accord the unsuitability of most people for the position and be all the more agreeable to my proposal. Furthermore, he's been away a good deal and I haven't had many chances at him. But it's time now to let him have it, before the coming of Davis the 12th [of] December, when he will certainly get another recommendation enforcing mine. Davis, by the way, writes very nicely about the whole idea of a review, and evidently relishes the chance to come and give us his own ideas.

Robb was mighty pleased to hear from Caroline. We are settled down at last very happily; sort of dug in for the winter, I feel, because this morning there's a three-inch snow on the ground. I don't think I can get down for Thanksgiving, since Robb hardly cares to try it. But if the president thinks I ought to go and talk it over with you, I'll come anyway. Lowell wants to come down to see you, though; I have told him I would tell you that he'll drive in Wednesday afternoon if you don't mind. If it's not convenient don't hesitate to say so. I think he would visit partly you and partly Starr,[1] and get away probably Saturday morning; he doesn't want to be in your way. But he says also that if he gets a wire from his Harvard friend Brown[2] that he's on the way here, he will wire you that he's not coming.

Avery Handly writes me about Jimmie Waller's accident; that's bad luck.[3] I hope it doesn't turn out worse than it seemed to be at time of his writing.

A nice note from the boys at Baton Rouge says they're printing my piece. I suppose they felt a little aggrieved at my high tone, but they don't extend the argument further. That's right about Shakespeare and the 19th C.—the critics went in head over heels for Shakespeare, and I should say Keats among the poets did too; the others had more immediate derivations.

Affectionately,
John

1. Alfred Starr, a minor member of the Fugitives, who became a prominent Nashville businessman.

2. Harry Brown, a young poet whose writing came to nothing.

3. James Waller, a Nashvillean, who contributed an essay to *Who Owns America*?.

To Allen Tate

January 1, 1938

Dear Allen:

Things didn't work out right, a great disappointment of 1937 for me.

Chalmers has been extremely anxious to get you here with me—he was converted 100%. But the budgetary thing was the difficulty. The *Va. Quarterly Review* has run consistently on a salary appropriation of around \$4200–4500, taking care of secretary, circulation, business and editorial staff. Chalmers thought he couldn't propose to his Board more than that. At the best it would have taken a good deal of time to negotiate a \$6000 or

$6500 salary appropriation, or enough to have brought you here on terms analogous to mine. When I got back from Indianapolis on a Tuesday I had a long talk with him thinking that maybe in spite of your latest letter you were not irrevocably committed to Greensboro, but the more we talked the more he felt that the prospect here wasn't of a kind to put up against the bird in hand there. He was sincerely regretful.

It sounds as if you and Caroline are mighty prettily fixed up there. I must hasten to withdraw my remarks about the Woman's College, because I saw it under no such circumstances as yours. I can't see how it will be more than a part-time duty for both of you, under conditions that are not definitely bad at all, though they might be better. I see the possibility also of you and Kendrick winning N.C. to an Agrarian program—*if you want to go that way.*[1] But I guess that will hardly be your object in making the move. I certainly want to wish you a good year, and many of them, right from the start.

One way in which I shall specially mourn the break-up of our plan is in missing your collaboration at some critical studies. I've just come back from the Modern Language Association at Chicago. The Professors are in an awful dither, trying to reform themselves, and there's a big stroke possible for a small group that knows what it wants in giving them ideas and definitions and showing the way. Crane spoke on my program. He's the best of them, and he's not quite up to the mark.[2] I picked a good nominating Committee in my section, with the result that Mark Van Doren is our Secretary. But the Chairman (my last-year Secretary) is the Germanic scholar, Ernst Rose; there's an interregnum. I have an idea that next year a group of us ought to organize and put over a permanent Council for our group. Van Doren, Austin Warren, Flint, and one or two others would be in on this.[3] But on the other hand I may think to myself that I'll not want to go to New York next Christmas, and will just stay away from the Professors. Shall we be independent Chinese war lords, or shall we come in and run the government? Another question of strategy. There's so much congenial revolutionary spirit in the M.L.A. that there's really something there to capitalize. I want to talk this [over] with you at my earliest opportunity.

I had a good talk with Don at Chicago. He's much more lively in spirit, and altogether, I think, because the new Dean (Pomfret) at Vanderbilt has unexpectedly turned out to be a good fighting man and has put over already a good half of the program which last year we "fit, bled and died" for without accomplishing.[4] Don is very keen about going to Scribner's with his Collected Poems and seeing how fixed is his idea there I told him I would write to Wheelock, though I don't know that I mean anything to Wheelock.[5]

Here's the first business matter, I dare say, that will have come to you in your new position; it is addressed to Caroline too. The sanest and most charming and at the same time most promising girl at the Boulder Writers Conference last summer was Jean Stafford. Her best work is fiction; she has a novel pretty far along. She has had a year of graduate study of some kind in Germany (last year), and is a B.A., perhaps an M.A., of Colorado. She's teaching, unfortunately, at Stevens College, in Missouri, of which you may have heard through Bill Bandy[6]—one of our most God-awful places, where they teach "communications" instead of composition, and have a required course or so in beauty-culture. Naturally she wants to get away next year. She would give up her salary as an instructor and take an English assistantship or fellowship at the right place. She is a fine person and competent scholar and teacher so that no risk is involved in dealing with her. She may have a considerable creative talent, I have not seen enough to tell. She is going to write you.

A letter from Cal says the doctors have been at him and think he may need building up, suggesting lumber camp, etc. He's not sure, but may stay out of school this spring and come back here in the fall. I hope he won't have to stay out at all. He is a fine boy, very definitely with great literary possibilities. I don't know whether he's better as critic or as poet, but he's making fast progress in both lines. He will be very sorry that the negotiations for getting you here have fallen through.

Now the main thing of this letter: What about your and Caroline's coming up to pay us a little visit this month before going to Greensboro? Any time. My round of Rhodes Committees, and my trip to Chicago, and our confusion all through the fall owing to Mr. Reavill's sickness, seem to have hindered me from going to see you, and I can hardly get away from classes to go now. Can't the mountain come to Mohamet? We will be delighted. It's a 450 mi. drive, best route via Louisville & Cincinnati, from your house; good roads if the ice doesn't interfere, and about every third week it seems to be icy. (Icy roads, I mean; slow going.)

What about this? We are going to expect you, and the sooner the better.

Yours
John

P.S. I've sent back to Scribner's the galley proofs.[7] But I have my extra set. The page proofs will be coming any day. I think I'll get you to look over a few matters when you come.

---

1. Benjamin Burks Kendrick (1884–1946), chairman of the history department at the Woman's College of the University of North Carolina from 1930 until his death, was coauthor of *The South Looks at Its Past* (1935).

2. Ronald S. Crane (1886–1967), professor of English at the University of Chicago and editor of *Modern Philology* for many years, turned from historical scholarship to Aristotelian criticism in the 1930s.

3. Mark Van Doren, poet and critic; Austin Warren, scholar and critic; and R. W. Flint, a critic, all shared Ransom's interest in a critical appreciation of literature.

4. John Edwin Pomfret was dean of the senior college and the graduate school at Vanderbilt from 1937 to 1942.

5. John Hall Wheelock, a poet who was an editor for many years at Scribners.

6. William Bandy attended Vanderbilt with several of the Fugitives. A distinguished scholar, he returned to Vanderbilt to teach French after many years at the University of Wisconsin.

7. *The World's Body*.

To Allen Tate

April 22, [1938]

Dear Allen:

I was much rejoiced over your fine letter commending my book; it was the first reaction I had had at all, and I fear it will be about the best one I shall receive, but all the better when I had just been going over the thing and wondering if it really came off.[1] In response to your question. Yes, it is certain that you are implicated to the extent of having "egged me on" in the general direction of publication; also in having put in the determining word to Perkins of Scribner's; and also, though this is ancient history, in having collaborated, often unintentionally, in the preparation of the content.

Meter and mythology are indeed neglected in this book, which is excessively on the side of generality: I have much more I would like to say to the topic of meters. I don't know what I want to say about mythology; I feel that there is a subject of first-rate importance which I have scarcely scratched; it needs some hard work; I doubt if you and I would differ on it finally, but at the present stage it's very far from finally. That is one of the things we ought to confer about.

I have been powerfully impressed by my belated reading recently of Winters' book.[2] That is about the closest study of modern verse from many angles that we have had. I have drafted, but not sent, a letter to Arrow Editions to propose another book of my own; not formally an answer or supplement to Winters', but in many respects taking off from the arguments of the book. It is unsatisfactory in several ways; in the discussion of meters, though they are discussed with far more understanding than we have seen elsewhere; in the moralistic locution, which is dragged in by the hair, and clutters up the scene almost fatally for the general reader; in the lack of any standard for distinguishing good poetry from bad, other than by the logical framework—there's a lot to be said about freshness, which is really only genuineness in a poetic experience, or even, a trite yet bold word, originality. Nobody can accept Winters' final evaluations, or the ground of them, though they are never as much as half-way off. I should like to turn in on some work a good deal closer than any I have done; closer than I am likely to do unless I can see some chance of publication. The official English publications (learned ones) are entirely unavailable for this purpose, and only Arrow Editions, plus occasional space in the *Southern Review*, offers any market. Yet close studies now are determining, the state of things being what it is, in seeing whether the generalities we utter so glibly will really work.

I have been deterred from writing to Arrow by the thought that perhaps you and I might do the thing together; perhaps this would appeal to you. The essay of yours on Confederate Dead would be very valuable in a book;[3]

and why not the essay on mythology which we know ought to be done? We might confer on this a little later. What do you think offhand about a collaboration? If Arrow Editions wouldn't do it, isn't it possible that the L.S.U. Press might come through?

Having gone so far, it is not fitting for you and me to go no further. We've begun a new chapter in poetics; why not finish it off for perpetuity?

The Note in Ontology is a central essay, and I'm glad you see it so.[4] Unfortunately, after clearing the ground in my first two sections of it (the Physical and the Platonic half-poetries) I don't denominate and define the true exhibit; it should be Integral Poetry, or Molecular Poetry, or True Poetry, or Whole or Organic Poetry, or Absolute Poetry, or something; the Metaphysical Poetry is just a variety, and it's a good variety to exhibit with, but its name should not have pre-empted the title and the general definition. I rather rode two horses in that essay, or tried to. I think I do have the right introductory matter in the last section, in leading up to the Metaphysical style, though I don't advertise it properly. I remember you once wanted the term Creative Poetry, and I demurred a little on the ground of something magical or mystical in the connotation. I don't mean to be disrespectful of your elected term.

That's enough about my past performance, which I certainly am in a mood to judge coolly.

Mrs. Reavill has at last come to stay with us, and will stay most of the year, though I think not in the wintertime.[5] The poor lady recently fell over a chair-arm and broke two ribs, but she is recovering not too painfully from that.

I have a hard summer ahead of me, as follows: University of Kentucky, June 13 to June 29, University of Chattanooga, July 4 to July 9, Murray Teachers College from July 11 to July 16, and University of Texas from July 18 to August 29. Then three weeks vacation. I am chasing the filthy dollar, being at last about to emerge from insolvency, but faced with huge expenditures in the interest of Helen's and Reavill's education. I wonder if you will be at Benfolly the latter part of the week of June 27; that is Thursday, or Friday, or Saturday, or perhaps a couple of those days, the 30th, 1st, and 2nd. That is about my only chance of seeing you and Sister Caroline, unless it may be in September. I'm sorry that Easter got by us. Or if you leave for Conn. before late June, why not come by Lexington a couple of days? We could have a big time.

I hope you have found your official duties not too binding nor uninteresting this year. You're going back, I suppose? I remember pleasant people at Greensboro, not exciting ones; not personally distinguished ones such as were to be found occasionally in our more absolute Tennessee South.

Randall [Jarrell] will return here next year on the same status as this. He is just back from Nashville, where Don [Davidson] accepted his work on an M.A. thesis, nearly completed. He is very unheroic in his pattern for the future; is thinking of trying for a Rhodes Scholarship; is so advanced in his thought that he wants just to pitch into some college department and work with the big professors; which is not too likely a prospect with his rather untactful manners and unimpressive public speech. I think highly of him and he has more than justified his position here; is very highly thought of. He and I don't talk together well; I have the feeling that he can't generalize, though he has taken a good deal of philosophy; but he is a very wise young man, and a learned, and a good-hearted.

And where is Nancy, and how does she get along in school? I thought she was mighty pretty as well as healthy the last time I saw her.

Best wishes from our family to yours.

Affectionately,
John

1. *The World's Body.*

2. Yvor Winters, *Maule's Curse: Seven Studies in the History of American Obscurantism* (1938). This book provoked Ransom to write "Yvor Winters: The Logical Critic," *Southern Review*, VI (Winter, 1941), 558–83; the essay appears in expanded form in Ransom's *The New Criticism* (Norfolk, Conn.: New Directions Press, 1941), 211–75.

3. Tate's essay "Narcissus as Narcissus," *Virginia Quarterly Review*, XIV (Winter, 1938), 108–22.

4. "Poetry: A Note in Ontology," *The World's Body*.

5. Robb Reavill Ransom's mother lived with the Ransoms briefly after Mr. Reavill died.

To Allen Tate

May 20, [1938]

Dear Allen:

I wrote you a longish letter two weeks ago, and I cannot find it, but I am certain it never got sealed up and mailed; at that time I was hurrying off to Richmond, where the ladies of the Poetry Society of Virginia (a pretty sad lot) met me and took me off to Williamsburg for their annual picnic at William and Mary. I was too rushed on this trip to get much fun out of it; and I was distressed to think of getting so close to Greensboro without being able to get still closer.

I relish your idea about a subsidy from the Guggenheims for us to do a joint book.[1] Please be sure to see Moe about it and represent me as highly in earnest about the proposition. We could take three months off, or a little more if it were necessary to bring it under the standard Guggenheim terms. And as you say, there are plenty of projects for us to work at. Improvise any project you please by way of an informal application to Moe.

I'm going to do a piece for Red, I suppose, taking up some of the questions Winters has raised and not settled.[2] That is, I had a nice letter asking for a piece, and I wrote back to ask if he would be interested in such a piece, but true to form Red and the boys have not got round to answering my letter yet. There's plenty of time to make overtures to Arrow Editions, as I think I will do.

For the time being I have gratified an old impulse and written to Macmillan (as the copyright holders) to see if they want an anthology of Hardy, with a critical introduction.[3] It's a shame that he is accessible to unacquainted students only through his *Complete Poems*, and some very bad general anthology selections, and no decent criticism at all. Haven't heard from them yet.

I asked in that other letter where I could get hold of your lecture-article on Tension; I thought you were pre-eminently the poet to handle that subject, and I wanted to see what you made of it precisely.[4] But now I see that the *Southern Review* advertises the essay as forthcoming in their pages. Forthcoming soon, I hope.

You must tell me what about our meeting in June or the first of July. They have six-day weeks at Lexington, where my stay is from June 13 to June 29. A week-end trip to Benfolly would very skimpy, i.e., before June 29. Maybe you and Caroline could come to Lexington as my guests for a little fuller session; though I don't know what sort of entertainment I could offer. Last fall in the home of President McVey, which is a pleasant case of Kentucky hospitality, I told them about their two great Kentucky authors, and they professed great chagrin at their unacquaintance; there might be some harmless good policy in your visiting there.

A number of pleasant private letters—for instance, one from Andrew [Lytle]—have come in as following my book publication. No reviews as yet that I have seen except one in Books, and one by Beatty in the Nashville *Banner*. A note from Cowley to the effect that he had asked Spencer to review it for *NR*.[5] I don't expect much, and in fact I've got pretty tough in my literary expectations anyhow.

A letter from O'Donnell speaks of his desire to land an open position in your institution next year, and I am writing a letter to Dr. Smith—whom I recall as one of the most eccentric men I ever saw. He would unquestionably be a great teacher. (I.e. O'D., not Dr. Smith.)

Randall is a very strange boy, and I'm not sure whether he's got a career ahead of him or not. Poetically, he's almost ruined by his attempt to put into practice Empson's doctrine of ambiguity.[6] As a teacher he's extremely animated when he is interested, and spares no pains, and gets pretty good results; but the other day he asked me if I ever got bored, and intimated that this was rather his stock condition teaching Freshmen. A man of his age and ill prospects has no business getting bored by his job. He's returning here one more year.

The Review is right on the edge of starting; just a little more work on printer's estimates and general budget to make sure we shan't start and then flop. It will be a handsome thing, and of the most distinction I can make it, and prompt and regular, and will pay a good rate to the contributors. My interest in it would be greater if it were a literary magazine, but it is so only in part. If we begin, I shall certainly want to ask you to serve on its Advisory Board, and one of the big items in our conference next month will be my solicitation of ideas from you.

I'm impatient to see you and Sister Caroline, and Nancy too. Before long, then.

Affectionately,
John

1. This project never came to fruition.

2. "Yvor Winters: The Logical Critic."

3. This book, edited by Ransom, finally appeared: *Selected Poems of Thomas Hardy* (New York: Macmillan, 1961).

4. Allen Tate, "Tension in Poetry," *Southern Review*, IV (Summer, 1938), 101–15.

5. *The World's Body* was reviewed by Thomas Merton, *New York Herald Tribune Books*, XIV (May 8, 1939), 8; and by Theodore Spencer, *New Republic*, XCVI (August 10, 1938), 27–28.

6. William Empson, *Seven Types of Ambiguity* (1930).

To Allen Tate

May 28, [1938]

Dear Allen:

The suggestion about packing the English Department of the Woman's College is quite exciting. If things should come up as you want them, and I had the power of making a strong lead for one "of our men"—I would hardly be in good ethics if I dallied with another offer myself at this time—which one should it be? I think Don is the best man if he would really forget his sore toes and go to work; Beatty and Monk fine men too, though not quite so impressive publicly.[1] Don might not be happy. Beatty might not be sufficiently "impressive"—to people who couldn't read. Monk has less publication or publicity in his favor. I'll be thinking about this problem with you and waiting for your further advices. I suppose there'll be nothing doing till well into next year some time.

Your cynicism is amply justified in the matter of Macmillan's wanting to publish Hardy freshly and intelligently—though the last adjective may seem to beg the question on my part. To tickle your vanity as a prophet I enclose the letter of the young man who wrote me. His name is not even included on the stationery of the house, though I observe he rates a secretary, or at least some of her time.

We have at last decided to go ahead with our publication, getting out an initial number next December. The only thing that now will stop us will be an order from the Board, which authorized it in general at its last meeting but expects to approve a detailed plan this June. The President had to beat the gun in order to sign up two new men who will have academic connections here but also, more importantly, publishing ones.

We have pledges of $5,000 annually, due Jan. 1 of 1938 (already in hand), 1939, 1940, and the theory is that we may not need to get out more than two years issues with this money, since a lot has to be spent before the time of first publication; and that after Jan. 1. 1940, the donors will review the question of whether to go on; they undoubtedly will if the magazine has made any reputation by that time. In addition we have my editorial connection already paid for. In prospect we have subscriptions, and a Secretary who will push them with all his might.

The personnel will be: Ransom, Editor; Philip Rice, now in Philosophy Department of U. of Cincinnati, and a frequent reviewer for *Nation, Poetry*, etc., Managing Editor; [Norman C.] Johnson, an Honors graduate of Harvard this year, one of the best men they have ever turned out, secretary. Rice will teach three-quarters time in the College, Johnson one-quarter time (in English). Rice is a good man though not a great one. He is a most competent philosopher, wishes he were a literary man.

There isn't money enough to get out a real Review, I am glad to say. We've canvassed printers, who charge a lot of money hereabouts; and have finally dropped the notion of a skimpy publication trying to compete with the comprehensive article represented by 200-pagers like Yale and Southern Reviews, 170-pagers like Virginia Quarterly Review. We will get out 100-page issues and devote the pages exclusively to literature and the arts. We must do something handsome and distinctive. The size is sufficient, I think; we ought to fill it with stuff of the highest quality. I want to see it solid but not dull. I think a good bet is to have a good deal of satirical or negative writing; there are enough deserving butts to pay our respects to; that is a popularizing feature, perhaps, but must not of course define the character of the publication. I think also that we want to use new kinds of writing, i.e. critical writing; the less standard and conventional in shape and tone, the better. We ought to make a little racket every time we appear. We will be able to pay five dollars a page, and a smaller page than Southern Review's; and in advance where requested; I shall have the checking account and we shall have money always ahead.

This is preliminary to saying that the last but not least I will be glad to have you and Caroline any weekend at Lexington, where you would be good for the community as well as for me.

Yours,
John

A. McLeish was here lecturing last week; very friendly; a good person, very definitely filled with social conscience.

---

1. Ransom is here speculating about the possibility of hiring Donald Davidson, Richmond Croom Beatty, and Samuel Holt Monk at the Woman's College. Beatty, a scholar in American literature at Vanderbilt, and Monk, a scholar in eighteenth-century literature teaching at Southwestern College in Memphis, were among the best younger Ph.D.'s of Ransom's acquaintance.

To Allen Tate

Lexington, June 22, [1938]

Dear Allen:

It has been a busy period for me, and I have neglected to acknowledge your valued letter; the one in which you seemed enthusiastic about the Review project.

I showed it, however, to my President, who seemed much comforted and fortified by your expressions. However, it will indicate setting when I tell you that he was a little alarmed at your reference to Rice as a Leftist. He knew that perfectly well, and Rice is as honest as a man can well be, and in fact he and Chalmers were at Oxford together; but I guess he had hoped that Rice wasn't publicly known as a Leftist. Many of the Kenyon faculty are decidedly "Liberal" if not Leftist; they are red-hot New Dealers, most of them, and I think Chalmers would be too if he were free; but I am afraid he begins to show that degeneration of the fibres which happens to a man with fine motives who is constantly exposed to the deliberations of a Board of Capitalists.

Rice has already come in, though Chalmers confessed to me that he would not have had Rice except that I insisted on him, and that he thought I might keep Rice straight. There's no difficulty in keeping Rice straight. Each time I have been with him I have liked him better. His Leftism is not a literary matter; he only sees collectivism as inevitable, he doesn't think it has anything to do with literature directly. And he's a good philosopher, and I thought we needed him at Kenyon in that capacity as much as we needed him as Managing Editor. He has a one-course allowance for this latter job; and the new Secretary, who came just before I left the College, has a three-fourths allowance and is almost full-time in his connection with the Review; a fine fellow.

We have $15000 pledged, and it's as good as gold. One third of it is already in hand. The other thirds are due next January 1, and January 1 of 1940. The budget we have worked out is $6700 annually, so that we can go two years and a little better without another penny revenue. If the pledges are renewed after the experiment, and meanwhile, we can go a year on the subsidy of $5000 provided we make up $1700 through subscriptions and sales. We can do that all right. The Kenyon boys—about 3000 of them, old and new, are terribly earnest, and will come through at once with a big bloc of subscriptions, and for a while regardless of whether they can read the publication. But I have indicated repeatedly, and it has been made well-known to the donors and the Board, that the success and permanence of the Review depend on our undertaking a publication on a professional level of distinction, with no reference to the local setting whatever, and on ultimately securing some sort of public recognition which we can pass on objectively to the subscribers and donors, and which will make them happy.

The Board met at Commencement and said go ahead. Just before that Chalmers and I had a definitive conversation in which we came to an understanding that satisfies me. He talked quite officially and formally about his responsibility in the matter; it's his project, and he is responsible to the donors and to the Board and to the Kenyon community. He could never have committed himself and the College to a Review but for his surprising confidence in me as a man with a "philosophy of life," etc., and but on the condition that I would keep my own personal rein on the whole conduct of the publication. A lot of kind words to that effect, whereupon I said: "It would follow from your confidence in me that I must have the utmost rope possible." I went on to tell him flatly that I could have undertaken a general Review without much conscience, but that now we had restricted it to a Review of arts and letters I had a professional interest which I must respect. He agreed.

There are several issues. One, that was not expressed between us, was the possibility of his interfering himself; not so much in matters of policy as in trying to get things into the Review which he would have liked personally—he has a good deal of unsystematic literary acquaintance; but it is clear that I won't have that. Another that was up before us was the name of the thing. I had come to the name "The Critic," or "The American Critic"; but that scared him somehow; and I thought it mattered so little that I waived my insistence in view of more important concessions on his part. So it's THE KENYON REVIEW; with some sort of sub-title or qualification like, "Devoted to Arts and Letters." Another issue was the matter of the Contributing or Advisory Editors. In the interests of Kenyon he wanted to have a lot of Faculty editors. But they would have been either dummies or meddlers; there is not one who has ever written for Reviews unless "learned" Reviews. He waived his point. And finally in the matter of the non-Kenyon and real Advisory Editors. He leaves that to me. But he does hope that I won't have Archibald MacLeish, who is Leftist, but who was suggested by Rice, on the ground, a very good one, that MacLeish would be a powerful name to get readers and library subscriptions with. However, I don't mind accommodating Chalmers there, as MacLeish has certainly abandoned poetry for social protest.

A funny thing was about Ridgely Torrence.[1] He is second only to Robert Frost in Chalmers' mind, and the last day he wired around and got Torrence, who is giving a little course in an Ohio college, to come to Columbus, where I went and spent the afternoon with him. Chalmers' idea was to see for myself if he wouldn't make a good Advisory Editor. He is indeed a fine old fellow, as I already knew. He said he had just one thing to say about the Review, about which he was enthusiastic: he would advise any Review, after his experience with the divided house of the *New Republic*, to have an absolute dictator; he approved me as a dictator, and advised me to dictate. I didn't tell Chalmers that, because I knew that Chalmers would be seeing him or hearing from him to that effect anyway.

Now I am committed, and the thing is on, and you can imagine how much I want to have that long conference with you. Much better if I had you at Kenyon, and we were Co-editors, with the simple agreement never to do anything that either of us disapproved. I'll wager my bankroll that would have worked perfectly; and I would now have a much more confident feeling.

We will get out our first issue as Winter, 1939, and must be on the stands and in the mails by the middle of December. You must help me plan that number.

And, against our imminent conference, please be thinking about a list of Contributing Editors. Here are names I have been turning over in my mind:—

Allen Tate;
Mark Van Doren; both these names are in universal favor at Kenyon;
Richard Blackmur;
Howard Baker; would he serve?[2]
Gilbert Seldes; he represents Movie-art (if any);[3]
Empson; could we land him?
Roberta Schwartz; she is Mrs. Chalmers; a very fine sweet thoughtful person, not a meddler, and a sort of proxy that we could deal with for the President; she's thoroughly good though not a high-powered literary person;
Marianne Moore; though I don't know if she would serve;
A painting man;
A music man;
Ridgely Torrence, I think not; he would be harmless, but I see no reason for him.

This is about as far as I have gone. I think we want the names of the Editors on the mast-head; I should think they would be infinitely valuable in prejudicing critics and literary subscribers and libraries in our favor.[4]

I'll be seeing you soon, won't I? Thursday of next week I'll be in Nashville for ten days. You'll be mighty busy, but I'm counting on a meeting anyhow. And I want to see Sister Caroline and Nancy too. You say when and where. I'm here through the 29th; then at my mother's house, 1610 17th Avenue, South. I think she'll have a spare room for the Tates; if not, I can find one.

Affectionately,
John

1. Frederic Ridgeley Torrence (1875–1950) was a popular poet and dramatist.

2. Howard Baker (b. 1905), a classicist who has written poetry and fiction as well as criticism, is best known for *Induction to Tragedy* (1939).

3. Gilbert Seldes (b. 1893) wrote *The Seven Lively Acts* (New York: Harper, 1924) and several critical essays on popular culture.

4. The first advisory editors were R. P. Blackmur, Paul Rosenfeld, Roberta Teale Swartz, Allen Tate, Philip Timberlake, Mark Van Doren, and Eliseo Vivas.

To Cleanth Brooks

Austin, Texas, August 22, [1938]

Dear Cleanth:

I read through with tremendous interest and admiration the proof, got it away by express for you yesterday.[1] Duties are very heavy just now and I can't write at length.

I made (with pen, to distinguish them) some proof-corrections, passim, though not a thorough job.

The book stands up. The most unified of all the fine critical books of our day, with possible exception of Empson, coming to a fine climax with the chapter on reform of literary history.

Your position is argued with patient and persuasive logic & illustration. It's an extreme position, as I think, or held with extreme almost dogmatic tenacity. You never discuss any *limit* to complication, and you tend to think that *any* complication in a modern is logical or functional complication, whereas poor Burns' *my luve's like a red, red rose* is not functional or logical. To most readers it will seem that *Waste Land* is excessive complication and no unit[ary] poem at all, after reading your exposition.

You do a similar disservice to Yeats. You put into the 17th C tradition poems that no 17th C poet would have approved. You use *wit* too broadly, or else you do wrong to the poetry in requiring it; and *irony*. *Lycidas* and Virgil and all Great poetry falls by your estimates. Etc. Etc. See my brief editorial 3 weeks hence on the new Joyce: Which is the perfection of literature so far as one would discover in your position.[2]

Yet I believe this is about the ablest book that's appeared. Its error if any is on the side of the angels. More about this later.

I must hurry back to Nashville where the family awaits me. Please come through Nashville next week—the 29th, the 30th, 31st, or 1st, and let's have a party, and maybe go to Monteagle to see Allen and Andrew.

By the way, making out my reading requirement for the course in 17th C lyric at Bread Loaf, next year, I've put down your book.

Many thanks.

My best to Tinkum, whom Jack will want to see.[3]

John

---

1. Cleanth Brooks, *Modern Poetry and the Tradition* (Chapel Hill: University of North Carolina Press, 1939). Ransom reviewed this book in the *Kenyon Review*, II (Spring, 1940), 247–51.

2. "The Aesthetics of *Finnegans Wake*," *Kenyon Review*, I (Autumn, 1939), 424–28.

3. Tinkum Brooks, wife of Cleanth Brooks.

To Allen Tate

October 1, 1938

Dear Allen:

Was mighty glad to get yours of the other day. I have written my mother to send me on at once the novel at 1610 17th Avenue South—I guess I got away just a little too soon for it.[1] I can also see from here that Mama and the girls have all been enjoying themselves with my book, but it is time now for them to make way. I am in a big hurry to see it.

You will see for yourself what our masthead is for the time being. Roberta Schwartz is Mrs. Chalmers, and she is a fine woman, more of a person than a poet, and not the sort to give us trouble, while on the other hand she is a person of mighty fine taste, and we will have things to refer to her beyond a doubt. Timberlake is our local faculty man, a good though unambitious man. Vivas is a Venezuelan, a professor of philosophy at Wisconsin, considered brilliant among the philosopher group, and a pretty good literary man; maybe you have seen his writings.

The biggest problem of a first number is not to fill up the space with rather good critical stuff, but to maintain a high standard of good *writing*. There are literally scores of willing and practised critics but as you know there are few literary men—men of letters, shall I say.

On the practical side our immediate problem is to increase the size from the projected 96 pages to 112; I believe we've got that worked out now, with a slight straining of the budget. We don't want to look thin. I believe we must reduce our page size by whittling away the margins (not to affect the printed page) in order to maintain a sort of relation between the thickness and the flat area. Internally, I believe we can show plenty of substance, or density, by careful editorial pruning and close allocation of materials, and also perhaps by reducing the type size in the book review section. I enclose a sample of the letter we are sending out, which is meant to indicate to contributors that we can't have verbiage though we do want good writing. By the way, if you have names of likely contributors to suggest, I will send to them; I haven't at hand a list of the 150 or 200 names to which we have already sent, or I would enclose it; in its absence perhaps you'll mention the names which it is rather likely we have overlooked.

I was delighted to hear about Ford's being here still, and am writing him in this mail; the Olivet boys, Nerber and Macaulay, thought he had gone to Europe.

About the review which you have gallantly allowed for doing in spite of your other commitments against your time: I wonder if you would abandon the Ford review for this number and review either Valéry's new book, *Variété*, which is a collection of essays that I haven't seen, or Eliot's forthcoming play, *Family Reunion*.[2] The point is this: I don't think we ought to double up by having more than one piece either by or about the same man. If Ford writes an article, which might be the lead article, I'd rather wait a number to review his book, which is of a kind to stand up well against time anyhow. The same consideration applies to a good many cases, and I have tried to evade the doubling up in all cases. I don't want our family to look too limited, nor our resources. On this principle I forebore to write to somebody, Winters I think it would have been, to ask for a piece on Tate's analysis of his best poem, and Valéry's analysis of his best poem, both of recent periodical publication, and a most beautiful opportunity: I'll get to that a little later, when no book of yours is at the moment under review by us. But I'm not going to absurd pains to avoid this sort of thing, so just say if you would be willing to make the swap now. We've written the publishers for the books named.

Only after I got back here did I read the summer number of *Southern Review*, and especially your "Tension." It's your ripest and deepest piece of criticism, I think. Again I reflect that it's exactly the piece I wish I could have done, and the piece toward which my thinking, though not perhaps my pedestrian writing, was tending. It will stand up as the best single specimen of our most advanced contemporary criticism.

You may not like my Empson article, about to appear in the fall number of So. Review.[3] It may be a little reactionary, or on the Winters side; it furthers a big argument I was having with Brooks orally during the summer; and I guess I don't bother about consistency.

Best affectionate regards from the family to all of you.

John

1. Allen Tate, *The Fathers* (New York: Putnam, 1938). Reviewed by Howard Baker in the *Kenyon Review*, I (Winter, 1939), 90–93.

2. Tate rejected many of Ransom's invitations to review books and write essays. His first review for Ransom was of George F. Whicher's *This Was a Poet*, *Kenyon Review*, I (Spring, 1939), 200–203.

3. "Mr. Empson's Muddles," *Southern Review*, IV (Winter, 1938–39), 322–39.

To Allen Tate

October 18, [1938]

Dear Allen:

I hope you got the Valéry—we told the publisher to send it direct to you. That will be a fine small feature.

The opening number will be good not great. The best thing so far is the Ford essay, thanks to your suggestion. It's a tremendous jeu d'esprit, on the Gallic spirit—brilliant and reckless. Thanks. Another good piece is Rahv (Trotskyite, editor of *Partisan Review*) on the dead novelist Kafka. Bishop is doing a piece on Wolfe.[1] All we shall use will be passably good; though we suffer from the lack of articles by Tate, Blackmur, (whose Adams is too involved in the matter of family permissions, etc., to use at present), Warren, Van Doren. Van Doren's Shakespeare offerings won't quite do—not compacted, pointed enough; I regret this. But he wrote very nicely in offering it, and I think won't bear us a grudge for not using what he feared would be unsuitable. We will have some good poems, none by a major poet for the present.

The make-up will be very handsome, I think.

Now about our second number, featured by the Tate essay. What about writing on some of the aesthetic values of good prose? Nobody's prose exceeds your own at its high. There's no standard of evaluation at present; [Gorham] Munson sent us in an awfully muddy thing on two proses (Thoreau and Williams) which showed the lack of standards; all he had was something half assimilated from what at its best was dubious—Saintsbury's scansions. Why don't you turn this over in your mind? So far as I know, Herbert Read's book on prose style is the best thing up to date.[2] You said you would do the symbolism of the young British Leftists, but that's too dreary a field for you I think; I'd like to spare you that; I'd like to be able to announce a title if we can arrive at it.[3]

I hear good things about the big meeting at Nashville, was homesick at having to be absent. Mama writes me that the novel didn't come to her address, and I guess the postoffice re-addressed it to me to some wrong point. The office copy came in and was sent out the same day to Baker, who will review it; but I'll get hold of a copy.

Yours,
John

1. The first number of the *Kenyon Review* contained Philip Rahv's "Franz Kafka: The Hero as Lonely Man" and John Peale Bishop's "The Sorrows of Thomas Wolfe."

2. *English Prose Style* (1928).

3. Tate did not submit an essay for this issue.

To Allen Tate

[December, 1938]

Dear Allen:

I separate this part as a sort of postscript, in the event that you might want to show the letter proper.

The novel is powerful and beautiful.[1] It begins a little slowly perhaps; after the first third the reader is caught and held there. I cannot quite agree with your critics that it has a thesis; it has a philosophical commentary. The issue is tragic any way it might turn out; tragic for your hero, the father and the son, tragic or something more ignoble than tragic for the son-in-law. It certainly does *not* oversimplify the human issue of the falling South; nor is it of peculiarly local interest. In that sense I think it rather escapes the classification of Southern novel strictly. But I'm going to re-look at it and try to send you some more reflective considerations. These are impressions.

Baker by the way does just a so-so job with the book in our Review, though he is very complimentary.

Our first number will be out in installments from the 9th to the 12th. We are printing 5,000, in order to supply all the alumni (2700) and pick up some subscriptions. Send me some names if you will and I will send either (a) a circular or (b) a complimentary copy, with subscription blanks in any case.

It will be pretty good, a little on the popular side probably. We have a most unusual and, I think, distinguished cover design, done by Norris Rahming, the painter here directing the art students. I'll ask you please to send me an informal but perfectly ruthless critique of the number after you have seen it.

Red and Cinina promise to come by at Christmas, Red on his way to New York to the Modern Language Association, where he is on the program and to which he therefore rates passage money from his university.

We all send love to all.

Yours,
John

---

1. *The Fathers.*

To Allen Tate

January 3, [1939]

Dear Allen:

Thanks for your critique. We've had 8 or 10 solicited ones, some others. I agree with most of your points, studying the others.

I can come along at nearly any time now. A date towards the very end of January or beginning of February would suit me the best, since that would be during our long examination period. But I can manage any time, I believe.

You are good enough to undertake the prose-technique essay, and I think that ought to initiate a new and useful topic—there's none more important.[1] Would you like to have till May 1 on it? That would work out fine for the Review *provided you would this month write us a review*, so that in any case we have Tate in our 2nd issue. It happens too that we want the Whicher book on Emily Dickinson reviewed, and you are obviously the one for that; you or Blackmur. Would this schedule suit you? I haven't read the book but it seems to be, or to want to be, fairly definitive as far as it goes. I think it, or rather you, ought to have 1200 words or a little better—say 1200 to 1500 words. I can get the book to you as soon as you let me know you want it.

Blackmur will give us his Adams essay for 2nd number. Then there's a philosophical symposium, with 3 short papers, which looks important. Then an unusually good paper by Dr. Williams on the Spanish (loyalist) late poet Lorca, with two translations from Lorca by the Guggenheim-fellow Humphries. Then a pretty good piece of aesthetics by Lawrence Leighton, called "Disorder." Then an essay on American Art and the Federal Projects by Forbes Watson, the boss at Washington—but more on the art than on the Federal feature. Then the 2nd and shorter half of Rosenfeld's piece, which I like better than his first instalment.[2] All those things are in hand or nearly. We're accumulating some reserve. And a fine set of reviews. But Tate is paramount for us. Warren, I think, will have a review for the number.

Red and Cinina, by the way, have just given us a 10-day Christmas visit, though Red was in New York and Boston for 5 days of the time. Red's novel is fine.[3] I only wish his material were more *conventionally* heroic instead of being about the odd and isolated Kentucky nightriders. It's one of the smoothest narratives I've seen.

It will be fine to see you and Sister Caroline. But I dread the difficult decision I'm going to have to make.

Yours
John

---

1. Tate did not write this essay.

2. The second number of the *Kenyon Review* included the following essays: "García Lorca" by William Carlos Williams, "Disorder" by Lawrence Leighton, "New Forces in American Art" by Forbes Watson, and "The Advance of American Music" by Paul Rosenfeld.

3. Robert Penn Warren, *Night Rider* (Boston: Houghton, Mifflin, 1939).

To Sara Ella Crowe Ransom

March 5, 1939

Dear Mother:

I had written you a little letter Saturday, in answer to yours of a few days before that, but did not quite get it into the mails; and then Saturday night came your second letter, Special, so that I'll just tear up the old letter and start a new one.

You may be sure that I have not failed to be thinking to the best of my ability about whether or not to make the move to Greensboro—it isn't likely that you have thought more than I have about it, or that Ellene has; or that you and Ellene have a better command of the things at stake. Still, I'm glad to get the advices. It's a very difficult problem.

I don't look at the thing quite from your angle, and Ellene's, for this reason: I'm not at my age interested in my "prestige" or my "prospects," I'm interested in the position itself. I don't know whether the new position is a "step up" or a "step down" because I don't know what that means; I suspect it means whether or not the ladies who come to tea will think it is up or down; it seems to me that Greensboro is up, very decidedly, in the two things that count, which I shall mention presently. Allen Tate's interest in the business has nothing to do with it; Dean Jackson said he went to Nashville in my Vanderbilt days and found out all about me and has wanted me since that time, but was told in Nashville that it was no use trying to get me to leave Vanderbilt, so that Allen's interest comes afterwards and is not in any way responsible; but I don't like to hear you abusing Allen, whose publicity in my behalf two years ago was what made my leaving Vanderbilt a matter of record at all; and when you mention the man's being told about Vanderbilt's mistake by somebody sitting next to him at the Symphony, that was because somebody had seen something about it in the papers, or had been told by somebody that had seen the papers, and wouldn't have known anything about it in the long run but for Allen's generous indignation and plain talk in my behalf; nor would the dinner have come off if Allen hadn't got it up, nor would the "testimonials" have come in if he hadn't wired people for them; etc. etc.; I think it's mighty fine to have friends who will fight for you and it's quite easy to point to what they have accomplished in this case. As between Chancellor Kirkland and Doctor Mims and Chancellor Carmichael on the one hand and Allen on the other hand, Allen's friendship is worth all theirs put together multiplied by 100. They have done nothing for me, these many years, except not to fire me, but he has gone to much trouble to get me what he thinks are my "deserts." And as to Ellene's view that I owe "what I am today" to the reputation of my former pupils—of whom Allen is chief—and that this is the cue to the kind of thing I am to aim at in the future, I beg to differ for this reason: the thing that brings me an occasional offer, such as it is, is my writing; and the thing to do now is to forward my writing as much as possible. Let the pupils look after themselves.

The kind of person I don't like is the kind who is always making calculations about the state of his "prestige" and "prospects." I don't think that kind of person amounts to anything.

There are two big advantages in the Greensboro offer, as follows:

(1) The salary, $6,000.00 unconditionally, plus $500.00 for an additional 6 weeks work any summer I please immediately after Commencement in summer school. It's hard to overlook that. (The summer work would leave me two full months of vacation, or more.) It's not only a cool thousand dollars or more per year extra, but it's at a place where the college education of

Helen and Reavill, which would be at Chapel Hill nearby, can be secured more cheaply than any way whatever and yet will be just about the choicest education to fit their respective cases.

(2) The nature of the position is ideal, and better than I have ever ventured to expect, anywhere, any time. The offer reads: "to act as head of the English Department and to teach not more than 6 hours per week." As to being head, they need one badly, and at first there would be plenty to do, but after that Dean Jackson told me I could run the Department "with my left hand." As to the teaching, President Graham said to me: "You will be the boss, and if some time you don't want to teach at all there won't be anybody to say a thing about it." What they want me to do is to write and publish. I have a system of criticism, and many projects to get on with, and I could edit a great many valuable studies, with the aid of the North Carolina Press, which (they think) would put the University of North Carolina on the map; they would like me also to return to verse-writing if I choose. So not only do they offer me more money than any professor at the University of North Carolina gets, and more than any Southern professor I know of gets, with the possible exception of somebody at Duke, perhaps, but they offer me the most liberal terms, I'm sure, that can be found anywhere. I have been kept mighty busy here, with little chance to do my writing; and editing is a big job which will always take up my time as long as I am at it. I might mention also the fact that not many institutions would like my brand of scholarship, or rather criticism, since it's somewhat in defiance of the old-line scholars; at the Men's College of North Carolina, for example, there isn't a chance that I could go in on these terms except over the dead bodies of the English professors; and my peculiar qualifications are not as marketable as they might from this offer seem to be. But at Greensboro they not only like it but propose to subsidize it; and I'll never beat that.

I had enough conversation with the dean and the president in North Carolina to fix up the offer in exactly the best terms I thought there was any chance of getting; I know they understand perfectly what I want, and what I can do, and they have come all the way and offered exactly that, and without any commitment on my part, either; just my statement that I would "consider seriously" such an offer. They want me, and I would go in under the best circumstances.

My principal hesitation is in being sure that I am not "letting down" President Chalmers. But we carefully avoided stipulating any length of tenure, and there is no contractual obligation on either party to go further. As for the Review, we will have completed the second year of the experiment, and it was defined always in the minds of the trustees and patrons as a two-year experiment. If the Review is a success by that time it will continue. The Managing Editor is Professor Rice, who came from U. of Cincinnati especially to take part in the Review, and he is entirely capable of carrying on, and will have demonstrated that amply within the two years. He writes about as much for the Review as I do, and he is perfectly familiar with its tone and policy. So I don't fear for that angle. Another thing: Kenyon is a very small community, and my salary is in excess of the normal full professor's scale by much more than I had thought, and that is embarrassing; I don't like that kind of position; I am sure that the professors would rather not have such exceptional positions, though they have been uniformly kind and agreeable to me. I venture to think that the President made a mistake, even, in opening such a handsome position to me. I wouldn't want to tell this to anybody.

I don't think that Greensboro will "wait for me." They have to make me a head in order to offer me the salary they do (and by the way, a part of it, the part in excess of usual salaries, is for a "lectureship" or something; I stipulated that in order not to run into the same kind of situation there) and they must make an appointment now; their old head is automatically retired at the end of this year, but they would invite him to continue one year more provided they have my acceptance for the following year. If I refuse their offer they must fill the position. It would be impossible for me to go on here more than two years while under engagement to another place, and I wouldn't suggest it, but would simply decline flatly the offer. It's bad enough for me to go on for one year while under an unpublished contract to go elsewhere, but I would of course undertake to make a good job of that.

I've been very careful to give the President every opportunity to talk me out of the thing, and I have definitely not closed the deal or even committed myself in a tentative way to accepting it. I wrote him a long letter after several conversations which he is reading now. He doesn't seem to think I am taking advantage of him, and if he takes that tone of course it may make all the difference.

It looks like "Ca'lina" from here.

I must say too that I've thought that in North Carolina I might find a good position for Ellene, either at Greensboro or somewhere else. That's not a thing I can talk with Dean Jackson in advance, though.

Robb took some pictures of Jack yesterday which she will be sending along in a few days. You will see what a young man he has grown into. (Robb says this part was to be a "profound secret.") I guess maybe Robb will be driving South before the spring is out.

Much love to Annie and Ellene, and here's wishing yourself the best of health.

Affectionately,
John

Robb encloses the cards for Annie—I don't know where they came from.

To Allen Tate

March 29, 1939

Dear Allen:

Many thanks for those kind words about the second number. It's my hope it will show to all the disinterested that there is real editorial direction behind it. We can't possibly guarantee *all* the contents, if we are going to run as many as 20 contributors, as we did; but it seems better to have 20 contributors, with some unevenness, and departures from direction, than to write it all at home, or in the family so to speak.

The prospect of your piece on fiction is exciting as you define it; it will clearly be a contribution along the same lines as the present number, which I think ought to be our regular line, for a long time. We can't get any more pamphlets from the Encyclopedia, as we got two sets of them rather under protest for this number; we couldn't get three. I think you will want Vol. I No. 2, Morris's *Foundations of the Theory of Signs*, and possibly Vol. I No. 1, contributed to by half a dozen of their big shots and entitled *Encyclopedia and Unified Science*.[1] They are paper-bound little books, should not be too expensive. The Morris one is really brilliant; he makes Richards look mighty small; his definition of designatum and denotatum would have special bearing on your topic; and in fact it's my feeling that now, with these definitive treatments of semantical and logical problems, the science boys have delivered themselves into our hands.

My thought about Greensboro has been in part that you and I might direct some important studies, and make some of them, and use the North Carolina press. Maybe something more modest than but analogous to the Encyclopedia; Encyclopedia of Unified Art and Religion. But we could get together and go as fast as we wanted. With a few other people like Warren, and Herbert Read, and doubtless others.

Now about the Greensboro business. The President has got to the point of saying he doesn't want me to stay unwillingly, and waives any moral claim on me to stay, if there is any, etc. etc., and is generally acting handsome; except that he keeps wanting more time and raising his ante and upsetting my decision as fast as I get one made. He wants to see now about matching both the salary offer and the hours of duty offer which Dean Jackson made; with the additional argument that running a Review is better than running a Department. So it is. But on the other hand. The President doesn't have the money; he has to go out and get it, first because it doesn't come to him, and second because for my sake it must be money outside the budget; I'm a little bit scared to have him going round to the rich trustees and patrons for fear it's premature; they may not be ready yet to plump for a permanent Review. The other consideration is that Greensboro is South, and perhaps the Tates will be there, and it's three times as comfortable in the South, for a

Southerner. Greensboro is secure, permanent, comfortable, solid; Kenyon is not any of these things. I'm to tell the President Monday whether I'll give him time and authorization to go raising my money and my terms from those that have them to give, and if I say go ahead it will mean asking Dean Jackson and President Graham (who sent me a big telegram the other day) to wait some weeks. My feeling is today that I shall tell him I'm going to Greensboro. I'm sorter tired of the problem, and apprehensive about the moves that have to be taken if I stay here. Am in daily negotiation with Robb on the matter, and we both have the notion it's better to take Greensboro. But I'm writing now to Jackson and Graham without committing myself, so don't give me away. I should say the chances are five to one I'll write in my acceptance next week. This may sound as if I'm trying to pry something else out of them, but I'm not at all; nor have I pried with President Chalmers, or done anything else except listen to his pleas and plans.

Johnson is sending the circulars to you, and presently to Dyer at Savannah, and I will write to Dyer.[2] Johnson says the figure of 1,000 plus which he quoted you was inclusive of only a little under 600 annual subscribers; the rest were consignments to bookstands, of which the larger part will certainly sell. We're not quite as good as his language led you to believe.

Don is a real problem to me. I haven't been able yet to write him about his book of selected poems, and I simply couldn't touch them in a published review; nor do I dare send them out to any good reviewer.[3] Don just stopped growing before the rest of us did; Don and Merrill are the boys in the bunch. Don's case is partly private but partly, I'm afraid, the effect of ideology; his peculiar patriotism, consciously or unconsciously, is one that calls for no action, just speeches and poems; and I'm sure many Southerners are in the same way their own worst enemies.

Affectionately,
John

1. Charles W. Morris's *Foundations of the Theory of Signs* (1938) influenced Ransom's "Wanted: An Ontological Critic," the concluding chapter of his *The New Criticism* (1941), and Tate's "Literature as Knowledge," *Southern Review*, VI (Spring, 1941), 629–57.

2. G. W. Dyer (1870–1948), professor of economics and sociology at Vanderbilt from 1907 until his retirement.

3. Donald Davidson, *Lee in the Mountains and Other Poems* (Boston: Houghton, Mifflin, 1939).

To Sara Ella Crowe Ransom

May 13, [1939]

Dear Mother:

Sorry it's not possible to take you to Church this Mother's Day tomorrow, but here's wishing you many happy returns. Robb and Jack send their best.

Have been waiting it seems a long time to write you something definite about my decision on the jobs offered. It is just now closed up, and the answer is that I shall stay here. I gave Dr. Chalmers every delay he asked for, with the result that finally he announced that the Carnegie Corporation had agreed to give the College a handsome lump sum which would go for the "encouragement of creative writing," and that their particular object specified was the employment of Ransom as editor to carry on the Review and do light teaching. The money won't come till next year, nor be announced till the Corporation Board meets in October, but I saw the letter from its president, and there is no doubt it will be as he says. My offer here will be, beginning with 1940, a salary of $5,700.00 and a house, with my time to go to the Review, teaching of one course only, and writing. That's better than my present contract by $1200.00, the work lighter by two courses. Besides, another much relished improvement: there's special provision for my salary, or a good deal of it; it doesn't come out of general budget, and I don't stand in the way of the other professors, as I felt I was doing. The North Carolina people were mighty nice, and gave me every requested time for consideration. But this looked better than that in the end, and besides I was already here.

A letter from Reavill is talking about coming home for the summer; time flies. He's out about June 5 or 6, I think. Helen not till a little later. She is enjoying college life very much, and doesn't know how well she is doing, but feels that it is better.

I go to Texas the middle of August again; have nothing for the early summer.

Thanks for the birthday good wishes.

Maybe Robb and Mrs. Reavill and Jack will be going down to Nashville to get Reavill, but it isn't decided. Mrs. Reavill has been here several weeks now. She had another fall this spring, you know; her broken wrist is still bothering her a good deal, though out of the splints.

Love to the gals.

Affectionately,
Your son,
John

To Allen Tate

May 13, [1939]

Dear Allen:

It turned out that I have passed up Greensboro, just as you have. Chalmers was right, he secured the Carnegie Corporation thing for my benefit; that is, I saw the letter from President Keppel, of the Corporation, saying that he would recommend it to the Board at the October meeting, and supposed there would be no question of it, as they already had the College down for a gift. It isn't a grant to the Review, but to the encouragement of literature, or something like that, but Keppel specifies that they have looked me up, and the Review, and that project is to use the money. My salary, beginning 1940, will be improved by $1200.00, and furthermore the bulk of it will be coming from a special gift, and I won't be standing in the light of the other professors. My work will be cut to the point of editing the Review and teaching one class. The job here is at least equivalent to the Greensboro offer in every respect, and in fact a little better. But Jackson and Graham have been mighty nice, and I would very cheerfully have taken their offer.

By all means I want to come by Monteagle and see you in July—if that is where you are to be. It appears that we are not drawing any nearer professionally as it seemed we might do.

I don't think the new Review is going to be so hot. In the lack of the essays from Blackmur, Schwartz, and Tate. We're about to go to press. Nearly everything depends on whether we get a good lead article out of Bishop on the World's Fair, due Monday. Or whether, behind that even, he comes through with an article at all. At one time we had Auden booked to do it, but he accepted a job which has kept him out of New York these two weeks. Then back to Bishop, with whom we had negotiated originally.

Now I must get to my piece on Yeats; a mean one, which I can see through pretty well at this stage, without having got it down properly[1]

Yours,
John.

1. W. H. Auden did not contribute prose to the *Kenyon Review* until many years later. John Peale Bishop's "World Fair Notes" and Ransom's "Yeats and His Symbols" appeared in the *Kenyon Review*, I (Summer, 1939).

To Allen Tate

Austin, Texas, [Summer, 1939]

Dear Allen:

You have every reason to seem pleased & confident over your return to verse.[1] The *K.R.* is just as glad to get it as it would have been glad to have the prose essay, which can wait. The poem is good. It's not best (for A.T.) but it's a lot freer, moves better, is more taken in stride, etc., than the last poems you were writing, in the previous dispensation. It's clean and strong. The climax, which I couldn't foresee, comes off. It's fine that your hand is in again. Please give us first chance at poems.

I enclose my PBK effort.[2] I *mean* effort. What started out as a lark became a burden, and I could have written several free poems out of the energies I spent on this one occasional poem. Hardly anybody has seen it yet. I'd *very* much like your word on it. The way that poem looks in print to me, perhaps even more to my friends, will determine my future avocations, pretty much.

You, Stevens (a fine informal Nature poem, longish), and I will figure in Autumn number.[3]

I'll make every effort to get back there about Aug. 31 or July 1. Can't tell yet. You and Caroline made me feel mighty at-home. Andrew is a great picker, by the way, I do like his lady.

Aff'ly
John

1. Ransom refers to Tate's "The Trout Map," *Kenyon Review,* I (Autumn, 1939), 404–405.

2. Ransom's Phi Beta Kappa poem, "Address to the Scholars of New England," *Kenyon Review,* I (Autumn, 1939), 406–408.

3. Wallace Stevens' "Variations on a Summer Day" appeared in the *Kenyon Review,* II (Winter, 1940), 72. Other poems in this issue included W. H. Auden's "For Sigmund Freud" and Theodore Spencer's "The Paradox in the Circle." Ransom had an essay in this same number, "The Pragmatics of Art," the piece to which he may be referring here.

To Allen Tate

November 9, [1939]

Dear Allen:

A recent note from Red says that they are to stay on a while longer in Italy. They have moved to Capri—very quiet and fine there now, they say. They are being advised by the American Consul at Naples, who will get them off if and when it becomes necessary. I have held the parts from the play to go over them once more and determine my ideas about them a little more precisely.[1] I think possibly Red's "business" is too complicated for plot, and some of it too trifling; and there's the boldest possible mixture of steep poetic symbolic bits, in Red's own tones, and of very broad satirical jingles; I don't know whether his scheme can carry any real poetry. But the whole business is interesting, and I can't say how well it might work. I'll send them off this week without fail to you. Then you can write him what you think. He asked me to get them to you.

We've asked Trilling to do the literary or aesthetic part of our Freud symposium. I think Krutch would do it better if he would do it—but I have had the feeling he wouldn't do it. And Trilling is mighty capable. He hasn't replied as yet. We asked Lovejoy to do the philosophical one but he declined. Whitehead is too old, I am convinced from what I hear of his now doddering state. We have asked Nagel to do it. The therapeutic and social one we have asked Miss Horney to do; her recent book on it is brilliant, the best written thing we have seen at all.[2]

Today Edmund Wilson sends us a long poem, pretty bad stuff. And Kenneth Burke keeps sending things, including a poem that was just impossible, and a long argument attached which is almost funny. Burke is good as long as you can tell him just what you want, but he fundamentally is short on aesthetic sense, in my opinion.

Our forthcoming number will be good but dull. Things we had wanted to liven it up didn't come through. My rejoinder to Morris is about ready to go to press, and when I get the proof I'll send you one—since we are both working on that line.

When you get a rip-roaring satirical impulse, to hit something pretty hard, and to talk downright fantastical, save it for us—I think some red-hot satire is what K.R. needs.

Your piece will go as you say; in one instalment or two.[3] I hope you won't forget what you first told me about it—that it was to show that there was a problem of meaning or "designatum" about those last sentences of "Turn of the Screw"; in other words, I hope you'll make it specific concrete literary talk while you are also being theoretical. Sorry you won't be coming to lecture this fall, but glad to count on you after Christmas.

I forgot to express my great interest in your editorship of the Agrarian paper.[4] I'm interested to the extent of planning Sunday to knock off a review of Smith's FORCES IN AMERICAN CRITICISM if you think that available.[5] Since he has many sneers at Agrarian philosophies in it, it might have political as well as literary interest. I guess you pay for matter? You know the financial complexion of worthy writers. Morgan Blum of N.O. will write it up for K.R.

Nancy's escapade sounds like our Helen all over. That younger generation beats me. I have no influence whatever for law and order with my children. Jack is in the stage of calling everybody "Stinkie" and "Pewee," the worst words he knows; he gets a great thrill out of it even if nobody laughs.

Regards to Sister Caroline.

Yours
John

---

1. Ransom here refers to Robert Penn Warren's "Proud Flesh," a play that became *All the King's Men* (1946).

2. Ransom was planning a symposium on Freud. Joseph Wood Krutch, A. O. Lovejoy, A. N. Whitehead, and Karen Horney did not write essays for the occasion, nor did Ernest Nagel (who became a contributor later). The contributors to "The Legacy of Sigmund Freud," *Kenyon Review*, II (Spring, 1940), were Lionel Trilling, Alexander Reid Martin, and Eliseo Vivas.

3. Tate's "Literature as Knowledge" was published in the *Southern Review*.

4. *Free America*.

5. Ransom's review of Bernard Smith's *Forces in American Criticism* appeared in *Free America*, IV (January, 1940), 19–20.

To Cleanth Brooks

November 22, [1939]

Dear Cleanth:

Wishing you and Tinkum a happy Thanksgiving!

I owe you a letter or two; and one to Albertus.[1] I'll come through Jan. 1 all right with the Hardy piece.[2] But the Ransoms will have to stay at home this Christmas, I'm afraid, and forego Baton Rouge, the Mississippi coast, the Modern Language circus, etc. Too many educable children in our family keep the exchequers depleted. We hate to think of not going to the sunny South, though, I can tell you. Isn't it possible that you will want to flee the scholars and pedants and head towards these parts? We have a fine latch-string, easy to pull, action guaranteed.

Thanks for the special autograph edition of the Big Book.[3] I already had the Review copy, sent by the publishers. I had planned to editorialize, and give it the very best send-off, with a haggling reservation or two towards the end to make the review decently "objective"—in this number, now just gone to press, for Winter 1940. But I had to write an answer to Morris and it took 12 pages; and I dare not appear on more pages than that of my own journal. So it will have to be Spring 1940. But it will be first in order then. As I have pondered on your general position I am most doubtful about your references to science. I have the idea that any definite and positive structural pattern discoverable in the poem, or anywhere on earth for that matter, is an act of science, not a peculiar act of poetry; unless you want poetry to rate merely as superior science. Science is not simple as you imply. The binomial theorem is pretty complicated. But everything in it, every term, is functional. You (and Red too, the two authors of UNDERSTANDING POETRY) seem to be primarily interested in displaying functional structure. For me, at the present, that's not quite the main cue. But wait till you see my argument with Morris; you will guess how I would apply it to your quarrel with science.

We have a bang-up article in proof from one Harold Whitehall on the *New American English Dictionary*. He is a young English (Cambridge) chap that has taught with me two summers out at Austin; regularly on the Wisconsin English faculty, now on a Guggenheim. He is a fine linguistic and phonetic scholar, not a dry crabbed one, and the best prosodist I know, especially in native English or accentual measures. He was easily the most effective and the most popular man on the staff at Austin. And he loves the South; it's wrong to let Wisconsin have him. He's a naturalized American now, with a nice little American wife. I wonder if you're not going to need a linguistic man soon, with [William A.] Read's retirement imminent. He's the best man in the country, I am persuaded. He ranks assistant professor at Wisconsin. If you want to give him a try-out, why not get him for a lecture before or after Christmas? He's got some dates in the Southwest and possibly in Cuba; I've heard he is a good speaker. He can certainly make language study hum. Address: Harold Whitehall, Apartment 49, 419 Sterling Court, Madison, Wis. He's going to New Orleans for the Christmas meeting, and I hope you will meet him. He's anxious to get acquainted with L.S.U., I happen to know. [Randall] Stewart knows him, by the way, I think. (Stewart is a great chap, incidentally.)

Red and Cinina seem to be settled down handsomely at last. I've seen most of the new play now, and am much impressed.[4] The poetry goes into Red's fanciest vein, but I believe it will come through on the broad farcical base under it. It's more daring than Eliot, a good deal.

Affectionately,
John

P.S. I'm at the office, but I'll sign for the family (Robb, Jack, Helen) and send their affectionate regards to T. and you. I know they'll honor my check.

---

1. Albert Erskine, the first business manager of the *Southern Review*, later became an editor at Random House.

2. "Honey and Gall," *Southern Review*, VI (Summer, 1940), 2–19.

3. *Modern Poetry and the Tradition*.

4. Warren's "Proud Flesh."

1940–1949

UCH OF Ransom's correspondence during the 1940s was related to his efforts on behalf of the *Kenyon Review* to attract essays and poems from the best possible contributors, to get editors and contributors for special issues, and to acquire individual and foundation support for special programs and projects (such as the *Kenyon Review* fellows, the Rockefeller fellows, and the Doubleday fiction prize). Nevertheless, he conducted an exchange of critical views with Tate, Arthur Mizener, Cleanth Brooks, Robert Penn Warren, and others. He continued to send Tate his essays and books for his reactions, and Tate always responded at length. He explained to Tate how "Wanted: An Ontological Critic" became a part of *The New Criticism* and how it changed completely the nature of the book he had written. Similarly, he always sent Tate or Warren or Lytle his immediate reactions to a poem, essay, or story that he had received from one of them.

The correspondence reveals Ransom's attempts to merge the *Kenyon Review* and the *Southern Review* as well as reasons why the merger did not occur. In 1945 the first edition of Ransom's *Selected Poems* appeared, and its reception clearly indicates that his reputation as a poet had become firmly established, though he had written little poetry for twenty years.

His reactions to Tate's commentary on *The New Criticism* clearly demonstrate Ransom's intentions and how he came to select the five representatives of the New Criticism: I. A. Richards, William Empson, T. S. Eliot, Yvor Winters, and R. P. Blackmur, whose critical emphases range from psychology to philosophy.

His letters to Tate also show the extent of Ransom's disappointment with Lytle's and Warren's fiction. "I've just been looking at Andrew's new book," he wrote on November 15, 1941, "and I'm disappointed, and also somewhat embarrassed." On December 15, 1941, he returned to the same subject: "Since writing you I've read Andrew's book very closely, and consecutively, and it's better than I first thought." On June 3, 1950, he wrote Tate: "I think Red's book is pretty horrible. It's like Tom Wolfe except that it's less consistent. Red's philosophy seems now to justify the guilt of his heroes (he never had much heroines) on the ground that they are implicated in the Universal Guilt." His opinion of Warren's poetry was always more complimentary. "The poems make a very beautiful book, Red," he wrote Warren on April 2, 1942. "I have found some extreme fans of yours among the boys here; and it takes a little book unit to show just what your distinction and personality and recipe for a poem amount to." And on September 4, 1942, he wrote: "The Eleven Poems are very brilliant. No important poet in our time ever was so successfully withheld from his natural public." He wrote Arthur Mizener on May 24, 1946, that Edmund Wilson's *Memoirs of Hecate County* was the "most amazing book for some time," with a "hero whose artiness is absolute" and "if he's not the Great Lover, he's quite a performer." Ransom added: "I have always defended Wilson. . . . But this will do him in." He wrote Caroline Gordon Tate why he had to reject Cleanth Brooks's review of A. O. Lovejoy's "fine big rich book on 'History of Ideas.'" His friends learned that they could not always expect immediate acceptance in the *Review*. He rejected a story by Caroline Gordon, fiction by both Lytle and Warren, and even one poem by Tate. Obviously, he was willing to sacrifice almost anything, including friendship, to enhance the quality of the material that appeared in the magazine that he was editing.

To Allen Tate

Gambier, April 19, [1940]

Dear Allen:

Mighty glad to hear from you.

Merrill is not a hero, and so far as I know that is about the worst thing you can say of him. I think his fingers have been burned in the Cal-and-Lowell-Seniors matter; it got beyond his control. He wrote me months ago that he had told the parents that they thought too much of the Cal-problem in terms of to marry or not to marry; that marriage would be better than a lot of things; that this one might be not so bad, but even if it were that it might be a good thing for Cal. But he should have come down harder than that. The fact is that he was retained by the *parents* not the son; and by the *mother* not the father. He has advised them in several matters well, to my knowledge. They made an issue of Cal's marriage: if he married that girl, he was not their dutiful son, etc. They got that no-marriage qualification sewed up in Cousin Lawrence's "Bachelor" fellowship which Cal could have had at Yale; a silly thing. This is secret still, better burn this up. But as you say Cal is married now, and any right man will have to be on his side.[1] I'm ready to do anything I can for him, and it is more and more likely that a job will develop here for him; I'm working hard for it.

Am much interested in the Princeton version of the war between creative literature and scholarship. About two weeks ago I wrote to Cleanth proposing that they and we run two parallel and hot-stuff symposiums at the same moment, next fall, calling attention each to the other's symposium, and get it into TIME's notice; then circularize the whole membership of M.L.A. with the matter, with an idea not only to the circulation of the periodicals but to some uproar at the next-Christmas meeting of the scholars in Boston; the rift has been steadily widening right in that body.

Cleanth is very enthusiastic, and I guess we'll go right ahead. I think we should have three pieces in each Review. The four most qualified writers would be Cleanth, Tate, Mizener,[2] and Ransom, probably. Then we might look hard and find two able undergraduates or graduate students to come in with their angle. Say: in Kenyon Review, Tate, Cleanth, and an undergraduate or graduate student; in Southern Review, Mizener, Ransom, and an undergraduate or graduate student. Would you be agreeable to that? I think these pieces should be just as uncompromising as they can be *provided that* they are circumstantial and accurate; that they be not those complaints and satirical remarks merely, such as have been got off here and there, but something really to carry persuasion.[3]

I'd like very much to get your ideas on such a scheme, and your suggestions as to the performers. I'm writing Cleanth that I'm writing you.

Meanwhile we all look forward to May 3.

Yours,
John

P.S. Title of Symposia: English Professors and Literary Sense?

---

1. Merrill Moore, the Fugitive poet who had long since become a physician, was Robert Lowell's psychiatrist for many years; and as Ian Hamilton makes plain, he often acted as an intermediary between Lowell and his parents (*Robert Lowell: A Biography* [New York: Random House, 1983], 63, 65). In this instance, as usual, Lowell ignored the wishes of his parents; he married Jean Stafford, who would become a distinguished fiction writer.

2. Arthur Mizener, a critic, who was teaching at Yale and would later write biographies of F. Scott Fitzgerald and Ford Madox Ford, was beginning his long relation with the *Kenyon Review* as one of Ransom's most prolific contributors.

3. In autumn, 1940, the *Kenyon Review* and the *Southern Review* published a joint symposium entitled "Literature and the Professors." The *Southern Review* contained essays by Ransom, Tate, Joe Horrell, Wright Thomas, and Harry Levin; the *Kenyon Review*, by Brooks, Mizener, Sidney Cox, Hade Saunders, and Lionel Trilling.

To Allen Tate

[Spring, 1940]

Dear Allen:

Thursday and Friday nights Pipkin called McDowell on the phone to get him to come at once to Baton Rouge to take up job as Review Secretary for the summer at $125 to $150 per month; the regular secretary (is that Erskine?) being about to leave for summer; and you know that beginning in autumn they were expecting McDowell there on a year's fellowship and extra-work proposition which would make him a living.

Well, on Friday we at last got a decision in the matter of appointing our own Secretary, and it had turned out to be McDowell. So my wire to you Saturday was by way of trying to get the L.S.U. combination job for Lowell.

I wrote at great length to Pipkin, after sending him a long telegram letter. I told him that everybody here, including Ransom, Rice, Coffin,

Timberlake, with the single exception of the President, had stood out for Lowell over McDowell; but that the President had nevertheless decided in favor of McDowell. (In justice to McDowell: we all believed he would be perfectly satisfactory.) I told him I would have only envy of him if he got that team (Cal and Jean) as it was precisely the team we had wanted here. Jean's qualifications for the summer thing are superlative, I should think. So I hope for the best. Am delighted that Cal is not sulking, is eager for the job, and it may well prove better for him than our job would, if he only gets it.[1]

President Chalmers expressed great regret at going over my recommendation, and entirely in the matter of Cal's qualifications as the part-time one-course instructor. He insisted that Cal is not mature yet. But I, and the others too, are so much better acquainted with Cal than the President that I am not too pleased at our recommendation being over-ridden. I think either that the President was just determined to assert his authority, especially since we turned down two names that he had defended; or, this is deeper and more dangerous, that he is beginning to be afraid I am too highbrow an influence, regards Cal as my man, etc. etc. . . . It is perhaps worth remarking that Cal is to make the Commencement oration, and is going to burn up the industrialist and Episcopal educational smoothies at least by implication; everybody here is delighted with his speech, which is along the lines of his mid-winter one, but I think maybe the President dreads the thought of his trustees hearing it. In other words, his courage is going. Though he overestimates the alarm of his trustees, so far as I can see. They won't understand Cal's oration.

Merrill Moore was here a couple of weeks ago, and did a nice lecture on Edward Lear, taking him apart as a psychologist. The most tactful, moderate, and persuasive thing I've ever known him to do. He was prepared to talk with the President urging him to appoint Cal for our job, but the President got back from a trip just in time to tell Merrill goodbye. I had Cal to breakfast with us just before Merrill left; and Merrill's patter was so bad and his insensitivity to Cal's sensibilities was so gross that I had to sit down and write Merrill a very sharp letter, immediately after he had gone. I therefore am prepared to move towards your position in regard to his status as a human being and a friend. But I think he is just obtuse, I do not think he is mean.

I'm awfully sorry about the headaches, I hope you can get to the bottom of them. I'm glad to hear of AMERICAN SCHOLAR coming out on the side of righteousness.

The Princeton speech is part of a series to be gathered up in a little publication, Stauffer says, but I think it is not part of an institute or symposium, like your affair at Columbia, which sounds fine.[2]

Helen is a little bit gleeful to hear such horrid reports about Nancy. But not so much on principle, I think, as because it will show her parents how common and "nice" it can be for girls to have academic troubles.

Tell Nancy we all send love, anyhow, and give my best to Caroline.

In great haste,
John

1. Charles Pipkin, an editor at the *Southern Review*, was offering David McDowell, later an editor at Random House and Crown, a job as business manager of the *Southern Review* as a temporary replacement for Albert Erskine. In the event Jean Stafford got the job, and Robert Lowell, her husband, went to Louisiana State to attend graduate school in English.

2. Ransom refers to his "Criticism as Pure Speculation," first published in Donald A. Stauffer (ed.), *The Intent of the Critic* (Princeton: Princeton University Press, 1941), 91–124.

To Arthur Mizener

April 26, [1940]

Dear Arthur:

Let's let the Tennyson essay ride till Fall; that's entirely satisfactory so far as the publication schedule is concerned from our angle.[1] I can see a mighty good essay coming; and there has never been any, not one, on the subject, if a generalization can be accepted from a man with as scattering a knowledge of things as mine is. Speaking of the conventions of that funny period, I am impressed with the sense that Matthew Arnold in his two essays, Function of Criticism, and Study of Poetry, is tops in the whole history of British criticism, unless we can verify our suspicion that tops hasn't been reached till just now. Right in the middle of the thing, Arnold saw the speciousness of the literary show all around him; a very rare performance; though of course he got wind of it first from his reading of the French critics of French literature. Lack of *disinterestedness* in criticism and in literature was his analysis of the thing. I am now giving a mild undergraduate course, introductory, in Tennyson and Browning, and I grow more and more amazed and offended at the heavy British coat-and-vest on that literature.

Robert Daniel sent me the clipping from Daily News on the Tate address.[2] I was much pleased. But I feel sure that the young reporter got Tate's tone down wrong. He has him exclaiming "Tommyrot!" in the middle, and speaking in a prophetic, earnest, almost oracular voice; I think surely he must have missed a Tatian irony. Otherwise I am forced to think that Allen is more excited over this issue than he has ever been in his mature literary life.

You let me down easy in the essay on the Sonnets of the Bard.[3] That is, your references were extremely handsome to this Ransom who has the surprising version of the 18th century criticism. Your actual argument is unfettered as it should be. But I don't think that substantially our controversy is quite becoming to either of us as a son of the morning. I evidently was intemperate and got myself way out on a limb; you in returning the compliment are pretty extreme yourself, and I seem to see you out in some such position inviting retribution. I have just read the essay once, though very closely, and don't have it by me, so that I shall have to speak from that impression, and doubtless will do you wrong in referring to the argument, for which I apologize in advance.

We don't come to grips really. You remark that Ransom represented Shakespeare as a metaphysical poet and then found fault with him on that ground. You seem to imply that this representation was not grounded, but I wonder if that is really your intention; you don't discuss the evidence. Then you indicate that Ransom compared the ordinary "romantic" sonnets unfavorably with the metaphysical sort of poetry, and give the impression that it is this heresy you wish to examine. But you don't discuss the ordinary "romantic" sonnets, not one. You look hard and find a strange sonnet which you examine from the Richards-Empson critique of multiple meaning. You don't offer any estimate of what part of the Shakespeare sonnets are composed on this principle; nor any sense that most sonnets don't offer that sort of critique at all. The net is that Ransom discussed some fairly metaphysical sonnets, and you discuss one multiple-meaning sonnet, and you are not discussing the same thing. I wonder if Ransom didn't at any rate indicate that the metaphysical sonnets, so-called, were greatly in the minority, while Mizener permits the innocent reader to believe that multiple-meaning was the normal method of composition in Shakespeare.

The only place where Ransom and Mizener really come to blows is a very little one—the bare ruined choirs passage. Here I would propose: that it's entirely possible Shakespeare had his eye on the bird-choir effect the minute he thought about denoting the time of life by the autumn leaves; that he knows (intuitively—I would tend to resist the thesis of the enormous deliberate calculation on Shakespeare's part, as I will mention below) that the singing birds don't belong very expressly to his tenor but almost exclusively to his vehicle, and is not deterred, as, I think, he should not be; therefore has an intermediate and transitional version of the vehicle, namely the cold bare boughs shaking in the winter wind, a perfect adaptation of vehicle to tenor; and then after this introduction of vehicle lets vehicle really develop itself into the choirs aspect, with the birds; knowing that Mizener or any decent reader will see at once that it is beautiful in itself (pure vehicular beauty) and then will see to it if he is a logician (and Mizener is that, a cannier one than Ransom) that some kind of no-singing-strains-now can be worked up in the tenor if necessary. That would be Shakespeare all over. The slurring-up and the slurring-down from one thing to the other sounds like a technical discovery in Mizener's careful locution and doesn't really refer to anything special that I can discover. It is an example of the "multiplication of entities beyond necessity" which Empson-Richards-Brooks-Mizener men are prone to.

I think there's something certainly to multiple meaning. But I think there's never so much to it as is made out by the enthusiasts. In the present case the sonnet is almost a metaphysical one; just the sort of main figure the metaphysical poets liked; the love, the psychological state, elaborated into a big physical analogue; with alternative descriptions of it, all equally physical; and even this sort of alternation, this doing the thing several times over in different versions, was not unusual in the orthodox metaphysical practice. By the way, Ransom never wanted to mean that a metaphysical poem was perfect logic; though I haven't reviewed him to see if he could have left that impression. Perhaps you remember hearing Ransom talk expressly on that subject in his recent unworthy Yale public address.[4] Here we have that pusillanimous thing, the issue that turns out to be one very largely in degree; which stultifies any argument, unless on the possible understanding that differences of degree do produce remarkable qualitative and therefore absolute differences.

I think the Empson-Mizener studies in Shakespeare's sonnets ought at once to be fortified by a research to discover to what extent, that is in what frequency, Shakespeare tried that method. It would have to be an effort in more than research to *evaluate* the cases in which he does try it. As to the present case, I think, candidly, that you destroy Shakespeare's public if it cared to adhere to your analysis; that the sonnet has a superb flash of power or so, and then runs quickly into almost impossible obscurities; and your analysis of the obscurity makes it the more obscure. And by the way: why is it necessary for the reader to keep firmly in mind all seven possible meanings of *state*, because each one will be expressly needed, when presently it is undesirable or fatal or something equally unfortunate for the reader to try to define the different possible meanings of some other key word: it is that the meanings of the new term are more than 7, and one must draw the line at 7? Or at any number of meanings for a single term that would require two figures to express? or is it three figures? And, again when does one focus on one of the separate meanings, when does one not focus? And doesn't the critical vocabulary of the Multiple-meaning School require a more definite term?

I can testify for Ransom that he has never touched on the metaphysicals without leaving out much of his own attitude; or at least without presently realizing that there is good deal more in his own attitude. Metaphysical poetry is certainly limited; that is a quarrel which I have made by letter and by voice several times with Brooks, though in my little recent review of his book that point didn't come up.[5] For instance, *wit* is a dangerous quality; it is as bad for poetry as it is good; and if *wit* is the predominant character of metaphysical poets I have to cross them off my list, with every reluctance. But on the other hand they are certainly not dry, as Mizener seems to imply. "For God's sake hold your tongue, and let me love"—etc. etc. They are very various in their images even in the same poem. In the Valediction Forbidding Mourning, there are at least four major vehicles, each one better and more loving than the last one. But Mizener will recognize all this, speaking in his true and non-disputational self.

Some time we'll talk all this out. I think it is healthy to find differences of opinion between Ransom and Mizener, Ransom and Brooks, Brooks and Mizener (see a remark in the letter about Tennyson), even Tate and Brooks or Mizener or Ransom. Healthy also to let the public see the differences. But fatal if the differences stop further collaboration and discussion. Old Victorian Ransom.

Sincerely yours,
John

Probably it's true—I'll look this up—that much of your argument about S's duplicity or multiplicity of meanings is a general argument about S's *looseness* of imagery and his ability to keep his romantic turn from getting out of hand. If so, you *were* replying to R's aspersions on the romantic method.

P.S. #2. Your nice note to hand. You were more than decent in *tone, air,* etc. Think no more about that. Concentrate on your intellectual sins (if any). But even *there* I guess your case is really pretty strong.

---

1. This essay never appeared in the *Kenyon Review*; instead Mizener wrote "Scholars as Critics" as part of the symposium "Literature and the Professors," *Kenyon Review*, II (Fall, 1940).

2. Robert W. Daniel, who was teaching at Yale with Mizener, had sent Ransom an account of Tate's Princeton lecture "Miss Emily and the Bibliographer," later published in the *American Scholar*, IX (Autumn, 1940), 449–60.

3. "The Structure of Figurative Language in Shakespeare's Sonnets," *Southern Review*, V (Spring, 1939), 730–47. In this essay Mizener replies to Ransom's "Shakespeare at Sonnets."

4. This lecture, much revised, appeared as "Honey and Gall."

5. Ransom reviewed Brooks's *Modern Poetry and the Tradition* in the *Kenyon Review*, II (Spring, 1940), 247–51.

To Robert Penn Warren

June 17, 1940

Dear Red:

The family all got in last night, and I am feeling more normal. Robb will be writing Cinina.[1] But maybe we can go to Bread Loaf via Bennington. I'll drop you a card if we can. In no case, I guess, will we be able to stop over a night, but maybe we could spend a few hours with you; that is, we'll hardly get off from here till the last thing; and we are due at Bread Loaf Friday the 28th. I'll work on that angle, I can tell you.

The letter in which I ventured a criticism of the play came back to me, not delivered, many weeks later.[2] I have the thing, but it isn't fit to send. I criticized chiefly the disparity between the ruling tone, the lowbrow tone, in which the action and the dialogue are cast, and the tone of the lyrics which come at the climaxes; you have almost outdone yourself in some of these lyrics, which are mighty fine; but I'm afraid there's too much interval between them and the choruses just before, or the action before the choruses. However: it's a grand close play, with special "features" à la Auden or Cocteau, only better and sounder than A. and C. Your course this summer is ideal; Fergusson will know what I don't know at all, he'll know *theatre.*[3] I think you couldn't do better than exactly what you are doing.

May I interrupt the summer's idyll to this extent: write us a review of Faulkner's latest book, HAMLET—won't you?[4] We are trying to keep our review section up to top notch, and not always doing it. Fewer and better reviews is our present intention. One thousand to 1500 words for you on Faulkner—we can get the book to you at once—by August 5. Please see if you can't do that. It'll just keep you in trim.

Yours, with everybody's best
to Cinina and to you,
John

1. Warren's first wife.
2. "Proud Flesh."
3. Francis Fergusson, author of *The Idea of a Theater* (1949) and many other studies of theater and literature, was teaching drama at Bennington College.
4. Warren's review appeared in the *Kenyon Review*, III (Spring, 1941), 253–57.

To Allen Tate

January 16, [1941]

Dear Allen:

Was delighted to have your note approving my recent essay.[1] It's about the only comment I've had at all; the boys at Baton Rouge said nothing whatever so that I don't even know whether they approve it.

The Winters essay is the next to last one in the new book, would have been the last one except for a chapter which I wrote in November and added after sending the MS in. I owe the suggestion for that to Delmore [Schwartz]. He said it was a pity I couldn't find an "ontological" critic; wished I might have made Tate or Blackmur or Brooks into one; I didn't do quite that but I wrote a Chapter IV entitled: Wanted: An Ontological Critic; naturally I was telling on my own what an ontological critic would do. It would take off from the Winters chapter which gets the thing down to terms of structure and distinguishes the poetic from the scientific structure. When I look for what is 1) universal in all the works of art, including non-moralistic works, abstract works, and music, and at the same time 2) absent from any scientific discourse, it's texture; or the extra dimension; or particularity; I try to put this as precisely as I can. It's an ontological interest behind the art-work; a speculative; I've stopped saying, because of possible ambiguities, a metaphysical. Outside of this new chapter, of which I don't have a copy, the thing nearest to it in my former writings would be my paper on Pragmatics of Art, Winter 1940, replying to Morris.[2] But I might say that I'm not satisfied yet with my terms and definitions. The future of aesthetics is ahead of us, as the man said.

You are right about the sub-title of the Winters essay. Structural Critic would have been better than Logical Critic, certainly for the independent essay form. The only thing was, I treated Richards (and Empson) as the Psychological Critic, Eliot as the Historical Critic, and that seemed to make Logical Critic the best caption for Winters; in the book, in other words, the title may go, I'm not sure.

Am keen to see your paper on the nature of the cognition.[3] My general point is not that in poetry the literal object-matter is different, but that it is ontologically or structurally distinct, as a different grade or level of cognition.

I'll be mighty glad to get the Cather review.[4] I've always had the greatest misgivings about that lady's work, and they are not mitigated by her latest. If you care to write up only the book itself, I'd suggest 1000 or 1200 words; but if you'll do a great thing for us, and make this book the occasion of a lookback into the author's sequence of books—Trilling did this with Lewis' late book for us[5]—then I'd say 1600 words. Is that all right? Deadline for Spring: Feb. 10. Of course we can wait till Summer. But I hope we'll have other matter of yours taking precedence of the review by that time.

Love to Caroline and Nancy.

Yours,
John

P.S. At Baton Rouge I learned that *Five Young Poets* was on the list for Blackmur's omnibus review, so I guess that'll have to be out, for us. I guess I'll do it myself; but I wish one of you could have handled it.[6]

P.S. Presently I have to help the President stage a financial campaign for the Kenyon Review. The old angels understood at the beginning that they would be able to get out after a little and fresh backers would take over; after the Review got established. I had a good interview with Carnegie Corp., though unofficial. We can get their backing if we can establish that we are something special. They have many applications, and don't know any way to make distinctions. I must get together the objective evidence in the form chiefly of letters from people they will respect. Please see if you can think of the people. Would Church do a discriminating thing for us?[7] The purity of our enterprise—arts and letters only—seems to me our distinction; I hope also the quality of the performance. Please think about this and give me some good dope. I think of some university people here and there, chiefly. Famous writers, if they would really go all out for us, would be wonderful. But I don't know what writers would.

---

1. Ransom's "Yvor Winters: The Logical Critic."

2. Another reference to Ransom's "The Pragmatics of Art," a response in part to Charles W. Morris. Parts of this essay in revised form appear in Ransom's "Wanted: An Ontological Critic," which would be published with the essay on Winters in *The New Criticism* (1941).

3. Tate's "Literature as Knowledge."

4. Apparently Tate did not review Willa Cather's novel *Sapphira and the Slave Girl* (1940), for the review was not published in the *Kenyon Review* or elsewhere.

5. Ransom refers to Lionel Trilling's essay-review of Sinclair Lewis' *Bethel Merriday, Kenyon Review,* II (Summer, 1940), 364–68.

6. Ransom's review of *Five Young American Poets,* a New Directions anthology edited by James Laughlin, appeared in the *Kenyon Review,* III (Summer, 1941), 377–80.

7. Henry Church, heir to the Arm and Hammer fortune.

To Cleanth Brooks

March 12, [1941]

Dear Cleanth:

Thanks for your letter and enclosure. I went to Vanderbilt and found myself giving six or seven speeches or fragments of speeches; a strenuous time. It was painful in more senses than one; partly pleasant, too, getting in touch with those superlative Southern-boy students, seeing Don and Owsley and Sanborn—not enough time with these because I was hustled. Curry propounded the Mims offering project, and I think he not Beatty is the elected man, the man holding the bag. Even Curry doesn't relish it. I talked very strongly against it, and he came back only weakly. That's about where the matter stands.[1] I shan't come in, and I'm writing Curry definitely to that effect. I heard from Don about Tate's letter and yours to the *Alumnus*, and thank you for showing me yours, copy of which I am returning. I don't know just what Vanderbilt ought to do with its brilliant graduates and young teachers. It can't keep them all, but it could keep more of them than it does, certainly. The letting go of Warren, who asked so little as a reward for staying, is the most nearly criminal thing in the Vanderbilt record. I have no resentment for their not keeping me. When I got here I was after a year extremely discomfited by the sense that I was getting more at the public trough than the other professors, and would have left here (to go to N.C.) had not the President provided for me with new money, Carnegie money, and eased my embarrassment. I have surprise and admiration for Hill Turner's desire to publish your two letters.[2] The general hush-hush attitude at Vanderbilt is appalling. I don't know what they are coming to there. Evidently the new Dean, Pomfret, is the ruler there, not Carmichael.[3] Whether Pomfret's first name (I don't even know his initials) is Michael or Lucifer cannot yet be said. There are signs it is the latter. Don has a great tragic sense, and I don't quite trust his objective view of the situation. Mims is like a mean old goat who's just been castrated and doesn't know what to do about it; though he only had a prostate operation. He evidently can't conceive of the fact of having done any harm or made enemies.

I was terribly depressed the other day to see in the Columbus paper that you are to have a MILITARY head at L.S.U.[4] The gentleman made the headlines because he commanded a post here recently; which doesn't make him smell any sweeter. I suppose the upshot practically will be that you are all now at the mercy of your Deans; a military man wouldn't know anything at all about literature. Bad, bad.

Will you, won't you, *can* you (along with all else you are doing) review Bishop's new (Scribner's volume) of verse for Summer issue?[5] Deadline May 1 or a very little after. Bishop would like to have you do it; he said so while here recently.

Love to Tinkum.

Yours,
John

---

1. A proposal had been made to raise money for a collection of books in American literature to honor Edwin Mims, soon to retire as chairman of the Vanderbilt English department. Walter Clyde Curry (who would assume Mims's post) and the others—Donald Davidson, Frank L. Owsley, and Richmond Croom Beatty—were against the project, in part because Herbert Sanborn, who was retiring as chairman of the philosophy department, was not being similarly honored by Vanderbilt or awarded a pension that Ransom and others had recommended.

2. Hill Turner, editor of the Vanderbilt *Alumnus*, had published letters by Allen Tate and Cleanth Brooks that protested Mims's refusal to retain Robert Penn Warren in the English department.

3. John Edwin Pomfret was dean of the senior college and the graduate school at Vanderbilt from 1937 to 1942; Oliver C. Carmichael succeeded James H. Kirkland as chancellor.

4. C. B. Hodges, a West Point graduate, retired from the U.S. Army as a major general in 1941 and was appointed president of Louisiana State University on July 1. Within six months Hodges had announced his intention to terminate publication of the *Southern Review*, whose last issue appeared in spring, 1942.

5. John Peale Bishop, *Selected Poems* (New York: Scribners, 1941).

To Allen Tate

April 14, [1941]

Dear Allen:

Have been reading intensively and intensely in the new number of So. Review. It is certainly a headache of dialectic; the most ambitious number I've seen yet; an astonishing piece of independence in a literary journal.

Nearly everything in it revolves around our science-poetry issue. But I don't think it is yet quite finished.

Christmas, I saw the Hook letter about Tate and urged Red not to use it; it was "beyond the pale."[1] He felt that they ought to, however, though he resented it. I imagine the boys thought that you could stand it, especially when they could devote their lead space to a new essay of yours elaborating your same position.[2]

Your book has come in—it looks fine, and I want to rush through it, but so far have only read the long new essay, and the version of it that is in So. Review.[3] Now, by quite a co-incidence, Roelofs was here one night last week, visiting Rice, and we had a little party at which over the drinks I jumped him about one thing: his injustice to Morris.[4] I argued that Morris never denied cognition, and on the other hand often seemed to assume it, quite non-behavioristically, quite otherwise than Richards. I said he "presupposed" awareness of the object, and in brief objectivity, and after a little while I caught Roelofs saying that "awareness" is presupposed in every mental activity whatever; I said that, again, Morris seemed also to presuppose it, and Roelofs finally said he might be in error about the cognition but he was not satisfied with Morris on universals; because Morris only said "the world was such" as to support the logical universal in some restricted sense; but there I believe Morris is afraid of Platonic universals; and I have been told by people who know Morris that he is a sort of "realist" in that he believes objectively that a universal has a real correspondent of some sort. I hasten to say that Roelofs is a fine chap, very brilliant as a talker, and more temperate as well as more incisive when he talks than when he writes. When he sent us his piece two years ago we urged him to cut out the paragraph about the babies and the baths but he wouldn't; we didn't succeed in making him change anything. It makes good "talk," not good writing.

One other thing. I have not re-read Morris since reading your paper, but I think his pragmatical dimension is meant to cover feeling and emotion and all the "subjective" side of knowledge; it embraces, I remember, whatever "psychological, biological, and sociological"—and sociological would include moral—implications the art-work might have for the maker or user. I have thought that dimension of the meanings might not be really coordinate with the others, and ought to be subsidiary, but it does make a disposition of the uses outside of the cognition proper. But one result of this if I am right would be that pragmatical is just one dimension, not all the dimensions, and I really don't think Morris means that it is the most important one in art.

Part of my knowledge about Morris comes from seeing a manuscript of his and sending it to Laughlin to ask if he wants to print it as a book.[5] It is in application of his aesthetic theory in the appraisal of an abstractionist New Mexico artist he greatly admires: Raymond Jonson.[6] But it fails. Morris doesn't really have a critical apparatus yet. But actually I incline to judge that "his heart is in the right place." In other words, he is better than Carnap, and a lot of others in his own crowd;[7] but the fact seems to be that they are a very mixed crowd; Lyle [Lanier] certainly has many affiliations with them. My own feeling about them is one of watchful waiting, not entirely unfriendly. They are pretty much "fed up" on the philosophical classics, but who is not? They represent starting at the bottom again, and pedagogically I rather think that is the right thing now.

Your dialectic is very keen and cogent. I am just raising the question of whether you are right in your disposition of Morris. And at that you do no more than Roelofs and Vivas both have done; one reason that Rice wrote a third paper for that discussion was his feeling that they misrepresented *some* though not all of the positivist-pragmatist-naturalist group.[8] But you will see when my book is out (within a couple of weeks, I believe) how painfully and laboriously I go over a lot of that ground, and in how many places.[9] I am far from satisfied with my performance.

Two weeks ago I heard an aesthetic paper from one Prof. Rogers of Western Reserve before the Ohio English Association. A good harmless but not very powerful young man who is to go to Woman's College of N.C. in charge of the English Dept. I told him I had once taught there and found it a nice place. But Jackson could have got a better man in the South a dozen times over.

Yours,
John

P.S. Your letter has just come in, to my great satisfaction. You don't say what is the gender of this young Lanier. . . . Glad you are on the Beach. You mean an essay, "notes on fiction," etc., or is it a review? I hope the former. Delmore [Schwartz] has just sent in a preview of his verse play, "Shenandoah," and it hit me so hard I wrote to see if we could get it.[10] It's slated for June number of Laughlin's Poet-a-Month; so Delmore is writing to see if Jay [Laughlin] could use it a little later and we use it first. Intensely appealing and amusing—a new sort of thing. The point is that it's longish, and if we use it in Summer number we'll put the fiction number off till Fall; if we don't, we'll use the fiction at once; carrying either one or two short stories of a superior sort (Delmore and Goodman), the Detective Fiction (Radford) I hope, a short estimate of Sherwood Anderson by Trilling, and—probably as our lead—you on fictional criticism.[11] If we hold it over till Fall we might have by that time what Warren has long been promising us, The American Short Story, a critique.[12] We haven't decided yet, and don't yet know whether Delmore can get loose from Laughlin's schedule for our sake. I say this because I wouldn't like you to put yourself all out to make our deadline and then have us postpone it. (Deadline May 1, or it may be just a few days (4 or 5) later—if we decide not to appear by time of Commencement here.) We've done that with one or two people and it has made us (or they have made us) feel so badly I don't want to do it again. Especially at your expense. As Jay is out in San Francisco it will take several days to hear from him so that I shan't be in a position to make this decision just yet—but will notify you just as soon as I am, and do. I wish you were here to advise on the decision. But I think Delmore is giving us something here which is very original and our readers will lap up. . . . As for Sanborn, it would be a great kindness to him if somebody should go over his letter (which I haven't seen) very closely with him and urge revisions in the interest of economy and objectivity and strategy.[13] But who it could be I don't know. If I were there, I would undertake it, though he would not like it and might show me the door. He insisted on showing me a letter he wrote to the Board of Trust on a previous occasion, and it was impossible; the conceitedness of it was the worst thing. And I don't feel, either, as you don't, like pulling his chestnuts out of the fire when the issue is a bigger one than just his own case; nor like using his case to whip the administration with in general. I haven't been sent the letters; Sanborn showed me a lot of them before I wrote mine. And I haven't seen his letter, or statement, but if I had I think I'd want to take up with him even by correspondence any revisions that looked urgent. I'll think about the "principles" and see if I have anything to send you before the meeting in May.

John

---

1. Sidney Hook's letter, "The Late Mr. Tate," *Southern Review*, VI (Spring, 1941), 840–43, is a response to Tate's "The Present Function of Criticism," *Southern Review*, VI (Autumn, 1940), 236–40, in which Tate attacked positivist theories of art and philosophy.

2. Tate's "Literature as Knowledge."

3. Tate's *Reason in Madness* (New York: Putnam, 1941).

4. Howard Dykema Roelofs (1893–1974), professor of philosophy at the University of Cincinnati since 1932, was an occasional contributor to the *Southern Review* and the *Kenyon Review*. Ransom's argument with Roelofs involved his interpretation of Charles W. Morris' *Foundations of the Theory of Signs*.

5. James Laughlin, publisher of New Directions Press.

6. Raymond Jonson, an American abstractionist painter, who founded the Transcendental Painting Group in 1938, which had an exhibit at the Guggenheim Museum in 1940.

7. Rudolf Carnap, a naturalized German, who was professor of philosophy at the University of Chicago and later at UCLA, wrote *Philosophy and Logical Syntax* (1935) and other books.

8. The second issue of the *Kenyon Review*, I (Spring, 1939), contained essays by Eliseo Vivas, Howard Dykema Roelofs, and Philip Blair Rice published under the title "A Symposium on the New Encyclopedists."

9. *The New Criticism* (1941).

10. Delmore Schwartz's verse play "Shenandoah, or, The Naming of the Child," appeared in the *Kenyon Review*, III (Summer, 1941), 271–92.

11. Since Schwartz's play was published, the stories by Schwartz and Paul Goodman did not appear, although both later had short fiction in the *Kenyon Review*. The essay on detective fiction did not appear; Lionel Trilling's "Sherwood Anderson" was published in the *Kenyon Review*, III (Summer, 1941), 293–302; the Tate essay did not appear.

12. This essay by Warren did not appear.

13. This is another reference to the controversy surrounding Herbert Sanborn's retirement from Vanderbilt. Sanborn had refused to contribute to the university's retirement plan and was now faced with lean years owing to his not having retirement benefits.

To Allen Tate

May 23, [1941]

Dear Allen:

Thanks for your good letter.

I don't know yet what to think of my book; there are times when I feel much depressed over it.[1] It's true that I sacrificed the critics in order to get my own oar in; in lieu of a systematic book on poetic theory I found myself using the given critics to point towards one. The ones who suffer most are surely Eliot and Empson. The only salve for my conscience is in the inordinately long samples of their method I carried. And it does seem to me that all my critics here really have the "makings" of the thing I want to talk about; the funny discourse which is opposed to scientific discourse by its multitude of "feelings" or its texture, as well as by the looseness of its logic.

I'd like to repel any idea of a political "strategy" behind it. I wanted it to have *no politics at all.* I don't think the Positivists will regard me as a convert, unless they are grateful for very small favors, which I think they are not. They have nothing as yet to show by way of poetic analysis. But they may turn out to have something when they get round to it. They are little boys dedicated to scientific or analytic principle; that's the most that can be said of them. But I despair of the old-school philosophers and their future as aestheticians; they are very indecisive. Sometimes they just make a mystery of the thing. Again, they are unwilling to admit that there's any given distinction between the scientific and poetic discourses, unless in subject matter; Wordsworth finds, for instance, that the topics of the poet are special, but argues that there is no difference between his talk about them and any other talk; unless possibly—this is a sort of rider—there's something very appealing to the *emotions* in his talk. That's about as far as we seemed likely to get.

I am forced to regard poetic theory as science, though a new science, because about a new or "different" kind of discourse. That's why I don't want any taboos, restrictions, philosophical censorship, against the analytic work. If that is Positivism, I guess I'm a member of the tribe. But so far as the absurd emphasis on scientific discourse as the only discourse goes, I'm far from being one. And I hope I didn't give them much comfort; I didn't mean to. You will recognize—because you have had the same experience—that the dissociation that was really binding on me was to get myself out of the public reputation of being one of a close group or clique or gang or confederacy. At the point where you and Red and Cleanth and I are, it is important that we develop our individual ideas; our community can be taken for granted now, or if necessary it can be easily made out afresh.

I concede your point about Winters. There are times when I'm disgusted with him; for instance, in a little review of Roethke which he has sent us and we have accepted in advance. When he proves that an alleged whiz-bang like Williams is a great classical artist, it's exhilarating; but not when he proves it for Roethke; and he has only one thing in the world he wants to prove.[2] He is the *reactionary* in my group of critics; that's his value; I have a powerful puritan straightlacedness about poetic technique that comes out more and more in me. And in individual bits of writing Winters is one of the most condensed and finished critics living; though he can also make a fool of himself as no other critic can.

Another thing, going back a couple of paragraphs. What the Positivists have done of most value to us is semantical theory; it never existed before; and people like Richards and Empson and Burke have made it live and do work for poetic appreciation. *They* have opened up the philosophical side of poetry as Eliot and Winters have not done. With all the errors that could possibly be made; notwithstanding this.

Our new number will be fine; featured by Delmore's play;[3] our best number yet. But the Autumn number should be fine too. A sort of fiction number, in which your notes on technique might very readily become our lead-off.

I am due at Bread Loaf about July 1, I think, maybe a day or so before that. So it would have to be in late June if I came by; and maybe that's too late for you. But I hope not, as I want to talk over many things with you, including our Review business.

Love to Caroline and Nancy.

Yours ever,
John

---

1. *The New Criticism.*
2. Ransom refers to Yvor Winters' review of Theodore Roethke's *Open House*, *Kenyon Review*, III (Fall, 1941), 514–16, and to Winters' review of William Carlos Williams' *Collected Poems*, *Kenyon Review*, I (Winter, 1939), 104–107.
3. Schwartz's "Shenandoah."

To Allen Tate

September 4, [1941]

Dear Allen:

Well, it's been a summer! and I didn't get to see you again following my brief but pleasant visit at your house. I was hoping to see you at Bread Loaf, and so were some of the boys (Yale, Princeton, Harvard), and we nearly sent you a wire to make it certain. But I guess you had to hurry along.

The seminar with Greene turned out very well on the whole. I have decided he is a decent person, indeed maybe magnanimous, for he certainly can take objection and argument. Not only I let him have it, but many of the students on occasion; and he was good enough to concede that there are mistakes and shortcomings in his book.[1] I think he really regards himself as just having started, with a system that is just tentative. He liked your book extremely—I mean the last one—up through page 86, or thereabouts; after which point he professed disappointment that you had dropped the special subject of the opening part and became more miscellaneous.[2] He is very much against the naturalists. I hasten to say, there was no issue between us there; what we argued was whether poetry is a tight unified logical whole or a loose almost disorderly one; that and similar subjects. I will add what is true, that he was quite good for me in his oppositions. Next summer I suppose we will try it again; I have arranged to have a house there, belonging to Robert Frost, several miles from the School, and we will be distinctly at home and demanding to see you, in short, on a better status than the one of this year, personally; and as for the course, Greene and I can certainly do a better job the second time than the first time.

Have just finished making up the dummy for Autumn, to be out about Sept. 24. The first time we've been late, almost, and this is because there was nobody here to go to press till I got back. A fair number, with a 24-page display of "Younger Poets." Almost none of our fiction pieces came through but we have had a good deal of material, too much in fact, in reserve.

I just wrote Stauffer (whom I got to like very much at Bread Loaf) asking him if he would "cover" the 5-man symposium on Ode on Intimations at the English Institute at Columbia and let us have a 5,000 word report and judgment on it as a piece of co-operative criticism. I am going on the impression that the Institute is next week, not this week, though I may be mistaken. The last of Stauffer I saw was him leaving for the West, to be back for the Institute.

At Bread Loaf I didn't get to do any work outside classes and students. It was close and confining, living in the same house with the Wilsons (two overpowering Old Virginians, to hear them talk), the George Andersons of Brown, and the Joyces of Dartmouth, with one common room and one bath room; and presiding over little tables of old maid students in the dining room; etc. etc.[3] I've been picking up lately the matter of the Review financing project. Our best trustee, a thousand-dollar backer of the Review, Wilbur Cummings, died this summer; though I think that doesn't mean the failure of our funds at all, it makes it the more obligatory to get on with the project of outside financing in whole or in part. I had a good interview with Carnegie Corporation and have some hopes of help from them; that remains to be seen. I found Bishop benevolent but obviously devoted for the moment to his own project, and thinking about nothing else. I lost the address of Church which you sent me; will you let me have it again, and I will write him a formal letter. I'll also follow up at once any leads you may have for me. And I'll travel if it is needed. I have two or three pretty good individual prospects. My idea is to go for nothing less than annual pledges to the amount of $500.00 and $1000.00.

Joseph Shipley has written both to me and to Rice about his Dictionary project, and in registering his approval of Rice's friendly letter of advice and tentative acceptance Shipley has now put him on his list of Advisory Editors, without consultation or permission; the new stationery has sprouted a list of editors two or three or four times as long as the one a month ago. Is this a bona fide project?[4] I've been thinking that the K.R. on a year's notice could devote one extra-large number to a critical dictionary that would be the real thing. We would start out with an Institute to lay out the work and agree on contents and contributors and policies; then get to work. Or your institute at Princeton (the Church-Tate one) could do it admirably. Or it may be that some real backing from a good foundation could be had for a real editor to undertake this job. So I find myself hoping Shipley may not go through with it unless he is doing better than he looks.

What about your reviewing for us Marianne's new volume of verse, of which we have page proofs?[5]

Helen is about to start for Vanderbilt; she's done really fine work this summer in French with Mrs. Larwill, and is definitely coming out of her revolutionary period I guess. Reavill wants another year at Kenyon. Jack is in school all day now, a first grader, very proud of himself. We are playing a lot of poker before school starts. Wish you and Caroline were around.

When does Caroline's novel appear?[6]

Yours ever,
John

---

1. Ransom refers to Theodore M. Greene, McCosh Professor of Philosophy at Princeton, with whom he had been teaching at Bread Loaf summer school. Greene's book *The Arts and the Art of Criticism* (1940) had recently been published.

2. Tate's *Reason in Madness*.

3. Ransom refers to these professors—James Southall Wilson (University of Virginia), George K. Anderson (Brown), and H. E. Joyce (Dartmouth)—and their wives.

4. Joseph Shipley was editing *The Dictionary of World Literature* (1943), which listed 264 contributors.

5. Tate did not review Marianne Moore's *What Are Years?* (1941).

6. Caroline Gordon's *Green Centuries* (New York: Scribners, 1941).

To Allen Tate

November 15, [1941]

Dear Allen:

This is mighty bad, your siege with that arm. I hope it's got to behaving right again. I can well imagine the upset it has meant to your projects; I find it's so hard at the best to get a piece of writing done to suit that the slightest irritation throws me off and I quit work.

I've just been looking at Andrew's new book, and I'm disappointed, and also somewhat embarrassed.[1] It seems to me he had the stuff there, if he really meant to give it life and handle it all in his characteristic style; and if he insisted on keeping the whole historical narrative in the story, that would have taken a big trilogy, nothing less than War and Peace anyway; and it might have been superb. As it is, he fails exactly as Shakespeare fails in the early histories and for the same reason: too much bondage to history. The last part is just hurried melodrama, good of its kind, but not Lytle at all; and it seems to me he's cut a lot of his fine military and economic and philosophical commentary out of the first part. It's a failure, on the whole, I guess; though I haven't gone through it at all thoroughly yet. And how can I review it in K.R.? We can't ask people for favorable reviews, and I figure an unfavorable review in this case would be worse than no review. Unless you can tell me a way out I guess we'd just better leave the book alone; though I'll write a personal note of thanks to Andrew for my copy.

I'm writing Church formally to see if he's "still" interested in what he once talked with me, the possibility of his assuming some editorial place and being responsible for some foreign-literature part of the K.R. But I guess from what you say that he has lost his spark. I have some hopes of help from the Carnegie Corporation: and I've one or two other small irons in the fire. I know of no early threat to our continuance. Our printers will go up 18 percent in their charges, and they are justified so far as I see. Rather than ask for a larger budget, or reduce our size, I think we'll accompany all acceptances from now on with a little slip stating that our rate will be "for the duration of the emergency" $4.00 per page instead of $5.00. Isn't that the best thing? That would make up the extra cost about as exactly as I can figure it.

If and when Knickerbocker gets out I should think the position at Sewanee should be yours for the asking.[2] I'd be proud to say so wherever you think it might do good. But I hope something superior financially will come to hand before then. I can't imagine a nicer situation other than financially.

Knickerbocker has just been having a crazy spell at the expense of Burke.[3] He reviewed Burke's book and mine together after his wildest manner, then started in writing a letter a day to Burke, and sending me the carbon copy. He spilled altogether 30 or 40 pages of single-space madness but apparently got no response till he insisted on one, and then Burke told him off, or so I would judge from the sign-off letter to K's. Once he had the same kind of passage with me (K did). I started to write to Burke to explain Knickerbocker to him, but decided Burke was able to look out for himself.

I lectured at Smith the other day, and spent some while with Fisher there, who is a great fan of yours and apparently a good man.

A new deluxe edition of Proust is out, and I have now a note from Katherine Anne Porter agreeing to write an essay on the work. I'd like to see a good fictionist passing on it.[4]

Our very best to Caroline and Nancy. We are all doing well. Helen is at

Vanderbilt, right under Cousin Meriwether in the dormitory, and apparently both having a good time and getting by very nicely in her classes. Unfortunately she doesn't have to work much to get B's.

We are being pressed to go back to Baton Rouge this Christmas, and probably will.

Yours,
John

---

1. Andrew Lytle, *At the Moon's Inn* (Indianapolis: Bobbs-Merrill, 1941).

2. W. S. Knickerbocker (1892–1972) edited the *Sewanee Review* from 1926 to 1942, when he was forced to resign. Tate became editor in the summer of 1944, after Lytle had been acting editor in the interim.

3. Knickerbocker published an essay-review of Ransom's *The New Criticism* and Kenneth Burke's *The Philosophy of Literary Form* (1941) in the *Sewanee Review*, XLIX (October, 1941), 520–36, under the title "Wam for Maw: Dogma versus Discursiveness in Criticism." Knickerbocker turns Burke's fondness for puns against him and goes overboard.

4. Katherine Anne Porter did not review this edition of Proust for the *Kenyon Review*, nor did anyone else.

To Allen Tate

December 15, 1941

Dear Allen Tate:

Since writing you I've read Andrew's book very closely, and consecutively, and it's better than I first thought. I suppose I had expected a kind of thing that wasn't there, and was led to reject it too soon. It's certainly brilliant in many places, and is mostly a failure in proportion, I believe; that is, instead of getting more and more minute, and slower and slower, with a sense of *dramatic* acceleration, it seems to me to reverse the process, almost precisely; so that the last parts are faster, and therefore more melodramatic and unrealized, than the early parts; and this is the worse in that it isn't the sort of book that has a positive or predictable ending. It's a tragedy, with the painful climaxes sort-of taken for granted. But I do feel a lot better about it than I did. My uncertainty over it is an incident of the fact that we general readers don't have, any of us, any standard conception of narrative form; because there isn't any standard. So that you ought to give us one. Anything you could say about the first principles of fiction would be all to the good. Therefore I do hope you can find the occasion pretty soon to write something for us on that line.

This family is going to Nashville this week, Wednesday the 17th in fact, to stay till Sunday morning, and then return with Helen for a Christmas at Gambier. We forewent the expedition to Baton Rouge. Does that mean we might meet? Couldn't you-all come by here, either going or coming? I'm writing to Andy [Lytle] at Sewanee today to tell him we're in Nashville. I don't know whether I could get up to Sewanee or not; I've made dates with my dentist for Thursday, Friday, and Saturday. I'm *not* going to Indianapolis. I decided to let the professionals alone and be an amateur scholar, from now on.

Merry Christmas to everybody.

Affectionately,
John.

To Andrew Lytle

December 15, 1941

Dear Andy:

It seems wrong to address you at Sewanee, but I have it on Brother Ab-bot's authority you are really there, with your greatly expanded family.[1] Congratulations about that baby, and affectionate regards to both the ladies.

Thank you for my copy of the brilliant new book.[2] I read it right through without stopping. It holds you that way. I wish it were three times as long as it is but admire it for what it is. I say to myself: Now De Soto has been done; nobody will think of doing him again; and I wish this writer, the only man who could have done it, had written up the march, the campaign, on the *minutest scale possible*; a regular War and Peace. I am so addicted to this particular writer that I would want to hold him up to his own standard at every point; that is probably most unfair, but it leads me to want him to be giving us a lot more reflection, philosophy, of his characteristic kind, as he goes along; and to give maybe also a sense of the *whole time* in the intensive way, on the theory that time intervals do not really reduce to actions already planned and noted, or to parts thereof, but they introduce new complications and have energy and growth of their own, so that in the last resort one time interval is almost as good as another and demands almost as full a treatment. But this is very dogmatic. I'm grateful for what you have done and hope you will do many other things as fine.

The Major and Jack and I are off Wednesday morning for Nashville, where we'll land for dinner that evening. We are there three days while I'm attending on my dentist. Then Sunday morning we start back home with Helen. I do wish I could get up to Monteagle to see the ladies, and yourself too, but I doubt if my dentist will let me. Is it possible you'll be getting to town in that period? I'll be at Mama's, 1610 17th Avenue South.

Affectionately,
John.

---

1. Abbott C. Martin, professor of English at the University of the South and occasional contributor to the *Sewanee Review.*

2. *At the Moon's Inn.*

To Allen Tate

January 28, 1942

Dear Allen:

We've been having a lot of turmoil here—as doubtless at Princeton, most at Princeton of all places as we hear in these parts—over speed-up curriculum. The Liberal Education is imperilled, though here we've tried to save it. Conferences, committees, faculty meetings, have made life pretty terrible.

The crisis is not merely military, it's total, and it affects the K.R. In other words, we will have to go on a reduced budget. There is in fact a possibility that we will have to discontinue, as follows: President Chalmers, in view of general college economies which he has urged and threatened, has invited the faculty to elect a committee to study the actual college budget with him; a nice and unusual gesture. So a committee is doing that, and inevitably they will come to the question whether the Review—which no one at all ventures to oppose openly—is not a luxury rather than an "educational necessity" and might not be cut off "for the duration." Faculty men whom I have talked with about the matter are opposed to such a stand, and I don't really expect such a thing. But the President, who seems to be behind us with all his might, has said that he doesn't know whether he could afford to go against a powerful faculty opinion in the matter; and that's the possibility of our discontinuing, right there.

I am sure that presently we'll have a little card for use with our contributors—but not with those whom we've accepted already, on our old terms—to the effect that we'll pay just half what we formerly did. And we'll shorten our office expenses, and after this spring go along on a student secretary rather than a graduate secretary. And I believe we'd better come down to an "occasional" publication, which in fact would mean three times a year, rather than a quarterly. This last rather than the policy of keeping our regular dates but issuing in abridged and scrappy form.

But here's a possibility. Upon the announced demise of the Southern Review I wrote the boys to please come in and "merge" with the Kenyon Review. We'd take their cover page and print both names; we'd take over their unprinted acceptances, and as many of their unexpired subscriptions as would consent. We'd have three editors, Red and Cleanth and me, perhaps with those two serving alternate terms; and we'd make this joint editorship real in every workable sense; and we could easily by arranging some sort of exchange have one of them up here a part of each year, on the faculty, and on the grounds. They replied very favorably, but it seems there are still friends there who are trying to do something and they've postponed formal extinction, till March 1 anyhow. I've written them to hurry up if possible, so that we could start our spring issue on the new basis if possible. I hope they do it. Then we'd be stronger here, as a public organ and also as a College project, because of the great name of the other Review.

We are now where outside angels would count double what they would have counted anyway. But I know no real prospects.

This is just posting you up on things.

I had a fine letter from Andrew, in reply to my thank-you letter and comments on his book. He concedes his errors, and the insufficient technique with which he undertook more than he could handle. But I thought his opinions were so sound, objective, and healthy that I wanted to tell you. It seems as if he has maybe learned a lot from this book, is not to be counted out.

No particular news otherwise. But I'd like to have a big talk with you. I liked your essay on Yeats;[1] perhaps partly because it jibed so well with my own position with regard to the "system" poems. My own essay was something of an impertinence, I'm afraid, because I was supposed to be paying tribute to Yeats and was really talking my own line.[2] I couldn't miss the chance, when I got down to it.

The family all well, and wishing you the same.

Yours,
John

---

1. Tate, "Yeats' Romanticism," *Southern Review*, VII (Winter, 1941), 591–600.

2. Ransom, "The Irish, the Gaelic, the Byzantine," *Southern Review*, VII (Winter, 1941), 517–46.

To Allen Tate

February 6, [1942]

Dear Allen:

I'm worried about your personal situation. Though you probably already know the answer to what I am saying, I have been under the impression that the endowment for Creative Writing at Princeton was precisely like the one for the Carnegie Professorship of Poetry at Kenyon, both being the gifts of Keppel of Carnegie Corporation. Our gift was a flat $60,000.00 cash with the stipulation that it be regarded as cash and not as capital, and be spent within ten years. If you are not sure about this, wouldn't Gauss be a safe man to call upon for information? I'll be wondering if there's any alternative to Princeton which I can think of, but at the moment I regret to say—there's none.[1] Except maybe this: McDowell comes back from Christmas at Sewanee saying that for the first time Knickerbocker has been telling people that he's leaving; which is inconceivable except on the assumption that he's been notified or told he is going to be. Ask Andrew about this.

About Church. I'll write him a nice but non-committal note, as our correspondence is sort of suspended, he having indicated a general but not a fixed disinclination. Our local situation is now worse than ever; I incline to think that we can't last beyond the fiscal year, which expires in July, without outside aid. The new thing here is not public opinion, or presidential sentiment, both of which are, I think, decidedly favorable; but the necessity of the College to go out and get some extra budget money for the sake of reviving aeronautics as an enrollment measure; we have no R.O.T.C., and correspondence is already showing how much store the boys and the parents set by military features. And there is no doubt whatever but that the College is faced with greatly increased expenses anyway, with a summer session coming in.

I am preparing a prospective budget, or rather two: one to scheme a *Kenyon Review* partially subsidized by Church; the other a somewhat larger *Kenyon-Review–Southern-Review* partially subsidized by Church. I cannot give you figures yet because the President asked me to show the two budgets to him and let him approve them, so that we may hold him to them if they (or either of them) go through. But we can say that the College will spend something like $3,000.00, representing salary of the Editor and Managing Editor and some cash for the office; and that we'd like to strike for $2,000.00 from Church for the KR alone, or $2,500.00 for the merger; that our earnings are over $2,000.00 alone, and should be $3,000.00 as a merger; and that we have taken printer's new estimates, and considered all possible economies in the office in making the computations. A 128-page quarterly alone, a 152- or 160-page quarterly as a merger. Don't hold me to these figures as they are not yet official.

Whether Church's assistance were to KR or the merger, I think we should offer him a literary stake in it as follows: a 12-page department of FOREIGN LETTERS or FOREIGN LITERATURE in each number. (More space if he can put in some money.) I rather boggle at the idea of a triple merger showing on the cover; awkward, and then MESURES is already extinct, and then it never had many devotees.[2]

I'll send you itemized budgets next week, after the president returns from a trip. I'll add one remark meantime: we are in a very healthy business condition so far as letters from new and old subscribers coming into the office daily would indicate. We have what seems to me a phenomenal rate of renewals now, and are fast adding libraries, who are the best of all subscribers. And we have a good budget record, these editors have; they've never failed to earn and lay by a little surplus over budget expenditures. Our net earnings last year exceeded $2,000.00, which would reflect about 1200 sales.

About the nature of the merger. We would keep our paper stocks and page make-up and typography, but switch to their cover. We would designate one or both of the So. REV. editors as joint editors with me; and this would mean real editorship so far as we could make it; especially would it mean, in the public eye, frequent essays, editorials, reviews signed by their initials—something we didn't get in the old So. REV. (But the boys would have to come in free, the way Rice and I do.) We would regularly send to them correspondence addressed to them, and strategic manuscripts. And we would manage to have one of them here for one quarter out of each year. In the matter of content, I note that So. Rev. has about three departments we haven't had: Southern Matter, a short story section, and politico-social matter. We'd come in on the last; and on the second to the extent of a story each time, which they might select if they wished; and perhaps occasionally on the first. We might occasionally offer a *Southern Review* prize, for poetry or fiction, and let them name the winner.

Church might have ideas about a cover; if so he'd be free to go at them. But offhand I should think their present cover would make their transfers feel at home with us.

Financially, it's extremely important to get the LSU people to consent to turn over the value of their unexpired subscriptions to us, or at least to recognize the order of the unexpired contributors to turn the money over to us. Perhaps it's necessary to make their president feel cheerful about a merger as more or less absolving him from the worst blame. I'm writing the boys about that feature. We don't want to stumble there. We could attempt to circularize their subscription list and doubtless get new subscriptions from many of them; hardly if they had just lost money on the demise of the magazine they had already subscribed to.

Please think these matters over and advise me and also advise the boys at Baton Rouge when you can get round to it.

Best regards to the family.

Affectionately,
John

P.S. Moe is now an Hon. Doctor and a great well-wisher of Kenyon's.[3] I'm glad he's in on this.

---

1. Tate, who had been running the creative writing program at Princeton since 1939, was not retained by Dean Christian Gauss and left in 1942.

2. *Mesures*, a defunct magazine devoted to the arts, had been founded and edited in France by Henry Church, who would contribute substantially to both the *Kenyon Review* and the *Sewanee Review*.

3. Henry Moe, executive director of the Guggenheim Foundation, had been awarded an honorary degree by Kenyon.

To Robert Penn Warren

April 2, 1942

Dear Red:

I was happy to get your long note of the other day, about Minnesota, and other matters. I didn't refer to it in my hurry-up letter to The Editors about merger day before yesterday.

There's no doubt you are scheduled to get some outside offers, and good ones. You suggest you'd like my impression about the Minnesota matter, and it is that probably you ought to take it. When I got your letter I had just had one from Austin Warren saying that he understood you had a Minnesota offer, and he was terribly sorry they weren't financially able at Iowa to make a counter offer. I'd kind of hate to think of living out my days at Minnesota, but it's a big important place, with high standards as to wage and teaching load, and doubtless a wonderful place to spring from, and you're young enough not to have to regard any new place as final.[1] I'd tend to take it; particularly if the Southern Review is at an end. I'd like to see you for once not overworked; I think you need leisure as much as you need anything else, and you'll never get it at LSU. I've often been worried by the idea of your undertaking too many things while having all the time a base load that was enough in itself. Better get into an *easier* job and reduce the speed. Surely life is endurable at Minnesota. I sh'd think it'd be about like life at Iowa; maybe a little better, because the community is bigger.

We are all pretty well, but miss seeing you and Cinina, whom we often are mentioning one way or another. I do hope you'll get by this summer. Robb is this week at Vanderbilt, helping to get Helen organized for her third term at Vanderbilt, and also—of this I feel quite sure—helping to start the golfing season off and the bridge season with her old cronies. She went by train, however; we were caught with tires that had 15000 mi. on them, and we don't drive one unnecessary mile. Reavill is finishing his sophomore year here, a very smart boy apparently, especially in mathematics, logic, and physics, though he's loaded up with Latin, Greek, and Italian courses on account of Santee's attractions. By the way, Fred has filed suit for divorce, to be heard April 23.[2] His domestic condition was intolerable and my sympathies are very much with him. But he is so easy and amiable and she is so brilliant and resolute that he may not get his decision, as she is contesting bitterly, with the aid of the meanest local lawyer. It's pretty messy. I don't know what will happen. He has done extremely well here as a teacher, though the last year or so she has nagged him a good deal publicly so that there's been a strain. The boys like him very much, and he has brought the Latin enrollment from about 6 or 7 to about 20 or more; not bad for a small place.

The poems make a very beautiful book, Red.[3] I have found some extreme fans of yours among the boys here; and it takes a little book unit to show just what your distinction and personality and recipe for a poem amount to. I haven't got two books I prize more than the Thirty-six[4] and the Eleven. There is no trouble about the book's having appeared before the poem in our Spring number; it makes no difference; and it's true we're a little behind schedule, having waited on the turn of events; we're actually to be out the first of next week.

Love to Cinina from everybody.

Affectionately,
John

P.S. Dooley (I think you know this wretch) has tried a second time to raise a family, and a second time she had to have a Caesarian. She's doing pretty well though it's worse than the other time, and she has two spotted pups to show.

---

1. Warren joined the English department at the University of Minnesota in 1942 and remained there until 1950, when he went to Yale, where he remained until his retirement.

2. Fred Santee, a brilliant classicist who later became a physician, had taught Greek and Latin at Vanderbilt in the early 1930s.

3. Robert Penn Warren, *Eleven Poems on the Same Theme* (Norfolk, Conn.: New Directions Press, 1942).

4. Warren, *Thirty-Six Poems* (New York: Alcestis Press, 1935).

To Cleanth Brooks and Robert Penn Warren

April 10, 1942

Dear Cleanth and Red:

I believe maybe I've struck a hot trail—assuming the merger goes through, which it will so far as we are concerned, but about which I haven't heard very definitely from you as yet.

I wrote Laughlin to the effect that we'd take a sizable gift from him, or if he liked we'd maybe figure with him on the matter of a handsome subsidy in return for exclusive advertising space in the Review, if we merged. Our joint list would give him pretty close to the perfect list to campaign with in pushing the N[ew]. D[irections]. books; and we could help him run a commentary, every issue, in the advertising pages. He wired right back that he was interested, asked to see our bookeeping figures, and I have sent them, and arranged (I think) for Pres. Chalmers to see him in New York this week end.

We are getting together a list of possible donor-prospects, and will canvass them in May and June. I really think we can come through in good shape—provided we can merge; and merge on almost any terms that you can get.

Please advise me about things just as soon as you can. I'm completely in the dark as to your own ideas, also the ideas of your financial authorities.

Please also let me have names of any good prospects who might be written to and/or seen about subsidies.

K.R. took to the mails yesterday, your copy should be in by Monday.

Affectionately,
John

To Alexander Guerry

April 16, 1942

Dear Dr. Guerry:[1]

Today a note from Merrill Moore, of Boston, tells me that Knickerbocker has asked him if he knew of a vacant position, from which my conclusion is that Knickerbocker has left Sewanee or at least arranged to leave. I don't want to be in the attitude of the scavenger bird, and I am innocent of any personal interests in the matter, but I do feel impelled to write you against the event that it may be in order to propose a candidate for the vacant position. If it is not in order, please disregard this note.[2]

My candidate would be Allen Tate. I happen to know that he has finished his work at Princeton (where he was in charge of Creative Writing under the Carnegie grant), having been employed for two years and then having been liked so well that he was made to stay another year. I rather think he is at a loss as to his next move, in fact, and would be approachable with respect to a position at Sewanee. Since I am at Kenyon, which is a sister institution to Sewanee, I know that Allen and his family would fit in entirely with the intellectual and social community at Sewanee. They are delightful persons, all of them, and even at Sewanee, where personalities are very choice, would be personae gratae. Then, on the intellectual and teaching and editorial side, Allen is really a towering intellect who is just coming into his prime. He believes in old-fashioned educational ideals, he is the soul of honor, he has the most precise scholarship and studies without stint when he comes upon the subject that he has not yet mastered, and he is about the best master of written English that we have in this country. I think he would make the Sewanee Review, our rival organ, flourish with a distinction second to that of no Review. I have never encountered an occasion, in fact, where the man and the opportunity seem so suited to each other as this one, hypothetical as it may still be, where I assume that Sewanee might want to consider the credentials of Allen Tate for an English position. But I suspect you know Tate, and are aware of all I am saying. Perhaps I am carrying coals to Newcastle. Or perhaps the situation is other than I have concluded on short evidence, and my letter is to no purpose.

At any rate it gives me a chance to wish you the best of luck, and to say that I have such a sentimental attachment for Sewanee as I have for no other Southern institution except Vanderbilt, where I taught for twenty years.

Sincerely yours,
John Crowe Ransom

---

1. Alexander Guerry, vice-chancellor of the University of the South.

2. Andrew Lytle was editing the *Sewanee Review* (under the title managing editor) from this time until Tate's appointment in the summer of 1944. During this period Tate was an unusually active advisory editor for Lytle.

To Allen Tate

May 22, 1942

Dear Allen:

I had your last letter yesterday.

At the last minute a wire from Baton Rouge advises us not to anticipate the final decision of the LSU Board, which meets not earlier than May 30 to wind up the merger action. The thing has been back and forth among editors, President, Board, Committees of Deans, etc. etc., down there, but apparently is really headed for final action. We have to hold back our circular letter to the subscribers of which I sent your copy. But I'm coming on East anyway to see a number of friends and get them if possible to see or to present me to some monied gentlemen who might commit themselves to helping us if the merger materializes. I'll be in New York Sunday morning to meet Weaver, our young man who went to sell advertising for us but whom I had to call off when we got the last Baton Rouge wire, and who is waiting for me. I'll call you up from New York Sunday.

I sort-of think I'd better go straight to Church's house. And seem to think that he's coming through. I enclose for your analysis his last letter, in answer to one I wrote him at the time I wrote you last. He's trying to hedge but is not very absolute about it, you will see. My idea right now is to urge him to put up a pledge of $1,000.00 right off, with $500.00 maybe to come later if we need it and if his affairs permit it. Though maybe I'd better name a larger amount to bargain from. I don't know.

It will be mighty fine to see you. I'll have to be mostly in New York. Seeing people like Moe who have some connections with money if they can persuade themselves that this is the occasion. I'm the last man in the world to do promoting but I guess I have to do it.

Yours,
John

To Allen Tate

[June 2, 1942]

Dear Allen:

It was fine to see you and the ladies.

Yesterday a wire from Cleanth said the Board of Supervisors there had unaccountably refused to sanction the merger, but he was still sure we could have the official right to take over their subscription list and fill it out, also take over their remainder money for the expense of doing so. Pres. Hodges had told him distinctly, and Cleanth had written several times to the effect, that this action would not require the Board's sanction. Cleanth is evidently at a loss as to why the Board rejected the Committee's proposal, which the President himself endorsed, but I think I know why: because Cleanth in his official memorandum to the President had specified as part of the deal that they pay an Editor down there (by giving him release in teaching load) to join in with us on official footing, and they were averse to that as they had already declared the University's effort to keep the Southern going as at an end. I was alarmed over that part of his proposal but didn't say anything as it may have been a matter of pride, or even of principle, on the part of said Editors. Anyhow the official "merger" is off.

Tonight I will phone Cleanth to know for certain that we will get the subscription list. If we also get the money (some $600.00) it will be fine, but it is much the lesser of the two considerations.

If that part of the thing stands up we are all right. I have rewritten the letter which we will send out, omitting the word merger, and just saying "we are authorized to announce" that the Southern Review is discontinued and has appointed us to take over its subscription list and the obligations attendant thereon. It doesn't affect our argument; it may affect our title, leaving it the same as always; it will preclude our using their cover design, but I feel sure we will come out in a new cover regardless. I don't even want to say publicly that we failed to get the "merger." I think maybe you'd better not say that out if you should be talking about it, though among friends it's no great matter. I feel sure that the arrangement will be referred to as a merger but it will be too late then for it to hurt.

If I don't write again tomorrow you may safely consider that we get the subscription list, and are the "literary heir" to the Southern even if there is no merger. Mr. Church, for instance, is one I'll be careful not to tell about our not having an official merger.

Were you in earnest about asking Brother Ben [Tate] to become a patron of letters in the amount of $200.00? I won't do anything about this without your sanction. If you want him to put in, shall I just write him, and count on your having tipped him off?

I really think our tire situation won't stand the trip to Tennessee; but maybe in late summer I'll make it by train, myself. We are having Helen come on home by herself. She seems, by the way, to be in less difficulties this time than at the same period of last term; maybe having broken our spirits she is relenting.

The dinner party at Cal and Jean's was mighty nice.[1]

There'll be a lot to talk over when I see you.

Affectionately,
John

1. Robert Lowell and Jean Stafford.

To Allen Tate

Bread Loaf, Vermont, July 12, 1942

Dear Allen:

I hope you're settled down again to proper life and letters.

The K.R. is all safe now; we've raised our required funds; small gifts have totaled so far better than $1,000, and then there's Mr. Church ($500.00), another large donor, and the appropriation from the *Southern* to fill their unexpired subscriptions. We're not rich but we can manage all right.

Our opening new number (to be out in September, dead line middle of August) troubles us. We didn't dare prepare contents till we were sure we would appear. We want to be larger and we'd like to be better. Haven't you something for us? Or would you like to do a review? We are short on reviews, fiction, and essays-not-about-poetry. Or will you make suggestions? Would any of those *Mesures* lectures of last spring do? Which would it be?[1]

Now here's another angle I'll just pitch into without beating the bush. We've taken on, for political reasons, Cleanth and Red, as advisory editors. That makes too many. But we ought to revise the list anyway. Rosenfeld doesn't write in our style, yet he's a fine gentleman, devoted to our success, sent us his check for $25.00. I think the best thing probably is, make a clean sweep, have about five names new altogether—not to hurt the feelings of Rosenfeld, and probably Vivas too. I've thought of pretty good persons, including Munro, of Cleveland Art Institute, to represent painting and to leave music represented in order *not* to seem to replace Rosenfeld. Trilling, Burke, Jarrell, are pretty good names. I'd like to get your reactions to this, thinking about the general public, certain present advisories like Rosenfeld, and yourself.[2] I haven't done or announced anything yet, other than to parade Cleanth and Red as now associated with us. I don't know what the institution of advisory editors is worth; a great deal at the start, I know, when your advisories are famous and your magazine is new. I guess it's largely front. You are the one whose advice I have consistently sought, the only one. I'd probably still seek it. But I can imagine the office has been of no conceivable profit to you.[3]

I'm here alone at B[read]. L[oaf].—couldn't move the family on old tires. It's pretty dreary weather here this week. Home by the middle of August.

Yours,
John

P.S. Don [Davidson] is here, and seems quite up to par.

1. Tate did not contribute to the autumn, 1942, issue of *Kenyon Review*.

2. Ransom removed the original advisory editors: R. P. Blackmur, Paul Rosenfeld, Roberta Teale Swartz, Allen Tate, Philip Timberlake, Mark Van Doren, and Eliseo Vivas. His new slate of advisory editors included Cleanth Brooks, Lionel Trilling, and Robert Penn Warren.

3. On the subject of advisory editors

Ransom wrote to Lionel Trilling on November 16, [1942]: "Now I gather you feel I ought to take 'advisory' much more seriously, play it more systematically, than I have been doing. But how can I? Here is some fact which may startle you. The members of staff who are closest (physically) to me here are Rice of course, Bentley who writes incessantly and has been here several times, Warren (who has helped judge S[hort] S[tory] contests), yourself next I believe. And take some of the items in Summer and Autumn which you disapprove; as follows: LeSueur, Hennemann, Balet: I can say that none of these had any champion in me but only in one or some of the others. Shouldn't I have come down harder there to have my own way? Wouldn't I even under the most favorable circumstances have to do some mediating? And do you think a democratic vote among all concerned would work? You know, probably, how HOUND & HORN went out; it went out fighting, with staff editors Allen Tate and Yvor Winters both appealing to Kirstein who had sent something round to them on which they differed very violently; and if Kirstein didn't just run out in consequence it was something very much like that. There is this also to remember though it will sound conceited in me, I'm afraid: the credit or discredit earned by the Review is on my head far more than anybody else's; I am *considered* responsible, so I *am* responsible; and naturally I just feel compelled to use my own best judgment. I will admit instantly that often it hasn't been much of a judgment; I hope it has purified itself as time has gone on; I hope I have learned some things, and not least from you, Lionel. But is there another practical base to work from other than the one we do work from?

"I feel all the time a little surer as to what is good and what is poor. Unless that is a delusion. Certainly I feel continually more in accord with your own tastes and judgments.

"I suppose I don't sense the importance of being *strict* in applying my judgment, as you do. I do sense the virtual *impossibility* of being that. We are pretty big as a magazine. We have 25 items or more in a number. I had just as soon as not some time have an item that I disagree with thoroughly; though I concede we shouldn't have one that in substance, that is in sensibility, is downright 'vicious' as you say. I don't feel that either the editor or the advisory editors are to be held responsible for every item; just for the general drift. Perhaps, as I fondly feel, there is an impression of vitality, of robustness, of fairness, in the *range* of views and accomplishments we exhibit in one number. I hope so, since it is impossible to obtain 25 items that will all suit any fastidious individual taste, even one on the easy-going side."

To Andrew Lytle

Gambier, Ohio, August 29, 1942

Dear Brother Andy:

The story is tremendously good; everybody has said so. And much, much longer than anything we've ever printed. But we are enlarging, to a point nearly midway probably between the Southern's size and our old size. So we will just print your story as a sign of our picking up speed. Though it will push us mightily. I don't think it would do at all to split ALCHEMY into two instalments, a quarter of a year apart.[1] And it's so much better than any fiction we have on hand that we just can't think of letting it go. It's about as clean a piece of good narrative as I ever saw.

But there's the price to haggle over, and maybe there's a rub there. We have thought of $100.00 as the price. It's not enough but we have cut our rates by half at least; had to for the duration if we were to survive. And that's more than we ever paid at our old rates for any one item, though we have never had such a big one. What do you say to that? I won't say we can't do any better since we have the old war chest full for the moment. But we have to piece it out and I think that's as much as we ought to do provided we are not cheating our distinguished contributor. Let me know what you think. The story is in press right now, and galley proof is very clean and there are no problems there. You may be sure we will do a good job of printing it. But what I started to say was, we can let you have the money as soon as we are agreed on the amount.

I like the sound of Headlong Hall.[2] I thought maybe I could get down there these few weeks between Bread Loaf and home teaching, but I have to save the pennies for Uncle Sam. But I'm going to make it Christmas anyhow. Reavill is going to Vanderbilt in a few weeks, to be a Junior. He has had two good years here. But the army will get him before long, since he's 19 next month. He's a good boy, and has a good head though he cares nothing about grades. He's best in mathematics and philosophy though he thinks he's a linguist. Helen is home, seems to be engaged to a Vanderbilt boy from Birmingham who's coming here to make a little visit next week, I believe. She has to get down to cooking and housekeeping in justice to the man of her dreams, whoever he turns out to be. Actually she makes salads and sometimes whole meals and seems wonderfully domesticated after her rapid tour of the institutions of higher education.

I saw a lot of old Don [Davidson] this summer in Vermont, had one or two big arguments with him. Over nothing. I guess we are both just argumentative. Don has become very critical, it struck me, he's agin the government, and so am I but with more moderation. I'm mighty fond of Don and argue with him as if he were my brother.

My best to Edna and the baby, when you see them. Good luck to the farm. You are the one practising agrarian and I know you are in your duty. As well as your pleasure.

Affectionately,
John

1. Andrew Lytle, "Alchemy," *Kenyon Review*, IV (Autumn, 1942), 273–327. This was the longest single piece of fiction Ransom ever published.

2. Lytle had asked Ransom's reaction to a name for a farm he had just purchased.

To Robert Penn Warren

September 4, 1942

Dear Red:

At Bread Loaf this summer, subbing for Perry Miller who couldn't come, colleaguing with me on the faculty, was one McDowell, of the English Dep't of Minnesota, with whom I talked about you.[1] He seems to be virtually a chairman of the Dep't, at least an important member of it, and a fine chap besides. He is determined to make your life at Minnesota worth while and is altogether a man of good will. I commend him.

Here's the big topic for this hasty letter: I did you some dirt without getting your permission to advertise you as coming onto our Advisory Editors Board. The way it happened, we waited and waited for the subscription list of the Southern Review to come through; as you know there was much red tape to cut. Finally when the critical decision was pending I called Cleanth over the phone and talked out everything with him; we were sending out some advertising circular matter at once. One of my questions: Will you and Red come onto our Board though not as joint editors (the L.S.U. people having spiked that)? Cleanth's reply was: Of course we will, I do herewith, and you can count on Red too though he isn't here now, has already gone to Iowa. So we announced you, and, resuming publication with an Autumn issue now in press, we carry you there. The fact is we just name two Advisory Editors: Brooks and Warren. To add names to our already bulging list would have been too much, so we just notified them of the change and dropped them. A little later we plan to accompany you with the name of Lionel Trilling, who has been very valuable to us; so there'll be three. We don't do this last now, because we don't want the old Advisories to think we've substituted new men for them except Brooks and Warren, which they quite understand as part of the Grand Strategy. (But to every one of them I wrote: their selection would be compelling anyhow, of course, but for the circumstance that we already have a perfectly good and full staff; and all have acquiesced cheerfully.)

You and Cleanth are now on the spot, though not a very hot one I hope. You do as much or as little as you will. You will see us improved. Our new number has [a] 168 pp book plus [a] xii pp advertising section; and 7 full pages [of] publishers' ads at $50.00 or a little better a page. Our features this first time are not extraordinary inasmuch as we had to prepare in haste: but two exceptions would be Andrew's long story about de Soto in Peru,[2] and a new cover design by Moholy-Nagy. I hope you'll not mind the step-down too much.

Now this: Henry James was born in late April 1843, and we plan a James whole number for Autumn next year. Will you be the special Editor of that number? It involves selection of content about James only. I have the feeling if you will consent that the authors invited ought to submit their brief outlines or at any rate topics early so that overlapping might be avoided. But you are the doctor if you will be the editor. We think we ought to announce it now in order to keep other periodicals out, or scare them away, if possible. So if you consent please wire me collect and let me run that item as well as the announcement of the issue.[3]

You and Cleanth will have to help us get good fiction, too. I hope you'll do this. And you'll have to regard yourselves as Contributing Editors as well as

Advisories. So get this general idea into your consciousness if you will.

Apologies for taking your name without permission.

I hope Cinina and you are well and fine. I think the Minnesota shift is a good one, and since I have used a football term I know you will benefit from the improved play in the best of all possible games. Nowadays you'll have to come to see us more often. Is there a chance following your Summer teaching now? I'm at home, following Bread Loaf, which went off pretty well as usual. There's much to talk about, and we grossly need some of Cinina's salads to improve the Ransom morale. All here are well. Reavill goes to Vanderbilt for his junior year. I guess the army will have him before long, since he's 19 this month.

Love to Cinina, and this would go for all the family, instanter and by acclamation, if I weren't at the moment in my office and not in touch. Be sure to send me a wire the very a.m. or p.m. you get this.

Affectionately,
John

P.S. The Eleven Poems are very brilliant.[4] No important poet in our time ever was so successfully withheld from his natural public. But I see from reviews that you are beginning to get yours.

Later. I just got your letter from Minnesota, and took this out of envelope I had addressed to Iowa. Cheerio.

---

1. Perry Miller, professor of English at Harvard and author of *The New England Mind*, was replaced by Tremaine McDowell, professor of English at the University of Minnesota, who also specialized in American studies.

2. Lytle's "Alchemy."

3. Warren edited the James issue of the *Kenyon Review*, V (Autumn, 1943).

4. Warren's *Eleven Poems on the Same Theme*.

To Allen Tate

February 27, [1943?]

Dear Allen:

Your letter came this morning. Good of you to answer so quickly. I'll be reading it some more, trying not to miss any hits that I ought to acknowledge. But at the moment I can't help but think you misjudge me at many points.

My book isn't ready; I've had too much distraction and work to keep at the book this winter very faithfully; I hardly think I can furnish it before another couple of months, and though I'll have to consult my publisher I imagine it'll be an early fall book.[1]

In this book I will try several approaches to the same thing, and here is the first and best one of all: A poem is an *argument* which does not abandon *images*. Arguments generally abandon images. Bryant Cooper, one of Dr. Sanborn's men, went to Germany and came back and read my "Ontological Note" essay and said I evidently didn't know what a "thing" was. He told me a thing was an undisposed-of or provisional image, an object still in its full particularity waiting to be used or, as we would now say, "reduced." As soon as reduction (or classification and use) happens the thing disappears forever; unless it occurs to us that we might find some other use and therefore call the thing an image and look at it again; provisionally, once more. Then the reduction and the disappearance act again. Well, you know that Aristotelian logic employs no individuals, only general and species, or universals, or "reductions." Logic can't use individual objects. Science can't.

But note that the economy of our knowing-and-using processes has a fatal flaw in it, from the scientific or Positivist view. We say we are through with the image when we have got the universal out of it; but are we? The image returns. We *have to have* the image while we are looking round for the uses (scientists have to have "imagination") and the images are expected to make off when we are done with them. Yet we record them automatically, as if we were motion picture cameras taking pictures forever. The pictures we take do return to consciousness. They creep into arguments and operations. They are actually "invited"—by artists, by sentimentalists, etc. The discourse which invites and enjoys them is art.

Why do we invite them into arguments to the damage of the arguments? You suppose I think they are "pretty" and "embellishing" but I seem to find far stronger words than that. The necessity is ontological; they make discourse realistic, objective, disinterested, etc.; yet they still don't help us biologically.

And why don't we take our images straight, without the argument? (Our biological rôle is a Positive rôle. We just barely evade it in our art.) The main reason is, our minds aren't built that way; we can't. Here are two illustrations. We've been doing work and we want some "relaxation"—so we take a walk. That is not an artistic experience; and it is a very feeble aesthetic one; we are just looking round, aimlessly, without a focus, too receptive, too passive, in fact "relaxed"; though if we really try to get everything into mind it becomes the most excruciating and difficult experience possible, or, rather, it's impossible, it's too difficult. So we have to be *walking somewhere*, getting somewhere, attending to some business, and let the landscape, or nature, slip into the experience if it is to amount to a real aesthetic experience.

Or take this one. The farmer gets considerable aesthetic enjoyment out of his labor; by having images in the course of his work. He doesn't go out to take a walk or to sit and look; he is plowing his field. The plowed field is the condition.

It's in that respect that I make a structural argument the condition of a work of art. The farmer's images are his texture; the work done is his structure; and in that sense I don't see any difficulty in conceiving the structural and textural elements in a poem. I don't know what you mean by saying I seem to be "reifying" an abstraction. When I say the farmer has done a morning's work I do not deny that he has had a lot of imagery to enjoy. When I say that he has had his imagery I do not deny that he has plowed his acre.

I do not value a poem in terms of the value of the structure; you seem to think I do. I do not think a structure is a poem at all by itself; and you seem to tax me with thinking that. The whole object of the poem is to get the imagery. But it has to get this as attached to its structure. My objection to the moderns is that they try to take their images straight; if they do; and I concede there is always an argument, and the possibility of hideous error, in analysing the individual poet and poem.

I don't really care what the Positivists, Pragmatists, or Naturalists think about me or my theories; I am not out to make friends; the chief luxury I have is that I don't have to do this. I find the Positive phrase "process" or the phrase "operation" the best single term (or at least the best two terms) for denoting the structure of argument, the heart of scientific action or practical action of any sort, and all the better that it has a fine "moral" flavor and represents the sort of human action for which all the sanctions exist. It gives a better definition of my "structure" than anything else; though in order to keep "texture" I have to have the companion word "structure" rather than process or operation. Then, besides, I like the naturalistic appeal to anthropology provided it's an open and honest one; I should want to found a non-Positivist activity firmly in the human constitution, otherwise it's just a vagary. (The Positivists have the most elemental, most central, and best view of what all human conduct is biographically, or with respect to its purpose, technique, and morality.) And I must confess I feel there is some prospect of humor if I make some Naturalists rise to my bait and attack me, because I'll want to see on what grounds. Therefore my strategy in the essay.[2]

I could never be a Positivist, however, except as I was a scientist; the Positivists explicitly declare there is no kind of discourse except the scientific one. The Naturalists seem more open-minded. I ask them what they are going to do about it.

I have no self-consciousness as to whether I sound like a Positivist or a Naturalist; let people read me to see if I am one. (*You* possibly have a self-cons. here, may feel that you are committed irretrievably. I am not in that position. If I am, I refuse to stay there.) And I do not see any necessity to reject them automatically and go on record in some heroic manner. On nearly every page I write I am careful to write in my reservations with regard to common doctrine. But I would have to have a doctrine never heard of before, and new at all points, in order to make sweeping rejections of common doctrines.

I don't even reject Eastman, or Sparrow.[3] I barely recall them as both cocky; and Sparrow especially as talking superficially about the conventions and proprieties rather than real existents. I'd not be surprised to learn that up to a certain point I might be on their side; provided they are on the same side and don't reject each other.

My last book was bad inasmuch as I tried to give some running account of the critical doctrines of my three or four critics, and also indication of my own doctrines in departure from them; I tried to ride two horses.[4] I should never have proposed structure and texture till I could put the case very much more fully. That is why I have to do this next book, though theory has now become a torment to me, and criticism has too. I want very much to get back to practice if I can. I'll start shortly by publishing Collected Poems, with some revisionary touches here and there. (I mean: Selected Poems.)[5] But I only have the great desire, no assurance that I can still work at the old trade. I must either do better work or none at all.

I feel very badly about the Eliot. I couldn't and can't use the essay and then dodge the natural issue. You can see the heavy apologetics going with the severe criticism; an uneasy combination. I shan't go into that here, though. Except to say that, after all, I know Matthiessen, and have read the Waste Land plenty.[6] The points you made here were familiar to me (*most* of them were, at least); I mean, the "explanations." And still I think my judgment holds. After all, that section is pretty long, though it seems skimpy to you, and though I write two or three times as much as I put in.

But I must say that to the best of my belief my new essay is thoroughly in tune with my World's Body.[7] I read some of God Without Thunder the other day, and also my Criticism, Inc.—I was astonished at how my views have held. (Have a look at *Crit., Inc.*) I've read a lot of philosophy these last years, and acquired a more flexible and accurate vocabulary, I hope.

Please tell Cal I'll write him just as soon as I can get Rice's examination of the poems. (Rice has been terribly over-worked.) Rice is really Assistant Editor, almost Joint Editor, not Managing Editor. We both together perform about every editorial action that takes place in our office. I like a couple of the new poems very much; especially the 17th Century formal religious ones. Cal is a more masculine Crashaw. That is something of an anomaly and an editorial objection. His free or contemporary thing I don't like so well. And please tell Jean that I sent her story to the place she said, after her second prompting.[8] I liked that story and hated to give it up. I wish she'd try me again. But I'll write her along with Cal. I like those two. In fact I have no friends like the old friends, and seem to myself very lonely without them at times.

Affectionately,
John

The proof was sent you after we were already in page proof and locked up for the printer; and your own poems were locked up too; in very fine shape though I did not have your latest version of Jubilo. I did have the revised

Sonnets.[9] We got behind and rushed the make-up period this time.—I'll go on a little anyhow. I can't give your message to Santee, he's not here. I'm sure you know about the horrible occasion of his divorce last spring. Well, in midsummer he married again; a very attractive younger woman but a strange personality. Last term he did many indiscreet things. He gave the boys heavily to drink, conducted a salon at his house, talked too much sex to them by all accounts; came in for much criticism, and I tried to defend him without entire success. He is pretty irresponsible. The draft board finally got him; ordered him to enlist or practice medicine. He left at Christmas with his father, failed to get a commission with the army, still has a chance with the navy, and wound up practicing medicine in some mean suburb of Baltimore where he wrote me recently that he had had one patient ($2.00) in a week, his wife had pawned her jewels, he had had to stop alimony to his first wife, Ruth the little girl was with her grandparents, etc. etc. Some boys and faculty here at my instance got up some $60.00 and sent him. I don't know what his future may be. He is hardly capable of managing his own affairs. Can give you a lot of interesting dope on him when I see you. His intellectual integrity makes him, in my judgment, a valuable man anywhere but does not keep him out of trouble.

We are doing pretty well. Reavill is just barely able to exist waiting to be called to service with Naval Aviation; he will go in April, by all accounts. Is here at Kenyon; left Vanderbilt after one term because he was told they would be ordering him into duty this term.

Mrs. Reavill died in December after two months' illness, greatly distressing to Robb, who is in poor condition. High blood-pressure; needs a good rest.

Helen has become a fine cook but otherwise not a perfect character. She is learning the hard way, little by little, that it takes more than charm to get along. She is immensely attractive to the gentlemen. Nearly got married to a boy in Birmingham after nearly a year's engagement, but that's now off. He was a rich boy, and a strong character, but had no literary sense at all.

And let me recur once more to our topic. I had to cut out most of my conclusion when we went to squeeze my long essay in; including the part about the thematic musical matter. That's arguable as you say. I have the feeling that Waste Land is much like Picasso's Guernica, which I dislike. Also much like Dali's surrealism, which has all sorts of fine detail and no composition. And of course like the kind of modern music that I don't approve. I can't help wondering if you have tastes in music and painting as advanced as your liking for Eliot in poetry. In any case don't we have to judge the advancement and status of a work of art by comparison with other works in the same art? How can we save a work of art by saying it would do very well if it were only in some other art?

Here's my parting shot. The way Eliot proposes in his note the business about the Hanged God is *so very much* like the drag-in method of Sidney MTTRON;[10] and I got so much of that that the method became odious to me.

"Don't you see in this word the lame man? Don't you see the going down? Isn't this about the serpent? Etc etc etc."

Aff'ly
John

---

1. This book was apparently abandoned by Ransom.

2. Some marginalia in this letter are illegible.

3. Ransom apparently refers to Max Eastman's *The Literary Mind: Its Place in an Age of Science* (1935) and John Sparrow's *Sense and Poetry* (1934).

4. *The New Criticism.*

5. The first edition of Ransom's *Selected Poems* (New York: Knopf, 1945).

6. F. O. Matthiessen, professor of English at Harvard and author of *The Achievement of T. S. Eliot* (1935), *American Renaissance* (1941), and other works of literary criticism and scholarship.

7. Probably the essay to which Ransom alludes is his "Positive and Near-Positive Aesthetics," *Kenyon Review*, V (Summer, 1943), 443–47.

8. Ransom did not publish any fiction by Jean Stafford.

9. Tate's "Jubilo" and "More Sonnets at Christmas" appeared in the *Kenyon Review*, V (Spring, 1943), 184–88.

10. Sidney Mttron Hirsch, one of the Fugitive poets.

To Robert Lowell

April 27, 1943

Dear friend Cal:

I'm sorry to have kept you all this time. We are not consciously obstreperous about holding verse; but we have drifted into this policy, which is at least practical, or has proved to be: We hold it as long as we can if we're not sure about it; and when time comes to get together a little exhibit for a number going to press, we select the best we have on hand. Last time it seemed that Tate and Van Doren had the call, and had enough volume to make our poetry section; and now we've got on hand about a dozen eligibles from which to make up our Summer number within a few days. I can say this: we'll print of yours either "Satan's Confession" or "To Our Lady on the Eve etc etc", if they are available. Your letter of the other day withdrawing most of the lot we had interested me very much, particularly because you sent along a couple of new ones; but I find now that my wife (or maybe it was Helen, they disagree) in cleaning up the living room deposited some papers of mine, including your letter, in the waste basket, whose contents were innocently burned by me. I'm sorry about this. Please let me hear about the two poems I've cited, and the new ones; though to a typist like yourself I realize how painful it is to supply a fresh copy.

I still think you are a fertile and ingenious poet. I feel that your modern things lack form, in my stubborn sense of that word; you go off so tangentially. The 17th Century things (Crashaw, not Herbert) are beautifully formalized, though they are naturally not so fresh as the modern things.

Here's also the little prose essay. I've read that too a great many times. I know how vain is argument with a Thomist, and I won't undertake any. At the time we got in your little essay I was working on my Maritain-naturalism-Eliot paper, that conglomerate, and I thought that had the first call.[1] And now I wonder if you'd be interested in sending a communication replying to my paper, and to Russell too if you like;[2] that's a perennial subject with us.

I'll give my objection to your position very briefly without documenting it. I think you argue that Thomism makes for human happiness, and I'm aware that it does, with *many minds*; with others it doesn't work. Thomism is philosophy as well as recorded "revelation"; as philosophy it's exposed to the liabilities of philosophy, and is countered by other philosophy. You are too easy about that, saying that "by guaranteeing certain demonstrable but arduous truths, Christian Revelation did actually confirm and liberate philosophy." But how can somebody else (was it the Pope, about 1870?) guarantee a truth to us? In what manner will compensation be made if it's found to be falsity rather than truth? And what were the specific arduous truths? You tend to want a kind of philosophy that subordinates itself, and quits applying its method, at a certain point; but that's not philosophy in my estimation. However, as to your views of substance I am with you 100% and I have many times argued that, and I'm sure that many philosophers are with us in that. If the Naturalists and Positivists cannot accommodate any religion or any art they have a defective perspective. But there is no reason why all science should not be *one* without involving the proposition that all knowledge is science; and this last proposition is the one that they are coming more and more up against.

Let me repeat, I did send Jean's story to the address she gave me, though it took her second prompting letter to do it. And we very much want a story from her. If she will try us again.

I will surely get to Tennessee this summer, very early after we close here, which is late June; and I hope you and Jean will still be in Monteagle.

Yours,
[J.C.R.]

1. Ransom, "The Inorganic Muses," *Kenyon Review*, V (Spring, 1943), 278–300.

2. Ransom probably refers to an essay by Bertrand Russell, "Non-Materialistic Naturalism," *Kenyon Review*, IV (Summer, 1942), 361–65.

To Allen Tate

May 16, 1943

Dear Allen:

That was mighty nice of you to write Church on our behalf and also to post me on his attitude. I wrote him a very long letter in reply to his to me, offering to come to see him if he liked to talk it still more fully; which I guess isn't what he wants, as he's softhearted, it seems to me, in actual presence. He wrote back that he was replying "next" week, which was last week; so maybe there's a note coming in this morning.

Actually, the College founded us (the President's idea) and got us $15,000.00 which ran us three and a half years; and still pays for my and Rice's time, and furnishes office and "auspices" which I like extremely. Now, the Faculty is on record wanting the Board to reduce expenses to the bone in order to save the faculty salaries, and the Board is doing so, and I can't in decency or even with real desire ask for a college appropriation. Our situation is this: we will have earned not far from $4,500.00 (subscriptions and ads) this fiscal year ending July 31; and we will carry over something round $1,000.00 for next year; and our minimum cash budget next year will be round $5,500.00; so that if we could earn as much again we'd be fixed up. But we can't; for one thing, the $750.00 from Southern Review was like a Christmas present when it's the last Christmas; and publishers are showing signs of retrenching and may not give us ads so much again; so that we need $1,000.00 or $1,500.00 to be on the safe side; and Church is our best single bet, I should think, for $500.00 or $1,000.00 of it. I do think we'll come through. For example, the Faculty here now thinks so well of us that I believe we could get them to pass a resolution asking the President to make us a small appropriation "in the name of the liberal college" which we have almost ceased to be in war-time. I'll let you know developments. In the meantime we're going right ahead planning; and first for the Henry James number. I was very glad a few weeks ago to have you remark as you did, and I forgot to answer that. I have been growing steadily in the opinion that James was pretty nearly the principal literary figure in the language for the latter half of the 19th Century. And you have a fine topic in what you have selected.

Robb is just about at rights again.[1] She had a fine series of meetings with Wolf, and has had treatments which he directed after she left New York, and his bill was awfully modest as such things go. Thank you very much. Robb is down in weight and down in blood pressure now.

We're using Cal's trilogy on Satan, which seems to me awfully spirited, an unusual very real "enthusiasm" for poetry in these days.[2] Nearly everything we get in here is too "labored"—good Yeats or good Eliot in manner, without anything real behind it. Except a general plaintiveness.

Love to the family.

Yours,
John

---

1. Robb had visited a New York specialist, recommended to Tate by John Peale Bishop, for treatment of high blood pressure and related ailments.

2. Robert Lowell, "Satan's Confession," *Kenyon Review*, V (Summer, 1943), 379–83.

To Robert Penn Warren

July 7, 1943

Dear Red:

I owe you the deepest apology—I had the line, "Robert Penn Warren is editor of this special number," in the ad which I fixed up in our recent issue looking forward to the James number. I then had to juggle the ad round a good deal to get it fitted in, and someway or other, quite without my consciousness, the line got left out. Naturally the Editor's name and function will be prominently displayed in the James number itself.

Besides: Oughtn't you to write an editorial introduction of two or three thousand words about the plan and the contents? (To lead off with; for an issue which is one single book.) I should think a good point of departure would be the old H&H James number of about fifteen years ago.[1] We could get all the pieces to you for consultation if they should come directly here rather than to you in the first instance. We have in hand Matthiessen and Austin Warren only; we jogged them all ten days ago, and will jog again the end of this week. But the editorial would go fine; it would be a binder, unifying the whole thing. I do hope you will do this. I meant to write a long time ago about this.

Trilling seems quite remorseful about his failure to get in and refers to his taking the lack of memoranda from you as leaping to his mistaken assumption that we might not really come through with the plan. He proposes that we approach Barzun for an essay on James's MELODRAMATICS; says Barzun is all primed, and a fast worker too; and it is a fact that B. did a fine job for us on his Shaw piece—isn't it? I have the feeling that you originally had Barzun in mind, too. So I have just up and taken the bit in my teeth, the hour being so late, and asked Barzun for the essay, telling him he might have the limit as to time, till August 7. Will let you know as to his answer. I hope you will forgive me. I had to run down to Nashville to see my aged mother for ten days when I could, and that got me back here only this past week-end, when I found Trilling's letter here about Barzun. If for some reason you really think Barzun wouldn't do, let me know and I'll cancel the order on some pretext, as he can't have done much with it by the time I hear from you.

Zabel has written a characteristic letter about suddenly having to change his summer plans and probably going to be a little late with his paper; that was his precise prelude to failing us on the symposium on the teaching of literature. I think his item therefore very doubtful. Tate is always doubtful; I saw him briefly while down south, and he had done almost nothing, in spite of having reserved so much extra space when you first approached him; he is doubtful, I think. Katherine Anne [Porter] is doubtful, so far as our editorial experience with her would suggest. These doubtful cases made the Barzun possibility seem all the more important to me.[2]

About Tate, though: he has really been doing some fine verse lately; the best unprinted as yet. He has one poem, "Seasonal Meditations," or something like that, which is his best yet with the possible exception of Confederate Dead, in my opinion.[3] I have got the rights to it for K.R. And he is going to Washington for one year, in charge of poetry at the Congressional Library, as you probably know. And he and Caroline spoke mighty well of your new book, which I had not seen.[4]

But since getting back here I've seen it and read it, and it's my pleasure and responsibility to tell you what I think of it. First, though, as you know I don't really "get" fiction unless it is in certain categories; I'm more reactionary about that than about verse, even; I don't trust my opinions. That being the case, I think the book has fine structure and finish and straightness. The Wyndham material is a sort of sub-plot that is awfully agreeable (I like it best in the book, I think) which gets triumphantly integrated finally, and doesn't constitute an episode merely. Under this head I believe I did feel that the lyrical passages in italics near the end of the book (not much there was of that) are a break that wasn't necessary. Otherwise, a book mighty well put together.

The materials and characters I don't so well like. They are not "sympathetic" for me. It's not merely a satirical book though the content is almost (sometimes) farcical. I may be too "close" to the Sergeant York, and the Hunt Club, and the Caldwell Company of fact. I feel that perhaps the graduate student circle in the latter part of the book, and the heroine's role therewith, are a bit unreal. Some of the characters are extremely well done, like the homefolks of the hero, and the disillusioned accountant, and maybe the Private, and, much of the time, the girl, and the rough boys. But the chief characters are characters you couldn't love; and doesn't that mean that there is maybe an ambiguity as between a satirical and a sympathetic intention? I find myself wishing that you would do a fiction analogous to your fine poetry; in the grand manner, in the magnificent manner. Nearly all current fiction (under the naturalistic impulse, I guess) is wasted on me; there's only Mann (whom in a flourishing period I think I wouldn't think so grand) and, on a small scale, Wescott and Wilder, little fellows, perhaps a few others. The rest are very smart, it may be, but I think they lack the highest aesthetic motivation. Is fiction to rate itself on purpose in a category inferior to poetry? I am painfully aware of talking somewhat like Dr. Mims.

You are the easiest, most flowing, prose artist we have; whether in critical or fictional prose.

We are all pretty well. Reavill is doing pre-flight school near here, at Ohio Wesleyan of all places; he gets home for Sunday now and then. Helen is in Vanderbilt again this summer. Robb and Jack and I feel like a very small family. We are moving in a few weeks, as soon as they fix up the house we have picked. It's up near Bexley Seminary, north; less house than we have now, but more grounds; in fact, a wonderfully nice location. The family send their best to you and Cinina, whom we wish we could see in person.

Yours,
John

1. *Hound and Horn*, VII (April–May, 1934), was devoted entirely to Henry James.

2. The James number of the *Kenyon Review*, V (Autumn, 1944), included essays by Jacques Barzun, R. P. Blackmur, David Daiches, Francis Fergusson, F. O. Matthiessen, Katherine Anne Porter, Eliseo Vivas, and Austin Warren. Lionel Trilling and Morton Dauwen Zabel did not contribute.

3. Tate, "Seasons of the Soul," *Kenyon Review*, VI (Winter, 1944), 1–9.

4. Warren, *At Heaven's Gate* (New York: Harcourt, Brace, 1943).

To Allen Tate

November 1, [1943]

Dear Allen:

At the moment I can't see your last letter with your home address on it.

Here's a proof, uncorrected in this office as yet. I didn't quite venture to entitle it—just the beginning of a title. I had the feeling that you needed something a little simpler than those on the list though they would do, any of them. "The Soul to the Seasons" or "The Soul Amid the Seasons" or "The Soul Amid Her Elements"? It will be as you decide.[1] I'm pretty sure this poem ought to lead off our number. It will be a "literary" number, with three short stories and a lot of poetry. The other poetry looks slight and tame, most of it, after yours, so it will be lumped together, yours separate.

The program you have had in mind for the Symbolist number is fine; what luck has there been in the responses? I agree that a small section of translations would be nice. The Ed. would insist on one from the Special Editor among these. When we turn the matter of the Winter number over finally to the printer (about November 15) I'd like to announce any detail of the Symbolist Spring number that was available at that time, provided several items were available; if not, then a general announcement.

Poor Cal! But he's not a man whose prison term in itself ought to be mourned for; it's his degeneration inside.[2]

Affectionately,
John

P.S. Please let me know of your expenses, the aggregate, an outside estimate in connection with the Symbolist business—the Review wants to pay that.[3]

1. Ransom is again referring to Tate's "Seasons of the Soul."

2. Robert Lowell was imprisoned for being a conscientious objector during World War II.

3. Tate did not edit a special number of the *Kenyon Review* on the Symbolists.

To Allen Tate

November 22, [1943]

Dear Allen:

There's been a bit of excitement since your last letter, and I've been terribly busy.

The corrections went through on the poem. The title seems fine. The *not* entered in an early line was not really put through, following your second message on that.

Last summer David Stevens, director of the Humanities Division of the Rockefeller Foundation, got up a warm correspondence with me about the finances of KR, the "burden" on the Editor, and the nature of the critical project in general. He had evidently become convinced that KR was a great instrument of education in the Humanities. Nov. 12 he came here and spent the day, and told me to put in application for aid, & it w'd go through the January meeting of his Board. He didn't say how much, but indicated various entries under which we might expect support. One is "relief to the Editor," which will take the shape of a dictaphone and a half-time professional stenographer to service it; so the ed[itorial]. correspondence, now snowed under, will flourish vigorously. Another is restoration of a decent rate of pay to contributors. Another is a full-time professional secretary for handling the business end. Then we've put in one or two fancy items. Apparently, we have at last found the angel. But I don't know for how long; and I don't even count this yet, and am not mentioning it in public, so please don't speak of it out.

Stevens is a fine person, modest and plain, devoted to the arts. So I told him in confidence about your tentative acceptance of the Sewanee position with the Review, and expressed the opinion he might get more for his thousand dollars there than anywhere in the world.[1] He seemed to like that, and took it down in his notebook. I don't know what it will come to, if anything. He asked me who Bishop was; said he understood Bishop was going into the Library under MacLeish.[2]

I think the Sewanee position is nice; wouldn't it be far more congenial than the Library position? I've always liked Sewanee. I can't imagine there not being enough market, too, to support SR as well as KR; but it will be an awful headache if they don't furnish you a bit of a war chest to pay contributors. I suggest you might get in touch with Kerker Quinn who (along with our Bill Moses and others) runs *Accent* at U. of Ill. They have a live, small review which finances by subscriptions only; and they pay something to all their contributors. They paid me $17.00 for an 8 or 10 p. fragment of my last book. And Quinn is very decent, w'd be flattered if you asked him how to do it. I believe there's some young Sewanee man who could take hold of subscriptions and make them *hum* before six months were out.

We've made a deal with Doubleday Doran whereby each year for 3 yrs we hold a SS contest for $750.00 of prizes, which they pay, and whereby also we receive $500.00 worth of annual advertising by DD in KR. We will therefore be very much in the SS game. And we intend to publish more verse, too.

Robb is in Nashville this week and I'm keeping house with Jack. Our best to the Tates. I don't think now I'll go East soon; my speaking engagement at Amherst, Mass., is off till next year.

Yours,
John

1. Tate was still negotiating with Alexander Guerry, vice-chancellor of the University of the South, about becoming editor of the *Sewanee Review*.

2. Ransom is alluding to John Peale Bishop and the possibility of his working at the Library of Congress for Archibald MacLeish. Bishop died soon thereafter.

To Lionel Trilling

April 11, 1944

Dear Lionel:

I wonder what you would think about our having a special exhibit of Melville pieces; and about your assuming editorial responsibility for it. As to the first, several people have suggested that, as topics of symposia go, this one is surely a must, the Melville criticism which we have being inadequate, and the interest in him nowadays among real critics being very great. And as to the second, I think it would be the very best thing for the health of a symposium, if we should have one. I assume that you are interested in Melville yourself.

Last summer, you know, we devoted a number almost entire to James. Our next number (Summer 1944) is going to be about Hopkins to the extent of maybe half; six papers promised, at least four will materialize. If only four materialize, I rather think I'll look for some further Hopkins matter, one or two papers, taking up where these would have left off, probably objecting to or supplementing them, continuing the feature into another number.[1] And there might be two ways of handling a Melville exhibit: by a lot of papers in one number, or by a serial attention to Melville lasting over several numbers. I'd like very much to know what you think of the idea in general, and the way to handle it; and then as I indicated I'd like very much to have you say you'd agree to plan it and edit it.[2]

Phil thinks you're the one to do it. But he didn't put the idea of your doing it into my head, where it already was.

The Wilson review will be coming in these next 20 days, won't it?[3] And very much welcome.

Sincerely yours,
John C. R.

---

1. Cleanth Brooks edited the special number of the *Kenyon Review*, VII (Summer, 1945), devoted to Gerard Manley Hopkins, which contained pieces by Brooks, Robert Lowell, Josephine Miles, Arthur Mizener, H. M. McLuhan, Austin Warren, and Harold Whitehall.

2. Nothing ever came of this proposal: no issue of the *Kenyon Review* was devoted to Herman Melville, and Trilling did not ever edit a special issue of the magazine.

3. Trilling did not review this book—probably *The Shock of Recognition* (1943), edited by Edmund Wilson—for the *Kenyon Review*; nor did anyone else.

To Allen Tate

April 24, 1944

Dear Allen:

Thanks for wanting me in your first issue. Assuming that it will be the autumn issue, deadline something like August 1, I accept.[1] I have two pretty nice-looking essays in sight, independent and self-contained, though as yet unwritten. As to a poem, I can't say; but that's not out of the question; and I will settle on that as your first choice if anything good should come through. The other day I wrote a 2,000-word review of Red's Selected Poems, a hurry-up call from Sat[urday] Review; I grudged making a hasty job of it, though I had long wanted to write on Red; and I think you would have wanted it if it were not taken. If they find it too long, or anything, I'll let you see it; and I don't care if they do.

I think Fitts may have partly been motivated as Arthur Mizener thinks, but it's more complicated than that. I met Fitts three years ago when I spoke at Yale. He was dying to get into Kenyon, if I'm not mistaken, and too proud to say so. He is a half-defeated man, a very good Latinist and a poor poet. In this piece he astonished me by the length and scope of his review; but I liked the scholarship and thoroughness on the whole; and as to his opinion of you, I felt like Cowser, our Secretary, who said that you would like it because you wouldn't care one way or the other about your Latinity and your reviewer did make you out to be a fine poet. Fitts is a bit stuffy and a bit precious as a writer, but a job of this kind, or a letter to the Editor, he is fitted for.[2]

Red told me about seeing Nancy, and about her husband's harsh treatment. That last is mean business, but it won't affect them in the long run, and I'm delighted with the whole thing as I think about it. Our Helen has fallen way behind at keeping up with Nancy. She is, however, getting very good marks, and applying herself quite well to her studies, and what is better, really getting a relish for critical studies, while there's no limit to her desire to do some creative writing; though nothing new at the moment to show.[3] She has taken to writing at the most tremendous rate to her mother, all about her dates, her love affairs, and her studies too, oh yes and her clothes; but her letters have a great deal of spontaneous literary quality.

Robb by the way is in Nashville a week or so, having been wired to by Trudy (Mrs.) Freeland her old friend [who is] there a few days from Florida. Jack and I are having a hard time but I suppose we'll pull through.

Blackmur told me two years ago about having written his views of the necessity of supporting creative literature, to the Rockefeller people, but I had not attached much weight to the matter. I believe I did tell him in a letter a few weeks ago that he must have been the prime cause of our success. (I write with a light accent.) But I have found the Foundation pretty tough; they are slow, and they don't give as much as they seem to be promising. It's likely that I'll see [David] Stevens before long, and I'll put in my little word for you whatever it may be worth.

Love to Caroline and Nancy.

Yours,
John

1. Ransom's "The Bases of Criticism" appeared in Tate's second issue, *Sewanee Review*, LII (Autumn, 1944), 556–71.

2. Dudley Fitts, translator of Sophocles and Aristophanes, reviewed Tate's *The Vigil of Venus; Pervigilium Veneris* (1943) in the *Kenyon Review*, VI (Spring, 1944), 303–308. He later reviewed other books in the *Kenyon Review*, but his poetry was never published there.

3. Ransom alludes to Nancy Tate Wood and her husband Percy, who would become a psychiatrist. Helen Ransom, who had transferred to Vanderbilt from Wellesley, would become in time an author in her own right.

To Wallace Stevens

June 15, 1944

Dear Mr. Stevens:

I've just been reading *Notes towards a Supreme Fiction*, some more. Nobody can do such poems, besides you. I like best the innocent, non-philosophical ones, like the Canon Aspirin ones, the "be-thou" one, the Nanzia Nunzio, the Catawba, etc etc.[1] Yet I'm absolutely *for* the philosophical position you occupy.

Please send us a sizable poem, or set of poems. We are a little bigger now, could do a whole series. I'd rather have you than anybody. We are printing just pretty-good verse, not-bad verse, from young poets-not-without-interest. Good poetry seems to me very rare now.

If we had something by early August, it would go in our Autumn number. But if you should be at work on something pretty big, which we would have to wait on but might have eventually, we'd rather wait.

With best wishes,

Yours sincerely,
John Crowe Ransom

1. All references are to the single poem *Notes Toward a Supreme Fiction*, which Ransom was probably reading in the Cummington Press Edition published in 1943.

To Wallace Stevens

August 18, 1944

Dear Mr. Stevens:

Your poem is truly magnificent I think. Somebody here says it is Stevens' Waste Land though I don't think the metaphor entirely apt. We are going to make it the lead of our Autumn number.[1] And just to make sure we haven't any error in it I am sending herewith the proof for your eye if you want to look over it.

It is nice of you to waive payment for the poem and as a sort of trustee of the interests of this Review I can't pass up the offer. But we would have paid double or triple for it if we had had to, and thought it sound business.

Sincerely yours,
John Crowe Ransom

1. "Esthétique du Mal," *Kenyon Review*, VI (Autumn, 1944), 489–503.

To Robert Penn Warren

October 18, [1944]

Dear Red:

Our Sec. has been away a few days, I haven't got to ask him about the copies of old numbers containing your two essays; I had thought they got off to you all right, but at any rate if they haven't they will. Naturally there's no charge.[1] We are indebted to you—no two ways about that.

I'm much interested in your words interpretative of the Billie Potts.[2] I wonder I didn't make out the symbolic intention. The medium didn't suggest that to me somehow, though I recall a lot of gnomic wisdom passim, especially at the last I think. I think perhaps you've written the hero *down* and colloquialized him to such an extent that the reader thinks this is just a new kind of ballad, realism married to balladry etc. But the intense seriousness of the piece (it's progressive) ought to wake up dull readers like me. My first chance, I'm going to give the poem a new and thorough reading. I still have a fear that Billie is too far from the Aristotelian definition of hero for us to get the pity and terror; but I want to read it and see; I'm chagrinned over my other reading.

Professor Roellinger of Oberlin (or maybe it's Western Reserve) sent us in the spring an essay for the James number. I replied that we would send it to you, the Editor of the number; and I guess I did, as we don't seem to have it on the premises. I intimated that there wasn't much chance of its going through, we had already made the assignments, etc. Now it seems he wants his manuscript. Do you have it there? Please see about this at your earliest convenience.

(I see that he's Professor Francis Roellinger of Oberlin.)

Yours,
John

1. Warren's "Katherine Anne Porter (Irony with a Center)," *Kenyon Review*, IV (Winter, 1942), 29–42, and "The Love and Separateness in Miss Welty," *Kenyon Review*, VI (Spring, 1944), 246–59, appeared in revised form in his *Selected Essays* (New York: Random House, 1958). Warren apparently anticipated an earlier collection of his essays.

2. Warren, "The Ballad of Billie Potts," *Partisan Review*, XI (Winter, 1944), 56–70.

To Robert Duncan

October 26, 1944

Dear Mr. Duncan:[1]

I am distressed, and I invite your opinion. We set up your poem time before last—that would be for the Summer number—but there just wasn't room for it; then we planned to use it for Autumn, but Stevens' long poem came along and we dispensed with all our shorter poems.[2] And now we have to make the decision.

Originally I thought your poem very brilliant, and it occurred to me that Africa was a fine symbol of whatever was dark in the mind, and that you explored the symbol well. I didn't think the particular darkness was defined; I said it was dark dissipation, or dark despair infecting love, etc. But since then you have written the courageous piece in *Politics* in which you say that the homosexual poets have usually symbolized their abnormality and palmed it off on the innocent "little magazines." And you propose in the future that they be less furtive.[3]

Well, in the first place, I entirely agree as to the cruelty of the general public attitude in such matters. But as to the course of the homosexualists, I think there cannot be much doubt: they have this superior perception, sensibility, I do not doubt, in many cases; abnormality provokes mind into being genius; why then should not they sublimate their problem, let the delicacy and subtlety of their sensibility come out in the innocent regions of life and literature: in the same sense, that is, in which repressions cause great works of art which have no recognizable relation to the repressed desires.

As to the present poem (Sections toward an African Elegy, you will recall) now that you have called public attention to it, it seems to me to have obvious homosexual advertisement, and for that reason not to be eligible for publication. But please tell me what you think. Is it not possible that you have made the sexual inferences inescapable, and the poem unavailable? Or do I misread the poem? Or misunderstand the situation as an editor should see it?

Sincerely yours,
John C. Ransom

1. Robert Duncan, who was born in 1919, had not yet published any of his many books of poetry. None of his work was ever published by Ransom.

2. Wallace Stevens, "Esthétique du Mal."

3. Duncan's "The Homosexual in Society" had appeared in Dwight Macdonald's short-lived magazine, *Politics*, I (August, 1944), 209–11.

To Robert Duncan

Nashville, December 6, 1944

Dear Mr. Duncan:

Mr. Rice, who has been carrying on the Review during my quarter's vacation, has sent on to me your letter, and at my request a proof of the African Elegy; he thought since I had started the correspondence I ought to finish it.

I am happy to withdraw my phrase about "palming off the homosexual symbols on the innocent little magazines." Clearly I misinterpreted your piece in POLITICS.

But I feel very sure that we do not wish to print the poem, and I regret very much to decline it after an original acceptance. I must say for the record that the only right I feel in this action is that belatedly, and with your permission, I read the poem as an advertisement or a notice of overt homosexuality, and we are not in the market for literature of this type.

I cannot agree with you that we should publish it nevertheless in the name of freedom of speech; because I cannot agree with your position that homosexuality is not abnormal. It is biologically abnormal in the most obvious sense. I am not sure whether or not state and federal laws regard it so, but I think they do; I should not take the initiative in the matter, but if there are laws to this effect I concur in them entirely. There are certainly laws prohibiting incest and polygamy, with which I concur, though they are only abnormal conventionally and are not so damaging to a society biologically. But I don't throw stones. I am very sorry to refuse publication. I return to my thesis about the artistic policy of homosexuals; you reject that, but I can't see any other option open.

I might remark just one other thing. The only use I can see the Kenyon Review making of homosexual material is a literary use which regards it as tragic altogether; or a critical discussion of what homosexualism means for literature and in literature. But neither of these uses would be exactly one that we should covet. Again, I am sorry.

I am sending this letter to the office in order that the secretary may put with it your original manuscript. This may cause a little delay, while she obtains it again from the printer. If the printer has lost it, since setting it up last summer, at least she will return a clean proof of the manuscript, and if this is all we can do I herewith offer my deepest apologies.

Sincerely yours,
John Crowe Ransom

To Robert Duncan

March 1, 1945

Dear Mr. Duncan:

This delay has been due to my traveling, while on vacation, and your letter not catching up with me till recently after I returned home.

But I am sorry to say, I am entirely averse to any publicizing of our differences as to the publication of the poem. I've got stakes in too many other public topics which have precedence over this one. I don't want my notes to you to be published; though please don't take this to mean that I didn't mean them.

With best wishes, I am,

Sincerely yours,
John Crowe Ransom

To Mona Van Duyn

Gambier, May 23, 1945

Dear Miss Van Duyn:[1]

I enclose for your information a circular we have been sending out here and there; and we will print it in the forthcoming number of the Review. The piece we had picked for the First Prize turned out to be ineligible when we learned that the author had published a book of fiction. We didn't have another out of 600 entries to put in its place.

But I want to say distinctly that the award we have made to you, though we haven't announced it and don't want to yet, is in no way imperilled.[2] If you don't win the Second Prize it will be because you win the First Prize. That is a possibility. We had the feeling that your story dealt with a young girl (though the minor characters were adults) and suited a Second Prize story rather than a First. It is on condition that we don't uncover a First Prize story that is both bigger than yours and equal to it in quality that we are fully prepared to give the First Prize to your story.

Your story gains by each reading. We have made no mistakes in this and I want you to know that we are not wavering in the least on it.

Sincerely,
John C. Ransom

1. Mona Van Duyn, who was born in 1921, is chiefly known for her poetry, which earned her a Bollingen prize in 1970.

2. "The Bell," *Kenyon Review*, VII (Autumn, 1945), 598–615, was awarded second prize in the short-story contest for 1945 sponsored by Doubleday and Co., Inc., and the *Kenyon Review*. First prize went to John Berryman's "The Imaginary Jew," *Kenyon Review*, VII (Autumn, 1945), 529–39.

To Robert Penn Warren

June 5, 1945

Dear Red:

I'm quite worked up over the prospects of the Ancient Mariner piece; have been from the beginning, got up all the more steam after you told of the handsome dimensions it was assuming.[1]

Here is my thought in the matter. To print it in any case (though this isn't the ultimate commitment). But especially if, as I think likely, we go from a quarterly basis to, beginning Autumn, a semi-quarterly basis. Didn't I write you about this? An Autumn I and II, a Winter I and II, likewise a double Spring and Summer. For commercial and educational advantages that seems obvious. To sell at 40 cents on the bookstands, which means, with conditions as they now are, that it would *really* sell, perhaps a thousand instead of three hundred as now. Subscriptions at $3.00 as now, but coming twice as often to the subscriber, or every six weeks. The matter to be of precisely the same quality as now, and only a very little more volume; 96 pp text each number as base size. The editorial work as now defined as getting quarterly material four times a year, then printing in two installments. The educational advantage (which I shall probably expound to Stevens of the Rockefeller Foundation) being that you get it *twice as often* and *not so much at a time*. It will put a premium on the sharp keen essay, the feature, and will forbid any merely academic content. But we have been looking after that these last few months, and have some very fine materials on hand and in sight, so that I think we could do it. The cost would be an extra GRAND a year, no mean bundle of hay. But 300 new sales on the average would pay for it and give us the moral advantage of the larger circulation. You're an Advisory Editor and should advise me about this. Rice is afraid of it. What do you think? Another commercial feature is that I believe we can combine this change with an advertising campaign and rake in a lot more money that way.

So much for the new plan I am brooding over. KEEP THIS UNDER YOUR HAT please. My competitors seem blood-thirsty cutthroats, Allen scarcely an exception even.[2]

And now for Ancient Mariner under this plan. It would be THE feature of one of the Autumn numbers, where it should be accompanied by just enough of our regular magazine features, quite highly selected, to impress the general reader with KR as well as RPW; then when normal sales were used up we would fall back upon that extra printing we would have made and begin to advertise the number for the sake of the Warren critique, which every scholar as well as bright reader simply must have.

If no semi-quarterly issue, then I think we'd just print it on its merits, length and all, and all to the good.

Now another little matter. I don't know for sure whether you're in Washington or gone to Conn. So drop me a word of your present address so that I can send you an autographed copy of the Selected Poems which is ready for you and Cinina.[3]

I'm sorrier than you are that you can't get here till late summer as you start west. Let it be then!

My records came, and they are admirable on the mechanical side. And yesterday a nice note from Evans thanking me on behalf of the Library, with no mention of any more substantial reward. I shan't claim any of course, but I am disappointed, as my mouth was watering, my paws were rubbing together, in view of that 6 × $50 which I thought might be coming up. But never mind.[4] Yesterday the President announced that a bonus was to be paid on this year's salaries in view of the high cost of living.

Helen and Robb as busy as wrens in the nest, making bridal plans for whatever-date-it-is-to-be. But Jack has come back home, and that is nice.

We all send love to the Warrens.

Yours,
John

P.S. The Melville critique might go *small* as Brief Mention (not more than 500 words or so) or large as a regular review. You can *make* it up largely by assembling quotations as you did for me.[5]

---

1. Warren, "A Poem of Pure Imagination," *Kenyon Review*, VIII (Summer, 1946), 391–427. This essay, which was accompanied by illustrations by Alexander Calder in the *Kenyon Review*, constitutes sections 3, 4, and 5 of the longer essay of the same title in Warren's *Selected Essays*.

2. Allen Tate was still editor of the *Sewanee Review*.

3. Ransom's *Selected Poems* (1945).

4. Ransom's reading of his poetry, with commentary, before the Writers Club of the Library of Congress on January 28, 1945, had been recorded. Luther Evans was librarian of Congress.

5. Warren's review of *Selected Poems of Herman Melville*, edited by F. O. Matthiessen, appeared in the *Kenyon Review*, VIII (Spring, 1946), 208–23.

To F. O. Matthiessen

January 12, 1946

Dear Matthiessen:

Just a line, to thank you for doing what I would surely have done if I hadn't been in the position of an editor with a possible stake in the thing: your communication to Tate about the Davidson essay on the negro problem.[1] And this is the second time: you had my proxy when you took up the editors of Partisan over the way they ganged up on Rukeyser.[2]

Let me say without fear of its coming back to embarrass us that anything you want to send us we'd be glad to publish. We aren't afraid of printing Matthiessen too often. I know you are working on James. And aren't there some other American authors you've been re-defining?

Sincerely,
John Crowe Ransom

---

1. Matthiessen's "A Communication," *Sewanee Review*, LIV (Winter, 1946), 144, was a response to Donald Davidson's "Preface to Decision," *Sewanee Review*, LIII (Summer, 1945), 394–412.

2. Ransom alludes to Matthiessen's letter to the *Partisan Review* in defense of Muriel Rukeyser, who had been vitriolically attacked by that magazine's editors for her propaganda work in World War II for the Office of War Information. See the *Partisan Review*, X (September–October, 1943), 471–73; XI (Winter, 1944), 125–28; and XI (Spring, 1944), 217–18. Matthiessen's letter appeared in the last number.

To Allen Tate

April 9, [1946]

Dear Allen:

I've got out of touch with you here lately, while so much has been happening, and I know there is little to be done about it via the mails. But I do want to write about one or two items of interest to the Review.

I hope we can have the Jarrell piece by the end of this month, for Summer.[1] That will be a fine time for it; we will have a good number to put it in. Now I find myself wondering what will happen to the *Sewanee Review*, and I can only think in answer that it is finished; whether formally or not I don't know.[2] Nor do I want to embarrass you in any commitments you may have made to it. But as you can imagine we here would be extremely interested in materials which you may have had brought to your attention or even have accepted, so far as they are negotiable; and in authors. You did a very fine job with your term of editorship, I needn't say; and this I must say, it stimulated us here, so that you profited us as well as your own circle of readers. We here are knocking along pretty steadily, printing and selling out 2500 copies quarterly and now faced with stepping the issue up to 3000, before long. We are steady. Do think about us insofar as you are free to do so. I scarcely dare to think we might inherit from you as we did from the *Southern Review*, by taking over unexpired subscriptions. But any help you can extend in a literary sense will be more than welcome.

We had a fine visit from Cleanth for three days. But I've seen nobody who has seen you.

Best wishes,

Affectionately,
John

1. This essay apparently was never written.
2. Tate had resigned as editor of the *Sewanee Review*. He was succeeded by J. E. Palmer.

To Allen Tate

April 22, [1946]

Dear Allen:

We are awfully happy to learn of the re-union of the Tates.[1] That was a bad chapter, for me and my friends who are the friends of the Tates, with a mighty nice ending.

Marshall McLuhan, now at Assumption College, Windsor, Conn., ought to make a good editor for the Sewanee Review. Brooks, who was here for three days not long ago, knows him personally and thinks he has a lot and "is one of us"—though he's Catholic. I believe he wants to get back into this country, but I am sure his status financially is a modest one, as he must be young. You saw his Hopkins piece with us, I suppose.[2]

A still better man, potentially a great man in my opinion, is Austin Warren of University of Iowa. He has been unhappy there at that awful place since Foerster went out.[3] I was there in November, and found him looking very bad—but he was over-working at his Rockefeller grant project and teaching, besides having an invalid wife at the point of death. She has since died, and it may be that Austin has an easier life at the moment. He is a genuine man of letters, I think; of gentle nature but uncompromising taste. He might like the peace of Sewanee with a Review to run. I don't know what his financial demands would be. He is religious, and of course from Boston.

Affectionately,
John

P.S. Would Heilman of L.S.U. be up to the mark?[4]

---

1. Caroline Gordon and Allen Tate, who had been divorced in January, 1946, were remarried in April, 1946.

2. McLuhan, "Analogical Mirrors," *Kenyon Review*, VI (Summer, 1944), 322–32.

3. Austin Warren, scholar and critic and author of *Rage for Order* (1939) and other books, had been at the University of Iowa since 1939. Norman Foerster, a leader of the New Humanism and the author of many books on American literature, had retired as director of the School of Letters at the University of Iowa in 1944.

4. Robert B. Heilman, a critic principally known for his criticism of drama (especially Shakespeare) and the author of *This Great Stage* (1948) and other books.

To Arthur Mizener

May 15, [1946]

Dear Arthur:

It's not a "slip-up" but a failure of conviction, our not sending those books on critical theory along. They don't amount to much. I had a note on my desk to write you about that, "*today*"—but it was put there 3 or 4 days ago. I hate to ask your time for them; they wouldn't deserve much notice. But here's a $30.00 set of books that in decency ought to be noted, and that might provoke a nice literary evaluation, maybe *re*valuation. It's the Centennial Edition of Sidney Lanier, complete works, Hopkins press; quite a thing.[1] Does that take you too far afield? I think a piece of goodish length, up to 2,000 words say at most, by a critic and scholar with entitlements in *both* fields, is called for: therefore Mizener in short. What do you say?

(Deadline August 25 for AUTUMN—but then he w'd be good for Winter if necessary.)

Thank you for the many kind words in your recent review of JCR.[2] I would never dare to expect a better response than that. Which being said, I remark that in the Dead Boy poem I referred to the *county* family, which has a good deal more substance than a *country* family would. Probably the printer's not the reader's slip. And I have to smile a little at being commended on Winters' grounds; when if I'm not mistaken (because somebody swiped W's book out of this office before I got through reading him even on me) W. credited me with only two lines somewhere that he could commend.[3] And I believe my "theme" is not nearly as consistent as you would have it; see the first poem and the last and about half of those between. It's true that I had a sort of formula for a poem, the ironical-realistic one, for a long time, and it gave me great delight; and I believe I could establish in about five minutes with you that this irony is one of the functions of poetry; but then it's far from being all the functions and it gets monotonous; I often felt entirely delivered from it, and later I forgot about it. And, finally, I am made to feel stuffy and self-conscious whenever they tell me that my studies have "killed" something that was better, whether creative or what not; when all I propose to do is to be myself, and that takes precedence over anything I might conceive as my goal, and I don't regard writing poems as a "mission" or a public responsibility which I have assumed; that's a false language somehow, a collegiate language. But no matter. You did me handsome.[4]

Affectionately,
John

1. Mizener never reviewed this edition for *Kenyon Review* (see the next letter to Arthur Mizener).

2. Mizener's review of Ransom's *Selected Poems* (1945) appeared in the *Quarterly Review of Literature*, II (1945), 366–70.

3. Winters' essay on Ransom was included in his *Anatomy of Nonsense* (1943).

4. Mizener had suggested that Ransom the poet may have been subsumed by Ransom the critic.

To Arthur Mizener

May 24, [1946]

Dear Arthur:

Thank you for your nice letter. I do want to affirm strongly that my main emotion over your review of me was SATISFACTION—not petulance. I concede all the rights of the critic in the premises—and this one surely did a handsome over-all job by me.

Here's the most amazing book for some time. (Agreeing that you haven't time to do Lanier, and the books in poetics aren't worth doing.) It's Wilson's

Memoirs of Hecate County—Edmund Wilson's, in case you haven't seen the thing. It consists in half a dozen little stories, or sketches, carrying an attenuated (i.e. it's spasmodic though sufficiently "hot") little romance forward, now and then, till on the last two or three pages the "I" marries the woman and they have a little honeymoon that's no happier than it should be. But the I everywhere is a hero whose artiness is absolute, and sticks out; he's the Great Aesthete of our times. There are two or three qualifications. He's rather leftist, which is odd, and it seems a lukewarm attachment in view of his great love for the fineries of life. He's pretty good-natured, but he does love those drunken parties where they put poison in each other's ears, and he uses a good bit habitually in his ink. And if he's not the Great Lover, he's quite a performer, and he gives us the plainest description of the techniques he uses with the ladies that I've ever seen from an American with a high-brow reputation. I think he destroys himself, in fact; I can't see how he dared to do it; though everywhere in the book you can see how he is oriented to the literary circles in New York, and the foreign countries, and the hinterland of America just doesn't exist for him. But what a book! I have always defended Wilson, e.g. against youngsters who wrote in scathing things against his literary dictatorship; I've thought he had good taste, and always knew a good deal about the pragmatic, or it may be the social, conditions, of the art-works. But this will do him in.

I hadn't meant to express myself at such length, and in such an opinionated way, when I am merely trying to put before you a book that you ought to review. My feeling is that your short story, and an allied effort like this, will presently get you out of an attitude which I have felt was academic; you have a career, a big one, which is less in the academic terms than we (I at any rate) have supposed. You know all about the gildings on our civilization (through Princeton and Yale and Fitzgerald and I don't mean to say you weren't fed with a silver spoon personally too, though I doubt it) and your version is so much healthier than Wilson's. Anyhow, you are the man I pick to ask to review this book for us.[1] It of course would be idle to get any of the literary drinkers round New York, for they wouldn't dare to be objective, nor would most critics in view of Wilson's standing. But you anyway. You have just the health and constitution, along with the know in this matter. For Autumn or Winter either. Though if we print a story of yours in Autumn what would it look like to be printing this associated piece?[2] I think it would look all the more interesting. But Winter if necessary.

I'm delighted to hear about Tennyson, but he can wait a little longer.

Yours,
John

---

1. Mizener did not review Wilson's *Memoirs of Hecate County* (1946) for the *Kenyon Review*, nor did anyone else.

2. Mizener's "You Never Go Back to Sleep," was published in the *Kenyon Review*, VIII (Autumn, 1946), 593–612, as the co-winner of the 1946 short-story contest sponsored by Doubleday and the *Kenyon Review*.

To Alexander Guerry

June 28, 1946

Dear Mr. Guerry:

I am flattered by your invitation to advise as to a right editor of the Sewanee Review in Allen Tate's place; I only wish I could reply with some certainty.

There's a good man who has written for this Review and yours too, if I'm not mistaken, and is excellent—Marshall McLuhan, now visiting professor at Assumption College, Windsor, Canada. He is an American, either a Catholic or an ex-Catholic but a thinker of his own; studied at Cambridge, England, among other places; and Cleanth Brooks knows him personally and thinks very highly of him. He is as good in the general prose field and the field of ideas as he is at the criticism of poetry. I would suggest that you write Brooks at Louisiana State for full information about him if you are interested. I have an idea McLuhan wants to get back into this country, and I predict he will have a distinguished career. He is youngish.

But I've been thinking of another and much younger man whom you know very well: Robert Daniel, now I think at the University of Oklahoma. He has some of the faults of youth and a good stock of its virtues, including strength and courage. He would make mistakes both literary and political, but what editor doesn't? Over the long run I think he might prove out very well. I have on my desk an essay of his, on Hemingway, which shows both critical capacity and character; it is very good writing, and the point of view is precisely what would be Tate's, or my own. I have a slight personal acquaintance with him too, and like him; once I felt he might be too ambitious personally, that is, impatient for fame and position, but I dare say that was just a chance impression. I do think he would bear your looking into. One could do far worse with a long-range publication than to enlist a young man to take charge of it.

I do hope you secure the man the Review deserves; I am convinced aside from good will towards everything at Sewanee that the prosperity and distinction of the Sewanee Review is very important for our Review here; that we do not compete so much as we re-inforce the common standard.

With best wishes, I am,

Sincerely yours,
John Crowe Ransom.

To Lionel Trilling

July 13, [1946]

Dear Lionel:

I'm sorry we won't have you here in August, and Eric will be sorry because he wrote the other day enthusiastically about seeing you here (he's going to spend the month of August here), but then we may have you later, and that is all right. Since we dismiss Summer term here Sept. 22, and take up again about 10th of October, I think we'd better plan towards a visit from you the latter part of October, and Pres. Chalmers says that will be fine. I haven't called my Lectureship committee together yet to issue a formal invitation, but will do so soon.

I am sending you three stories, for your valued opinion. One in proof, the second prize story we picked in May, whose author we notified, and then told that we were going to stand by this selection however the extension contest might turn out; in fact we said that if we failed to name this story as Second Prize story it would be because we *might* make it a first prize story, but that we had the feeling that with its juvenile content it looked like the Second Prize rather than the First Prize story. The other stories by Mrs. (Robert Maynard) Hutchins, and by the musician Krenek, just sent in by Eric. I suppose Krenek isn't good enough for a prize but it might be worth publication. A fourth story too: by Herschberger. A revision just rec'd. I'll probably send you one or two other items a little later, as I believe some good prospects are yet to come in.

You understand that we can't name the winner now, must wait till July 31 when all entries are in; but no harm surely in making preliminary canvass of matters. We have about a dozen stories in hand, mostly not real candidates. The Hutchins is much the most interesting if provocative entry.[1]

Here is an essay project dear to my heart, but useless if we can't get some very choice mind to undertake it. On the topic: Is Politics all? Is freedom compatible with the Revolution, i.e. with the Dictatorship of the Proletariat? Is censorship and control of art function in the Marxist economy? But you see my drift. I think that noble young men like [Eric] Bentley are being heroic, therefore romantic, *at a distance*, that is, recommending a polity that is fine for Russia, and fine for us in the unattainable future, where it does not encroach upon our own actual freedom; and that there is something fundamentally immoral in supposing that they have to endorse everything that a historic dynasty, like the Lenin-Stalin one, chooses to do. I even sense that Eric has to take an uncritical attitude to the Russians whereas Tate does not take an uncritical attitude to anybody; and that in this controversy Tate even appears to the moral advantage. This topic exercises me because I see as well as anybody that Marxism is the last great Idealism which has appeared, and it enlists all generous souls with its motive of the classless society and the brotherhood of man. Yet how mean (in the popular sense: vindictive, contentious, braggart) is the way in which many of the Idealists seem to participate in their Ideal. Of all the Marxist writers I have felt that Wilson is the most critical, yet even he seems to think that history turned its last page when Lenin got to the Finland station. Isn't there room for a good man to elect a lot of Marxism with fundamental humanist reservations or cautions? Must this cause like most others in the dark past be pursued uncritically, that is, without the exercise of intelligence and the moral sense? Can't we have a really vital expression of good men on this point, or must they remain bitter and uncritical partisans pro or con? The case of Bentley is the one which at the moment most fills me with the sense of urgency in this matter.

In short. Wouldn't you want to do this essay? You would be my pick of the men to do it. How would it do for your speech here in latter October? You see I'm trying to rope you in for a performance both oral and written, to the advantage of this Review as well as this College.[2]

Needless to say, however, a topic in American lit would do wonderfully well. And for that matter, any topic you choose.

Sincerely yours,
John

Parker Tyler in a curiously prim and verbose communication has accepted our decision to take the Proust part if his Romains-Proust essay is cut down appreciably.

---

1. M. P. Hutchins, "Innocents," *Kenyon Review*, VIII (Winter, 1946), 14–28. The other stories mentioned here were not accepted.

2. The subject that Ransom proposes was not taken up by Trilling but by Isaac Rosenfeld. See Rosenfeld's story "The Party," *Kenyon Review*, IX (Autumn, 1947), 573–607. Trilling did not visit Kenyon College until September, 1947, when he delivered "Manners, Morals, and the Novel" as a lecture, which was published in the *Kenyon Review*, X (Winter, 1948), 11–27.

To Allen Tate

July 17, [1946]

Dear Allen:

Of course you know Red is with us this summer.[1] A big idea has taken hold of us. Next year Faulkner is fifty years old; why not a very fine Faulkner number of this Review? We think as we talk of such items as—a new story by Faulkner, two or three essays on Faulkner by Americans, one or more each by Englishmen, Frenchmen, and Italians. Apparently F's *literature* is not *engagée* enough for New York critics, so that he is in the position of a prophet who will not be honored at home till the visible honors come from abroad. Besides, we think of one briefly-biographical and fully-bibliographical piece for completeness.

Red is writing Cowley, who has come over to Faulkner now, and, more important, knows F. well and might get us access to him. Red is telling him for the Lord's sake to keep it quiet, too, so that our scheme won't get stolen. Then we have some lines to Italy and France, where F. is highly regarded. We don't know who is our man in England; though I recall in 1931–32 they were teaching F. in the modern novel course at College of the South West (Exeter) as one of the great artists.

So I write you. First, wouldn't you write a piece? You could do it better than anybody, along with Red or Katherine Anne [Porter], though we wouldn't want too many Southerners I think; I don't know who the Yankees might be, though somebody like Blackmur perhaps who admires and studies the Russian novels for other than political reasons. I think we'd make April 15 our deadline, hoping for a Summer Faulkner issue.[2] Then, give us your advices, about writers anywhere, especially Eng., that we ought to approach. And whatever other advices occur to you.

My feeling is that either you or Red ought to edit this number, but that we'd reluctantly give up that connection for either of you that might care to write an essay.

Please write me as soon as you have time to feel this topic out in your mind.

Our best to Caroline.

Yours.
John

1. As a *Kenyon Review* fellow.

2. Although Warren, Ransom, and Tate all expended considerable time and energy on the planned Faulkner issue of the *Review*, it never appeared.

To Lionel Trilling

August 5, 1946

Dear Lionel:

There is just one opinion possible on your new piece—it is extremely good, and we are glad to have it, and will set it up as you suggest.[1] No doubt we can send you proof too. At this time you can add the title if it doesn't come to you before then.

I've long been wanting you to do just this sort of thing.

My own feeling is that you say the determining thing when you mention Eleanor Clark's saving, freeing *sense of humor*.[2] I know that you know well Freud's Wit and the Unconscious; I have been lately finding a great deal of effective aesthetic doctrine therein and thereabouts. In humor (of all sorts) the id gives an explosion of relief; he doesn't *have* to make the delicate adaptation recommended by the ego; and his noise may be even like the horse laugh, directed *at* the ego with its fussiness and stuffiness. In Clark's book nobody in the end is quite capable of being taken seriously except that fine natural woman, unless perhaps the bank clerk has grown up, in our estimation.

Liberals can become fussy and stuffy just as much as other people, in fact it is probably peculiarly the "hazard of their profession." They cut things too fine. Especially when they live together and make each other more serious even than they tend to be by themselves. As in New York, I think I must say. They are likely to conclude that salvation depends on a concatenation of doctrines and policies which is quite unlikely, and the turn of events within a generation will show that. I don't feel that Communism has come out of the fire unscathed; since it's a move in practical politics and power politics (involving such a contradictory technique as Dictatorship of the Proletariat) it proves as vicious as it is heroic, and greatly disturbs its romanticist followers, in fact alienates by far the most of them. But what is good is your *caritas*, and that's just Christian doctrine. It is my doctrine. But not everybody who says "the brotherhood of man" seems to me my brother. A humorous Christianity is my ticket. I cannot but feel what an awful fool I am capable of becoming when I think I have the political technique, so I need the humors. Or the poetries; the "precious objects" to love and honor, regardless of our progress and evolutions. Maybe this sounds quite disjointed, but it is what I am writing now and I hope before long there will be something for you to see.

I'm coming to your city next Saturday night, to be there Sunday, Monday, Tuesday, and if necessary Wednesday. So I'll call you probably round noon Sunday. But if you aren't at home then I'll call you Sunday night, and if that fails Monday, at chaste intervals. To see which day you'll go out to lunch with me.

Sincerely yours,
John

This is one of the days when I *cannot* make my typewriter obey me, and it infects my style of thinking even, I'm afraid.

---

1. Trilling, "The Life of the Novel," *Kenyon Review*, VIII (Autumn, 1946), 658–67, an essay-review devoted largely to Eleanor Clark's *The Bitter Box* (1946), her first novel.

2. Eleanor Clark, a writer who married Robert Penn Warren in 1952, is best known for *Rome and a Villa* (1952) and *Baldur's Gate* (1971).

To Allen Tate

August 22, [1946]

Dear Allen:

It was fine to see you and Caroline, and I enjoyed all my three evenings with you—not to mention the fine dinner that last evening.

I thought I should write about the Faulkner project about which I have just this minute been talking to Red.

1) There's no doubt you are the man to edit it if you have sufficient enthusiasm for it and it won't tax you too much. Red hopes you will do it. I would feel we were honored if you did.

2) For American writers who ought to be in the issue there are Red, Caroline, Cowley, Katherine Anne Porter, Fergusson, Troy,[1] and Matthiessen; these have all been mentioned, and all would be good; Red says he thinks he can write a piece on F's idea of Nature, provided you look over his recent New Republic essay to see what you think of that item as he has it listed there.[2] Cowley we are pretty well committed to, and he has written about a piece he wants to do. Nothing has yet been written about F. that's better than Caroline's piece. As to the others named, I have no information what they think of F. Then in addition there would need to [be] a biographical-bibliographical piece, for which you mentioned Daniel, and there is always Robert Stallman if we need him.[3]

3) For English writers I have no leads; but I know he is well regarded in England.

4) For French critics Red thinks Cowley would have leads, and Red and I both think there would be some advantage in getting either Camus or Sartre; though Hytier is a more catholic critic and a very fine one.[4] We wouldn't know how to get this item anyhow; we'd probably consult Cowley if we were left to our own devices.

5) For Italian critics there are Vittorini (I think that's right) the novelist and translator of Faulkner, and also Mario Praz whom Red knows.[5] The latter the more philosophical critic. But Pierre Pasinetti is here, just going back to his job at Bennington, and he will write to the Italians for us if you say so.[6] Just let me know.

6) Pasinetti says there were some good German critics of Faulkner before the war, and that Auden would know them, and know if they were still available. Incidentally, Auden might be considered as one of the English critics, or the one English critic; I don't know.

7) There should be a fine and if possible hitherto-unpublished story by F. himself. Cowley says that Ober the agent reports that F. has a fine Indian story not yet placed, very dear to himself (Faulkner).[7] We'd try to pay out pretty well (for us) for such a story. I suppose Faulkner ought to be written to personally or seen.

8) The date. I don't quite know how it would help F's publisher, or F

through his publisher, if we timed the issue to be simultaneous with his next book. Wouldn't it be just as well to come out ahead of the book, and make a build-up for the book? Seems to me Autumn 1947 is a good time, and more than a year hence. We could put deadline arbitrarily at June 1, which would allow a 2-months leeway for getting copy to the printer for Fall publication. This would be like everything else, however, as you say.

9) And why shouldn't Holt bring out the thing later in book form if any publisher does? But this would also be as you say.[8]

Please feel free to exercise your own judgment; I've just entered all the items we've talked about as far as we had gone with them.

10) Red says now that we ought to get one of those artists who make professional sketches of writers to do one of Faulkner to put into the issue. I like the idea.

Now a minute or two about the connection which might conceivably be made between KR and Holt, or some other publisher. Trilling talked to me at some length about this the other day, as he had done a year ago; he has at all times thought we ought to make the deal with Holt. He figures we could be worth $2,000 (if some round figure needs to be named) to our publisher. We could carry all the advertising that could be devised for one publisher short of a multitude of similar ads about different books. We could doubtless steer many young authors, if few prospective best sellers, to our publisher. And turn over every little while something book-size from our own publishing. The difficulty about this is the embarrassment I feel, and doubtless you will feel, about pushing your friends with your own house. Trilling thought I ought personally [to] have gone to Brandt just to avoid this.[9] Since I am not there to do it I think Trilling would do it, and do it very effectively. We will need before long to see several publishers to make a deal, but Holt would be our first choice if we can manage it.

Yours ever,
John

1. William Troy, a critic then teaching at the New School for Social Research, contributed only one essay to the *Kenyon Review* (on Balzac).

2. Robert Penn Warren, "Cowley's Faulkner," *New Republic*, CXV (August 12 and 26, 1946), 176–80, 234–37.

3. Robert W. Daniel had compiled *A Catalogue of the Writings of William Faulkner*, in 1942; and Robert W. Stallman, author of books on Stephen Crane and other authors and editor of several critical anthologies, was also an established bibliographer.

4. Jean Hytier, author of *André Gide* (1939) and several works on Valéry, would soon join the faculty at Columbia University.

5. Elio Vittorini was a novelist and journalist who had translated many British and American authors (including Shakespeare and Faulkner). Mario Praz, a distinguished scholar and critic, wrote *The Romantic Agony* (1930), among many other books.

6. Pierre Pasinetti, an Italian novelist who was naturalized in 1952.

7. William Faulkner's literary agent was Harold Ober. The story was Faulkner's "A Courtship," *Sewanee Review*, LVI (Autumn, 1948), 634–53.

8. Tate was then an editor at Henry Holt and Company.

9. Joseph August Brandt had become president of Holt in 1945 after having directed three university presses.

To Allen Tate

September 19, [1946]

Dear Allen:

Thanks for your two letters, or maybe now it is three. I didn't reply right away to your letter accepting editorship of the Faulkner feature because Red was about to start for New York and was particularly intent on seeing you and talking Faulkner. I suppose he did, but I haven't seen him since. He was going to assure you that my suggestions were just that—you have the final decision at every point. We'll even splurge, spend money, as you require, in order to do something of unusual distinction; though naturally I hope we can get out without shedding too much blood. I'll do anything you want in preparation too; e.g. writing to some contributor, though I don't know of any special use there would be of me there. As to the art-sketch of Faulkner, that would be too good an item not to have; and if you want me to do something about that just tell me.

I might say that my sentiments about all this are just the same as Red's.

About the Ghiselin poems: thanks a lot; I am sure we'll take something of this batch; he has come along; and I've got a special feeling of wanting to go a little way to meet him if necessary because he is such a fine person; I think even yet we may have to go a very little way, though I haven't had time to do justice to the reading yet, because there is a romantic lavishness which is short of an artist's severest standards of selection, or so I seem to note on the surface at a glance.[1]

Many thanks for that suggestion that Trilling and I both write to Brandt. I wrote, the other day, at some length; and have a note from Trilling today that he wrote. And here to day is another item, a real book-project for us to hand on to our publisher if we get one, that I will describe. Our young man Southard is a naval intelligence officer attached to Marshall's staff in China, and the only American in North China who knows Russian.[2] (He previously was employed in landing Amer. supplies on the Russian Pacific coast.) He's been there already nearly a year. So prodigious is his capacity that already he's written up China for us, or is doing it, upon our suggesting a China letter. But from his note today it seems it will be a China book, for he outlines 4 Letters instead of one, explains the necessity of them; and I am writing him that he must just send us the whole thing, and let us use excerpts from it as from a book, and let us give it to a publisher for next fall publication. I will wager anybody 5 to 1 that it will be an intelligent and highly readable and original view of China by an Occidental born to sympathy with the Orient, and that it will be a publisher's beat in that it will be both timely and masterful. It will have some political implications, frank ones, but will be largely an appreciation and understanding of the country. Seems to me that's the best publisher's project we've yet had.

Last night Jack Kershaw of Nashville was here, and we, as Nancy said of her grandmother, were "talking about the Tates," and we went through that handsome copy of VERVE which Caroline so rashly gave me. I want to thank her again for that. And for that hospitality.

Affectionately,
John

1. Brewster Ghiselin, then an associate editor of the *Rocky Mountain Review* who was teaching at the University of Utah, had published his first collection of poetry, *Against the Circle* (1946). Ransom would publish three of Ghiselin's poems, including "To the South," *Kenyon Review*, IX (Winter, 1947), 29.

2. W. P. Southard, at one time secretary of the *Kenyon Review*, was graduated from Kenyon College and commissioned in the U.S. Navy in 1943. He contributed "The Religious Poetry of Robert Penn Warren" to the *Review*, VII (Autumn, 1945), 653–76. Southard also wrote fiction and poetry for the *Kenyon Review*, but the book on China was apparently never written.

To Andrew Lytle

July 19, [1947]

Dear Andrew:

Had a wonderful evening two days ago reading THE BOOK.[1] It is a very big achievement.

I offer first impressions strictly. For 25 or 50 pp I wasn't sure; the style and intention are not decided; I didn't know how to take it. The speaker (the 1st person reporter) is a bit garrulous, has a lot of *general* commentary about things; e.g. is an agrarian, etc. But slowly the book got hold of me. The latter half of it is cumulative & powerful.

It's a ghost story. But all ghost stories (or so I used to say in my brash days) should have a naturalistic version as a possibility. In this case it would be: that Major Brent is a symbol for something in the 1st person-reporter's heroic and somewhat fevered imagination; that the ghost is a figment of *his*, and he is the source, and also the victim, of the tragedy. But that w'd tie up with my opening remarks this way: he ought to have been made more *distinct* and even more *queer* from the beginning. We can love him all right though he has a phoby and some passionate ideas.

Some of the writing is very beautiful.

It's a great book with one reservation: I wish it could have *sat* and got one more revision. This is a small reservation. You have lots of power, always.

We're kinda waiting on a new car to go to Tenn. in. But one way or another we're going there before summer's out. I'll write you, because I want some hoecake and fried corn. Helen, you know, is going to live in Nashville, out at Thayer Hospital, where Duane is a young surgeon assistant, now getting the apartment ready.[2] She's here with the baby now. Red & Cinina are in this town for the summer. All send love to you and Miss Edna.[3]

Affectionately,
John

1. Lytle's *A Name for Evil* (Indianapolis: Bobbs-Merrill, 1947).

2. Helen Ransom had married Duane Forman in 1945.

3. Lytle's wife.

To Wallace Stevens

October 7, 1947

Dear Mr. Stevens:

The poem is very fine, and we are delighted to have it—doubtless for immediate publication. I think it even better than your *Esthétique du Mal*—it has a slightly warmer, more obvious humanism. I remark—but irresponsibly, don't take me up on this—that the climax is almost in # IX rather than # X, so much do I like the rhetoric of that part. But then # X has the happy-unhappy dialectic.[1]

Thank you very much.

Yours faithfully,
John Crowe Ransom

1. "The Auroras of Autumn," *Kenyon Review*, X (Winter, 1948), 1–10.

To Allen Tate

November 17, [1947]

Dear Allen:

You will have Coffin's letter in this mail, inviting you to take part in our school of criticism (technically a School of English) and I do hope you will accept.[1] All the information is down there in his letter. I would gladly have talked this over in advance with you if I'd got to see you. We're counting on you. I very much hope we can get either Eliot or Empson; I hardly dare to hope for both, though we're asking both.[2]

Bowling's Faulkner is good enough.[3] It's a close study of the technique of one novel: *The Sound and the Fury*; but it will make a few cross-references to technique in other novels, so that it is a good paper in that field. So I thought we might get a paper or two to go with it, and have a small Faulkner feature next fall; and Richard Chase has promised a paper on the *substance* of a novel, probably *Light in August.*[4] And now I wonder if we couldn't get a new story by Faulkner himself; you'd know how to get that, though perhaps Cowley might be a man to work through. And I do wish you yourself would consent to write a general paper on Faulkner, or a paper on some other novel, critical in the widest sense; couldn't you do that?[5] Or couldn't Caroline if you didn't want to? We need a paper by a Southerner. Then I think we ought to get an artist to do a sketch of Faulkner's head, and put that in. How does that sound to you? While not a whole number all that would amount to a very sizable Faulkner item, and I'd be proud of it.

Yours,
John

And should we get Stallman to do a Bibliography?[6]

---

1. Charles Coffin was chairman of the English department at Kenyon and dean of the Kenyon School of English.

2. William Empson taught in the School of English, as did Tate; but T. S. Eliot did not.

3. Lawrence Bowling, "The Technique of *The Sound and the Fury*," *Kenyon Review*, X (Autumn, 1948), 552–66.

4. Richard Chase was a frequent contributor to the *Kenyon Review*, and his "The Stone and the Crucifixion: Faulkner's *Light in August*," *Kenyon Review*, X (Autumn, 1948), 539–51, would later appear in his *The American Novel and Its Tradition* (1957).

5. This essay was not written.

6. The autumn, 1948, issue of the *Kenyon Review* did not include a Faulkner checklist.

To Caroline Gordon Tate

February 8, [1948]

Dear Caroline:

We are mighty glad you will be with us this summer; and Nancy too, whom Helen will be mighty glad to see, not to mention her young fry Choppie (*Robb*, to some people). I'm sorry to think of you not having your garden, but you will have to advise me about mine; flowers exclusively, except for tomatoes, which are an old specialty. Charles Coffin says he will find a house for the Tates all right.

I'm worried about Cleanth. Lovejoy, of Hopkins, has a fine big rich book on "History of Ideas," of which C's review has just come in to us. After much pain I've had to tell him no. He notes Lovejoy's book perfunctorily, then writes at lengths to inform Lovejoy what disposition of a historian's work a CRITIC is obliged to make, then is reminded of an attack on his critical position by one Mr. Pearce in the *Journal of Aesthetics*, and devotes the remaining 6 or 7 pages to refuting Pearce without further mention of Lovejoy. I told him I was writing to him as "one of the family."

Affectionately,
John

To Wallace Stevens

September 7, 1948

Dear Mr. Stevens:

It seems that our forthcoming Autumn issue completes our Volume X of this periodical, and our Winter issue starts us into our 11th year; an age as venerable for a Little Magazine as 60 years is an age to make an Elder Statesman (apparently) out of a pedagogue-poet. I can't think of a better distinction we could start out the year with than a Long Poem or Group of Poems by yourself; we'd be going to press with it in early November.[1]

Your remarks in the Sewanee Review were, I'd like to think, most humanistic if flattering; you make a case out for me that I'd like to believe in.[2] Many thanks. I felt very much touched over the whole affair. With best regards,

Sincerely yours,
John Crowe Ransom

1. After "The Auroras of Autumn" was published in the *Kenyon Review* for winter, 1948, Stevens contributed no more poetry to Ransom's magazine.

2. Wallace Stevens, "John Crowe Ransom: Tennessean," *Sewanee Review*, LVI (Summer, 1948), 367–69. This was the leading piece in an issue celebrating Ransom's sixtieth birthday and largely devoted to his work.

To Allen Tate

September 7, [1948]

Dear Allen:

Thanks for your nice recent letter; I'm glad you are enjoying yourself, and happy to think you didn't mind the strenuous program you went through with us here.

My most important item right now is about T. S. Eliot. As soon as he is in this country I hope you'll see him on behalf of the School of English, tell him how much we want him to teach for us next summer, and give him an idea of the sort of thing we do, the freedom he would have, etc. We are ready to pay him $2500.00 inclusive if the Fellows don't mind making that exception in his honor; and I have no doubt he would have invitations from nearby universities to make a few addresses during our session if he cared to increase the emolument in that way; I should say offhand, at $500.00 a lecture. I'm thinking of places like OSU, Iowa, Minnesota, and other Big Ten places. Please let me know . . . if there is anything you think I might do to persuade him; I'd gladly make a trip to Princeton for this purpose but I really don't imagine that this would have a telling effect. Our President Chalmers would write him on behalf of the only Episcopal College founded on English philanthropy. I am sure we couldn't high-pressure him, of course. If you are at expense getting to see Eliot, let the S[chool]. of E[nglish]. repay you.

Reavill is with us this week, on his vacation from the job with the gas company in Nashville. He is really very good company, and a fine boy, if I do say it.

I felt mighty bad every time I thought of Caroline's poor doggie; I hope it wasn't too bad for her. When our Sealyham terrier which we brought from England died of distemper, after being inoculated before we left England, the affections of Robb and the children were so wounded that I said we'd never have another pet; but of course I really didn't have anything to do with that, and it didn't come about.

Best love from the family.

Yours,
John

To Arthur Mizener

March 14, 1949

Dear Arthur:

This is a nice essay; we'll take it; thanks.[1]

Now for the argument from the Old Man of the New Criticism. You've got precisely to the point where, so far as I know, all the New Critics of poetry got and where they are still stranded: viz., the poem (or the novel) deals with the concrete or particular, and the more show of the concreteness or particularity by the New Critic, to make it indefeasible and beyond controversy, the better. At the same time there must be some solid scientific matter—the categories of abstract use—under or behind the particularity; this is to be identified with the Argument or Logical Paraphrase of the poem, the "social truth" of the novel. (I'll waive the point that some fictions don't deal with Society but with God or Nature, like *Moby-Dick*, or *Pecheur d'Island*, just as there are poems that do the same, like Wordsworth's; but no matter at this moment.)

I said concreteness and particularity so long and ritualistically that I finally came to see that I was saying nothing to the pragmatical or positivistical naturalists. I therefore began to ask myself, What's the good of particularity, pure particularity? If we are dealing with human uses why do we want to clog them with particularity? What do we want with objects over and above the uses of said objects? The fact is that the positive ethics has no use for individuals, any more than the positive logic.

The next phase for *you*, as surely as for the New Critics, seems to me, is to show what concrete individuals are for; how they are the appealing factor for the reader; and *what they mean* for him. Meanwhile you can establish over and over how the good novelists offer individuals, with their feelings and intimate ways of thinking. The fact is important. But presently you'll feel obliged (if you don't want to go on repeating) to speculate on what they are for. It is my hunch that the critics of literature are going to recover for literature, perhaps incidentally for religion, such sanctions as these human behaviors can boast. Formal philosophy has proved unequal to that job.

Excuse this preachment.

Yours always,
John

P.S. May we say that the author of this essay is preparing a work on Fitzgerald? Or even that it is part of that work?

---

1. "The Novel of Manners in America," *Kenyon Review*, XII (Winter, 1950), 1–19.

To F. O. Matthiessen

August 17, 1949

Dear Matty:

I'll just report very briefly about things to you; and propose something for your consideration. I do hope you've had a good summer, however, in the first place, after a strenuous year or two. I feel more like personal talk than I can afford, at least at this rather rushed moment.

The second session was pretty good. It left me quite convinced, definitively convinced, that we have an educational mission and can discharge it if we continue along present lines. I came back at mid-session and felt that things weren't going as smoothly as last summer, but before it was over I sensed the right feelings nearly everywhere, and a great community of feeling, almost professional. The Fellows didn't have a common table as they should have had, therefore didn't get together as soon as they should. The Forums weren't so much on leading and general topics as they were the first summer, and that was a mistake too. The importance of the Forum is beyond measurement. It is the Common Life of the School. Then the Staff did well. Winters was a chance, but he came through with a solid course, administered with great pedagogical conscience; and wasn't disagreeable personally. Rahv surprised me; he gave a solid course and he was the model of propriety; respected by everybody, and in every way scrupulous in his relations. Schorer was very good; so (I heard) was Read,[1] who must be a species of saint as well as a good head. His course and mine, the 12-hours-a-week concentration courses, were much too hard and laborious; we mustn't repeat that kind of course under any circumstances, I think; bad in itself, and demoralizing to the schedule. But I don't mean to indicate that we didn't get through our work in these courses.

Coffin has reported to you in great detail, so now let me get into the business.

At the Foundation, Stevens is retired, and Fahs has come on as assistant to Marshall who is in charge. Fahs came out and spent two days poking into everything and holding many interviews with all sorts of people; sorry to say it was while I was out. There is indicated for me a very serious interest on the part of the Foundation, and some desire to have the intelligence on which to talk the matter of renewal with us presently. And I think if we don't approach them at once with respect to 1951 and afterwards they will wonder what sort of people we are. We had a good deal of talk among the Fellows, and some students too, about the future. This is what we all thought should happen: The Foundation should renew for 1951–53, or preferably for 1951–55, at the same rate of subsidy as now; there should be added a sum annually sufficient to bring to Kenyon College through the school year a Fellow in Residence who could work with a seminar of School-of-English students and supervise some M.A. theses, with the idea that the School of English should give the M.A. degree. The requirements might be for one summer, or maybe two summers, in the School, plus a year-round job with the Fellow in Residence at this College. This Fellow would have to be on leave of absence from his own institution; but I can think of half a dozen men who'd probably be quite willing. I think of the students under him as being something like a dozen. We'd enroll them without trouble at the summer sessions; in fact the summer session would be our means of picking them; and there'd be intense interest. We might build up such a good M.A. that it would be just the right qualification for a man when the Universities were considering your instructors in criticism. It would help in many ways.

There has been revival of the opposition to modern schools of critical and creative writing, as doubtless you have noticed (your sense of smell could have detected it). The Foundation should adhere to its policies and back them up all the more. And I think it is well to suggest that to them. I'm thinking now of the possibility that you may be able to go in and talk with them. But first I'd like for us to agree on a proposal of some kind. President Chalmers will be back the first of September. Please let me hear about the representations you think we should make to the Foundation right away, so that Chalmers can initiate the talk with Marshall; then let you and Trilling and me follow up as we can. I'm going to Indiana University in September for one year as visiting professor of English, to give a critical course or two, but I'm due to give a reading at Wellesley the last of November, and I would want to see Marshall while I was in the East. (By the way, my idea in going to Ind. is simply that they want me, have been after me for some time; and I *need* to get away from the Review for a time, not to grow stale in the office; I've stuck here a long time, pretty close.) So much for Foundation business.

Of course there's also the matter of our Staff for 1950. Indicated already, through commitments formal and otherwise, are Rice, Mizener, Lowell, Knights,[2] and Empson if he can get out of China as he thinks he can; E's wife is a Communist, I think, and he likes the Communists, and the British who direct him like him to get around as he did last summer. I've just written to Trilling to see if he will come next summer, but to indicate also that the 3-week courses don't seem advisable in any case, and that we need to have our staff made up by early fall, not later. I should have thought it would be useless to take up this matter with him, but Rahv said that he believed Trilling would come; that his absence was due to his extravagant devotion to his baby, and his wife with her whims; but baby has been doing so well that he would probably be able as well as desirous to get off next summer. So we'll see. If he doesn't come, will you? Of course I wish you'd come anyway. But it seems almost imperative if he doesn't come. It would never do for me to have a third straight go. I'll keep you posted. I'm also writing Blackmur and Red Warren, who stand very high on our list.

With best wishes, always,

Yours, affectionately,
John

---

1. Mark Schorer, a short-story writer, critic, and literary biographer, who taught at the University of California at Berkeley, and Herbert Read, an English man of letters, were on the staff of the School of English.

2. L. C. Knights, a scholar and critic, who had already written *Drama and Society in the Age of Jonson* (1937) and *Explorations* (1946) and had helped F. R. Leavis found *Scrutiny*, also taught at the School of English.

To Denham Sutcliffe

October 5, 1949

Dear Dennie:

I'm greatly touched by your solicitude for my feelings, and your (and Phil's and Charles') defense of me while I'm *in absentia*.[1] It makes me feel mighty good.

Reading the *Collegian* article in question, I'm not much excited.[2] Am awfully tired of people wondering about the *politics* of my, or anybody's, critical position; I find even here, where they don't know much about it, the tendency for people to read a lot of ambition, and racketeering, and some sort of party line, and deep plotting, into a speech, paper, essay, etc. That Kenyon boy was sure to crop-up. I'd have laughed at him, I think. But his cropping up *does* show the harm that the sailor-poet's tactics have done.[3] He's raised up the middle-brows against the high-brows; like the woman in Yeats who "set the little houses against the great," though you mustn't probe into that *great*; and I'm afraid he'll offer a cheap currency which will drive out the dear (in the sense that his exercises will be easier than ours). But then he may be regretting his summer's madness himself for all I know.[4]

Our best wishes to the family and you. We're pleasantly situated, but scarcely "at home" yet.

Yours,
John

1. Ransom spent the academic year 1949–50 as a visiting professor at Indiana University.

2. The issue of the *Kenyon Collegian* for September 30, 1949, reported that during the summer "Robert Hillyer set off a political-cultural powder keg that ultimately may serve to loosen that strangle-hold on American letters held these many years by mad Ezra Pound, T. S. Eliot, and other high priests of incomprehensibility worshipped by the 'New Critics.'" The article concluded with a derogatory reference to Ransom—or so Sutcliffe (now chairman of the English department), Rice, and Charles Coffin interpreted it, and they wanted to write letters to the *Collegian* defending Ransom.

3. Robert Hillyer (1895–1961), winner of the Pulitzer prize for poetry in 1934, was visiting professor at Kenyon from 1948 until 1951.

4. For an account of the controversy that erupted when the Bollingen prize for poetry was awarded to Pound in 1949, see Thomas Daniel Young, "The Little Houses Against the Great," *Sewanee Review*, LXXXVIII (Spring, 1980), 320–30.

To Caroline Gordon Tate and Allen Tate

December 10, [1949?]

Dear Caroline and Allen:

It was mighty fine to be in your new house with you, and thank you for that royal entertainment. Seems to me you-all are mighty well settled now, mighty well adapted to the world as the anthropologists would say, and it gave me great comfort. I don't mind the advancing years if they advance as becomingly for me as they do for you. Of course that is not a proper remark to make, because you are just youngsters by my standards, but let it do prophetically anyhow. Robb wanted to know about everything; she learned from Helen about Percy's commitment to the Navy, and thought that fine.

I have another morsel of bad news which you are entitled as Members of the Party to know at once. The other day the President wrote me that he had "changed his decision" about one of the two halves of our petition to the Foundation: the one about a Resident Fellow and the M.A. work. This came after a long session of the Senior Fellows at which not an ugly word was said, and the President seemed to brim over with enthusiasm; and a session with John Marshall and Chet D'Aurno[1] in the evening at which ditto, i.e. everybody seemed to brim, though the President (perhaps in a panic, but pleading that he was weary with travel) absented himself from the business part of the session. He explains himself in one sentence as follows: "From our discussion of the last several years with respect to the Review and the School of English, you will remember that I am necessarily concerned that the College itself as it deals with literature shall not be predominantly one thing." This is somewhat cryptic to me. All I remember is that after Hillyer's appointment to the College (without benefit of consultation with the English staff) he told me he had felt that other literary interests besides my own ought to be represented in the College staff and curriculum. But during November I had written at some length to him more than once that I felt we ought to be very clear at our New York meeting about the kind of Resident Fellow we would want and the method of his appointment; and without disputing his legal right to make a Presidential appointment in the School as in the College, I had said that I for one wouldn't care to undertake the Resident Fellowship, or bring it up before the Foundation, if he would not renounce that method for the School. He replied twice to say that he meant no harm, or something equally vague, and quite obviously refused to give me this assurance. At the Fellows' meeting, however, I think he must have decided that he couldn't dictate the School without running into resignations from all the Fellows. So now we have the result. (Perhaps one of the *courses* will never publicly appear; what happened when he gave his report to his home backers.)

I am for going ahead with the rest of our business, as usual, but I can't say what the other Fellows will say, or the two members of the Board we talked with.

Love to you both from Robb and me,

John

---

1. Officials of the Rockefeller Foundation.

1950–1968

N THE LAST DECADE of his association with the *Kenyon Review* Ransom was convinced that the age of criticism, to which he had contributed so much, was nearly over and that his quarterly should participate in the new "surge of creativity" that he anticipated. As a consequence he exerted considerable effort in securing friends from the Rockefeller Foundation to establish *Kenyon Review* fellowships in poetry, fiction, and criticism. These fellowships were awarded to some of the most promising young writers of the period, among them Flannery O'Connor, Andrew Lytle, Irving Howe, W. S. Merwin, R. W. B. Lewis, Howard Nemerov, and Richard Ellmann.

When the School of English moved from Kenyon to Indiana University to become the School of Letters, Ransom continued as a senior fellow, attended the planning sessions, and three times offered courses during the summer sessions of the school. He continued to plan very carefully for each issue of the *Kenyon Review*, requesting specific essays, poems, or stories from his most dependable contributors. These requests brought him some of the best of Allen Tate's essays and a long section of Robert Penn Warren's *Brother to Dragons*. But he continued to reject Warren's fiction, refusing to publish a long chapter of *Band of Angels*.

On May 3–5, 1956, Ransom returned to Vanderbilt University for the Fugitive reunion sponsored by the university and the Rockefeller Foundation. His letters to Warren during this period are warmer and more personal than ever: he responded with great delight when Warren announced his second marriage and, later, the births of his children. After his retirement from Kenyon in the late 1950s, Ransom accepted visiting professorships at Northwestern, Ohio State, and Vanderbilt; and despite the debilitating effects of an inner-ear infection, he continued to accept twenty or more invitations each year to give papers or read his poetry on college campuses from New York to California. When he was retiring as editor of the *Kenyon Review* he was deeply involved in choosing his successor, and many of his letters to Tate and others concern details related to this appointment.

At the request of Warren and many other of Ransom's friends and former students, he often wrote his impressions of their poems, essays, or novels. He continued to write, completing essays on Hardy, Stevens, and Eliot; revising slightly and adding a lengthy postscript to the new edition of *The World's Body*; and, as he expressed it, "tinkering" with his verse. During the 1960s two editions of his *Selected Poems* were published; each included more poems than he previously had been willing to leave in print, and each showed the extent to which Ransom was altering poems written many years earlier.

During his last years Ransom lived so quietly in Gambier that most of the students and some of the faculty at Kenyon were not aware that they were sharing this village in middle Ohio with one of the most influential literary men of their time, one who, one critic has said, made Gambier the literary capital of the United States. Despite the growing discomfort resulting from his inner-ear trouble, he continued to make a few public appearances, presenting readings and collecting an increasing number of literary awards. His last reading was at the University of Florida when Andrew Lytle received an honorary degree. His last public appearance was to introduce Robert Penn Warren when he came to Kenyon on February 23, 1973, to read his poems. Warren's visit motivated Ransom to write a late poem, "Four Threesomes or Three Foursomes," which was published in the *Sewanee Review* a few months later. Among his last letters was one complimenting his oldest friend, Allen Tate, upon the birth of twin sons, born to him and his third wife, Helen Heinz.

To Allen Tate

March 28, 1950

Dear Allen:

A few minutes ago the Director of Frick Museum called me to see if I might replace you as their lecturer April 22; said you were retiring from your work for the moment, on the doctor's advice. That is bad news. I do hope it's nothing serious. Incidentally, I have to read a paper on Wordsworth that very day at Cornell, so I had to decline the Frick invitation.

A letter from Evans at the Library [of Congress] today invites me to become one of the Fellows, and that I am extremely glad to do. I look forward to seeing the crowd at January meetings, if I am able to attend, as I shall try to do.

This which follows is not official, and still confidential. Rockefeller turned down the plea of the School of English for renewal of funds. With a pretty enough letter, of course, about our having done such a good job as to be in large part responsible for the opinion they have solemnly come to on the Foundation board: that this special concentration of critical courses is no longer needed now when the type of thing is so widespread and so universally authorized. So that's that. Chalmers, and Coffin too, who is very much hurt by this turn of events, seem to want to approach other angels, but I don't think of any help I can be, nor do I think that any others are really approachable. The Bollingen people might be the most eligible for approach but for the strange recent conduct of my President; but I guess those beans are entirely spilt. Probably before long you'll get an official confirmation of this news; I am sure we must tell the Fellows just as fast as such news becomes valid.

We're doing pretty well in most ways. Tell Caroline her heart would bleed for me if she knew how these nicer early-spring days I long to be out digging in the soil, but have only the range of a small stream-lined apartment which does not permit digging.

Be sure to do what the doctor says so that your period of disability will be the very miminum.[1]

Affectionately,
John

1. Tate's illness was eventually diagnosed as emphysema.

To Allen Tate

Bloomington, Indiana, June 3, 1950

Dear Allen:

Red and Cinina came through here in late April, and we were awfully pleased with Cinina's apparent recovery from her troubled condition; she seemed very much on her best behavior, and the two of them in normal good relations except of course intensely self-conscious about it. It is evident that part of her prescription (she has evidently been analysed) is to look after Red, and Red's part to demand a little looking after. Fine. But I don't know what the expense to Red may be. And this brings me up to the fact of his new novel which I've just read.[1]

When Red and Cleanth were together, it was clear (as we have many times felt) that Red supplied the ideas; but now it becomes clear, I think, that Cleanth supplied good stern moral principle, and that both of them suffer now that their close relation has been broken up. I think Red's book is pretty horrible. It's like Tom Wolfe except that it's less consistent. Red's philosophy seems now to justify the guilt of his heroes (he never had much heroines) on the ground that they are implicated in the Universal Guilt. It makes him philosophize sententiously about Truth, Innocence, Justice, and what not. All that I feared from the ambiguities of All the King's Men has come out strong and clear in this volume, where there's no ambiguity at all. It's most depressing. How can Red be the soul of honor personally (as I still feel sure he is) and dally with the themes he does in the fictions? Of course all this objection of mine may well be met by the contention that Red is presenting his characters as they are, or were, and it happened that they were weaklings, so that they must be presented so. But what about the phony style which Red falls into? It doesn't have any metaphysical timbre to it now; it's just bad rhetoric and pseudo-philosophy. I can't but think that Red is going to take a terrible panning from the serious critics.

There's just one honest man in Red's book, the one who assisted in the defense of the hero at court; and he isn't *realized*.

Well, there's that. Thank you for your recent note about coming through Gambier the night of July 15. I get out of Writers Conference here that very day; that morning, I guess. I have looked up Penna. time tables and find that I can get to Columbus that evening at 6:45. I can get Robb to meet me, and be home shortly after 8. If you'd come round at 8:30 we could talk a little, and let Phil and Charles join us at 9:00. I think we must do that. It's true that Hudson (who runs the Writers Conference) says if I will stay over here a night or two he'll take care of me; but then you & I wouldn't get together with Charles and Phil.[2]

We can't afford not to have you help us save the School if it can be done. Now I can talk about one move, the one you mentioned earlier. It seems that Charles raised with Chalmers the question (suggested by you) of approaching Bollingen; but was told that this party was on the regular College preserves, and couldn't be approached for our extra-curricular project. That's an old story. The Review has always been estopped (since 1942) from approaching the "friends of the College", or those who were down as prospective donors to the College proper; and heaven knows the College needs are great, and come before everything else, even in my interest, so that I have made no complaint about the principle. Well, Chalmers himself approached Bollingen; I suspect it was Paul Mellon himself, at any rate it followed a build-up through Huntington Cairns; and C. told me here a few weeks ago (when he was here making a speech) that he got a kind and perhaps promising reception. You can imagine how GKC must have humbled himself in the first place. Now it seems that the special thing which C. wants from Bollingen is to endow my own chair at Kenyon; within the coming year the original endowment, not a capital fund but an aggregate to be spent, put up by the Carnegie Corporation, will be exhausted. He has talked to me before about that, saying that I was to do nothing, that the College would assume the full cost of my regular salary from now on, but that in the meantime he was trying to raise the money from some foundation or philanthropist; and now and then, as recently, he has repeated this, always with the assurance that the College would underwrite the salary fully if the benefactor could not be found. Carnegie declined to renew the chair. GKC is mindful, I suppose, that I w'd have left Kenyon and gone to North Carolina in 1940 if he had not got the money for me from Carnegie; I felt that I had no business getting more than my share of salary from the regular Kenyon budget. However, you can see that it is a little embarrassing to me. I was so keen about your idea of Bollingen saving the School [of English] that I feel badly if it reduces to Bollingen saving Ransom. I've no ideas specially. I'd like very much to have a full talk with you about the whole business. My mind is quite open.[3]

It will be nice to see you and Caroline even if briefly. But can't you make a more leisurely stop as you return East later in the summer?

Affectionately,
John

P.S. Tomorrow (Sunday) a.m. Robb takes off for Tennessee in an empty car, to bring Helen, Choppie, Jack, and Duane (for 1 wk. vacation, in his case) back to Ohio about next Friday the 9th. Then Duane will drive back here (275 mi.) for me and our stuff. I'm promised to make the PBK speech Saturday night the 10th at Indiana, so am not out of school yet. Helen will audit at the school. Empson has cabled that he's coming.[4]

1. Warren, *World Enough and Time* (New York: Random House, 1950).

2. Ransom refers to Philip Blair Rice, Charles Coffin, and Richard B. Hudson (who was running the writers' program at Indiana University and would run the School of Letters).

3. Ransom was describing to Tate the various efforts to save the School of English. In the end no further help was received from the Carnegie Foundation, nor was any new support received from the Bollingen Foundation, whose directors included Huntington Cairns, a lawyer and supporter of the arts who edited *The Limits of Art* (1948). Gordon K. Chalmers (whom Ransom refers to as C. and GKC), Kenyon's president, ultimately let the School of English go to Indiana University, where it became the School of Letters; Chalmers was able to make arrangements satisfactory to Ransom about his salary, and he remained at Kenyon until his retirement in 1959.

4. William Empson had said he was coming to what would be the last session of the School of English.

To Allen Tate

Gambier, Ohio, June 27, [1950]

Dear Allen:

I'll send this to Princeton to be forwarded, since I haven't unpacked all my papers, which would include the letter giving your itinerary at the moment. I think you're at Salt Lake City, in which case give my best to the Ghiselins.

I exchanged letters with President Chalmers about the Mellon and Old Dominion matter, and eventually he called me for a conference, as he ought to have done in the first place, and we talked a whole hour or so, about everything.

It seems he is well aware of the Old Dominion side of Mellon's interests, and counting on tapping it for his own purposes. His purposes, however, I must say, are the whole Ransom program: keeping Ransom, keeping the Review and paying off some $3,000 deficit which has accumulated in four years (without the College's having paid out a cent in cash), and keeping the School of English. He wants them all. I told him that he didn't have to keep me against his own wish, since Indiana University has invited me to join them permanently after this year; it is in his response to that that I would gauge his feelings about me. They have had a rough time at Kenyon during the past year, with a committee reporting adversely on the President's way of operating a college without much consultation; it hung fire all the year and the report was made just a week or so before Commencement;

a bad time, and of course inconclusive. He wants peace very badly; I take it the faculty does too; and that he is prepared to be more conciliatory and consultative in the future though he would never say so, or admit having done anything wrong.

He thinks he made a good start with the Bollingen people, and plans on getting to Mellon and making an appeal which will all turn on me and the College's supplying me with the place to do my little kind of work. I don't know whether he has a chance or not. At any rate I don't know for sure that he has no chance; I told him I feared it would come to nothing net, instead of its possibly coming to something if we gave you the chance to take the initiative and strike for the School of English alone, but when he went into the particulars of his conversations there I had to tell him I had no specific information whatever about it. I was especially firm in indicating that you had not offered to discuss anything with the Mellon interests except the School of English, and had no reason to. I told him frankly that I felt he must have lost any favor he might have had there by continuing Hillyer in employment after the attacks H. had made on the Mellon interests and on the sort of thing with which I was identified—taking Chalmers at his word in saying he thought they were interested in that sort of thing. I said he ought to have fired Hillyer then. He took it pretty quietly; but I really imagine it is too late to fire Hillyer for that now. However, he said he wanted to talk with you and not be judged by you without talking. He is not willing to authorize an appeal for the School of English exclusively. And on the ground that you aren't in the East anyway, I suggested that we let things ride till I talked with you on July 14 or 15.

I am very much at sea about my own course. It is embarrassing to know that my salary is more than $2,000.00 better than anybody else's here, to the best of my information, and that the College budget is extremely straitened now. I wouldn't want to stay, I think, unless I can be taken off the budget, and I won't wait this time so long as I did when the offer from Carolina Woman's College, which you will recall, was up. Chalmers insists that I'm to let *him* worry about my salary, which will be paid regardless. I have told them at Indiana that I will give them a reply this fall. Having lived a year at Indiana I know that I can make out there. In fact, it is very nearly a virgin field for building up creative literature and critical studies, and one likes to think he is doing good, especially when one gets well paid for doing it. They gave me a good welcome, and the graduate seminar was stimulating; I should get a good deal of writing done there, whereas it is easy to slack down at Kenyon. I shouldn't mind dropping the editorship in favor of doing more writing at this stage, though it is not an objective. I suspect that your own teaching and lecturing in new places these past few years has had something to do with your immense activity in writing. Going on here would be nice, I will admit, for this is the best place I have ever lived, but I won't endure very long the consciousness of waiting on while the President is passing the hat to get support for me. I might add one other item, not of extreme importance: at Indiana they retire their professors at 70, at Kenyon 68; and it looks as if I would hold out pretty well to that advanced old age.

I am assuming that all these facts and considerations are material to your own interest in the School of English. The fact seems to be that I am pretty well heeled, though heaven knows it feels tragic to have settled arrangements blown up under one, and to have to make other arrangements perforce. So you are at liberty to act with entire freedom in so far as your actual interests are concerned, and despite your unfailing thoughtfulness for my interests. Even here I hate to set all these things down in cold blood.

The School is starting off in fine style though the numbers are a little off in both students and auditors. Nowadays the plight of the literate graduate student is pitiful, with the end of Veterans' benefits, and the need of placating every possible power in order to stand high on the list of those wanting jobs. Our new dispensation, if we get one, must have a very handsome item for scholarships, including scholarships that pay all expenses; the men are there waiting, but they can't get to us without help. Our new staff seems very strong. A big session the other evening here with Rice, Coffin, Burke, Empson, and Knights gave me the sense that we'd have unusually intelligent and civil discussions this summer. [Austin] Warren didn't get here, but he had the smallest enrollment, and we have easily managed. Cal [Lowell], Mizener, and Delmore [Schwartz] are in good form. Mizener is impressive, though I have the feeling that he has slipped into an academic manner since I last saw him. I hear many times how the Tates are missed. The Mizeners have your house.

Love to Caroline; I'll be glad when we can all have a big talk at Bloomington.

Yours affectionately,
John

To Allen Tate

August 22, [1950]

Dear Allen:

Have just written a long letter to Trilling, about K[enyon] S[chool] of E[nglish], and I felt obliged to tell him *in confidence* about the I[ndiana]. U[niversity]. offer to take over. As I see it, if and when GKC[halmers] says Kenyon can't keep the School, I.U. will invite all the Fellows to carry on under their auspices; no School will exist till the Fellows indicate that they want to go under I.U. as formerly at Kenyon. I felt Lionel ought to be posted, so I wrote him what I'd have preferred to say to him.

But I told him I'd suggest to you that you ring him up sometime soon while in N.Y.C. and have a good talk with him about any of the angles in which he might be interested. He is discreet, and I really believe him *interested.* (Sounds funny, saying that—but I haven't seen him at close range in a long time.)

Mighty sorry I couldn't get to Princeton on this trip. The Harvard Conference dragged out through Thursday. It was a nondescript affair, with high moments. I believe now for the first time Wm. Elliott sees that his own verse (which on one occasion he read) doesn't have poetic *texture* or quality.

And guess who put up the money for this Conference: Bollingen! And Spender came up with the proposition of holding it next year at Oxford, England, and Bill Elliott is probably going to work that with Bollingen too.

There's no news, except that the School was very fine in its 3rd session. And Charles [Coffin] announced that it would open next year in all probability, though not necessarily at Kenyon.

G.K.C. doesn't act in the summer, but he has on his docket now two letters from me, the latter one asking him to make his decision on the School pretty soon, so that if it's not to be at Kenyon the other institution can take over in plenty of time for next summer's arrangements.

Reavill is with us for a month, preparing to go to Iowa to get help with his fiction. He has GI benefits still, and I think has done just enough with his writing on his own to feel it worth a more professional try-out.

Our best to Caroline.

Aff'ly,
John

To Allen Tate

September 6, 1950

Dear Allen:

Reporting progress, if there's anything under that head in what follows.

Yesterday the President returned to his office, and called me in for a conference at once; the first time in many years that he hasn't sat back and waited for me to break through the dragon's guard to call on him. I should say he's had a change of heart, somewhat, over the summer; I don't know what has happened. He is apparently anxious to retain me and the School of English too. Wanted to know how long I thought he could decently withhold decision on keeping the School, without imperilling its continuance next summer at Indiana. I said I thought maybe six weeks. He has just come from the Old Dominion keepers, who seem to be a different crowd from the Bollingen. Thinks he has a real prospect for the School as well as my chair, maybe better with Bollingen than with Old Dominion. I can't judge that. I believe at any rate that these two Foundations are his last recourse so far as the School is concerned, and maybe the less of a prospect inasmuch as he puts my chair ahead of the School with them. The chance of his getting the School are certainly slim by any calculation. I told him that I had the same mind as you did in the matter, if I understood it: I wanted to keep the Review going by remaining at Kenyon if possible but I was satisfied that the School could be kept going anyhow, either here or at I.U. He seemed much pleased that you wanted me to stay on here with the Review, and very grateful in advance for any move you might make in favor of that event. So should I be; for I am of the same mind as he is in a few things, it would appear. I really am fixed in the determination to leave Kenyon if my salary, in order to remain at its present figure, has to encroach on the general College budget; and I don't know what the prospects are. There will have to be an angel, so far as I can see.

The clouds hang a bit low on our College opening. Attendance has dropped here as everywhere else, and the tuition fees will not justify the present large faculty. I think we are reduced probably to our final size, something above 400 students, and for that size we are overstaffed, and worthy professors will have to be let out, which is always painful. Rice and Coffin are inclined to think that with reduction in the number of our Freshmen sections the English staff is excessive, and Hillyer will go. I have no evidence on earth to support that; nobody knows unless GKC himself.

The Harvard affair was very mixed, with some bright moments. Bill Elliott was a little obstreperous but as gentle and kind as he could possibly be. He hasn't grown imaginatively but he is at least a man of character. I was delighted with Marianne Moore, and with Spender, and some of the programs (of which there were about six formal ones) were very good.

We made up the dummy for Autumn yesterday, leading off with Credos from four critics: Fiedler, Read, Chase, and Empson. You will see that we very much need some old-line new-critic Credos, and most of all that means you, as I see it. We have Credos coming up immediately from Northrop Frye and Cleanth, promised from Trilling and Rahv, whom I will jog right away. I think also of asking Spender (who has turned conservative enough, and is a sort of Shelley when it comes to his view of poetry, with emphasis on spontaneity and creative imagination); he's finished as a poet, I should think, but has a distinction in his prose, always something fresh. Also maybe Jarrell, Mizener, one or both; and maybe Fergusson, if he would expound his sense of literature as proceeding under religious auspices, in which he is pretty close kin to Eliot.[1] Do you have any suggestions? But please set about a Credo of your own if you will, and as soon as you can. I'd like us to finish up in two more numbers, though I'd hope for a strong set of papers for Winter, deadline November 1. The papers we are printing now are very serious and carefully composed; so much beyond our expectations (from the authors concerned) that more than ever I'm sure we will have a choice book for a publisher. The publisher will be Random House, if they want it; we have just made a deal with them whereby we call young authors and new manuscripts exclusively to their attention and in return receive a thousand dollars a year for the budget.

Blackmur, by the way, has done a long piece for us (it is in our Autumn number) on Trilling's book, admirable in many ways but under one of his fuzzy captions: The Politics of Human Power.[2] He also has written an essay for Hudson of which mimeographs (originating at University of Virginia) appeared here in the summer, and in which they tell me he dissociates himself rather strongly from some other critics including myself. In the course of our exchanging a couple of letters apiece he explains that he doesn't mean any harm, is trying to clear the air or something to that effect. He also is glad I corrected Trilling in my essay on the point of the Wordsworth Ode;[3] but he isn't zealous to correct Trilling in his own essay. I've rallied him a little about the necessity of his not being exclusive of his friends and inclusive of the aliens, but he's pretty sure everything is all right. We haven't asked him for a Credo; it couldn't be very clean cut, I think. Nevertheless, I like and admire Richard much more than the contrary.

I don't see any prospect of seeing you till I go to NYC to make a lecture at the Frick Collection December 17. My title, by the way: The Odes of Keats.[4]

Love to Caroline.

Yours,
John

---

1. The *Kenyon Review* published ten credos: Richard Chase, William Empson, Leslie Fiedler, and Herbert Read contributed to the autumn, 1950, issue; Cleanth Brooks, Douglas Bush, and Northrop Frye to the winter, 1951, issue; and Arthur Mizener, Stephen Spender, and Austin Warren to the spring, 1951, issue.

2. R. P. Blackmur reviewed Lionel Trilling's *The Liberal Imagination* in the *Kenyon Review*, XII (Autumn, 1950), 663–73.

3. Ransom, "William Wordsworth: Notes Toward an Understanding of Poetry," *Kenyon Review*, XII (Summer, 1950), 498–515.

4. This essay by Ransom was not published.

To Allen Tate

November 4, 1950

Dear Mr. Tate:

By this time you may have seen the announcement that Kenyon College has given up The School of English, and Indiana University has taken it over. Of course we are sorry at Gambier that the School could not remain here. But the College simply could not afford the cost, now that the Rockefeller subsidy has run its three-year limit; and I know Indiana University quite well, since I taught there all of last year, and am confident that the school will be properly housed and cared for in every way. They really wanted the School at Bloomington, and they have many facilities for a special summer project; it is their intention to keep the School in its new existence as continuous as circumstances permit with the School as it was at Gambier; with respect to the educational ideal and operation, for instance, and the personnel of the staff.

Replacing the late F. O. Matthiessen as Senior Fellow is Austin Warren, of the University of Michigan. Lionel Trilling and I hold over. I speak for President Wells of Indiana University and the Senior Fellows in hoping that you will still be associated with the School as a Fellow and (occasionally) Teaching Fellow.

It seems likely that a small change of titles will have to be made. "School of English" invites confusion at Indiana with the Graduate School of English. The "Dean" will become the "Director."

We should inaugurate the new tenure of the School at Indiana University by arranging a very strong program of courses for the summer of 1951. I presume the calendar will be about as usual, the School opening in the 20's of June, and lasting 45 days into early August. The stipend for a session of teaching will be $1,500.00 as it has been for the past two years.

Please therefore write me as soon as possible as to whether you (1) will remain a Fellow (as I have great confidence that you will), and (2) will be in a position to teach a course in 1951. If your reply to (2) is affirmative, please indicate two or three possible subjects, in the order of your preference, from which we might select with a view to the general balance of our courses; though it is most likely that the one you name first would be entirely acceptable.

With very best wishes,

Sincerely yours,
John Crowe Ransom

JCR:r

P.S. Excuse the formalities, Allen. We think you ought to come to I.U. *this summer*—it would be great reassurance to a lot of people. And mightn't it be on Modern Poets, or some of 'em? Dick Hudson (the new Director) is here this week-end, getting the dope from Charles [Coffin].

Aff'ly,
John

To Allen Tate

November 28, [1950]

Dear Allen:

Was much relieved to hear from you by phone, with such good response to my letter; and the next day to hear by letter (a week after its sending).

I guess I don't think on my feet very well, or at least in my seat at the phone. Upon reading your letter and thinking things over, seems to me we'd want exactly the subject you preferred: Dante and Poe; and your subtitle explains what might not at first thought appear to be a connection between these authors. I like the idea behind your course very much. We are now the School of *Letters*, perhaps you know; so comparative literature or *any* literature is in order. Not that Coleridge wouldn't be good, but it seems to me not so good as the other. So I'm writing to Fergusson explaining that perhaps we'd better settle on his second suggestion for his own course, the dramatic form of certain of Shakespeare's plays. If you like, call him up. But I dare say it's all the same with him. I can't remember whether I wrote and plumped for his Dante course; I do remember I hoped, in my original letter, he might give a Dante course. I do believe this arrangement is altogether to our advantage.

And I guess I'll write in a minute to accept Eric [Bentley]'s offer. I just hate to think of dragging out negotiations for our summer staff; and I believe Eric will be all right.

Love to Caroline. Hope your weather is better than ours. Ten inches of snow here, and still adding a little day by day.

Yours,
John

To Allen Tate

February 3, [1951]

Dear Allen:

I'm going to NYC the day before Washington, on a little business; to Washington (Statler Hotel) the evening of Feb. 9. So why can't we have breakfast at the Statler at, say, 8 o'clock Friday morning? If you want to suggest another place, drop me a line at the Statler. Otherwise I'll expect to see you there; I'll probably be reading a newspaper in the lobby.

Naturally I was 100% surprised at the Bollingen award;[1] and 99% pleased, of course; the small reservation being the faint suspicion that I may have owed it in some degree to the Committee's (unconscious) idea of using Ransom as a stick to beat Hillyer & SRL with.[2] But this reflects on me as a suspicious creature, as well as on the Committee, and it hasn't been more than just a sneak of a suspicion, as I said above. So, flatly, I'm mightily pleased.

Love to Caroline.

Yours,
John

By the way, Hillyer has resigned, and after this year won't be back at Kenyon.

1. Ransom received the Bollingen prize for poetry in 1950, which then entailed a cash award of $1,000.

2. Ransom is referring to Robert Hillyer's "Treason's Strange Fruit" and "Poetry's New Priesthood," articles published in the *Saturday Review of Literature*, June 11 and 18, 1949. Hillyer vehemently protested Ezra Pound's being awarded the Bollingen prize for his *Pisan Cantos* (1948).

To Allen Tate

February 12, [1951]

Dear Allen:

Mary is sending you today (with our compliments) a copy of KENYON CRITICS.[1] I was sorry we didn't have you in there, with an essay on "modern literature." But we do have Vivienne Koch's essay on your poetry, and you will find it is a fine essay if you will read it again.[2] I cut it a great deal, and she was good enough to consent. It really pleases me.

Today a letter came that is worth a good deal to me, yet has its comic side. I am to be recipient of a prize from National Institute of Arts and Sciences, in the amount of $1,000.00. In the letter it seems they like to "recognize" work all the more if it has not been publicly "appreciated." Evidently they didn't know about Bollingen when they were in session.

It was mighty fine to see you and the "chillern." Love to Caroline.

Aff'ly,
John

1. Ransom (ed.), *The Kenyon Critics: Studies in Modern Literature* (New York: World, 1951).

2. "The Poetry of Allen Tate," *Kenyon Review*, XI (Summer, 1949), 355–78, was reprinted in *The Kenyon Critics*.

To Francis Fergusson, Philip Rice, Allen Tate, and Austin Warren

March 13, 1952

Brethren:

This is an ignominious occasion. After many tries, I am unable to write to Dr. Hutchins of the Ford Foundation the letter which you delegated to me. Never in my life have I made such a sorry showing.[1]

I think my inhibition is partly moral. I don't have much conviction in the matter; and the more I hear of the intellectual if not the ethical scruple of

Dr. Hutchins, the less I wish to beard him with a proposition which becomes further and further from a "must" in my book.

On first undertaking this last fall, I thought the idea was for a kind of enlargement of the School of Letters project; but you disabused me of that. I don't know what to think of an Institute, with a lot of money, and standard-making committees and Fellows. I can't think I believe highly in our American capacity to run this sort of project gracefully, as the French can. And I don't know if I am really to plump for a "prestige" job, that is, an honorific institution "honoring" people, the right people. It is very hard to plan such a thing in black and white, at any rate. I think fundamentally I am a one-gallus homespun country fellow, like the fox-hunt at Murfreesboro. Such an immense power, through an Institute, might get into the wrong hands. On the other hand, as long as the good books get written and distributed, I incline to feel that everything else will in its time and way get done.

I have come to feel, even, that the path of literary criticism in the academy has been so smoothed during the five years since the School of English got started that we don't need much further help with that; we do have one good and (I hope) permanent project going at Bloomington, right at the center, and I think personally there's no occasion to ask to have that duplicated and the idea elaborated; though I do want that project to succeed, and for a very long time.

On hand here is the composite statement which Rice made of the several manuscript notes you made last summer, and the further extended comment upon them which Charles Coffin supplied. I must turn over these materials to the man designated. I have delayed the thing seven or eight months, and I do not like to think about that. (I heard the other day, from President Chalmers, how frantic was the Ford Foundation, even today, over how to spend its money; so maybe the wait hasn't been fatal.) You have my fullest apologies.

Fraternally,
J. C. Ransom

1. Ransom had been delegated by the fellows of the School of Letters to propose an institute of criticism to be funded by the Ford Foundation. Robert Maynard Hutchins was then its associate director. Nothing came of this plan.

To Allen Tate

March 19, [1952]

Dear Allen:

I guess the enclosed letter in carbon will speak for itself; I'll only add that my feeling there must be in the long run a matter of politics, the form of the good action.

We've just been informed that Rockefeller will not renew our Fund-to-Pay-K.R.-contributors, so that after the Spring issue we'll have only our old low rate of pay available; it comes to something like 1¢ per word *vs.* the 2½¢ a word we've been paying. And this will apply to acceptances in hand, I'm afraid; it will have to. Therefore to the Poe essay. Naturally we must invite the authors to recover their MSS if they like in view of this change. We want the Poe; but don't hesitate to take it elsewhere if you need the money.[1] Our feelings can't be hurt under the circumstances. Quite the contrary; it's the other way round.

The Dante issue is exceedingly good.[2] You'll have it very early in April.

Helen was writing the other day to ask all about Nancy and her family. It may be she's not willing for her family to fall behind Nancy's.

I wish you and Caroline will be coming by to see us before long, on one of your through trips. For a good stop-over.

Affectionately,
John

---

1. Ransom alludes to Tate's "The Angelic Imagination: Poe and the Power of Words," which would be published in the *Kenyon Review*, XIV (Summer, 1952), 455–75.

2. Tate's "The Symbolic Imagination: A Mediation on Dante's Three Mirrors," *Kenyon Review*, XIV (Spring, 1952), 256–77, appeared in a special number of that magazine devoted to Dante; the other contributors were Erich Auerbach, R. P. Blackmur, T. S. Eliot, Francis Fergusson, Robert Fitzgerald, Jacques Maritain, and Charles S. Singleton.

To Allen Tate

April 9, [1952]

Dear Allen:

As to Poe, I'm happy to say that the Foundation boys appeared much taken aback upon learning that a communication from Fahs to the President was regarded as a final brushoff; by GKC[halmers], Phil [Rice], and me equally. Apparently they had not intended that. Our informant is D'Arms, who is a former Oxonian chum of Phil's, and has now talked with him.[1] They have given us a broad hint to make them another proposition which won't involve direct subsidy to contributors but will get us the money, which we then can spend on contributors; they've even indicated the kind of proposition, and we'll get a letter off tomorrow about it. So the Poe essay may yet be paid for at usual rates. In fact, D'Arms says we mustn't relax our rates even temporarily, and is going to find us a small tide-over grant, he thinks, to enable us to keep on the old rates.

The letter from Regnery surprises me. I don't think hard of the President for his conversation. But he thought poorly of an idea of mine, which was to approach the Foundation for help in a strong editorial policy over some years which would have focussed on just such problems as Corrigan indicates; though perhaps less "committed" on the religious side. Chalmers is wonderfully "for" the Review just as it stands, considering that he doesn't and can't read it. Quite willing for us to carry on at the expense to the College of a little annual deficit if necessary. And I'd rather go on just as we are. I am showing to the President your letter from Corrigan. I can't think it's a violation of confidence, as I really don't think there was anything secret about it. And if there is, I need to know and have it in the open.[2]

I hope you were pleased with the Dante number. It turned out brilliant, I feel. The only ordinary piece there was Fitzgerald's, and it certainly wasn't less than ordinary.[3] The editing of quotes, translations, etc., isn't uniform, because I never had all the pieces before me at once; they were many weeks coming in. Could do a better job with a second Dante number. Let me know how you like it when you write again.

Our best to Caroline. Do come by to see us this spring or early summer anyway.

Affectionately,
John

1. Edward Francis D'Arms, who had been a Rhodes scholar with Philip Blair Rice, was now associate director for humanities at the Rockefeller Foundation. With the help of D'Arms the *Kenyon Review* offered fellowships to "distinguished younger writers" for the next three years, and the $4,800 granted each year for administrative costs for this new program was to go mainly for contributors' fees paid by the *Kenyon Review*.

2. Tate had approached the Henry Regnery Company, a conservative publisher in Chicago, on behalf of the *Kenyon Review*. Corrigan, an editor, had responded. Gordon K. Chalmers, Kenyon's president, was again involved in Ransom's continuing efforts to secure outside support for the *Kenyon Review*.

3. Robert Fitzgerald, "The Style That Does Honor," *Kenyon Review*, XIV (Spring, 1952), 278–85.

To Richard Wilbur

June 19, 1952

Dear Mr. Wilbur:

I feel badly at our not having published any poems of yours, a poet as eminent and admirable as you are. Can't we still remedy that?[1] We'd like very much to see a group and publish a few poems at an early date; as a matter of fact, we could publish in Autumn number; deadline July 31, but of course the sooner we could have them the better.

I'm a little vague—so hectic has the Commencement season been here—about your latest honors, but I have the strong impression that you are to be away next year on some good Fellowship or Grant.[2] In any case, best wishes,

Sincerely,
John Ransom

1. Ransom had lost a batch of poems from the manuscript for Wilbur's first collection of poetry, *The Beautiful Changes* (1947), and was here trying to make amends.

2. Wilbur had recently received his first Guggenheim fellowship.

To Josephine Piercy

June 29, 1952

Dear Miss Piercy:

This is a belated note to thank you for your many kindnesses, and to say that Mr. Blackmur and I are enjoying our summer home very much.[1] It is extremely hot, but that happens everywhere—except perhaps in California?

I read the Blue Book devotedly, and we have been going by all your instructions and directions.[2] The cleaning lady is coming according to schedule; the lawn man has come and cut the grass and dusted the roses; the garbage is being disposed of in the sanitary way you described, though we do not create much in the kitchen with our private breakfasts and occasional luncheon sandwiches; the 2nd-class mail is being stacked up in the study, though we do not fail to read *New Yorker* and other periodicals. The one thing that worries me a little is the matter of the service bills. None has come to the house in the mail. I rather think that during the coming week I'll call at the Telephone and Gas and Electric Companies to pay up current bills, as a friend occupying the house during your absence, or however I should put it in such a way as to make no change in the name of the contracting party.

We think the house is awfully pleasant, and the lawn. And we have a lot of room.

I hope you are having a good summer yourself.

Sincerely yours,
John C. Ransom

1. Ransom and R. P. Blackmur lived in Miss Piercy's house during the summer of 1952, while they were members of the faculty of the School of Letters of Indiana University.

2. Miss Piercy, a member of the English department at Indiana University, left detailed instructions, which Ransom called the Blue Book, for Ransom and Blackmur concerning their use of her house.

To Robert Penn Warren

November 3, [1952]

Dear Red;

The poem is magnificent; more specifically, has a world of pace and fury, but always built up to, in order, convincing; in fact, has everything, including drama and poetry.[1] I haven't any major objection *at all*. Phil [Rice] also is impressed, equally so; and says he wants to wait till proof (and copy) comes back from the printer at Antioch so that he can give you a matured and philosophical judgment.

A piddling comment or so. *Heorot* (not *Herreot*) was the king's castle in Beowulf. *Albemarle* is, according to my geography, not *Albermarle*. And should Isham refer to his mother as *Mammy*? I had thought *Mammy* was the black wet-nurse, and the mother was *Mother*; especially among the proud Virginians *then*. My impression is (away from copy at the moment) that Lilburn says *Mother*; and perhaps you want to give *Mammy* to Isham to help characterize him. So probably you've thought this out. Anyhow we wouldn't be so presumptuous as to edit this; I guess I did edit to *Heorot* and *Albemarle*.

We sent in everything up to a point on p. 144. I was afraid to use quite so much as you had suggested, in view of the permission we had officially from Random House. Besides, isn't it better to get a whole and perfect context, situation, not only tragic overwhelmingly but with the motif clearly indicated, and us able to guess *more or less* what will come next though not exactly. To get clear through to the prediction of the specific action (as we would if we carried to where you suggested) would seem nearly to tell all, to leave too little unsaid; that isn't as true as it would seem because you make a great deal of the "reconciliation," of the next-best ideal which Jefferson takes to, giving an ending which I like and admire; besides the dramatic detail of the final action, which is fully up to its advertisement. But still if we stopped with Lilburn "leaning to Isham"—a phrase you play on—after we infer very clearly the sort of thing he's about to tell him: don't we then get the right stopping place for the instalment of the serial whole?

However. Perhaps even that calculation was academic. For after sending it to printer I went back and read the words of Albert's letter; and the official part said: ". . . provided an outside limit of 3,000 lines is set."[2] Your pages have 23 lines each, and therefore 130 pages of your manuscript contains 2990 lines and is our offical limit. So this morning I called up our printer (Antioch Press, Yellow Springs, Ohio) and asked him to set up 125 pp and send that much and the whole copy of the 144 pages (your pages) back for us to figure the ending again. Have you any suggestions? One thing I'd not like, but it might be best: to drop the Meriwether Lewis section out in order to get on further with the central story. Another thing I figure is not in our power, unless you'd care to intervene, and I can imagine you might not care to do it at all, is just to go on to the ending I had marked, or the one you have suggested or might suggest. The third thing is to stop between pp 125 and 130 somewhere, and I don't think it's likely that'll be quite good. But lacking the copy at the moment I can't tell. I have an idea the proof will be back here about the end of this week or the first of next. Maybe I'll call you up when I see the copy again. Can you give me your telephone address?

Here's an ignominious thing I hate to bring up. We are sworn to try to keep in the black this year, and we actually made out a budget, the first one yet. We undertook to print down to our base contract size of 168 pp of text; and to hold payments to contributors to $1550 per issue, which would average out as right for that size. Now the 3,000 lines in our pages of 34 lines would make up as I figure to about 94 pp; I had hoped it would run over 100 pp, so that we could figure $550 for the balance of the issue, contributors' pay. But as it stands it looks like $900. I know this won't affect your advice or action. But at the moment I'm wishing we could get permission anyway to run to p. 144, which would mean 500 ll. over our permission. Maybe I'll up and call Albert anyway. But I hope you can write me any ideas you have right away, so there'll be time for that.

We're well, and hoping to see you in the Christmas holidays; earlier if possible.

Yours,
John

1. Warren, "Brother to Dragons," *Kenyon Review*, XV (Winter, 1953), 1–103.

2. Albert Erskine, Warren's editor at Random House, was writing on behalf of the publisher, which would publish the entirety of *Brother to Dragons* later in 1953.

To Monroe K. Spears

November 19, 1952

Dear Monroe:

I am sending herewith the Empson MS, with his letter of directions (sent to me, but I have since told him I'd like permission to send one of his MSS (Hamlet and Falstaff) to you and he has agreed), and with an altered beginning of the essay sent later. I hope you can use one of the two essays he indicates as possibly excerptable from the whole.[1] It is very good writing, and good thinking, with just enough controversy and meanness in it to make it exciting to the literary mind; and the typography is as always in execrable shape. We'll try our luck with Falstaff, which is the less good of the two. Even that will have to wait, for our Winter issue will contain 100 pp of a novel-length and novel-like poem by Warren, another epic of Kentucky.[2] I hope you'll find a place for yours; if not just return it to me. Empson is so important, I think, and has been so handicapped alone in China, removed even from any sort of library, that I very much like to serve him if possible.

I'd better stick in my review to the Matthiessen,[3] I think; I'm over-extended, as the saying is. And the Blackmur essays I am doing elsewhere.[4] But I'm anxious to do my bit by Matty, and I think I have a line on his gifts and limitations as a critic, and they are well worth writing about.

Sincerely yours,
John Ransom

Please take care of that part of MS which you don't use, if you do decide to use some of it.

---

1. Monroe K. Spears, editor of the *Sewanee Review*, published William Empson's "*Hamlet* When New," *Sewanee Review*, LXI (Winter and Spring, 1953), 15–42, 185–205; Ransom published Empson's "Falstaff and Mr. Dover Wilson," *Kenyon Review*, XV (Spring, 1953), 213–62.

2. Warren's "Brother to Dragons."

3. Ransom's essay-review of Matthiessen's *The Responsibilities of the Critic*—"Responsible Criticism," *Sewanee Review*, LXI (Spring, 1953), 300–303.

4. Ransom's review of Blackmur's *Language as Gesture*—"More than Gesture," *Partisan Review*, XX (January–February, 1953), 108–11.

To Robert Penn Warren

December 22, [1952]

Dear Red:

We were mighty happy to have the ANNOUNCEMENT—and we are looking forward to seeing you and Eleanor with us in late January.[1] Sorry it cannot be for Christmas. Be sure if you find that Christmas is the right time after all, you come right on here. It would be fine for us, for there are only Jack and Robb and me. Reavill and Shirley[2] in Nashville, so are Annie and Ellene my sisters, and in Baton Rouge there are Helen, Duane, Choppy and Elizabeth.[3] A big scatteration, what?

You know how to manage a long poem, Red; all the pace, variety, vitality, suspense, in the world. I think the poem is magnificent. We have it in good shape, in press now, with page proofs only to see.

It's so good that I hate to make piddling comments, as you suggest; but since this is right when you are putting the last touches on it, I'd better now—or else hereafter hold my peace. I'm not sure of my points, and only invite your consideration; and there are not many places I have noted to comment on. But here goes.

I don't think the title is happy; and I don't think it matters, as for that, that we have already given you a title in KR—'twould make our version all the more attractive to the historian if it wasn't the authoritative title. BROTHER TO DRAGONS isn't euphonious somehow; hard to say; hard to remember, as to which noun is singular, which is plural, and why there's a distinction; and it's a bit Tennysonian, isn't it? I'm thinking of the dragons that "tear themselves in their slime," or something like that; I admit I haven't looked it up (In Memoriam) to check on. And now I have to confess that I haven't one to suggest. However, I'll keep my mind on it and if in the next two weeks a name occurs to me I'll suggest it. Other people here aren't notably taken with the present title.

Stylistically you have done a wonderful job; there's just enough High

Poetry, while the Mean Poetry is always vital and dramatic; what more could you ask? A few places bother me, only; you have tinkered precisely along the lines I would have suggested, in the alterations you sent; maybe I'd suggest a little more tinkering. For instance, in this kind of locution:

RPW: The scream came. Came once. Came twice, and came
Again. . . .
Laetitia: . . . . said Now,
Said Now. And Now. . . .

(But you've taken some of the Nows out already.)

Laetitia: She . . . . said Hesh. . . .
And she said Hesh. Said Hesh.

(Somehow this locution seems especially unsuitable to the quiet emotional effects of L's speech.)

Laetitia: . . . . And he said Ah. And said:
Ah, Laetitia. . . .
. . . .
. . . .
. . . . And he said Ah.
. . . .
Said Ah. . . .

(Same speech, a little higher.)

. . . . I wanted to say No.
. . . Say No. Say Stop. But I couldn't say No, say Stop.
Laetitia: Said Chile. Said Chile. . . .
. . . .
. . . Said Chile. Said Chile, yore Mammy. . . .

(And there are a half a dozen other cases in this speech.)

Aunt Cat: Sing Lil. Sing Lil. . . .
Sing Lil. . . .

That is a dramatic locution, but it doesn't have the right texture somehow; kind of chorus or vaudeville drama.

On your p. 155 I'm wondering if the Sacco-Vanzetti business you want to identify with President Lowell so explicitly.[4]

A little matter: shouldn't it be *sweated* for *sweat*, your p. 165? Elsewhere with a common speaker you can say *sweat* in the past, but this is Grand Style (RPW's) about how Hercules *sweat* in the Forum.

I think the finest verse is in our section, the first half. But the ending is all right. It marches. By that time there is tremendous momentum; the verse can be a little simpler. So that is all right. There is the general katharsis to attend to, out of the elements already at hand. And the Meriwether episode is a surprise episode that counts heavily.

That's about all. There's a world of comment possible on the substance of the thing, but still that is the heart of it, not to be challenged. Except one thing occurs to me: I don't believe you ought to refer to "old Hobbes" as the type of naturalist: it's a little bit academic; too pat; or so I fear.

It's great, Red, and will make a great impression.

We wish you and Eleanor a Big Christmas and a Happy New Year.

Affectionately,
John

1. Robert Penn Warren married Eleanor Clark on December 7, 1952.

2. Reavill Ransom's wife.

3. Helen Ransom's husband Duane Forman and their daughters Robb (Choppy) and Elizabeth.

4. A. Lawrence Lowell (1856–1943) was president of Harvard University from 1909 to 1933.

To Babette Deutsch

April 22, [1953]

Dear Miss Deutsch:

Your verse is always *poetry*: I believe my feeling is adverse on one point only, but pretty steadily—I miss *formality* in it. I think I'm probably prejudiced.

Thank you for sending this, and the nice note too.

Sincerely,
John Ransom

To Monroe K. Spears

May 2, 1953

Dear Mr. Spears:

I think mighty well of [Flannery] O'Connor, and I'm told she *needs* the help. And of course it's really up to *you*. I'm a little bit jealous on behalf of democratic principle of scattering our benefits; but in this case I'm sure I'd be tempted, and as I say I don't feel entitled, or obliged, to form an opinion, which might be worrisome. I can say I'll be happy to know she's looked after.[1]

Thanks for your remarks about Reavill. I visited him (& family) Easter

Sunday, and he proudly showed me an essay on Dryden which I liked, as he said you had liked it.

Best regards.

Sincerely,
Ransom

1. Ransom is responding to Spears's request to recommend Flannery O'Connor for a *Sewanee Review* fellowship (also underwritten by the Rockefeller Foundation). In the end O'Connor won a *Kenyon Review* fellowship but not one from the *Sewanee Review*. (She contributed fiction to both magazines.)

To Robert Penn Warren

August 28, 1953

Dear Red:

We were much thrilled by your account of the adventure of July 27, and with the net consequence in the person of Miss Rosanna Phelps Warren; who is doing fine, I hope.[1] I find myself this summer a generation removed from my young relatives but we've had 'em right here; at least we've had Helen with her two, Robb III (act. nearly 7) and Elizabeth (2); and next Monday for a few weeks we'll have Reavill and his, Master John Farley; all are bouncers of the first water, and give me great satisfaction.

Then it was quite an event to hold in my hands the final book of *Brother to Dragons*, for that *is* a poem. It is firmed up everywhere. You are a fine reviser. Robert Lowell is reviewing it for our Autumn issue but I felt that he didn't write it as well as he had talked it, and his talk was what led me to ask him to do the job for us.[2] I haven't yet seen reviews though I've heard of several; I don't want to see the one in *Time*; they have made an error there, for this is going to be an important book which will have active currency for a good many years, and even when it is laid on the shelf will never be staying there very long. Orally I have heard the finest testimonies to it. I agree with most of them that this is your best book.

What is the chance of getting you to [do] a Conrad essay for us?[3] We're leading off in Autumn with two essays and expect to carry a number of others. We especially want one from you; on whatever topic is most on your mind when you think of Conrad.

Jack is going to brave Ohio State's Freshman Engineering this fall. He may make it, then again he may not. He has nothing much to recommend him as a scholar except that he graduated from High School. But he is a young engineer, no doubt about that. I hope the interest of the subject, etc etc. He is due back today from two weeks summer camp with a Marine

Aviation reserve unit at Cherry Point, N.C. He doesn't want to fly the babies exactly, just to keep them flying with his ground service as a technician. If he should not succeed at O.S.U. I believe he'll just go on and serve his stint in the army (or rather the Navy), and I'd hope that he'll want to get his money's worth by coming out and using the allowance which the government will make him for more education, assuming that he'll [be] more of an age to appreciate it.

You and Eleanor must not lose a chance to come by and see us, with Rosanna, the very first time you get out this way.

Our best to all of you,

Affectionately,
John

---

1. The first child born to Robert Penn Warren and Eleanor Clark Warren.

2. Lowell's review, "Prose Genius in Verse," *Kenyon Review*, XV (Autumn, 1953), 619–24.

3. Apparently this essay was never written.

To Lionel Trilling

October 20, 1953

Dear Lionel:

Thanks for your good note about our reviewing our own staff-authors—with sometimes painful results. I've waited to mull over the question before replying; and I haven't yet had occasion to talk with Phil, but I will show him this before sending it to you.

My disposition is—to keep on living dangerously; perhaps I could put it, sportingly. I know of the passions of authors; but then we've never, I think, had any exhibition of them on the part of members of our staff who got mauled in our reviews. I should think the general understanding, and surely their own understanding, is that we leave all to the reviewer, and pick the best reviewers we can though with the reservation: not the friends, in any close sense, of the authors. When my book THE NEW CRITICISM appeared, Phil wrote to Richards, whom I had mistreated in the book perhaps, to review my book and have his innings; with my entire consent; but Richards replied that I had misunderstood him and he would probably misunderstand me, so he declined. I have always felt that it was becoming for us on the staff to reproach one another, too, though in good temper; there has not been much of that, but something, as for example when I have let go against Brooks; and no heads have ever been broken, or even, so far as appears, hurt. Isn't it good to seek the impression that we are willing ourselves to take the chances that other writers do? Blackmur reviewed you, and I doubt if there was a word changed or held back for the reason that you were on the staff of the reviewing organ, and he was formerly on the staff. And now Lowell has reviewed Warren, and Goodman has reviewed Bentley. Both writers (i.e. writers reviewed) were apprised in advance; and indeed Goodman's name was one of several that Eric had suggested; I was a bit taken aback when it turned out more adverse to Eric than I thought quite just, but it was open and aboveboard, and the points were intellectually and objectively argued, and I couldn't for a moment ask the reviewer to make a single modification. However, I'll write to Eric right away, to express some deprecation of the review, though I wrote him before we went to press to this effect, already.

I'll keep your wise words in mind, however; there's nothing to do at the moment anyhow.

Blackmur is back from a year in the Mediterranean culture, and in the hole financially, and wants to teach for us at Bloomington again. I believe we should let him; and I should not offer myself at all. The only thing I want to teach there right now is some of the major critical problems which are current with American writers right now; I think that is important, but it's not the kind of course we seek particularly. Empson, Blackmur, Jarrell, and a fourth would make a fine front window, and live up to the advertisement too. The fourth is a little dubious right now; I've written Zabel, knowing he has a lot of modern fiction at his fingers' ends, but then he is sure to say he won't know till next March. There's time for that fourth to be recruited, I think. Blackmur, by the way, took the hardest possible books in his summer-before-last job with us: *Ulysses* and *Counterfeiters*, chiefly; and they were pretty tough for some of the students; if he should do fiction again he ought to take Proust, James, Dostoevsky, perhaps, the biggest things and straightest achievements possible, to show how a fertile critic finds to say about great works; and everybody does better on the second try. But I haven't replied to B. except to say that we were very much interested, and he'd hear from me presently. What do you think?

Yours ever,
John

Phil seems to feel strongly as I do—that it hasn't yet caused us real difficulty, this business of reviewing our staff-members.

To Andrew Lytle

March 25, 1954

Dear Brother Andrew:

Mighty glad to hear from you. It's been quite a spell since we were in touch. I'm glad to hear that things are busy and well with you, and that you've got Langdon to match our Jackie.[1] Jack is a mechanic, for the time being at least, with small interest in other things. He is disgusted if I put him to working with his hands, helping me clean up for the garden, but he'd work day and night too if he could get a tractor to bear on the labor. He keeps our car in the pink of condition. He's a pre-engineer Freshman at Ohio State, but comes home every Friday night for [the] week-end.

Helen and Duane, and their two little girls, live at Baton Rouge, where Duane practises brain surgery. But Reavill is finishing up his Ph.D. residence work at Vanderbilt, through with it this summer. He has the MA in Fine Arts from Iowa, but his stories are not the money kind, and he thinks he'll make teaching his profession and backlog. He and Shirley have young John Farley, who's just passed his first birthday.

By all means let me see some of that novel, and don't hesitate to ask the good young writers you have there, for me, to send us stories. We have a hard time finding fiction of any distinction. Some stories we publish aim at distinction, and that's the most you can say for them. Take a look at our Spring number when it comes out (round April 1) and see our four stories there. The one by Flannery O'Connor is first-rate, I think, and the one we published this time last year from her is the best story I've seen in years, if I'm not mistaken.[2] Most of the other stories are just good tries.

As you return from Salt Lake, come by Bloomington and stop over a night. I can put you up. I'll be teaching modern poets in the School there.

Yours ever,
John

I don't know if it's practical, but I wish you could take the *family* out to Salt Lake City, and then by Bloomington, and after that by Gambier, where Robb will be presiding over Helen with her two, Shirley with her one, not to mention Jack. We'd love to see Edna and the girls.

---

1. Jackie is Ransom's younger son, John James; Langdon, Lytle's youngest daughter.

2. O'Connor, "A Circle in the Fire," *Kenyon Review*, XVI (Spring, 1954), 169–90. She had earlier published "The Life You Save May Be Your Own" in the *Kenyon Review*, XV (Spring, 1953), 195–207.

To Allen Tate

September 28, [1954]

Dear Allen:

It was mighty fine to see you and Caroline—I hope you'll not fail ever to stop by in your crossings. You have great friends here, besides the JCR's.

I just can't see my way to joining up in the National Institute.[1] Am trying to simplify my existence these days. And I do hate the feel and the reputation of "honors" of all sorts. But thank you anyway.

What do you say to reviewing *The Identity of Yeats* (Dick Ellmann) for us?[2] It's very good; philosophical as well as very knowing poetically. I do hope you will. Or shall I send you the book to see first?

Till mid-October at the Senior Fellows meeting.

Auf Wiedersehen,
John

1. The National Institute of Arts and Letters. At Tate's urging Ransom later changed his mind and accepted membership.

2. Tate never wrote this review.

To Wallace Stevens

October 5, 1954

Dear Mr. Stevens:

I am sorry I could not come to the Birthday Dinner which your (and my) publishers had for you.[1] That was a historic occasion. But the best I can do is to wish you many happy returns of the day, in writing, and to say I am overjoyed at seeing at last a Collected Edition of the Poems. There will now be a great Stevens revival, which is altogether right.[2]

Sincerely yours,
John Ransom

1. Alfred A. Knopf. Stevens was seventy-five.

2. Ransom contributed to the revival in "The Planetary Poet" (*Kenyon Review,* XXVI [Winter, 1964], 233–64), an appreciative essay in which he argues that Stevens is a major American poet.

To Robert Penn Warren

April 14, 1955

Dear Red:

I don't want to feel, don't want you to feel, there's any particular difference between us in the matter of our tastes. Here was the way my ideas were running when I thought we'd better not do that chapter.[1] The time: right in the middle of a bang-up fight between South and North again, which may lead God knows where, over the desegregation order; with my own mind torn between its sympathies but, if I have to have one sympathy strong and decisive, on the side of deseg.; a time, though, when everything seems weighted that bears at all on the matter. The occasion: that chapter in which such a handsome attractive rascal, with an adoring concubine of the slave race in bed holding and kissing his hand, tells her of his running the slave trade. He acts and talks like the Hero. But there's not a speck of thought that he's done anything bad. So what would be the response of the ungentle reader who sees the Big Issue in that sort of argument? I wrote you that I felt sure this would be assimilated, and the moral commitment made all right, in the book at large.

A funny coincidence. We have the best serio-comic story Flannery O'Connor has yet written, in this Spring issue. But it's entitled: "The Artificial Nigger." I was for using it, but Phil pointed out how sensitive the people of color are, so I wrote and proposed to her another title. Her reply was in effect that the responsibility would be ours, we could change the title if we liked, but she believed that if the people who read her title would also read the story they would see that the only reflection on anybody is on the whites. We kept her title. In your chapter, though, we don't get enough of the whole to get perspective, and it *reads* like an extraordinarily fast streamlined piece of a-moral action by a most attractive son-of-a-gun.

I'm sorry I've got so sensitive.

Yours,
John

P.S. Our best to Eleanor, and Rosie Posie whom we thank for giving a special value now to that spoon.

---

1. From Warren, *Band of Angels* (New York: Random House, 1955).

To Robert Penn Warren

September 1, 1955

Dear Red:

I'm proud to have been presented with a book by the Author.[1]

Let me say that the fears I had concerning the drift of the Hamish Bond story, as printed independently, don't hold up at all in the context of the whole book. H. B. is a first-rate Kentucky gentleman as a character when he's matured; the best character in the book, I think; so human that his youthful history is like one that must have belonged to another man.

You show the "peculiar institution" of slavery from many angles, all of them unhappy ones, and that is responsible showing in my book. I never stop being surprised by remembering that the settlers, North and South, came to this country for liberty, and immediately they were withholding it—the North by Puritan codes, the South by buying and keeping slaves. And Hell to pay for either crime. But slavery was the worse, the more explicit and elemental.

The writing is mighty fine, as one must expect from this author. More power, or at least continuance of the power, to you, Red!

Meanwhile that is a happy coincidence that your son and my grandson have the same birthday.

With kindest regards to Eleanor,

Affectionately,
John

1. *Band of Angels.*

To Randall Stewart

October 29, [1955]

Dear Randall:[1]

Thanks for your letter, and *by all means*, I'm for the Fugitive reunion. Seems to me a wonderful idea for the Fugitives themselves, and I'd hope some of the passion might spill over and be a credit on the public side.

I'm very much in the air right now as to whether Rockefeller will renew our *Kenyon Review* help for another 3 years, and therefore whether I'll stay on here—though capable of more or less extended forages elsewhere—two years beyond retirement time next June.

Yours ever,
John

1. Randall Stewart, a scholar who wrote *Nathaniel Hawthorne: A Biography* (1948) and other books, had succeeded Walter Clyde Curry as chairman of the Vanderbilt English department.

To Richard P. Blackmur

December 5, 1955

Dear Richard:

Thanks for the wire; and remember that I think you are the most faithful and valuable contrib. we have at KR.[1] Know too that I am having trouble of my own with releasing a screed about *Emily*; what with some absurd but extremely distracting special extra-curricular jobs that have cropped up here for me, as well as the ambiguity of the whole mass of the Dickinson canon when somebody tries to give it a push to make it fall one way or another.[2]

But I guess we have had to close the book now. We were late sending copy this time; waiting on the news from the Front (at 49 W. 49) to see if we were going on at all.[3] We don't know yet, but news I think is imminent. We know our proposal was brought up to the Trustees just as we had it. So the President said we must go on with the Winter issue, hoping to go on a couple of years or so beyond even that. However, time is short and we must rush it, and the fact is that we have a little more than copy enough in already (much of it already back here); and would like to put you off till Spring which is *almost* in sight. I hate this. Is it OK? If you react strong against it I'll still see if we can.

Yours,
John

1. Blackmur contributed more work to the *Kenyon Review* while it was being edited by Ransom than any other author except Ransom himself.

2. Blackmur, "Emily Dickinson's Notation," *Kenyon Review*, XVIII (Spring, 1956), 224–37; Ransom, "Emily Dickinson: A Poet Restored," *Perspectives USA*, XV (Spring, 1956), 5–20.

3. The address of the Rockefeller Foundation.

To Andrew Lytle

January 12, 1956

Dear Brother Andrew:

I wonder if you'd be interested in standing for our Fellowship in Fiction for 1956. The money (Rockefeller Foundation) came through only in mid-December, so that we're a little cramped in defining tenure and dates of payment of stipend. A 1956 Fellowship may be for the calendar year or for the school year beginning next fall. Semiannual payments of stipend will accordingly be made on March 1 and July 1 (for the calendar year) or July 1 and January 1, 1957 (for the following school year). The stipend is $2,700 for an unmarried Fellow, $4,000 for a married one.

We have a form for filing application, and it will need to show just what leisure time the Fellowship would contribute to some specific writing project. The time, considering our rate of stipend, would hardly be expected to mean relief from a whole year of professional duties.

Then the form will ask for copies of published work already done. What I'd want my advisors particularly to see would be *Long Night* and that latest book whose title I can't recall.[1] I've had and cherished both those books, but I have a way of losing books to my boys; and the better the boy, the better the book he takes.

I've come to have the notion somehow that you haven't had your "feet in the trough," as Red Warren expresses it with respect to getting into the Fellowship scramble, and that this is a scandal. But then of course I can't anticipate the decision of the judges.[2]

Best wishes for 1956, and regards to the family.

Yours,
John

1. Lytle's *A Name for Evil.*

2. Lytle was appointed a *Kenyon Review* fellow in 1956 and worked on *The Velvet Horn* (New York: McDowell, Obolensky, 1957) while on this fellowship.

To Randall Stewart

February 18, 1956

Dear Randall:

Thanks for the provisional program, for a meeting to last from noon of Thursday, May 3, through early afternoon of Saturday.[1] I was off on a trip all this week till Thursday evening late, when I found the letter waiting for me, and now after looking hard at it I feel that my response has crystallized sufficiently to answer it. A provisional answer, of course. For I shan't hold out at all against the wishes of the majority if my views aren't accepted.

I can't accept the role of a leader in any sense, however. We were too democratic or communal for that sort of thing. And much too equal in any objective sense. And I find that what I would like would be some long sessions together with the old crowd, and the chance of taking some decisions, and just a little bit of joint publicity and applause.

Nothing I know, even from a limited experience, is quite so painful as being "honored"; and especially when the socialites who don't know anything about one's work are enlisted to shed their own glory over the occasion. We did not call ourselves Fugitives for nothing. I can't tell you how I hate the social pages of the Nashville papers; I keep thinking of being in Nashville during the last war, and seeing Mrs. Guilford Dudley and her handsome son a young officer (at home on leave) spread over the whole front page of the society section, with the back pages filled with hundreds of other notices of mother and son reunions in an exactly diminishing degree of space per head, as social status declined.[2] I also know how one is hounded by the old Vanderbilt reporter girls when one is back in Nashville, and pretty notices must be got into the papers. Etc etc.

This is of relevance when one sees that there are to be 500 "*or more*" invited guests to the big tea, and a cocktail party and dinner at the Country Club at the expense of the Chancellor and Board of Trust, with 100 invited other guests of proper stature, and myself slated to address Board and guests about matters on which one cannot speak intimately because of the disparity between the subject and the audience. Horrors.

I'd rather meet humble persons who kept up with what we were writing than any number of Big People who are ready now to come over to us briefly.

These big occasions under the eye of the society reporters are so much out of order, and the Fugitives then or now are such an independent breed, that there are pretty sure to be many broad ironies dropped in speech or informal talk alike, to the benefit of nobody that I can think of.

It is likely that what I have in mind as the nature of the "memorial" of the Fugitive bit of history is not what was contemplated in the terms to which the Rockefeller grant was applied for and extended. If so, then just cancel this paragraph. I think I'd sort-of like to hold our expenses for the meeting down to some comfortable minimum ($1,000 or $1,200?) and reserve the rest as a capital fund to be used by an Executive Committee, with Davidson as Chairman, on the right occasions; when there is a strong group or even a strong individual with some real literature in the making and no means to get it published. An occasional year book with the Fugitive indorsement on it, or little magazine, or small book of one author's, or literary meeting which seems of importance. I don't know what there might be, but I'd like to see us thresh out the problem. I'm thinking entirely of Vanderbilt or ex-Vanderbilt students drawing the advantages. I think history will give the Fugitives themselves as much honor as they merit, and it is a slight failure of confidence to assume that we must superintend this bestowal, and can do it because of the present lucky break, realized because of your own spirited initiative. But as I said, if this is not the use contemplated in the grant just lay my idea aside.

Accordingly, I'd like for the Fugitives to meet at some very peaceful and private place for the mornings and noons of at least two days; all of the visiting Fugitives and Donald Davidson besides spending full time in these meetings, with such part time from other Fugitives as they can afford, those like Stevenson and Wills and Curry and (I'd say especially) Alfred Starr, and Sidney Mttron Hirsch. (And what about Bill Elliott at Harvard? It will break his heart if he is not invited.)[3] The place might be that nice hotel (used to be nice, anyhow) down at Murfreesboro. There would need to be free access to most of these meetings, informal meetings, specifically imposed upon certain key people outside of the Fugitive membership like yourself, Cleanth, and Beatty.

I feel that as you say the University *does* want to show some appreciation. Couldn't that be by some undertaking to support the memorial fund, help with its projects, as occasion and circumstances permitted?

As for the reading programs, I think I'd favor two of these, one in connection with an open tea (of the most inexpensive sort), the other during one evening. And I'd like to see Donald putting together two programs, much as the program director arranges the concert of music; I'd certainly go along with his wishes. In one or the other of these meetings or programs *any* of the old Fugitives who willed would be assured of our wish that he take part too. Maybe at the most Donald could have the publishing Fugitives speaking (i.e. reading) twice. They would be memorable programs, with some definition to them.

That's as far as I've gone. Just mull over the ideas and see what you think. And please show this to Don and get his reactions.

My wife does want to come. And we'll be seeing you before long.

Yours,
John

1. Through a grant provided by the Rockefeller Foundation to the American Studies Association, all the living Fugitives were invited to a reunion held at Vanderbilt, May 3–5, 1956.

2. Guilford Dudley, Jr., later became president of Life and Casualty Insurance Company in Nashville and then ambassador to Denmark.

3. Ransom calls the roll of the minor Fugitives: Alec Stevenson, Jesse Wills, Walter Clyde Curry, Alfred Starr, Sidney Mttron Hirsch, and William Yandell Elliott.

To R. W. B. Lewis

February 23, 1956

My dear Mr. Lewis:

Thanks for your note and I'm very glad that Marks is working on Johnson.[1] Your piece will be in time if we get it by the very last day of this month.[2] That would be just about the latest possible time. Since I presume it will be of major length, it will be all right coming in by that date.

I had wanted very much to write myself about your book on the American Adam.[3] I found it very good and useful, particularly in view of some cultural reflections which I had been making about the state of things. Surely you use a great deal of learning very modestly when you write. I have the idea that the book on Symbolism in the Nineteenth Century in America by Feidelson two or three years ago, and now your own book with a slightly different thesis, together make an invaluable picture of the early attempts at a new American literature.[4] And as for the crisis at present, after we might have thought that the nineteenth century crisis had been resolved, I should say that the new one is the result of the late developments of capitalism or industrial revolution in the form of mass production and its corollary mass consumption. At any rate surely things are breaking down from the standpoint of the old professors, and that is the reason I would assign. In a later number anyhow, if you will pardon the present delay, I hope to get round to your book.[5]

Sincerely yours,
John Crowe Ransom

JCR/mas

1. Ransom did not publish Emerson R. Marks's "The Uses of Dr. Johnson" in the *Kenyon Review*.

2. Lewis, then teaching at Rutgers with Marks, was writing a review of Alfred Kazin's *The Inmost Leaf* that would appear in the *Ken-*

yon Review, XVIII (Winter, 1956), 140–45.

3. Lewis, *The American Adam: Innocence, Tragedy, and Tradition in the Nineteenth Century* (1955).

4. Charles Feidelson, *Symbolism and American Literature* (1953).

5. *The American Adam* was not reviewed in the *Kenyon Review*.

To Andrew Lytle

February 28, 1956

Dear Andrew:

I don't know why we should not say here and now that you are our Fellow-elect for 1956. We have several other applications entered, but none to compete with yours. I feel very happy over this.

I do hope you will go ahead with short stories, and not feel yourself obliged by one project or another specifically. I confess to feeling a little antipathy, which I don't doubt would disappear when I saw the work itself, to the novel on the subject of incest.[1] That's pretty strong medicine. But you are the doctor. You have our carte blanche.

With best wishes to Edna and yourself.

Yours faithfully,
J. C. R.

1. Lytle, *The Velvet Horn*.

To Randall Stewart

April 2, 1956

Dear Randall:

Thanks for your recent notes. I guess I'm whipped, and therefore with every possible becoming show of reluctance I concur with your plan to seat me at the high table with the Chancellor and be prepared to make Remarks. And here will be the poems for my reading:

Janet Waking
Antique Harvesters
The Equilibrists
Prelude to an Evening.

OK? I had a nice note the other day requesting this list for the printer, but I haven't the note by me just now.

Oh, yes, Robb will come along and I'll be much obliged if you will reserve us a room at the Allen arriving the A.M. of the 3rd. She has stayed there several times; all of us spent a night there after Christmas vacation in Baton Rouge.

Yours ever,
John

To Robert Penn Warren

August 28, 1956

Dear Red:

I think your letter came about three days ago, and today came a letter from Miss Elizabeth Cray of the Poetry Center of NYC to say that under the circumstances of your being unable to participate the Fugitive program would have to be postponed for this season. I have replied to her that I heartily concur. The fact is that Allen conducted the negotiations, got them (along with Robert Richman at Washington[1]) to raise the ante, and as I thought had worked out the calendar acceptable to you because the agreement came for me to sign for the specific January date; and I did sign it but over the express condition that all three parties would participate. So there we are. It would have been fine to have some private talk with you and Allen, but I was not looking forward especially to the public talk.

I imagine you know, through Peter Taylor,[2] of Charles Coffin's death (by sudden massive coronary occlusion) several weeks ago in the Huntington Library at Pasadena. Within six months we lost Rice, Chalmers, and Coffin; a very dreary record.[3] I can't feel that the place is quite the same without them. And I guess of the three that I was closest to Charles. I'll be glad when Peter gets back here; there aren't many of his time that I am particularly intimate with, I guess. I'm glad you like him and Eleanor;[4] Robb and I have a weekly bridge date with them, and exchange garden products and secrets, and think they are wonderful.

I'm glad things are happy with the Warrens. If you are writing with that feeling that you aren't sure it is right, I know that feeling, and have far more reason to fear it; but I suppose it's a good sign, like a little of stage fright just before you make a speech.

Love to Eleanor and Rosieposie and Gabriel,

Sincerely,
John

---

1. Robert Richman, literary editor of the *New Republic* during 1952–54, had been director of the Institute of Contemporary Arts in Washington, D.C., since 1953.

2. Peter Taylor, author of *The Long Fourth* (1948) and many other collections of stories, was a graduate of Kenyon and had returned to teach there.

3. Philip Blair Rice was killed in an automobile accident on January 25, 1956. Four

months later Gordon K. Chalmers died of a cerebral hemorrhage. On July 20 of the same year Charles Coffin died of a coronary occlusion.

4. Eleanor Ross Taylor, Peter's wife.

To Robert Penn Warren

October 16, 1956

Dear Red:

Last Saturday I joined Cleanth Brooks and I. A. Richards in a panel all about poetry at the Hill School in Pennsylvania. They kept our noses right on the grindstone, but I did have a few asides with Cleanth, and he told me about the new kinds of poetry you were writing. I am now talking to my machine, and my special editorial secretary will be typing it up tonight, and if I were not writing about something else I would be writing to say that K.R. *demanded* to see some of that new verse. As it is I am saying with great emphasis to the gadget that we are mighty glad to have the poem which came in yesterday without waiting to be demanded.[1] But we cannot print it in the Spring issue, as you suggest, because it will already have appeared in the Winter issue. OK? You are extending the genre of the art here, Red, it's a fantasy full of melody and history, and it progresses, and your reader feels good progressively. I'm glad you have cut loose from the other arts for the time being and taken up this one again.

I am glad to hear that you are homesick a little bit, you and Eleanor, for A&P, and other of the Americana. But I know that doesn't prevent you from having a wonderful and profitable trip over there.[2] We are about as usual, with a telephone call just now from Trudie Freeland, an old friend of Robb's and mine in our Nashville days, who is coming to see us next Saturday to play bridge, etc. So we'll be thinking old-timey thoughts.

Our best to Eleanor and you, and we wish we could see the children.

Yours ever,
John

---

1. Warren was writing the poems that would be published in *Promises: Poems, 1954–1956* (New York: Random House, 1957), for which he would win a Pulitzer prize. "Ballad of a Sweet Dream of Peace," *Kenyon Review*, XIX (Winter, 1957), 31–36, appears in *Promises*.

2. The Warrens were in Rome.

To Andrew Lytle

March 25, 1957

Dear Andrew:

I have taken a terribly long time to tell you, now, how pleased I was to see a chapter of your Big Novel in the *Sewanee Review* some issues ago.[1] And I have not acknowledged a nice note or two from you in the meantime. Over my head in the routine.

I am delighted to think that Dave McDowell is going to print your novel next fall among the first of the imprints of his new firm.[2] It is a grand thing. And I thought of you when I read the novel by that Nashville man (whose name I can't recall) dealing with the wildcat distiller out on the bluffs of the Cumberland in Cheatham County.[3] He is touched with a little of your philosophy and your spirit for the epical.

We are thoroughly satisfied with the Fellowship in Fiction during your tenure. You equalled all my expectations. I am awfully anxious to see the volume as a whole.

I wish I could have been with you more during our celebration in Nashville last May.[4] Much as I enjoyed the occasion, we were terribly rushed about, and I came away quite disappointed with the poor allowance I had for seeing you and the Cheneys and other of my best friends.[5] We have not yet staged a big get-together after long years. But I hope we'll get round to that somehow before long.

This is just a letter of greetings. I think of you a lot, and wish I could see you and Edna and your children, who now are pretty big girls, as I imagine. I hope they take a good deal after their mama in good looks.

We have Peter Taylor here with us, teaching the writing of fiction and now of drama, and perhaps you have already seen his new play, Tennessee Day in Saint Louis. Anyhow our local actors are going to perform it next month. I have very high hopes about Taylor's eventual eminence.

Love to you all,

Affectionately,
John

---

1. Lytle published a sequence from his novel in progress, *The Velvet Horn*, as a story, "What Quarter of the Night," *Sewanee Review*, LXIV (Summer, 1956), 349–97.

2. *The Velvet Horn* was published by McDowell, Obolensky in 1957.

3. Madison Jones, a native of Nashville, had recently published his first novel, *The Innocent* (1957).

4. The Fugitive reunion, May 3–5, 1956.

5. Frances and Brainard Cheney, longtime friends of the Fugitives and Agrarians and authors in their own right.

To Robert Penn Warren

July 3, 1957

Dear Red:

I wish you folks were here, or nearby. The Taylors are coming over for a picnic on the Fourth, with their two children to romp with Reavill's two children, the old folks hoping to settle down to some good Bridge later in the evening. Shirley is here with Farley and David, while Reavill is home (at Boulder) working on his dissertation on Dryden, and telling us over the phone that it's going well. But the Taylors are moving in a few days; to OSU, where he has a very superior job almost on his own terms (at least with respect to the hours of labor and the small picked classes). He wouldn't have left us but for a misunderstanding with the Acting President about his house, not entirely unfriendly, just stupid on the AP's part. And it may be that Peter had a foot that wanted to rove a little more, I don't know. In any case I believe it means that KR will go out after the Spring issue next year, just before my final retirement. No use going on just to be going, especially in a field (more or less "new" criticism, which has now decayed in the editorial sense, its fight being won and tucked away) that doesn't have the interest or urgency it had 19 years ago. What we would have done would have been to make Peter the editor, and Bogardus the managing editor,[1] of a KR devoted to new fiction, theatre, and poetry, with just enough reviews and essays to keep the reader up; I think it might have been something very distinguished. You don't by any chance have any suggestions, do you? I can't in my mind hit on a competent man to take the place of Peter in this set-up. And maybe Peter feared the job a little, that it might use up more time than he wanted to spend on it, as he is very productive right now. You've read his Tennessee Day in Saint Louis, haven't you?

The big question of this letter, though, is whether you'll be so good as to review Andrew's new novel for us.[2] I want somebody not immersed in the social novel, or the naturalistic novel, with a real sense of the historical and the epical. And such critics are few and far between. Wouldn't it be possible for you to do it as briefly as you wished, and objectively, not personally, no matter if you are old friends? I think your job wouldn't be picked up by anybody as an act of friendship. Dave McDowell of McDowell and Obolensky says he can supply advance pages pretty quick, and direct to my reviewer, and we'd all like an Autumn review. Our deadline would be at best August 15, and at latest, say August 25. No specification as to length.

I'd like to hear you all on Italy and other good topics. I can imagine Rosy Posy talking idiomatic Italian even at her tender age. Katie Taylor, who is about 9 years old, hated the French and won't talk French but she got up her Italian better than her parents, they say.[3]

And I'd like to know how Eleanor's novel has proceeded.[4] I know it is a big novel, but I guess it must have gone a long way since I saw that opening. Love to you all.

Affectionately,
John

P.S. I admired your disposition of the Madison Jones novel, the finest Cheatham County art I've ever seen.[5]

1. Edgar Bogardus, a promising poet whose work Ransom had published regularly since 1951, would soon be selected as managing editor of the *Kenyon Review*; but owing to a defective flue in his house, he was asphyxiated and died in Mount Vernon, Ohio, on May 11, 1958.

2. Lytle's *The Velvet Horn*, which was reviewed by Robie Macauley in the *Kenyon Review*, XIX (Autumn, 1957), 644–46.

3. The daughter of Eleanor and Peter Taylor.

4. Eleanor Clark, *The Song of Roland* (1960).

5. Warren reviewed Jones's *The Innocent* in the *Sewanee Review*, LXV (Spring, 1957), 347–51.

To William Empson

August 3, 1957

My dear Empson:

I am shocked to learn that you don't now like the long Donne Essay.[1] I know the feeling, because I have often, and in fact always, felt that if I were doing an essay over it would be an improvement in substance as well as otherwise over the thing I have published. I should guess that always a sensitive author dislikes the thing he has just done, and in fact the next time he takes a step forward in doing the new thing better. But this is a commonplace. Let me urge you to my own view of the essay.

It is one of the best pieces of exposition of a sustained point of view that I know of in the literary field. I would have hazarded the opinion that you might not have been familiar with all the writing on Donne which has come out in these twenty or thirty years, because there has been a tremendous lump of it. But in some ways it must be better for the writer not to take into account all the other writers on the subject, because then he would be intimidated from doing what no one has done so well before, even though somebody somewhere has done a little of the same thing he is doing. I must say that I had the greatest satisfaction in having your essay show in *The Kenyon Review*.

Now about my part in it. I do not have that original set of corrections to the copy which you sent in before the copy had gone to the printer. The reason is, I cut out so many of your sentences and pasted them onto the pages of your original manuscript, for the printer, that I destroyed every single page of the corrections in the process, even though most of the corrections I made by way of interlinear additions in my own hand. So at the end I threw away the rest of your correction pages because nothing was left of them. So I cannot send back your original set of corrections, but I am sending back the essay itself as it went to the printer with corrections which followed your directions. My impression is that I did not fail to make a single correction you had indicated.

Now we had big trouble in making the corrections which you had returned on your galley proofs. The printer tried to do a good job in the galleys, and held that part of the copy till the very end though we had sent it to him first of all. As a result, you were late seeing the galleys, and when they came back to us we had not only returned the galley proofs, but the printer had set up the pages and we had returned the page proofs. The printer's place of business is near Springfield, a hundred miles or more across the State. It takes either one or two days for a communication to go from him to us, or the other way round. So such corrections as I had him make in accordance with your reading of the galleys were indicated over the telephone, and we did not see them made until we had the magazine itself. I recall sending in a handful (five or six perhaps) of short and very explicit corrections, and I believe he made them properly. But I think you are under the impression that your corrections included many which involved a few historical items in your original essay.

I am sending your own corrected galleys, and you will see that this is not the case. In general, it is our rule, and I think that of every other magazine, not to enter at the page proof stage any corrections that make substantive additions unless they are very urgent; nor minor corrections unless they be required. Printers are very difficult about that. In the first place they make errors in resetting a single line, as often as not, and sometimes a difference of a few letter spaces in resetting a line will call for the resetting of many subsequent lines, and cost a lot of money, and sometimes cause a page to go beyond its size.

In looking over your proof corrections, I see one bad place where either I did not make a required correction or the printer disregarded it if I did make it; it is towards the bottom of the first galley and shows on page 339 of the published essay. Where there is an insert quoting Coleridge, the last sentence was to come out and [be] placed down into your own text where it belongs. So far as I know that is the great blemish of the text which we have furnished; and I am sorry. You will see that on your own corrected galleys several times you wrote in the margin an opening new sentence for a paragraph, and then crossed out what you had written; as if you did not think it essential, and knew that it would disturb a good deal of the text following it and cause much resetting.

It is too late to have offprints of the essay made. They will have long torn down the type. But the secretary is sending several additional copies of the magazine and can send still others if you need them.

Sincerely,
John Crowe Ransom

1. Empson, "Donne the Space Man," *Kenyon Review*, XIX (Summer, 1957), 337–99.

To Andrew Lytle

August 31, 1957

Dear Brother Andrew:

I hear that it was a mighty fine party they had for you in New York, and it mortifies my spirit that I was unable to attend.[1] (I seem to have developed a great repugnance for flitting around, and in this case it was countered by my intense desire to be on hand to Do Honor but reinforced by the sense that Duane and Helen and their two daughters were all on hand here with us, Duane just come to take the others home. So I abstained, but I regretted it.)

You will hardly imagine how much I was touched and pleased by your dedication page, for which I feel humble and proud at the same time.[2] I didn't notice it for some weeks after the book came in, till one of the local camp-followers who get into our books pointed it out. Then I hastened my continuance of the reading, which was subjected to many interruptions, and just the other day I completed it with immense satisfaction. I should say, editorially, that our 1956 Fellow in Fiction has just about proffered as the fruit of Fellowship the finest achievement we have had. I can see now how mistaken I was in not using that magnificent section we had a chance at, in the course of the composition a good while back.[3] I'd say that your novel is a series of lyrical & dramatic achievements, on a base of philosophical attitude founded on the sense of nature and the paradoxes of sex, and grounded firmly in history and the old (and maybe timeless) South. This is the same Andrew we have known so many years, maintaining himself over a big novel at the top of his powers. I can't but imagine this book establishes you firmly, as many readers will come to testify, who might not have known *The Long Night* and that next-to-last one about Evil.[4] (By the way, Red thinks the *Long Night* is one of the great books of our century, and I have taken up with several paperback publishers the matter of re-printing it; they all admired it immensely, when they had read my copy of it, but found it did not fit into their plans for the time being; they will come to it.)

Robie Macauley's review of the work is already in proof for the Autumn issue. I wanted a non-Southern reviewer for it, as a proper sort of triumph, and Robie has done right by you, without any solicitations from me, of course. But he didn't let himself go as I would have liked, not only because that is not his nature, but also because (as I learned after I had invited him) he feels himself a close friend of the author's.

We are doing fine and hope you-all the same. This is my last year in the harness, and I am getting mighty willing to take to the pasture.[5] Reavill is starting his fourth year of the instructorship at Boulder, where he is supposed to be completing his Vanderbilt dissertation; I know he has been at work on it, but he is such a good family man, and so sedentary and reflective by disposition, that I don't know if it is yet in the final stage. (His two boys and wife Shirley were with us earlier in the summer, but he stayed at home on the job.) Duane and Helen and children live at Baton Rouge, where he is a brain surgeon. Jack finished last June at Ohio State and seems to be a well fortified young business man, now in a responsible position with the State Tax Office. He and Loa (whom he married a year ago and who is herself a Gambier girl) are great home-comers, and I'm glad to say they rush home as soon as they are through working at Columbus, to spend Friday night and Saturday and some of Sunday with us. And we'll settle down here; it's the easiest thing in the world, and we're thoroughly at ease in the community and the landscape, which is much like that of Middle Tennessee, only with better grass and less heat.

Our best love to all of you.

Sincerely,
John

1. Andrew Lytle's publishers, David McDowell and Ivan Obolensky, had a cocktail party for him in New York to mark the publication of *The Velvet Horn*.

2. The novel was dedicated to Ransom.

3. Ransom had returned the sequence that was subsequently published in the *Sewanee Review* as "What Quarter of the Night."

4. *A Name for Evil*.

5. Ransom retired from teaching in 1958 but edited the *Kenyon Review* for another year, completing his twenty-first volume.

To Richard P. Blackmur

October 15, 1957

Dear Richard:

All these months, since you got back last Winter (or was it Spring), the old KR–Blackmur road hasn't been functioning.

To bring you up to date, Kenyon has a new President, former-President Lund of Alabama College, apparently a fine man, who hasn't talked to me these two weeks he's been in office, and snowed under, but I have it on the best authority that he means to continue the Review, and presently will be on me to name my successor.[1] Any suggestions? Now I've been uncomfortable these last few months because in checking my stock already in the barrel I found that we had just about enough on hand to use up all our space for the Winter and Spring issues which will be my last; but if I can get the right man in to follow me I might leave some things in his lap for publication later, and have a bit of the usual freedom in determining content issue by issue. If so I'll put in a strong plea very soon for a *Big Essay from you, say in Spring*. Right now all I can discuss is book reviews.

Victor Gollancz, the English publisher, is an old acquaintance of mine from Oxford days, and he kindly sends me advance galleys, cut up and assembled in book shape, of a new book by one of the Cambridge mythologists, *F. A. C. Wilson*, about the late plays and occasional lyrics by *Yeats*, in which Yeats uses the regular or "traditional" heterodoxy, the occulted doctrines we generally call "mysticism" in this country, or at least my old crowd from Nashville does. But it's an important and systematic book; I'm afraid it will nearly ruin Yeats, to make him so didactic. I looked up yesterday that old issue of Southern Review, the Yeats issue, about 1939 perhaps, where you led off. Many of the writers there paid their respects to this effect in Yeats, and you did it. (I was the most stubborn, refusing to allow that the value of Yeats depended one bit on it.) Still with this new book in hand, deadly in systematically tracking down the sources of all the mythology in Yeats, you might be interested in reviewing your estimate of Yeats, and maybe saving him. Shall I send the book to you, while I write the publisher to ask who will do the book in this country, and arrange for advance reviewing?

Or there's another book I know nothing about, except the occasion and the author, Shahn's *Shape of Content*, the Charles Eliot Norton lectures of last year. What do you say?[2]

I have to make my annual Senior Fellows trip to New York next week, but I'll rush right back here. But November 4, a Monday, I have to go again to make a reading at City College, and maybe before or after that I can toll you to town for a dinner?

Yours,
John

---

1. R. Edward Lund succeeded Gordon K. Chalmers as president of Kenyon College.

2. Blackmur reviewed F. A. C. Wilson's book along the general lines that Ransom indicated he thought important. See "Obscuris Vera Involvens," *Kenyon Review*, XX (Winter, 1958), 160–68. He did not review Ben Shahn's *The Shape of Content* (1957).

To Allen Tate

October 18, [1957]

Dear Allen:

Jack and Dillie [Thompson] will come to tea (or cocktails) at five Wednesday, and I think I'll say to my hotel, Prince George, where they have a good bar and dining room.[1]

It does seem to me to be a matter of Robie or Jack Thompson. You've mentioned Howard Nemerov and Mr. Smith; maybe.[2] But I thought Howard was a little foolish in finding his praise for *Lolita*, Nabokov's naughty novel that I had found pretty pointless (Howard reviewed it for us).[3] And I don't know Smith, though I've just been looking at some verse of his (in a new book by him, if I'm not mistaken); I do know Barbara Howes' work.[4] As between Robie and Jack, I'd say Robie will quite certainly be a good editor, and I think he'd like to get out of his present livelihood.[5] And I believe I think Jack Thompson has a better critical head and will bring up that side of the Review better than Robie; perhaps without failing to know all about contemporary letters. I have always felt that Robie is one of the best technical critics, but commonplace (rather commonplace, anyway) in the categories to which he submits the arts in the last resort. I'd look for a little more elevation (and style) in Jack's judgments. But I'd back either one of them. And yesterday the new President, who seems admirable at this stage, told me he meant for the Review to continue, and after his first Trustees Meeting this week-end (which has taken up all his time since October 1 when he began on his job) wants me to tell him whom I want for our job.

I rather think I'd like to ask Jack, and in Dillie's presence, how he'd like to come back to Kenyon as a teacher of English, in order that I may have his name when I talk to Dennie Sutcliffe the Chairman about filling in the gaps. But I'm very anxious to hear him talk and to get your own reactions, with reference to another job entirely.

It seems that Victor Gollancz, the English publisher, belonged with me to an English-American group when we were students at Oxford, and now he sends me a nice note by way of supplying me with a new book made from the galley-proofs by F. A. C. Wilson, one of the Cambridge mythologists, about Yeats. It is entitled, *Yeats and the Tradition*. But the tradition he refers to is the mystical one we used to be exposed to out on West End, as formulated by Theosophy, Cabbalism, the Greek esoteric religionists,[6] Plato, and moderns like Blake (the chief if not the only representative among the first-rate authors) and Swedenborg and Boehme. He is at great pains to derive the symbols of the late plays by Yeats (The Clock Tower, The Herne's Egg, etc.) and to refer to the derivation of many symbols in the lyrics, from these *regular* religionists, and not from Yeats's own *Vision*. The effect on me is depressing. So I turned to that Yeats number of Southern

Review, where I found that nearly all except myself (and I was ludicrously stubborn in holding that the lyrics don't need special symbolic systems for our understanding them) dealt seriously with his symbols, and some (like you and Blackmur) seemed apprehensive about the upshot.[7] The faith of the mystics of this eclectic sort seems childish in comparison with Christian theology, and after the recurrence of the same symbol a certain number of times it grows tiresome. Now I should imagine that you went further than any of us in handling a mythological symbol, in your verse, or making up a fresh one, but you kept it spontaneous and strong. By the way, Jung's archetypal ideas come in for praise as being of the true faith, but surely these are far too casual and naturalistic for serious religionists. I say all this without much commitment on my own part anywhere, but a sense for a theology that wants in any case to be serious philosophically. Probably you haven't seen Wilson, unless you like me have been asked for an advance comment. But if you haven't, you'll be faced with Wilson presently.

Affectionately,
John

P.S. I've got plane reservations by which I arrive in N.Y. about 7:00 Tuesday evening, and go out at 9:15 Thursday morning. Austin Warren always meets me at Prince George—any chance of your going there?

---

1. John Thompson, a Kenyon graduate and a contributor to the *Kenyon Review* after this time, did not make an academic career.

2. Howard Nemerov, poet and critic, and William Jay Smith, poet and translator, were among the people being considered for editorship of the *Kenyon Review*.

3. Nemerov, "The Morality of Art," *Kenyon Review*, XIX (Spring, 1957), 313–20.

4. Barbara Howes, a poet and editor, who was then William Jay Smith's wife.

5. Robie Macauley, a writer who had taught in various universities, had published a novel, *The Disguises of Love* (1952), and a collection of stories, *The End of Pity* (1957), but at the time had no academic or publishing connection.

6. Ransom was referring to Sidney Mttron Hirsch's influence on the young Fugitives.

7. Ransom, "The Irish, the Gaelic, the Byzantine."

To Allen Tate

November 5, 1957

Dear Allen:

I've been so rushed since the Senior Fellows meeting that I don't believe I've written you since; I had to go back to NY last Monday, the quickest flight I could make, to read at City College; then I had a little bout with the flu, but it wasn't the bad kind, and after three days of sitting in and reading several books I emerged all right. Except that my schedule was badly thrown off.

I had a fine meeting with Jack Thompson and his wife, cocktails at the Plaza Hotel, near which they live; but I decided that Jack wasn't quite my man; he didn't seem to me quick in his responses, though he was just trying to be amiable, I guess, and he never suspected that I had a special object. I can't think he's ready for it.

I find it hard to think of Robie [Macauley] as the editor; I'd be afraid the Review would be undistinguished as compared with its rivals; it would lack the tone of criticism which is built into the Reviews as they have come to be. (The old Southern Review established this tone, then KR started up and sort-of drifted into it, then you came along with a complete articulate concept of the critical review and founded one from the whole cloth at Sewanee; then somewhere along the line Hudson appeared as a conservative review in the metropolis, sort of foil to Partisan.) Robie would conduct a good and readable Review but I don't know if he would satisfy our present patronage among the readers who like critical writing almost better than literature itself, or at least as expressing that understanding out of which the reception of literature rises. But it would be very easy to name Robie and let things take their course.

There are two men in my mind right now as worth thinking about. One is Joseph Frank, who is extraordinarily admired by Blackmur and perhaps yourself; B. says write you about him, as you are bringing him to Minnesota (after his year abroad?); and a lot of my friends admire him too.[1] You mightn't want to let him go. But anyhow there is this hitch in my mind, that the President here is further from having any acquaintance with Frank than from his knowing any other man I've mentioned. And while President Lund has said that he wants a man so strong that he can stand on his own feet and conduct the magazine without any Presidential advice or supervision whatever, I do feel that since I am retiring *completely* from the picture, and Rice and Coffin and Chalmers (who always supported me and never made a cavil) are quite gone, it seems in order to consult the local reception of the new man. At the moment Kenyon is without much literary distinction on the part of the faculty. And President Lund's point is not how he himself reacts to the editor, for he's very humble about that, but as to whether there's any wide response publicly to the new man. Here I have to feel that Frank is probably not a poet or fictionist himself, and that his critical principles are very high and would seem to many general readers (of you and me for instance) as rather subtle and attenuated. I do wish you'd write me briefly about your thought on this; I'm not conversant as I should be with Frank's later and current publication. I know he is a good man.

The other man brings up the possibility of a pretty big shift in the intention of the Review; towards the side of publicity and even the spectacular. I have said to the old President, and the present one too, that Jarrell is too polemical and stylistically too journalistic and personally too fond of his enemies (of having enemies) to be acceptable. But right now I'm inclined to think he might be the right man for our unusual situation. His way of life in a small community would make a riffle, and there would be many incidents, but after Santee's stay here I think the town can take anybody; and then I have yet to find in Jarrell a lack of courage or of principle. I've always respected him for the way he will pitch into a question which puts the Jew at a disadvantage; even though he might pass for a Gentile if he kept quiet; and of course for his readiness to fight for unpopular causes, which indeed, being aggressive on principle, he rather enjoys. Now Randall has a great journalistic or publicist flair, and in the main it is directed against the Philistines. He is more or less sensational. And yet he showed enormous scruple and loyalty to a going institution during that year when he replaced Miss Marshall on the Nation.[2] I suspect that his selection might please the President a great deal, and that the Review would at any rate prosper under his hands, and have readers, even if many of whom would be those whom he had provoked.

That's about where we stand so far as I can see right now. The President is away this week but I'll be talking to him next week and opening this topic. In whatever you wish to say about this I'll find a great deal of reason for taking my own stand. I hate to pester you with our problem so much, but you are the statesman and strategist for us all in these matters.

Oh yes, one thing more. I told the Senior Fellows that I thought I could teach one last time in the School [of Letters] next summer, but suggested that the Secretary sound out you and Rahv. (Rahv was absent for the same reason you were.) I'll retire in favor of either of you.

Affectionately,
John

---

1. Joseph Frank, who was leaving Princeton to continue teaching at the University of Minnesota, had been publishing many of the essays collected in *The Widening Gyre* (1963), especially "Spatial Form in Modern Literature," a three-part essay that Tate published in the *Sewanee Review*, LIII (1945).

2. Randall Jarrell had succeeded Margaret Marshall as literary editor of the *Nation* in 1952.

To Allen Tate

November 23, [1957]

Dear Allen:

That was a mighty fine letter of yours, about Jarrell, and I was happy to get it.

The fact is that I had had my doubts about Jarrell myself, and I want to bring them out and get a decision with myself, and certainly, before we should close a deal with Jarrell, I'd go to him and ask him some questions, and satisfy myself about his real literary intentions, and his attitude at taking over a magazine already established. I have wondered if Randall was going to write any more poetry. What he has done is impressive if you look only at his *Selected Poems* (and that's the test I've put up for myself), but it is imperfect, and always verging into prose. I have wondered if the career he really wants is not that of a humorist, the place where he gets the laughs to enjoy in person. He might settle for the title of a wit, like the old title of professional Toastmaster; not exactly a University wit, either. What is he up to really? I'm writing to Huntington Cairns and Robert Richman, to have their impressions. Then Munroe, the Librarian, has written to ask me to take the Consultant job after Randall, and indeed it is now a nice job, paying $8,000 and allowing for the incumbent's private trips round to make speeches, and his private writings, and holding him to only 9 months residence, and lasting for two years as the defined tenure. (Would you be interested? Though probably not.) I've declined to think of anything but retirement and private life (and work) after Commencement next spring. I've missed my point here. I've asked Munroe, provided he feels free to do so, to give us *his* impression of Randall.[1]

The informal committee here working on the appointment of an editor consists of the President, and Sutcliffe the Chairman of English, who is interested because we want the editor to continue as a professor of English, teaching one course, and myself. They depend on me a good deal, but they have views about the sort of man, and these are quite to the point. They want most for the new man to have some drive, and great capacity, and if possible some name already as a writer.

Here is a development I've worked out with Dennie just now, as something possible. We have on hand here Ted Bogardus, who is a good poet, and a good critic, and an omnivorous reader, and standards very like those of the Review in the past; and we count on him as the Managing Editor, provided he suits the Editor. We are asking ourselves about the editor, and not depending on Jarrell either, though he has the reputation as our other candidates don't. Always there's the possibility of Robie or Randall, though we have our hesitation about them, and especially about Randall, with your letter as a valuable caution if not a deterrent. But what would you say to three other possibilities as follows: Howard Nemerov, who is certainly good, as you have said, in fact made to order as far as the continuance of the Review in its old line goes; young Guerard, who is very good in fiction, and has a great name academically at least, and who knows the Review very well and has stood up in public in defense of modern criticism—please give me your reaction there; he is mighty well placed already, of course, at Harvard, but I believe the President will not stand out against what it takes in the way of salary for any desirable man.[2] Finally, and this may be a shock, Stanley Hyman, at Bennington;[3] Dennie had his eye on this man, and so did I but hadn't got round to mentioning him; Hyman used to be poisonous to the people he didn't approve, and I took him to task and closed our pages against him for five years, but he came back in the last issue with a very informed judgment of the Brooks-Wimsatt book, a difficult thing to handle;[4] and then he has always been pretty close to right in his antipathies, those against the anthropologists for example, even those at Indiana, where they flourish and hate Hyman; on behalf of Hyman, he is a tremendous worker, and grows more learned by the hour; I don't know him personally, but I do know that he is an honest man. Tell me what you think. I'd say that Hyman or Guerard would make more of an initial splash than Nemerov would, and may have more drive and enterprise than Nemerov though not necessarily. Neither of them can write as well as Nemerov, but Hyman writes very clearly, for a more general reader than Nemerov does, while Guerard writes very well in an academic sort of style, if one has to characterize it unfavorably; not too academic, I think.

Thank you for telling me about the Medal which they have assigned to me at Brandeis.[5] I'll certainly want to accept it, coming from that committee you mention, and that institution, but I do hope they won't ask me to make the trip just for receiving it! I hope there will be some adjustment of the time possible, so that I can be East already.

Stallknecht writes that he wants me to teach this summer in any case, even if it means two Senior Fellows there at once.[6] So I guess I will, and that means that you, Blackmur, Chase, who has grown back (away from social causes) more or less into his Yankee inheritance, and myself, will be the visiting staff, though Stalky himself is going to give a course. I like the idea.

Yours,
John

---

1. Ransom was referring to Randall Jarrell, then consultant for poetry at the Library of Congress, and L. Quincy Mumford, librarian of Congress (whom he calls Munroe).

2. Albert J. Guerard, a professor at Harvard, had published books on Hardy and Gide and was completing *Conrad the Novelist* (1958).

3. Stanley Edgar Hyman, a critic who wrote for the *New Yorker* from 1940 to 1970 and taught at Bennington College, was, like most of the candidates considered as Ransom's successor, a contributor to the *Kenyon Review*. His best known book, *The Armed Vision* (1948), was reviewed by Ransom in the *Kenyon Review*, X (Autumn, 1948), 682–88.

4. Hyman reviewed *Literary Criticism: A Short History* (1957) by Cleanth Brooks and W. K. Wimsatt in the *Kenyon Review*, XIX (Autumn, 1957), 647–57.

5. On January 27, 1958, Ransom was notified that he had been chosen to receive the Creative Award Medal presented by Brandeis University.

6. Newton Stallknecht, chairman of the English department at Indiana University, became director of the School of Letters in 1953.

To Robie Macauley

February 20, 1958

Dear Robie:

Would you be interested in succeeding this editor on the Kenyon Review? Your name has been high on our list all the time; and the "our" refers to Dennie Sutcliffe, Chairman of English, the new President Dr. Lund, and myself; I have no voice, except to recommend, while Dennie is immensely interested because the position involves a faculty status and teaching of one course, very important to the English boys, and of course the President appoints, and he's thinking of the continuation of the Review, whether on the old lines or some new lines.[1]

If you are interested, we'd be very happy if you would come out at your earliest convenience to talk with us. Could you stay overnight, and as much of the two days as your convenience allowed? We'd meet you by train or plane, and see you off again, and of course the College would take care of your expenses.

I should state that we have offered the position to Randall Jarrell, and he has declined it, on the ground that he is too happy where he is, and fears the editing would keep him from writing. He is something of an anti-critic, and he would have liked to devote the Review largely to new fiction and theatre and verse, with not too much technical literary criticism. All agreed to that plan, because the President's idea is to get the right man and turn him loose without meddling from the College; and I thought the Review had seen a certain period pass when criticism bulked large in everybody's consciousness, whereas now the new criticism is the old criticism, and the results of criticism are widely known and not up for disputation so much as formerly. Perhaps a halfway-between position might be advisable, with good criticism going right along with a larger body of creative writing. I rather think that might be the saving course for a Review now. But that would be as the editor thinks.

In any case the President wishes the Review to continue, and commits the College to its maintenance.

Please let me know if and when you might come out and talk informally about it.

With all best wishes,

Sincerely,
John Ransom

1. Robie Macauley was editor of the *Kenyon Review* from 1959 to 1966.

To Allen Tate

April 21, 1958

Dear Allen:

I've got off a strong letter of nomination to Lowry, of the Ford Foundation[1]—proposing to write again in such form as may be directed, and saying that if Allen is ready to write some more verse or fiction that will be a literary event. I'll let you know what I hear from him. I had just last week declined to be one of the five judges of the competition; 350 applications expected in complete form by April 18 (though I suppose and hope that there would be later lists too); and $50.00 a day and expenses to a meeting of the five judges in NYC. I would have required 10 days to work over this material, and I didn't have time to earn money that way.

Randall [Jarrell] declined our invitation, for reasons that I respected. First, he wasn't sure that he was sufficiently in touch with the critics; perhaps not sure that he was interested in that phase. Then, after his unhappy childhood and previous existence generally he at last is in bliss, with a congenial job, a home which he owns, and a honeymoon still going with his new wife, so why should he give all that up? I think it may be that he won't write a lot more, or at least a lot more that is distinguished; but I'm not sure, because his mind is very keen, and he impressed us a great deal.

But Robie is obviously a good man, and he and Bogardus make a fine team. We thought of the team a good deal. And this is not discounting Robie individually, because he is a man of taste, and a very good and fast-improving writer, and as to his literary convictions they are just the same as this Review has always held to, without ever defining them. So why not Robie?

Affectionately,
John

1. Wilson McNeil Lowry (b. 1913), a teacher, newspaper editor, and foundation executive, was a director of the Ford Foundation during the years 1953–64.

To Richard P. Blackmur

November 10, 1958

Dear Richard:

I wish I might have heard your lecture on Muir; I was prepared for your going out in favor of that good head, with whom I'd made my own pretty favorable although slight acquaintance. I turned up Saturday noon at Baltimore, heard Marianne [Moore] (who gave a circus with her beautiful animals, and made some nice wisecracks mostly about the reading and remarks of Yvor Winters that morning), and then I read and remarked a little—but Marianne didn't speak quite clearly enough for my bad ears and I didn't catch everything. I liked the informality of the occasion.

I'm glad to hear from Stalky this morning that you have signed up, and I will make it a point to go over there on Wednesday of the session to see you and hear the Forum. I want to hear about the house. I'm in the act of earning the new furniture for mine, which is up and almost finished inside; so I've done a bit of barnstorming; came back from a week on the road with $1200!

I'd like to get last season's Forum speech of yours just as soon as I can, because the next issue will be slightly tailored and several of the essays will be coming late in the month. That's your intention, isn't it? And later we'd be just as glad to have the Muir paper if you haven't already placed it elsewhere. We'd like RPB in Winter, Spring, and Summer if we can; after that I'm a retired man. I speak casually, but you know how strongly I want this, desiring to leave the office with a bang not a whimper.[1]

Affectionately,
John

1. Ransom did not retire as editor until after the fall, 1959, issue was published. In the year 1959 he ran three pieces by Blackmur; "The Logos in the Cathedral: The Role of the Intellectual," XXI (Winter), 1–22; "Edwin Muir: Between the Tiger's Paws," XXI (Summer), 419–36; and "Homo Ludens" (essay-review of *The Literary Works of Matthew Prior*), XXI (Autumn), 662–64, 666, 668.

To Robert Penn Warren

September 2, 1959

Dear Red:

Well, what a time I've taken. It's been a hectic time for me, trying to get on with some new writing which hasn't gone too well, while I kept the home fires burning about 7 weeks after my retirement waiting for Robie to come on duty, and that stage of the job was a chore!

But mainly, you know it's mighty hard for a friend to make a critique on a friend's pieces. A little preface even now, before I do it. You're the only one of us who hasn't put his head in the clouds, and the only one that has a Great Public. Which last would seem to be so important that probably no criticism which reflects the least bit on it ought to prevail. The rest of us are at the dead end reserved for the Highbrows when the age has rushed away under them; I find myself writing that out publicly in some of my recent pieces; but not thinking of getting out, or trying to, which may be my own epitaph. So it is with this sort of reservation that I hold back from admiring every bit of your writing. I'd never deny its force, or its modern aptness.

However—You asked for it. And I have to say that the new collection of poems is mighty tough, mighty hard-boiled, for my poor old taste.[1] On the whole, that is. You upset my sense of the value of poetry which is in a word—piety, of the free and pagan and non-religious sort. On your side I'd have to say that poetry is what it is empirically, what poets make it; and you don't quite make that of it. But you know how stubborn I am.

The book has got a grand tight though informal organization; it is a book in the sense that a collection almost never is. And it's fascinating, readable, as nine-tenths the books are not.

These are the poems which I like very much; many others I like not quite so much, and a good many seem too hard in their tone. My poems would be especially (these aren't all of them, but the conspicuous ones): Clearly About You—for its lyric quality, and its perfection as a preface, Switzerland—for its ending, The Self That Stares—for its fine execution, Fatal Interview—for being a tragedy in the classical mode, and the section Some Quiet, Plain Poems—for the mood and the execution too.[2]

I could do better if I named some good ones which for one reason or another I like though not so much as these. So forgive me.

We are well, and had Reavill and Shirley and the three kids with us a few days, and had a fine time. We put 'em in the Big Room in the basement where they said it was fun. I wish you folks could come and see us. But we would put up non-members of our family in sleeping quarters somewhere else, no basement.

Robie and Ann—who is a Memphis girl—are fine and he is going to make a fine editor.

Love to you all, from us both.

Yours.
John

1. Warren, *You, Emperors, and Others: Poems, 1957–1960* (New York: Random House, 1960).

2. Ransom had published "Penthesilea and Achilles: Fatal Interview" and "Switzerland" in the *Kenyon Review*, XX (Autumn, 1958), 599–603.

To Robie Macauley

Evanston, Illinois, February 14, 1960

Dear Robie:

About ten days ago I delivered my public lecture, using just about the script or copy which I enclose.[1] But I learned so much from hearing my own reading, and chatting with people afterwards, that I had to make changes in it. They are made now, but what I show here does not include the last 3 pp or so which I have not had time to copy. My job here is not heavy in hours, but there are so many responsibilities on a visiting strange teacher that he is always surprised by interruptions he had not allowed for.[2]

I had a long full day and evening yesterday to get this new typing done, but still there was interruption, and I could not finish the speech part. I wish I had; they come from the literary critic, and must not be taken as from the *acknowledged* legislator of mankind, any more than the poet's words; as modest as I can make it, that is. But these missing pages would bear out the crucial sense in which Hardy represents the modern naturalist wanting to find his God, as my title (special for your occasion in the K.R.) indicates.

After this main part on the fables of Hardy, I turn to some other poems, fine ones but not too well known, outside of course of the "Satires of Circumstance." It is comfortable to find a poet furnishing good things even in his second-best line. That part of the job is ready for final re-typing, all the selections made; including the final part which I have not mentioned, concerning the likelihood that Hardy will rate after Browning and Tennyson (early Victorians and orthodox mostly) as the third of the major Victorian poets, a late-Victorian one whom the period needs very much if it is going to be represented in its naturalistic or disaffected phase. There may be round or close to 30 pp altogether; but the latter half (nearly half) of it is easily subject to cutting.

If you like, do send this part to the printer; the rest when I send it, I think, on Wednesday from here. I have a free day Tuesday; and some time Monday and Wednesday mornings.

There would be this afternoon for work too, since it is now only noon on Sunday. But Cal [Lowell] and Allen and Isabella [Tate] are in Chicago,[3] and I am spoken for attending upon the joint public readings by Isabella and Cal, then a little party and private dinner. I can't pass this up, and shouldn't, and wouldn't.

The copy enclosed is final enough; I promise not to make editorial changes unless I see some egregious error not of style but of fact or reference; which isn't too likely at this stage.

I could never get manuscripts out of Blackmur and a few others except two weeks after the deadline; I scolded, and wrote and wired and telephoned. But I never dreamed I would be as difficult as Blackmur, and it mortifies me that I am being so.

Yours,
John

1. Ransom, "Thomas Hardy's Poems," *Kenyon Review*, XXII (Spring, 1960), 169–93.

2. Ransom was spending a semester at Northwestern University as visiting professor of English.

3. Allen Tate was divorced by Caroline Gordon during the summer of 1959, and on August 27 he married Isabella Gardner, a poet.

To Allen Tate

Nashville, October 21, [1960]

Dear Allen:

Your nice note makes me feel mighty bad. I've had to tell Frenz that I can't get to the meeting, and I've not missed one before.[1] I have to be talking to the East Texas teachers of English, at Nacogdoches, Texas, on the evening of Friday, Nov. 3. Since the nearest airport is Shreveport, 90 mi. away, I can't possibly be in New York Saturday AM—unless Jack Kennedy sends his private plane to pick me up Friday a little after mid-night. What a bad meeting to have to miss, after reading your plans. Do give everybody my best.

Thanks for your ideas about my publishing. I haven't had any news better than yours, about the fresh start *you* made at Florence. I'm pretty sure I shan't take any more teaching jobs, as I have a lot of things frying over the fire on my own.[2] I do plan to use that Library of Congress piece[3] (leaving out the opening part and extending the rest)—and I do have some other essays in hand and ready; and am working on a quite long essay which grew too big and fateful for use by John Palmer in his anniversary number of Yale Review—he commissioned it, but I couldn't deliver.[4] I'm teaching that paper as I write it, and I do find that kind of stimulus in the academic life.

Knopf is after me for a new book of essays, or another *Poems and Essays* if I have a further version of the poems, and the new essays. As a matter of fact, I've promised myself to bring my selection of poems up to 50, adding a few others (revised vitally) of the old ones, and—as I hope—two or three new ones.[5] I'm eager to try my hand at verse again just as soon as I can get through (a) my present essay, (b) the Emily Dickinson (for the fine U. of Minn. pamphlets), and (c) an introduction to a very unwieldy collection of Valéry's essays, in the Bollingen Series, for Matthews.[6]

So I don't think I have a MS for Swallow, though I'm much impressed by what you say, I'll be ruminating over it. I've had proposals to re-publish *World's Body*, and *New Criticism*, and *God Without Thunder* too, but I can't read my old things with pleasure now. *World's Body*, with considerable excision and perhaps supplementation, I've felt nearest to doing.[7]

Let me see some of that new verse before long, won't you?

Affectionately,
John

P.S. I want to pay tardy compliments to that other poet in the family. I liked that new book of hers.[8] It seems to me that those elegiac poems in honor of the public dead are the best things we have in that kind now; they're just right.

As for Robb, she isn't with me here yet. Jack's family, who is to be increased by a fourth member before very long, engages her attention and protection—especially as Jack is away at his business in Columbus most of the week.

---

1. Horst Frenz, chairman of the comparative literature department at Indiana University, was running the School of Letters, and the senior fellows were meeting.

2. Ransom was spending the fall semester at Vanderbilt as visiting professor of English.

3. Ransom had delivered his 1958 Whittal lecture at the Library of Congress under the title "New Poets and Old Muses." It was published in *American Poetry at Mid-Century* (Washington, D.C.: Library of Congress, 1958), 1–14.

4. John E. Palmer, editor of the *Yale Review*, had requested an essay for the fiftieth anniversary issue. Ransom did not complete this essay on Blake.

5. Knopf published a new edition of Ransom's *Selected Poems* in 1963 that contained fifty-three poems, but a revised edition of *Poems and Essays* (1955) was never published.

6. None of these projects came to fruition.

7. *God without Thunder* was reprinted by Archon Books in 1965, and *The World's Body* (rev. ed.) was published by the Louisiana State University Press in 1968. Greenwood Press has announced a reprint of *The New Criticism*.

8. Isabella Gardner, *The Looking Glass: New Poems* (1961).

To Allen Tate

April 16, [1962]

Dear Allen:

Glad to get your letter. I've noticed that there is a school or schools of critics who just don't know that we are here, and especially because they identify us with a section that they don't hold with. But we can't bother with them. Least of all yourself. You are thoroughly rooted and established in a form of poetry that nobody else has adhered to or *can* manage. But then I haven't seen this particular new anthology.

You'll enjoy your Fugitive meeting. Wish I could go along.[1] You'll like what Jesse [Wills] is doing. I read them my first stab at a new "Conrad" which Don responded to, but which even as I read it didn't come up to any solid unit.[2]

So I've tinkered and tinkered, at various moments. I don't know if it is a whole; if it is, it's a queer thing. But here is my latest (I'm pretty sure my last) version of the thing. I don't want to expand it, as it's meant to be terse; so I've sectioned it. The value of it for me has been to get me back in the groove of poetic language, even though I emphasize the technique of the tetrameters, try out its capabilities. Well, well.

I do hope before long to explore some Ideas which are on my mind for verse. Some new ones.

Our love to Isabella.

Yours,
John

1. Tate had been invited to participate in the Vanderbilt literary symposium later that month.

2. Ransom was referring to a new version of an old poem, "Conrad in Twilight" (1922). Two versions appear in the *Selected Poems* (1969): "Conrad Sits in Twilight" and "Master's in the Garden Again."

To Allen Tate

February 27, 1963

Dear Allen:

It will be mighty nice to visit you, and therefore to make a reading for the Walker Art Centre.[1] June 3 is the best date for me, in view of my several appearances round and about during May. Thanks.

What a confusion the Poet's Festival was.[2] I scarcely more than exchanged greetings with you and Isabella. I handed back the letter you had written to Don before I had had a chance to read it.[3] But I'm glad you are having such a good correspondence with him. He writes me that for the first time he is devoting long and serious study in his poetry class to yourself. And that your verse stands up beautifully, etc. etc. I find of late, myself, that I have grown up to it, it doesn't baffle me much. I have always admired its elevation and passion, and of course I have always had some very great favorites among your poems which never gave me anything else but pleasure.

Am glad you concede me my Revision.[4] I'd advise against any such thing from a poet, but still I felt compelled to rewrite this one. And not honestly and completely to recant from the old version and commit it to the flames, but to leave it in the book too.

Since Washington I have put on again just about all the weight I had lost in the past two or three years, and I am in good health. But at my age I can't work as fast or as long as I could a few decades ago. I feel the need to work but it takes time. I do hope, however, to get a few new poems done.

I felt very sad about Frost, though I didn't go to the funeral.[5] I generally had the curious feeling about him of being indebted to his achievement, in this sense: he was at his best a fine poet, but he chose not to be at his best generally, and therefore discharged the debt to the less literate society which we can't find it in us to take seriously. That's a sort of missionary feeling, with relief that somebody else is doing the job. But in saying this much I don't mean that I have let the question worry me.

We'll have a big conversation, at least a three-way one, when I see you. I don't know if I can persuade Robb.

Yours,
John

P.S. Robb and I returned last night from a 10-day visit to Reavill and his family at Purdue.

---

1. The Walker Art Center is located in Minneapolis, where Tate continued to teach at the University of Minnesota.

2. Ransom was alluding to a symposium held at Kenyon in connection with his seventy-fifth birthday. Ransom, Tate, Robert Penn Warren, Robert Lowell, and Stephen Spender participated in conversation on a panel moderated by Robie Macauley and devoted to the topic "Quo Vadimus? Or the Books Still Unwritten."

3. Ransom was probably referring to Tate's letter of January 10, 1963, to Donald Davidson, *The Literary Correspondence of Donald Davidson and Allen Tate* (1974), 389.

4. Another reference to the Conrad poem, probably "Master's in the Garden Again."

5. Robert Frost had died on January 29, 1963.

To Allen Tate

September 21, 1963

Dear Allen:

I am delighted to think of you and Isabella as in London, a different world for you, especially at this time. Have a good holiday.

I gave Robie your address; he wants to sew you up if he can in making a contribution to the Hundredth number of *Kenyon Review*. I have to offer something, and it will be at long last a piece on Wallace Stevens; a poet and man I have much admired.[1] I am more than ever anxious to do this after my second reading, just now, of Pearce's *Continuity of American Poetry*.[2] I don't care for his taking exception to the *matter* of poems as crippling the freedom of the artist; and my commendation of Stevens, as perhaps the best natural poet our country has produced, does not mean that Stevens hewed to the best poetic line, or that poems in general must not suit their own honest occasions.

I have also copied and sent to A. A. Knopf Inc. the part of your good letter relating to the distribution of my new *Selecteds*. I do think, however, that Knopf distributes me under its own name in Britain, or at least my other *Selecteds* seem to have become known there.

Robb and I are well. Though we live rather retiredly, life seems (by a comfortable illusion) almost busier than ever.

Aff'ly,
John.

---

1. Ransom, "The Planetary Poet." Tate did not contribute to the issue.

2. Roy Harvey Pearce, *The Continuity of American Poetry* (1961).

To Newton P. Stallknecht

January 22, 1964

Dear Stalky:

I haven't been idle exactly, just more or less inconclusive in my thought about some sort of reorganization of the Senior Fellows' part in the program. I think there will be sure to be much good talk about it when we assemble in March.

It seems to me that *you* are the people whose wishes and needs now have to be consulted. You've been so faithful to the letter of the old constitution that obtained at Kenyon—if there really was any actual transfer of any actual constitution in the communications that passed between President Chalmers and President Wells. After thirteen years of operation of the School of Letters at Indiana it is your turn now to fix the procedures exactly as you want them. The Senior Fellows all think that.

I ask myself: Why a staff of Senior Fellows determining the visiting instructors and their subjects every summer session? I guess that was the question in my mind principally, when the Rockefeller people gave Kenyon College the money, and the President designated me to set up the affair. The same situation had risen earlier when President Chalmers initiated the Kenyon Review, with me as Editor and Rice as Associate Editor. Both times we wanted to get something superior if that was possible; and that meant: to staff the Review, or the School of English, with the brightest possible *outside* people rather than Gambier people, so that our standard would surpass the local College standard by aiming at an absolute excellence. We had no four or five or six people at Gambier qualified as our designated Contributing Editors of the publication, or designated Senior Fellows of the School, had to be; we looked round and shopped for them, but we were pretty successful in getting those we picked. Our idea was to conduct a Review which would be beyond the local talent of the College to conduct, very decidedly beyond that; and to conduct a School for summer instruction in the critical approach such as must be far beyond the instruction we could have tapped in the College. I believe we even put it this way: the operation of a Review that would be far better than Harvard or Columbia or Chicago could do it, since we drew on the whole American (and even English) market for our contributors, and Harvard or Yale or Chicago would have decided to go it alone; and the operation of a School of English, ditto. The Review and the School of English went after *professional* writers of criticism who could teach critical writing professionally; and in those days that would have been a little different from going after regular competent academic writers. Nowadays I suppose there is not so marked a difference, partly because we have succeeded so well in our instructions.

I think you at Indiana University are doing something wonderful by way of those students who stay on over the winter, or over several winters, and study the nature of literature in your seminars. The look-in on your class in December caused me to get a new and vivid impression of how much spirit and mass there was in that operation. That's "tying-in" the summer work with the full-time university program of student studies.

But I would hope that the Senior Fellows would survive; I mean in principle, though I think it's time to get a new slate of them; a group just as various and catholic, but even more aware of what is going on critically, and of who are the men to notice when it comes to summer appointments; our crowd has grown old in the service, and less active than we might be.

And I agree altogether that as Director you need to have something continuous in the group-office of the Senior Fellows, so that you can always get in official touch with them when you need to.

I'll keep thinking about it, and looking forward with considerable sense of excitement to our meeting in March. And thanks many times for the good time you showed me when I was there in December, and the lovely dinner and party afterward when our business had gone as far as it could.

Yours,
John

To Newton P. Stallknecht

April 21, 1964

Dear Stalky:

I'm sorry I didn't write to Rahv—I wasn't sure I should, or had undertaken that. I did write a very long letter to Austin Warren, to acquaint him with our plans and relieve his fears, and to ask him to send some nominations for the additional Senior Fellows to add to our list. He has not replied to me and evidently not to you. I think it is difficult to write letters in his strained long-hand. Won't you write Trilling asking him to talk with Rahv?

As to my own additional nominations, the item which came up on the second day's session when I had to go, I send a few here:—

I find myself thinking of the need of another kind of Senior Fellow, and not be found on our list of ordinary Fellows: either Wallace Fowlie, master of the French language and literature, and well versed in our own verse, even the contemporary, whose teachings are wholly just,—unless you know some impediment to his performance with us,—or Erich Heller, who dittoes Fowlie in German language and literature—just for the improvement of our Comparative Lit. offerings.[1]

But I think I would exclude some otherwise very suitable persons who happen to be close to Allen and myself, and whose addition even in part would tend to give an excessive weight to a single group: Lowell, Brooks, Jarrell.

So here would be my list of nominations in the order of my preference:—Mizener, good at fiction and in general; Leslie Fiedler, a critic of traditional poetry and criticism, but representing an attitude that has come strongly into a fashion, and perhaps needs to be taken into account—he is saner and less exclusive than Shapiro—see Fiedler in KR for January—; Fowlie, ahead of Heller for our purposes.[2] And do we need any more?

Austin's queries addressed to me before I went to our last meeting had to do with matters which I don't believe we got round to clearing up during at least the first day of our session. Who selects the new Senior Fellows when it comes to replacing an old Senior when he has to be absent? And what of the salaries (as they are denoted by the University) or the honoraria of the Fellows when they number seven or eight? And might not the list appear top-heavy in our publications? And a better definition seems needed than I have heard given (even when I was talking) of the inner council or executive committee of the given year, and its functions.

I've been awfully busy for several weeks, and am off tomorrow on a five-day trip to Mississippi College for Women, where my sister died, the Dean and Professor of English, last June, and where I take part in a Southern Lit. Festival which is also a sort of memorial to her.[3]

I like very much the new poster.

Yours,
John

---

1. Wallace Fowlie, who like Francis Fergusson and Stanley Edgar Hyman was long associated with Bennington College, is a scholar, critic, and translator who has written books on Gide, Stendhal, Proust, surrealism, Dante, and other subjects. Erich Heller, a scholar and critic who has taught at Northwestern since 1960, is the author of *The Disinherited Mind* (1952) and other books.

2. Leslie Fielder, a professor of English at the State University of New York at Buffalo since 1964, is the author of *Love and Death in the American Novel* (1966) and other works of criticism. Like Fowlie he was a regular contributor to the *Kenyon Review* when Ransom edited it. Karl Shapiro, a poet and critic who has written many books, including *V-Letter and Other Poems* (1944), *In Defense of Ignorance* (1960), and *The Bourgeois Poet* (1964).

3. Mississippi State College for Women, at which Ellene Ransom was professor of English and academic dean during the last ten years of her life.

To Allen Tate

February 16, 1965

Dear Allen:

I'm sorry to be so tardy answering your good note of the 3rd. But I spent last week in Texas; reading at Rice, then being a member of a 4-man team at a Symposium (on Theory of Poetic Form) at U. of Texas; and the previous week I was more than fully occupied with my preparations. At Rice I observed that you were to make an early appearance there—it is a delightful place. Perhaps you are already on tour, and won't see this till you get back.

But I'll write an essay on Eliot; I have notes of a speech I made but never wrote; and an intense sympathy at last with that tortured soul who achieved serenity. So, yes, to that.[1]

And yes about the A.A.A.L. [American Academy of Arts and Letters] matter, where your urging supplements Malcolm Cowley's. Since Cowley seems to be in California at the moment, and I don't know where, I won't try to reach him. But I feel very grateful to you both, and I would be just plain obtuse if I held out.

I too felt that Pratt of U. of Miami in Ohio had done a good job by the Fugitives.[2] I wrote him to that effect just now and made no suggestions. I had taken no umbrage to what he wrote about my "Necrological," as a critical slip that wouldn't do any particular harm. He is indeed a good man. I recommended him to the Kenyon President, who is looking for a new Chairman of English. I am extremely glad that he has got well into your own verse; I don't think that he would have coped with it till now—he's a comparative youngster. And I had meant before this to write you about my great pleasure in Geo. Hemphill's pamphlet book on yourself;[3] I've not seen anything so full and good on your great accomplishment; though I see a lecture on Tate listed among the four Spring lectures wh. Don is going to deliver. (Duncan, the Acting Chairman, said they hated to retire him after he had reached the age stipulated in the rule, but did so with request for a series of lectures anyway.)[4] Don will be another able voice testifying.— And it's just possible that I might give the topic a whirl, for the Summer issue of *Southern Review*, though I might not be able to furnish it in time for them.[5]

Our best to Isabella and yourself.

As ever,
John

---

1. Ransom's essay, entitled "Gerontion," did not arrive in time to be published in the special Eliot number of the *Sewanee Review*, LXXIV (Winter, 1966), edited by Allen Tate; but it was published in the next issue, LXXIV (Spring, 1966), 389–414.

2. William Pratt (ed.), *The Fugitive Poets: Modern Southern Poetry in Perspective* (New York: Dutton, 1965).

3. George Hemphill, *Allen Tate* (Minneapolis: University of Minnesota Press, 1964).

4. Donald Davidson was presenting four

public lectures during his last semester at Vanderbilt, partly at the instance of Edgar Hill Duncan, acting chairman of the English department.

5. This essay was not published.

To Allen Tate

August 1, 1965

Dear Allen:

Thanks for your good letter, with so much news in it.

I wish you could have been here for Andrew's entitlement.[1] We had a good party at our house, for Andrew and Polly and Andrew's fine son-in-law and the good theologian who accompanied him. I got in a bit of private talk with Andrew in my study but just as the party was arriving at the proper hilarity the guests of honor had to take off in the night in order to reach Sewanee punctually on the next day.

About my commitment to write a "review" of the Stewart book. I had just glanced at it when I got the request from Matchett, out at Seattle, editor of the Modern Language Quarterly; and I liked Matchett when I was out there last year, and have had to decline several invitations of his to write for him. But he thinks he is full-up for the Autumn edition, so that there's no rush; except that nowadays I am in a constant rush trying to get some other commitments in shape. I will write Matchett presently, perhaps to say that I won't have time, and I wouldn't care to write briefly anyhow; what I would have to write would be an essay going over much of the ground that is taken in Stewart's book.[2]

I'm not sure if we should answer Stewart at all. Here is my acquaintance with him.[3] First of all, he was a graduate student at Ohio State about 1938 or 39 when he wrote to me asking leave to submit a paper for the joint symposium which the Southern Review and the Kenyon were about to offer (in our Autumn 1939 issues); which request we accepted, publishing the essay he wrote about the teaching of English in the graduate departments; he wished to use an assumed name, and did so, calling himself Hade Saunders. I met him in person at Bread Loaf and became well acquainted with him over three summers when I taught there. He was well behaved and did his work well, without being a star. Ever since, until the appearance of his Pamphlet book about me, I have wondered if he was ever going to write for the public.[4] But perhaps you don't know that he had a dreadful stroke of some kind, Polio I think, and became a hopeless cripple. So I was told about four years ago by Roy Harvey Pearce, at Ohio State. But he was recovering; and it seems by the most heroic exercise of his will, going through his exercises and never giving up hope. I think his own feat was in his mind when he wrote about you relying on Faith when there were other cultural possibilities by which men without the Faith could secure themselves.

If I should write up his performance I would of course be objective and call attention to the many qualities he lacks as a critic. I should deprecate his attention to the Agrarian book because he has an animus about that; he is a sociologist and amateur economist; I should have to point out that his work on that has been anticipated by many other sociologists and economists and we ourselves were well acquainted with these fields insofar as we were making our case, and he missed the train entirely from being too young to get into the controversy when it was warm. I should have to note his curt and often brutal judgments on the poems of all of us, as if he were an oracle rather than a critic expected to go to a certain depth in his pronouncements. He is most brutal dealing with Don and you; he remarks later that Davidson did some good poems, and was a very good prose writer, "brilliant" being I think the word describing his history of the Tennessee River. He seemed most afraid to pronounce upon your verse, but you did make him get up his Dante and his St. Thomas, though for a monstrous purpose: to convict you of Belief! and I thought it rather mean to picture the declining days of poor Sidney [Hirsch] when we had abandoned him; and to give that ugly picture of Warren in his youthful desires.

What I would have liked to continue with would have been the idea of how he might have chosen his topic and treated it. He should have written up the five poets who became professional after their Fugitive apprenticeship: me (if he wanted to keep the order of age), Don, you, Merrill [Moore], and Warren. And I think he might well have added Brooks (if he goes into the prose work), who wasn't converted to Fugitive poetry and Agrarian ideas till he went to Oxford; visiting us when we were in Exeter during his summer vacation in 1932, and paying his penances; then masterminding one section of our movement as critics. And if the prose fiction of the members of the group, then by all means Lytle, who came to some of our meetings in 1924 or 1925, and became not a poet but a very distinguished writer of fiction. A big job, but done with proper economy the book would not have been bigger than the one he did publish.

As to Merrill [Moore], that is another case where Stewart did not read his authors to the end. I feel sure you know *The Phoenix and the Bees*, which was finished just before his death and published the next year of 1957. There are many fair sonnets of Merrill's, and enough very good ones to get into anthologies; but after Merrill went to Boston he sent me some of the first of his meandering but innocent and often charming strings of quatrains, which I didn't later know he had ever rounded up into the hundreds of them in the Phoenix set. They are strictly Celtic in their charm (they often have charm) though not highly consecutive. Merrill followed through as a doctor but he had the most tender sensibilities of all of us on tap for the poems. It makes me sad to think that I didn't see that last book, or know of it, till publication.

This is [what] I would like to have said if I had written or decided to write for Matchett. I don't think I will. And of course it would only be a vain rebuke to Stewart to plan for him when he had already done his worst. The more I think about it—and this is the first time I have written anything out—the less useful it seems to be to write of Stewart publicly. Our standing is many times better than his and for my part I can shrug him off. I do mean to write out to Davidson my indignation, and to write a note to Merrill's widow about Merrill's last book.

I'll write to the Taylors presently. We can't get to Monteagle this month; Reavill and his family will come by here for a few days on their way to New York and abroad; Reavill has a half-year of sabbatical, and they all want to go to Spain. But I imagine Peter and Eleanor staying at Monteagle indefinitely, or at least till it gets too cold for them, because Freund of the Rockefeller Foundation wrote me a fine letter about Peter's special fellowship for the year.

Robb and I send our best to you *all.*

Yours,
John

1. Andrew Lytle had been awarded an honorary degree by Kenyon College during its spring commencement.

2. Ransom did not review John L. Stewart's *The Burden of Time: The Fugitives and Agrarians* (1965) for *Modern Language Quarterly*, edited by William Matchett.

3. Donald Davidson had suggested to Tate that one of the principal Fugitives should write a formal response to Stewart, and Tate had asked Ransom his opinion. In the end none of the Fugitives responded to Stewart.

4. John L. Stewart's *John Crowe Ransom* (1962), like George Hemphill's *Allen Tate* (1964), was published in the University of Minnesota's pamphlet series on American writers.

To Allen Tate

August 24, 1965

Dear Allen:

Thanks for the new letter. I'll be glad to sign Don [Davidson]'s letter to the Princeton Library, or make any kind of endorsement.[1] Later I'll write to Stewart to express my resentment towards his patronage, and my distaste of his critical methods. It probably won't disturb him, by your own account of his sickness.

What has shocked me most was R. W. B. Lewis' enthusiastic reception of the book as expressed in some ad. I saw—I forget now where.

Here's a matter for you and Andrew to confirm if you think best:—I notice from your list of contributors you are inviting to the Tribute to Eliot that you'll have a lot of MSS. on hand; and so I'm thinking of a general word or so of honor, as a preface to my own job, and then a detailed study of "Gerontion." It has always interested me very much, especially as to how he poeticizes the lapses from prosody by finding the odd scraps of information and the unexpected words that make the style fresh and vital as if it were straight verse. I think there's no poet who can satisfy the modern taste without the leap into not-quite-relevant images. I'm thinking of a piece of about ten pages, which is assembling itself now in my mind. What is Andrew's deadline?

I wish you a good season in Italy.

Aff'ly,
John

1. Davidson had suggested that a letter be sent to Princeton University Press, signed by Ransom, Tate, Warren, and himself, protesting Stewart's book, especially the errors of fact. This letter was never written.

To Allen Tate

November 20, 1965

Dear Allen:

I have just found, under my papers, the enclosed letter I meant to send you, and thought I *had* sent you. But since then, I think it was, I got your wire.

Probably it is too late to think about my entry now. Monday morning I leave to make a speech and reading at Emory and Henry College in Virginia; but I am back home by Tuesday evening. Today and tomorrow I must be getting my speech (written, a Lectureship Series paper) in final shape. Wednesday and Thursday, and part of Friday and Saturday, I can work to see if I can get it into the mail for you to have Monday the 29th. If that isn't too late, as it well may be.

I have written an introduction in good faith about Eliot and his faith, and then talked a little of the more indefinite faith of most poets such as myself.[1] But most sympathetic; and concluding with my describing briefly the "Gerontion," both substantively and prosodically (where I say it is a revolutionary and successful experiment in loosening the strict bonds of the old pentameter verse). Then to the poem. I enclose a page containing the text of the first paragraph of the poem, and under each line my readings of the prosody. The great point Eliot was after, and got hold of, was the prosody of the *phrases* of his text, where time after time there is a rhythm, i.e. a *repetition* of the phrases containing one, two, three, or four stresses, while the unstressed syllables don't disturb. The first stanza is the most important, almost 100% old English and therefore rather the hardest to make melody of. But I have marked the first five stanzas, and the little eighth and final one; leaving the sixth and seventh only for remark. I am under the conviction that the well-voiced linguistically-trained readers do not have the slightest sense of the *expression* which they either don't follow, or don't dare to render. It is an important poem, and I'd like to hear a "linguist" try to read it. As for myself, I regret that I haven't heard Eliot read nor followed his readings on the records. I think he has launched a new age for the poets who attend to their prosodical advantages.

I find I don't stand very well too many hours of working closely at my writing. But I am in good shape; I think and hope I'm approaching the physical stage of a gerontion but am yet in the senescent rather than the senile stage.

I heard you were getting on well with your own poem, and that is good news.[2] Robb sends with me best wishes to you and to Andrew.

Aff'ly,
John

P.S. Suppose I'm too late with the schedule I've suggested. Andrew might want it for his next number, and could have it if he does.

---

1. Ransom was discussing his essay on Eliot's "Gerontion."

2. Tate did not publish any new poetry between 1953 and 1970.

To Allen Tate

December 4, [1965]

Dear Allen:

The enclosures should reach you Monday, airmail. They include my opening paragraph, for your own pleasure; and the insets in which I try the scansions of several of the sections, including a final one as the third and ultimate coda. In between them I shan't do much except a little general talk about the other sections, prosodically. And my remarks on the substance will be very much briefer than my running comment on the prosody of the insets.[1]

It is these insets which will give the printer a headache, and will start him off on my piece. Not later than Monday I'll mail you my prose parts, which are well under way. You should have it by Wednesday morning. I should guess some 12 pages length in the essay; a little more if anything.

There is just one excursion from *Gerontion* which follows my introductory paragraph. I speak of the man as a deeply religious one, even in the early poems where he has apparently lost his Faith somewhere, but is still wrestling with the problem; and it seems imperative to spend a page or two on the *Prufrock* because, true to form, he makes his reader use all the head he can to read him rightly; and even the best critics—about all I have read—take that poem as an uproarious comedy at Prufrock's expense; who appears to be unable to sue for his lady's hand. The complementary fact, in my judgment, is that he finds her unworthy, because she is incapable of religious understanding, and I cite the phrases which show that he thinks there is no use putting the "overwhelming question" to her, for she would turn away. So the joke is on the common reader who is not interested in that feature; as Eliot even with all his piety must have expected. He had a great wit.

The reason I can't send the whole piece today is because Jim Wright and his friend Bly came by and took up the better part of yesterday, Bly driving a rented car and taking along Wright, who has been at his old home place at New Concord, Ohio.[2] I liked Bly much more than I could have anticipated; we got on famously. It is Jim I am worried about; he's developed into an alcoholic, and rather looks the part. I didn't speak to him about it, but I hope he can recover himself.

Aff'ly,
John

1. Ransom is again referring to his essay on "Gerontion," which was selected for the first *American Literary Anthology*, edited by John Hawkes and others (New York: Farrar, Straus & Giroux, 1967), and sponsored by the National Endowment for the Arts, which paid Ransom $1,000 for the essay.

2. James Wright (1927–1980), the Pulitzer prize-winning poet who wrote *The Green Wall* (1957), *Shall We Gather at the River* (1958), *This Journey* (1982), and other books of poetry, was a graduate of Kenyon College. Robert Bly, who won a National Book Award for *The Light Around the Body* and has written many other books of poetry, collaborated with Wright on several books of translations.

To Allen Tate

April 18, 1966

Dear Allen:

Thank you for your fine remarks about JCR in your postscript about your splendid understanding of TSE. I was touched.[1]

I'm sorry I was away (at Purdue, with Reavill and his family) when you came by Sewanee and you and Andrew tried to reach me over the phone. I never worked and read so hard as I did last summer and ever since in trying to round up two essays at once, both overdue. The other one was the elaboration of the remarks I had made at the University of Texas last year in a symposium about the Form of Poetry; the management told us we might extend our remarks in the written piece which they would publish; first in the *Texas Quarterly* which is forthcoming, then in the book to be made of them. I'll ask them to send you a copy of the Quarterly.[2] I compared notes constantly between the two essays in order not to have any repetitions, and it was strange but fascinating. I sent in the Sewanee piece first, the other a week later, just before Robb and I took off for Purdue. Either of them would have been a little firmer if I had had the time, but I could not delay any longer.

In my Texas essay I used three quotes to show how a poem is a miniature universe, reaching out always to extend the area, by vocabulary and metaphor. One quote was "Death of Little Boys," which is such a fine poem, and one of the most metaphorical ones in the language. I wrote to your publisher to ask about the fee for its use, and that nice Secretary there wrote me a lovely little note that there would be no fee for me (too bad for you) but only proper acknowledgement, which I think they have followed to the letter. I can't recall quite her name, since I sent it at once to Texas, as I have had acknowledgement.

I hope some of these days you may come by and see us. Robb is looking fine, since she has been eating freely again, and in fact is pretty handsome.

I have one more biggest of essays to do (as the lead in a big book of essays long promised to Jay Laughlin) and I shall be doing it this summer.[3] About the improvisations of the critic who wants to see the whole metaphysical mind of the poets he is reading. It will theologize in an amateurish way.[4] I made a speech about it at Emory and Henry College in Southwest Virginia; the President who invited me had just come on from being Dean of the Theological School at Vanderbilt.[5] He wrote me afterwards that my views would be quite acceptable to the present speculative theologians (who are wild enough to take anything) but, he thought, perhaps not to my colleagues the other critics of poetry.

Aff'ly,
John

---

1. Tate, "Postscript by the Guest Editor," *Sewanee Review*, LXXIV (Winter, 1966), 383–87.

2. Ransom's "Theory of Poetic Form" was presented in a symposium on formalist criticism and published in the *Texas Quarterly*, IX (Spring, 1966), 190–201.

3. For many years Ransom had been promising James Laughlin, publisher of New Directions, a sequel to *The New Criticism*. This book was never completed, nor was the big essay to which he alluded here. In the event Laughlin published Ransom's *Beating the Bushes: Selected Essays, 1941–1970* (New York: New Directions Press, 1972), which contained "Wanted: An Ontological Critic," nine previously uncollected essays from the *Kenyon Review*, and a new essay, "The Concrete Universal."

4. This lecture was not published, but some of Ransom's remarks may appear in "The Concrete Universal" (*Beating the Bushes*) and in the postscript to the 1968 edition of *The World's Body* (in the commentary on Eliot, especially on pages 375–78).

5. William Finch.

To Allen Tate

September 14, 1967

Dear Allen:

Your breath-taking note came to hand—dated Labor Day the 4th, reaching me about the 7th. The news is magnificent.[1] Please give Helen my love, and eventually I hope to have the acquaintance of John Allen and Michael Paul. One of them will have to be, like his father, a Man of Letters.

Apologies for this belated note. Reavill and Shirley, with their three fine children, were with us for 10 days, left us the day after Labor Day. It was very hectic, with Reavill and me working morning at literature, then playing Bridge with the ladies. Just before they left an old ailment of mine broke out—the dizziness caused by the bad state of my right ear. I found I couldn't get out of bed in the night without holding on around the walls,—I refused to crawl, I haven't ventured to work in my garden or drive the car; but I've recovered, nearly, though my walking is not firm yet. Next week I've an appointment with my eye-and-ear doctor, who's now on his regular vacation which he takes in the hay-fever season. He'll help me, I'm sure. But already I'm at my writing as usual.

And now I want to talk about the writing I'm engaged on as a duty and pleasure, on your behalf.

I can't imagine why Roger L. Stevens, Director of the National Endowment for the Arts, and Carolyn Kizer his able assistant through whom all letters to him go, and herself (I imagine) more knowledgeable than he is, could have honored us five "older writers who have not had the attention they deserve"—and left you out.[2] I don't think there is a single one of us to whom you as a literary man are not at least the equal.

But I have decided I won't accomplish much by even a warm though general letter, such as I sent to him last July. Miss Kizer has written me about how many people spoke and wrote on my behalf. Somebody, as I imagined, spoke up against yourself. I shan't ask them about that. But what I have already started on is a paper, numbering quite a few pages, in which I shall type out a fine group of your easier poems—though they are all wonderfully perfected in that pithy and yet graceful line you have. On each of them I shall remark as fully as seems necessary, though I can't see how anybody could fail to make a great find as soon as he looked at them.

My list takes them in the order you have put them into your Poems of 1948. Here they are, on the next page.

The Mediterranean (where you have seen Europe and come back home)—
Aeneas at Washington (where the shade of Aeneas judges the doomed city)

To the Romantic Traditionalists (where you reject them—I use the first 4 stanzas)
Winter Mask (half-sporting in Cummings' vein, and absolutely uninhibited)
Causerie (some passages)
The Wolves
(Then three grand poems which you have placed consecutively—)
The Meaning of Life
The Meaning of Death
The Cross (which I think now I understand)
(and finally)
Death of Little Boys (as exhibiting such a *profusion* of metaphors)

You and Hart Crane were born in the same year, and you looked hard at each other's verse. He wrote some beautiful poems, which beside yours lacked starch and substance and the sense of doom. Then he wrote "The Bridge," where his gift wasn't working but dead. You and Eliot are the unique poets of that period, and your performance was much pithier than his, more memorable; until the greater parts of "Four Quartets."

It feels good to study your poems again, harder than I ever did. I'll send you my little essay when I've done it, and at the same time send it to Stevens with "Attention Miss Kizer" on the envelope.

Affectionately,
John

This is written very hastily, and I'm not quite in form yet.

---

1. Tate had announced the birth of twin sons—John Allen and Michael Paul—to him and his wife, Helen Heinz Tate.

2. The other four were Yvor Winters, Kenneth Patchen, Louise Bogan, and Malcolm Cowley.

To Newton P. Stallknecht

March 22, 1968

Dear Stalky:

I've been meditating hard about your last note, and by all means I must give you an answer. But I, at my age, am not up to par. I have still a case of vertigo, due to an ear trouble; I can't walk in the dark, and at times I simply stumble along instead of walking. (I don't dare to drive a car.) My ordeal will be to participate in the three-day Southern Literary Festival at Dallas in late April; I have to do that because the "Fugitives" and "Agrarians" will be the speakers and the panels.[1]

I am working away, slowly but not too badly, at some prose writing to which I am committed; and I do not often furnish it on the date-line.

I wonder if Allen Tate is not your man; or Francis Fergusson. If needed I can write out a page-or-two statement about the history of our move at Kenyon, and then of the transfer to I.U. Fergusson didn't come to us at Kenyon, but Allen knew all about it and was there. And Allen has become a first-rate platform man, of great dignity and considerable wit. I might add that Trilling did not attend the Vanderbilt "School," nor Ellmann.

I'm so sorry. With all best wishes.

Yours,
John

P.S. Allen is of the English Department, his last year, at U. of Minnesota.

1. Tate, Warren, Lytle, and Mrs. Frank L. Owsley also attended this meeting.

To Robert Penn Warren

July 9, 1968

Dear Red:

I was thinking I couldn't reach you in Vermont, but since your good letter I can see now that I only have to give Redding Road plus *Please Forward.*

Your essay on me in the *Kenyon* is simply fine; the points are so clarified, and the praise is so sweet, that I am immensely pleased; and the general readers will take good notice.[1] I have always thought you a fine critic. There is great dignity in the style of it, too.

We were mighty sorry to miss you at the Big Event of my life, but I know you couldn't help it. Our fine foursome at U. of Dallas was wonderful in itself.[2]

I enclose three improved poems about poor lady-people. In my *Selected Poems* with Knopf I have promoted about a dozen poems which I had not thought worthy of *S.P.*, all of them re-worked pretty well. The one of that list in this sending is a sample: Youngest Daughter.

Robb sends her love to all, with mine; though we're not sure which ones of you are at home.

Affectionately,
John

1. Warren, "Notes on the Poetry of John Crowe Ransom at His Eightieth Birthday," *Kenyon Review*, XXX (Autumn, 1968), 319–49.

2. Warren had attended the celebration of Ransom's eightieth birthday in Dallas but not the one held in Gambier.

The Eye Can Tell

Three times he passed our park where with me went
Sweet Hope, the fair and gentle, and it was strange
That not once glancing did his vision range
Wayward on me and my dear innocent,
But strictly nursed his own predicament.
Dying before his death? His eye seemed true
As ours, he walked with it, it was as blue,
Yet could be monstrous in its fixed intent.

And I'm for telling how. In his long years
Close-watched and dangerous, many a bright-barbed hate
Burning had smote upon the optic gate
To enter and destroy; but his quick gears
Blinked shut the apertures. Else those grim leers
Had won the inner house, where sat my Hope
Who fancied him. He made her misanthrope,
But bled her courage with his softer spears.

He's given to scorn. For he must guard as well
Against alluring love, whose brave engine
Was perilous too for long sitter-in
So hard consented with her little cell;
Her tender looks vainly upon him fell,
He would not answer them, lest one light arrow
Be sharpened with a most immortal sorrow;
So had he kept his ticket shut of hell.

Nearly upright he walks for one so old,
Thrice-pondered; and I dare not prophesy
What age must bring me. But I look round bold
To seek my enemies out, and leave untold
The side-ways watery dog's glances I
Keep fawning on her; Hope will never scold.

March 7, 1973

"This poem was written in the late winter of 1973 as John approached his 85th birthday," Robert Penn Warren writes. "He read it to me at Gambier in March & later sent me this copy."

INDEX